Mastering Amazon EC2

Unravel the complexities of EC2 to build robust
and resilient applications

Badri Kesavan

‹packt›

Mastering Amazon EC2

Copyright © 2024 Packt Publishing

All rights reserved. No part of this book may be reproduced, stored in a retrieval system, or transmitted in any form or by any means, without the prior written permission of the publisher, except in the case of brief quotations embedded in critical articles or reviews.

Every effort has been made in the preparation of this book to ensure the accuracy of the information presented. However, the information contained in this book is sold without warranty, either express or implied. Neither the author, nor Packt Publishing or its dealers and distributors, will be held liable for any damages caused or alleged to have been caused directly or indirectly by this book.

Packt Publishing has endeavored to provide trademark information about all of the companies and products mentioned in this book by the appropriate use of capitals. However, Packt Publishing cannot guarantee the accuracy of this information.

Group Product Manager: Preet Ahuja
Publishing Product Manager: Suwarna Rajput
Book Project Manager: Uma Devi
Senior Editor: Roshan Ravi Kumar
Technical Editor: Arjun Varma
Copy Editor: Safis Editing
Proofreader: Roshan Ravi Kumar
Indexer: Rekha Nair
Production Designer: Shankar Kalbhor
DevRel Marketing Executive: Rohan Dobhal
Senior DevRel Marketing Executive: Linda Pearlson

First published: May 2024
Production reference: 1120424

Published by
Packt Publishing Ltd.
Grosvenor House
11 St Paul's Square
Birmingham
B3 1RB, UK

ISBN 978-1-80461-668-0

www.packtpub.com

I dedicate this book to the pillar of our family, my wife, Parimala Radha, who is always there for me, and to my wonderful children, Neya and Shri Reyan, who make every day special. To my grandmother, Parimala, who raised me with resilience and love, and to my late grandfather, Lakshmi Narayanan, whose memories and upbringing continue to guide me. A heartfelt thanks to my mother, Chitra, and father, Kesavan, for their sacrifices and unwavering support throughout my journey. To my brother, Madhan, for his steadfast support that has been my great strength.

– Badri Kesavan

Foreword

I remember launching my first EC2 instance on AWS back in 2010 and feeling awed by the on-demand convenience of the cloud. However, as a developer back then with limited infrastructure knowledge, I felt quite uneasy about the provisioning and configuration choices I was faced with, especially with limited guidance or documentation. The funny thing was that the instance crashed and became unrecoverable through my own experimentation, and I was forced to re-provision. That minor setback and many others gave me a deep desire to master the tech I was working with and encourage others such as Badri to do so as well.

Fast forward 14 years, and the offerings and complexity of AWS have greatly increased. New and even seasoned AWS adopters face a steep uphill climb when trying to keep up without good guidance and mentorship, with the AWS EC2 service probably being the first and most important foundational service they will work with before progressing on to anything else.

I could not think of anyone better than Badri to be the one to help others to master the AWS EC2 service. He lives and breathes AWS, has almost all the AWS certificates, and is officially part of the AWS Community Builder and User Group Leader programs. More importantly, he gives back his time to the community by being part of my core team running the AWS User Group Community in Singapore, running monthly meetups and workshops in the workshop track, as well as being a regular speaker at AWS conferences.

I am glad Badri is writing this book to share his wealth of experience and knowledge to help you master working with AWS and the EC2 service. It completes a cycle of knowledge being passed on to the next generation of users and adopters, as I have passed on my own knowledge to Badri previously. This book is an excellent guide written by a deep practitioner, giving you something that certifications and documentation will not be able to teach you.

Now go build.

Steve Teo
Director of Cloud Security Engineering
Horangi – A Bitdefender Company

Foreword

I have known the author, Badri, as a friend for well over four years. He boasts 12+ years of extensive experience, firmly rooted in the ever-evolving realm of cloud architecture. His passion lies in not just mastering the intricacies of cloud platforms such as EC2, but also in engineering innovative solutions that push the boundaries of what's possible. Beyond his technical prowess, Badri is a passionate community builder, actively co-organizing the AWS User Group in Singapore. Witnessing his insightful speeches at these meetups, where he shares his real-world experiences and challenges, has been a privilege for me personally. He truly embodies the spirit of learning and collaboration that thrives within the cloud community.

The cloud computing landscape has undergone a seismic shift in recent years, with EC2 standing at the forefront of this revolution. Its ability to provide virtual servers on demand, with scalability and flexibility unmatched by traditional infrastructure, has empowered businesses of all sizes to innovate and grow like never before. For anyone looking to harness the power of EC2, mastering its intricacies and nuances is crucial. This book, meticulously crafted by Badri, serves as your comprehensive companion to achieving just that.

Whether you're a seasoned IT professional or a budding developer taking your first steps in the cloud, this book caters to your needs. Its carefully curated learning objectives ensure you gain a deep understanding of EC2's core features, components, and benefits, empowering you to confidently navigate its dauntingly vast capabilities. This book recognizes these challenges, as outlined here, and equips you to overcome them:

- *Challenge 1: Choosing the right resources and managing costs*

    Feeling overwhelmed by the sheer number of instance types, storage solutions, and networking configurations? This book breaks down the complexities, helping you select the optimal resources for your specific workloads. You'll learn to balance performance, cost, and scalability with practical guidance on identifying the most cost-effective options.

    Worried about keeping your cloud spending under control? This book arms you with cost optimization strategies, including right-sizing instances, utilizing Reserved Instances, and leveraging Spot Instances. You'll gain the knowledge to monitor and manage your cloud spending effectively, ensuring your cloud journey remains cost conscious.

- *Challenge 2: Ensuring security, compliance, and effective monitoring*

    Feeling lost in the labyrinth of security best practices and compliance requirements? This book offers a clear roadmap to securing your EC2 environment. You'll learn to implement robust security measures such as IAM policies, security groups, and encryption, ensuring your data remains safe and compliant with industry standards.

    Struggling to set up effective logging and monitoring? This book provides practical guidance on configuring CloudTrail, CloudWatch, and other essential tools. You'll gain the ability to monitor your EC2 infrastructure for security threats, performance issues, and operational insights, enabling proactive troubleshooting and informed decision making.

- *Challenge 3: Optimizing performance, resource placement, and backup strategies*

    Concerned about scaling your applications effectively on EC2? This book delves into scaling strategies, including Auto Scaling groups and Elastic Load Balancing. You'll learn to maintain optimal performance by understanding factors such as instance types, network configurations, and load-balancing techniques.

    Unsure about utilizing placement groups for strategic resource placement? This book explains the benefits of strategically placing your instances to optimize network performance and cost. You'll gain the knowledge to leverage placement groups for specific use cases, enhancing your application's efficiency.

    Worried about data loss and downtime? This book covers reliable backup and recovery strategies for EC2, including EBS snapshots, Amazon S3 backups, and disaster recovery solutions. You'll gain peace of mind knowing your data is protected and readily available in case of unexpected disruptions.

    Modern cloud environments are rarely confined to single platforms. This book recognizes this reality by exploring AWS CloudFormation, a powerful tool for automating and managing your EC2 infrastructure. This allows you to build and deploy infrastructure as code, ensuring consistency, scalability, and reduced human error. The ever-evolving nature of technology demands a forward-thinking approach. This book doesn't disappoint, venturing into advanced EC2 concepts such as containerization and serverless computing. Additionally, it delves into hybrid and multi-cloud architectures, equipping you with the knowledge to navigate the complexities of modern IT landscapes.

In conclusion, this book is more than just a technical manual; it's a comprehensive roadmap to mastering Amazon EC2. Whether you're looking to launch your first application in the cloud or optimize existing infrastructure, this book provides the knowledge and practical skills you need to succeed. So, embark on this journey with Badri as your guide, and unlock the full potential of Amazon EC2 and your career.

Raja SP
Leader, Centre of Prototyping and Customer Engineering Excellence, APJ
Amazon Web Services

Contributors

About the author

Badri Kesavan is a cloud and DevOps enthusiast with a deep-rooted passion for application development, cloud system design, and automation. He leads a dynamic team in the financial industry, focusing on cloud system design and platform engineering. Badri's role also extends to driving application modernization, implementing DevOps methodologies, and safeguarding information security. An active AWS Community Builder, he co-organizes AWS user meetups in Singapore, spreading knowledge and fostering community growth. His academic credentials include a master's degree in computer science from the National University of Singapore and a bachelor's degree in computer science and engineering from Anna University, Chennai.

About the reviewers

Omkar Kadam, a confident Lead DevOps Engineer and AWS Community Builder, is among the youngest DevOps ambassadors globally chosen by the DevOps Institute. With a knack for simplifying complex concepts, Omkar's expertise in AWS/cloud computing allows him to deliver innovative and scalable solutions.

His commitment to mentorship is evident through his active participation and mentorship in several hackathons, fostering collaboration and empowering aspiring developers.

Omkar embodies collaborative innovation and knowledge dissemination. His contributions extend beyond conventional roles, marking him as a dynamic and influential figure in the ever-evolving tech space.

I am profoundly grateful to my family for their unwavering support and encouragement throughout this rewarding journey. Your belief in me has been my greatest strength. Heartfelt thanks to the talented author, Badri, for the invaluable opportunity to contribute to this book. Thanks to Packt, who have my sincere appreciation for their guidance, professionalism, and unwavering commitment to excellence.

Ashok Kalakoti is an IT professional with an insatiable curiosity and a penchant for staying ahead of the tech curve. He dives deep into the realms of cloud technologies, unraveling the mysteries of scalable infrastructures and the seamless integration of data in the virtual sphere. His journey extends into the fortresses of DevSecOps and cybersecurity engineering, and he is deeply passionate about automation, where he focuses mainly on designing and delivering the most secure digital solutions, dissecting threat landscapes, and exploring the frontiers of digital defense. He is on a mission to unravel the intricacies of the AI and ML space. He strongly believes in the power of community and knowledge sharing.

In the vast realm of AWS cloud computing, my gratitude extends to giants such as my friends/ mentors, the AWS Community Builders program, AWS User Groups, and cybersecurity forums. These open communities, where knowledge flows freely, are my foundation. Special thanks to my family for unwavering support amid a busy schedule. Together, we stand as a community of learners and collaborators.

Prem Ananth Selvaraj boasts an impressive 23-year tenure in information technology, with a substantial portion of his career dedicated to the financial services industry. His expertise lies in designing and deploying reusable architecture, with a keen emphasis on big data, low latency, high resiliency, and operational efficiency.

His proficiency in data extends to the design and implementation of robust data architectures and the adept utilization of advanced analytics techniques.

Notably, he served as a principal solution architect at a renowned cloud service provider. Currently, Prem Ananth Selvaraj holds the esteemed position of **chief technology officer** (**CTO**) in a leading company specializing in payment technology.

In this captivating work, I extend heartfelt gratitude to the insightful author for crafting a masterpiece. Special thanks to my cherished family for unwavering support – a journey of words and emotions that wouldn't be the same without you.

Heartin Kanikathottu is an accomplished cloud architect renowned for leading technological transformations in cloud computing and security at prestigious organizations. He is also a prolific author recognized globally, with his book being named the eighth best in cloud computing in 2020. His impressive career includes roles as founder and director at Trainso Training Solutions, vice president at Morgan Stanley, principal architect at Societe Generale, and cloud architect at VMware. He has also worked at TCS, SAP Ariba, and IG Group. He holds over 15 professional certifications from Microsoft, Amazon, Oracle, Pivotal, and IBM, and dual master's degrees in cloud computing and data analytics. He is also a regular speaker at many technical forums.

I'm immensely thankful to God for guiding me to opportunities such as this book review. I would like to thank the Cloudericks.com team at Trainso whose assistance has been invaluable. A special note of appreciation goes to my wife, Sneha, whose unwavering support has been the backbone of my endeavors. Also, a big thank you to my children, June and Novanah, for their patience and understanding amidst my busy schedule of work and authoring.

Rajesh Daswani is a seasoned solutions architect with over two decades of expertise in IT infrastructure services and cloud computing. He specializes in AWS and Microsoft 365 platforms and helps clients navigate and achieve their digital transformation goals.

As a corporate trainer in cloud computing, Rajesh has supported thousands of IT professionals in honing their real-world skills, which has enabled them to better assist clients in adopting cloud technologies.

When not engrossed in the world of cloud computing, Rajesh enjoys watching re-runs of his favorite *Star Trek* shows (*The Next Generation*) and spending quality time with his family.

To my mother, Vandana, and in memory of my father, Devkrishin; I am grateful for their sacrifices and for showing me the power of persistence. To my beloved wife, Divya, my best friend and unwavering anchor; thank you for your constant support. To my incredible daughter, Ryka, who has taught me that simplicity is the key to creativity; thank you for inspiring me every day.

Table of Contents

Preface — xix

Part 1: Diving into Amazon EC2 Fundamentals

1

Introduction to Amazon EC2 and Its Benefits — 3

Unveiling Amazon Web Services and EC2	3	Web application hosting	10
		Big data processing and analytics	10
Benefits of EC2	4	A multitude of other use cases	11
Amazon EC2 versus traditional hosting	8	Amazon EC2's standout features compared to other cloud platforms	12
EC2 use cases	10	Summary	13

2

Understanding Core Components of Amazon EC2 — 15

Introduction to core components	16	Example of an instance identity document	24
Amazon EC2 instances	16	Steps to retrieving an instance identity document	24
Definition and types of instances	16		
Instance lifecycle and instance states	19	Instance purchasing options – On-Demand, Spot, and Reserved Instances	25
Instance state and instance lifecycle use cases for instance management	21		
Instance metadata and user data	22	Amazon Machine Images (AMIs)	27
What is instance metadata and user data?	22	Core components of AMIs	27
How to avoid instance impersonation attacks with instance identity documents	23	EBS	28
		Types of EBS volumes	29
		EBS snapshots and backups	32

ENIs – fundamentals, configuration, and use cases 39

Understanding ENIs, their properties, and configuration options 39
Attaching, detaching, and managing ENIs 39
Security and performance implications 40
Use cases for multiple ENIs 40

Enhanced networking – fundamentals, capabilities, and use cases 40

Supported instance types and enabling enhanced networking 41

ENA use cases 42

EFA – fundamentals, capabilities, and use cases 42

Significant features of EFA 43

Security groups and key pairs 45

Security groups – virtual firewalls for your instances 45
Key pairs – secure authentication for your instances 45
Best practices for security groups and key pairs 46

Summary 46

3

Creating and Managing Amazon Machine Images (AMI) 47

Exploring AMI virtualization – types, boot modes, and user-provided kernels 47

AMI virtualization and its types 48
AMI boot modes 49
User-provided kernel 49

Types of AMIs – an in-depth look 50

EBS-backed AMIs – the Flexible and Durable options 50
Instance store-backed AMIs – the high-performance choice 51

Creating and sharing custom AMIs 52

Creating custom AMIs 52

Sharing custom AMIs 56

Launching EC2 instances from AMIs 61

Selecting an appropriate AMI 61
Configuring instance details during launch 62
Reviewing and launching instances 65

Best practices and cautions while creating custom AMIs 67

Best practices while creating custom AMIs 67
What to watch for while creating custom AMIs 68
Troubleshooting common AMI issues 68

Summary 69
Further reading 70

4

Choosing the Right Amazon EC2 Instance Type and Size 71

Quick recap of EC2 instance types and sizes 72

Understanding workload requirements 73

Analyzing CPU, memory, and storage needs 73
Networking and performance requirements 74
Application and infrastructure resiliency 75

EC2 instance purchasing options 76

On-Demand instances	76	**Benchmarking and performance**	
Reserved Instances	76	**testing**	**80**
Spot Instances	77	Tools and techniques for performance testing	80
Savings Plans	78	Rightsizing your instances	81
Comparing costs and use cases for each option	78	Best practices for instance selection	82
		Summary	**82**

5

Networking and Connectivity in Amazon EC2 — 83

Overview of VPC	**84**	**Elastic IPs and Elastic network**	
Importance of AWS VPC	84	**interfaces**	**107**
Significance of networking in EC2	**85**	Understanding Elastic IPs and their use cases	107
Creating and managing a VPC	**86**	Elastic network interfaces	111
VPC settings and configuration options	88	**VPC peering and**	
Modifying and deleting VPCs	90	**connectivity options**	**116**
Subnets and route tables	**92**	VPC peering concepts and setup	117
Understanding subnets	92	**AWS Direct Connect and VPNs**	**121**
Understanding CIDR blocks	92	**VPC endpoints and their user cases**	**122**
Security groups and network ACLs	**99**	**VPC design principles**	**122**
Introduction to security groups	99	**Summary**	**123**
Network ACLs overview	102		

6

Implementing Security Best Practices in Amazon EC2 — 125

Introduction to Amazon		Data at rest encryption for EBS volumes	
EC2 security	**126**	and snapshots	132
Shared responsibility model	126	Data in transit encryption with TLS/SSL	133
IAM	**127**	Key management with AWS KMS	133
IAM in the context of Amazon EC2	127	**Network security**	**134**
Creating and managing IAM roles for EC2		Additional network security best practices	134
instances	127	**Operating system and application**	
Understanding instance profiles and policies	131	**security**	**135**
Data encryption	**132**	Patch management and updates	136

Application-level security considerations	137	Logging with AWS CloudTrail and CloudWatch	137
Introduction to Amazon GuardDuty for threat detection	137	Auditing and analysis techniques	138
		Summary	139

Part 2: Building a Resilient Application on Amazon EC2

7

Load Balancing and Auto Scaling with Elastic Load Balancer and Auto Scaling Groups 143

Introduction to ELB	144	Understanding the concept and components of ASG	167
Types of load balancers	144	Use cases and benefits	167
Setting up and configuring an ELB	149	Configuring and managing ASG	168
ALB	149	Launch templates	168
Setting up and configuring an NLB	155	Scaling policies	171
Creating and configuring listeners	156	Life cycle hooks	179
Setting up target groups for the NLB	158	Integrating ELB with ASG	182
Configuring health checks for targets	161	Associating target groups with ASGs	183
Load balancer best practices	163	Distributing traffic among instances	187
Cross-zone load balancing	163	Health check settings	187
SSL/TLS offloading	164	Best practices for using ELB and ASG together	188
Monitoring and logging	166	Summary	189
Introduction to Auto Scaling groups	166		

8

Understanding and Optimizing Amazon EC2 Storage Options 191

Amazon EBS volumes	192	Instance stores	210
Types of EBS volumes	192	Characteristics and use cases	210
Use cases and performance considerations	193	Performance and limitations of an instance store	211
Provisioning and attaching EBS volumes	194	Launching instances with an instance store volume	212
EBS snapshots and lifecycle management	201		
Sharing and migration	207		

Data persistence and backup strategies	214	Choosing the right storage option	224
Amazon EFS	**214**	Assessing application requirements	224
Understanding EFS and its use cases	215	Comparing storage options – performance, durability, and cost	225
Performance and durability	215		
Setting up EFS and mounting it on EFS instances	216	Best practices for optimizing storage configurations	225
EFS backup and security considerations	221	**Summary**	**226**

9

Optimizing Performance with Amazon EC2 Placement Groups and Pricing Model — 227

Introduction to Amazon EC2 placement groups	**227**	On-Demand Instances	233
		Reserved Instances	234
Types of placement groups	228	Savings plans	234
Benefits of using placement groups	229	Spot Instances	235
Strategies for deploying placement groups	**230**	**Choosing the right pricing model**	**236**
		Cost optimization strategies	236
Choosing the right type of placement group	230	Use cases for different pricing models	237
Best practices for placement group creation and management	231	Balancing performance and cost	237
		Monitoring and managing costs	**238**
Optimizing performance with placement groups	231	AWS Cost Explorer	238
		Budgets and alerts	239
Introduction to Amazon EC2 pricing models	**233**	**Summary**	**239**

10

Monitoring, Logging, and Maintenance with Amazon CloudWatch, AWS CloudTrail, and Backup Strategies — 241

Introduction to Amazon CloudWatch and AWS CloudTrail	**242**	CloudWatch dashboards and visualization	244
		CloudWatch logs and log insights	245
Overview of monitoring and logging in AWS	242	**AWS CloudTrail for auditing and security**	**246**
Differences between CloudWatch and CloudTrail	242		
		Setting up and configuring CloudTrail	246
Amazon CloudWatch essentials	**243**	Analyzing logs for security and compliance	249
Metrics, alarms, and events	243		

CloudTrail integration with other AWS services	250	Capacity planning and resource management	260
EC2 maintenance best practices	250	Key strategies for capacity planning and resource management	261
Patch management for EC2 instances	251	Backup and recovery strategies	261
Performance tuning and optimization	260	Amazon EC2 and Amazon EBS backups	262
		Disaster recovery and automation	262
		Summary	263

11

Automating Amazon EC2 – AWS CloudFormation and Infrastructure as Code 265

Introduction to AWS CloudFormation and IaC	266	Creating and updating CloudFormation stacks	273
Why is IaC essential for cloud management?	266	CloudFormation best practices	276
AWS CloudFormation overview	266	Integrating EC2 with CloudFormation	278
AWS CloudFormation basics	267	Launching and managing EC2 instances and other resources with CloudFormation	278
CloudFormation templates, stacks, and resources	267	Automating EC2 infrastructure provisioning with CloudFormation	279
CloudFormation template syntax and structure	268	IaC with AWS CDK	280
Template parameters, outputs, and mappings	270	Summary	282

Part 3: Advanced Amazon EC2 Concepts and Use Cases

12

Containerization and Serverless Computing in Amazon EC2 285

Introduction to containerization and serverless computing	286	Amazon ECS overview	287
		Amazon ECR overview	287
Containerization in EC2 with Amazon ECS and ECR	286	Deploying containers on EC2 instances with Amazon ECS	288

Running containers using AWS Fargate	295	AWS Lambda overview	302
Introduction to AWS Lambda and serverless computing	302	Deploying and integrating AWS Lambda functions	303
		Summary	305

13

Leveraging AWS Services for Hybrid and Multi-Cloud Architectures 307

Introduction to hybrid and multi-cloud architecture	308	Data management and migration across clouds	316
AWS services for hybrid cloud integration	309	AWS DataSync	317
		AWS Transfer Family	318
AWS Direct Connect	309	AWS Database Migration Service	319
AWS Storage Gateway	310	Monitoring and security in hybrid and multi-cloud environments	320
AWS Outposts	311		
AWS VPN	312	AWS Organizations	321
AWS services for multi-cloud integration	313	AWS Security Hub	322
		AWS Config	322
Amazon Route 53	313	Case studies and best practices	323
AWS Transit Gateway	314	Summary	324
AWS Resource Access Manager	315		

14

Optimizing Amazon EC2 for High-Performance Computing, Big Data, and Disaster Recovery Strategies 325

Introduction to HPC and big data on Amazon EC2	326	Redshift for data warehousing	332
		Designing and configuring HPC and Big Data Clusters	333
Understanding the importance of HPC and big data	327		
		Network configurations for low-latency communication	334
HPC-optimized EC2 instances	328		
Instance types for HPC workloads	329	Storage options and performance tuning	335
GPU instances and accelerators	330	Introduction to DR strategies	335
Big data solutions on Amazon EC2	331	Importance of DR	336
Amazon EMR for big data processing	331	Key DR concepts and terminologies	336

AWS services for DR	337	DR planning and risk assessment	339
Amazon RDS Multi-AZ deployments	337	RTO and RPO	340
Amazon S3 CRR	337	Monitoring and testing DR strategies	340
AWS Global Accelerator	338		
Designing and implementing DR strategies on AWS	339	Summary	341

15

Migrating, Modernizing, and Ensuring Compliance in Amazon EC2 Environments — 343

Migrating legacy applications to Amazon EC2	344	Compliance and governance in Amazon EC2 environments	353
Assessing the current application architecture	344	Understanding compliance requirements and frameworks	353
Identifying migration strategies and tools	346	Implementing security controls and policies	354
Planning and executing the migration process	347	Auditing and monitoring for continuous compliance	355
Modernizing applications in Amazon EC2	349	Case study and best practices	356
Refactoring and re-architecting applications	349	Case study – Migrating, modernizing, and ensuring compliance	356
Leveraging managed services and microservices	350	Best practices for a smooth transition and compliance	358
Implementing DevOps practices for continuous improvement	351	Summary	359

Index — 361

Other Books You May Enjoy — 374

Preface

Amazon EC2 is a web service offered by AWS to rent servers on a pay-as-you-go basis. EC2 allows businesses to quickly deploy, scale, and manage applications in the AWS cloud. EC2 not only streamlines IT operations by eliminating the need for purchasing physical hardware and reducing the time and effort required for infrastructure management but also stands as a prime candidate for migrating legacy applications to the AWS cloud.

In this book, you will embark on a comprehensive journey through Amazon EC2. You will start with the basics, learning what EC2 is, its benefits, and how it can help you build secure and scalable applications. By starting with the fundamentals and progressing to more advanced topics, you will gain a thorough understanding of EC2's core components, from instances and storage options to networking and security. You will learn how to select the right resources, implement security best practices, effectively manage your cloud environment, and optimize the resources for performance and cost-efficiency. As you progress, navigating the chapters and learning about EC2 foundations, you will gradually transition into advanced areas such as load balancing, auto-scaling, cloud formation, containerization, and high-performance computing to equip you with the skills required to design efficient, resilient, and modern cloud-based solutions.

This book will be crucial for you because it empowers you with the knowledge of EC2, aligning with the industry movement toward cloud computing. At the end of this book, I am confident that you will be equipped with the skills needed to deploy and manage secure and scalable applications on EC2 and to be able to tackle complex scenarios involving high-performance computing, disaster recovery, and big data. Whether you are an IT professional, developer, or someone curious about cloud computing, this book serves as an indispensable guide to harnessing the full potential of Amazon EC2, propelling you toward a future in which any form of cloud expertise is increasingly indispensable!

Who this book is for

Software developers, cloud architects, cloud engineers, IT managers, IT decision makers, students, academicians, and any individuals who are curious to learn more about AWS and EC2 will benefit greatly by expanding on their basic understanding of cloud computing, general knowledge of AWS, basic knowledge of operating systems, and experience in virtualization.

What this book covers

Chapter 1, *Introduction to Amazon EC2 and Its Benefits*, sets the stage by providing an overview of EC2's powerful features and advantages. This chapter is essential for you to comprehend the service's potential in building scalable, cost-effective, and secure cloud-based applications, forming a strong foundation for the subsequent chapters.

Chapter 2, *Understanding Core Components of Amazon EC2*, provides you with an in-depth exploration of essential EC2 components such as instances, AMIs, instance types, EBS volumes, and security features. Gaining knowledge of these core elements empowers you to effectively utilize EC2 for creating, managing, and securing cloud-based applications and infrastructure.

Chapter 3, *Creating and Managing Amazon Machine Images (AMI)*, delves into the intricacies of **AMIs**, a foundational aspect of EC2. This chapter helps you understand how to create, customize, and manage AMIs, equipping you with the skills to streamline application deployment, simplify scaling, and enhance the overall management of EC2 instances.

Chapter 4, *Choosing the Right Amazon EC2 Instance Type and Size*, guides you through the process of selecting optimal EC2 instances for your specific use cases. Understanding the nuances of instance types, families, and purchasing options enables you to efficiently allocate resources, improve performance, and manage costs, enhancing your cloud infrastructure's effectiveness.

Chapter 5, *Networking and Connectivity in Amazon EC2*, offers you valuable insights into the complexities of EC2 networking, including **Virtual Private Clouds** (**VPCs**), subnets, route tables, and security groups. Mastering these concepts allows you to design and implement secure, scalable, and highly available network architectures, enhancing the overall performance and stability of your cloud-based applications.

Chapter 6, *Implementing Security Best Practices in Amazon EC2*, equips you with essential techniques and guidelines to bolster the security of your EC2 environments. It covers crucial topics such as IAM roles, instance profiles, encryption, and patch management. This knowledge empowers you to safeguard your cloud infrastructure, ensuring data privacy and compliance with industry standards.

Chapter 7, *Load Balancing and Auto Scaling with Elastic Load Balancer and Auto Scaling Groups*, delves into Elastic Load Balancing and Auto Scaling groups to ensure high availability and fault tolerance for applications on Amazon EC2. You will learn how to effectively distribute traffic, dynamically scale resources, and maintain optimal performance, enabling you to build robust and resilient applications.

Chapter 8, *Understanding and Optimizing Amazon EC2 Storage Options*, provides you with a comprehensive understanding of various EC2 storage options, including EBS, Instance Store, and EFS. It highlights their unique features, use cases, and performance characteristics, enabling you to make informed decisions about which storage type best suits your application needs. Additionally, the chapter offers optimization techniques for maximizing storage performance, durability, and cost-efficiency.

Chapter 9, *Optimizing Performance with Amazon EC2 Placement Groups and Pricing Model*, equips you with strategies for optimizing performance and cost in your Amazon EC2 environment by utilizing placement groups to optimize network latency and throughput. It also demystifies the various pricing models available for EC2 instances, helping you make informed decisions on instance selection to maximize cost efficiency while meeting your application's performance requirements.

Chapter 10, *Monitoring, Logging, and Maintenance with Amazon CloudWatch, AWS CloudTrail, and Backup Strategies*, equips you with the skills to efficiently monitor, log, and maintain your Amazon EC2 infrastructure using Amazon CloudWatch and AWS CloudTrail. By understanding these tools and implementing effective backup strategies, you can proactively address performance issues, ensure security compliance, and safeguard your applications and data against potential failures, resulting in a more resilient and reliable cloud environment.

Chapter 11, *Automating Amazon EC2 – AWS CloudFormation and Infrastructure as Code*, empowers you to streamline and manage Amazon EC2 resources by utilizing AWS CloudFormation and **Infrastructure as Code** (**IaC**) techniques. You will learn how to create, deploy, and manage reusable and modular infrastructure templates, enabling efficient and consistent EC2 provisioning while minimizing human error and improving overall cloud management.

Chapter 12, *Containerization and Serverless Computing in Amazon EC2*, explores containerization and serverless computing in Amazon EC2, enabling you to leverage these cutting-edge technologies for efficient resource utilization, scalability, and reduced operational overhead. You will gain valuable insights and practical knowledge to modernize your applications and drive innovation in your projects.

Chapter 13, *Leveraging AWS Services for Hybrid and Multi-Cloud Architectures*, explores the process of leveraging AWS services to build hybrid and multi-cloud architectures. You will learn how to integrate different cloud platforms, enable seamless data sharing, and manage workloads across various environments. This knowledge will empower you to create flexible, resilient, and scalable solutions that can adapt to changing business needs.

Chapter 14, *Optimizing Amazon EC2 for High-Performance Computing, Big Data, and Disaster Recovery Strategies*, empowers you with the knowledge to optimize Amazon EC2 for high-performance computing and big data workloads, ensuring maximum efficiency and scalability. Additionally, you will learn how to design and implement robust disaster recovery strategies, enhancing the resilience and reliability of your critical applications and infrastructure.

Chapter 15, *Migrating, Modernizing, and Ensuring Compliance in Amazon EC2 Environments*, equips you with the knowledge and tools to migrate and modernize legacy applications to Amazon EC2, reducing costs and improving efficiency. Additionally, you will learn how to implement and maintain compliance and governance in your EC2 environments, ensuring that your workloads meet regulatory requirements and industry best practices.

To get the most out of this book

Having a basic understanding of and/or experience working in AWS, EC2, networking, virtualization, containers, and creating applications in AWS can significantly enhance your comprehension and contextual grasp while reading through the chapters of this book.

Software/hardware covered in the book	Operating system requirements
EC2, AMI, VPC networking, EBS storage, virtualization, load balancing, automation, high-performance computing, containerization, and serverless	Windows, macOS, or Linux
AWS CloudFormation CDK	

If you are using the digital version of this book, we advise you to type the code yourself or access the code from the book's GitHub repository (a link is available in the next section). Doing so will help you avoid any potential errors related to the copying and pasting of code.

Download the example code files

You can download the example code files for this book from GitHub at https://github.com/PacktPublishing/Mastering-Amazon-EC2. If there's an update to the code, it will be updated in the GitHub repository.

We also have other code bundles from our rich catalog of books and videos available at https://github.com/PacktPublishing/. Check them out!

There are a number of text conventions used throughout this book.

Code in text: Indicates code words in text, database table names, folder names, filenames, file extensions, pathnames, dummy URLs, user input, and Twitter handles. Here is an example: " Use the `sudo mount -t efs -o tls <efs-file-system-id>:/ <mount-point>` EFS mount helper. Here, `<efs-file-system-id>` represents your unique EFS ID, and `<mount-point>` represents the desired mount location."

A block of code is set as follows:

```
Parameters:
  InstanceTypeParameter:
    Description: Enter the instance type
    Type: String
    Default: t2.micro
    AllowedValues:
      - t2.micro
      - m3.medium
      - m3.large
```

When we wish to draw your attention to a particular part of a code block, the relevant lines or items are set in bold:

```
[default]
exten => s,1,Dial(Zap/1|30)
exten => s,2,Voicemail(u100)
exten => s,102,Voicemail(b100)
exten => i,1,Voicemail(s0)
```

Any command-line input or output is written as follows:

```
sudo yum install -y amazon-efs-utils
```

```
sudo apt-get install -y amazon-efs-utils
```

Bold: Indicates a new term, an important word, or words that you see onscreen. For instance, words in menus or dialog boxes appear in bold. Here is an example: "Select System info from the Administration panel."

> Tips or important notes
> Appear like this.

Get in touch

Feedback from our readers is always welcome.

General feedback: If you have questions about any aspect of this book, email us at customercare@packtpub.com and mention the book title in the subject of your message.

Errata: Although we have taken every care to ensure the accuracy of our content, mistakes do happen. If you have found a mistake in this book, we would be grateful if you would report this to us. Please visit www.packtpub.com/support/errata and fill in the form.

Piracy: If you come across any illegal copies of our works in any form on the internet, we would be grateful if you would provide us with the location address or website name. Please contact us at copyright@packt.com with a link to the material.

If you are interested in becoming an author: If there is a topic that you have expertise in and you are interested in either writing or contributing to a book, please visit authors.packtpub.com.

Share Your Thoughts

Once you've read *Mastering Amazon EC2*, we'd love to hear your thoughts! Scan the QR code below to go straight to the Amazon review page for this book and share your feedback.

https://packt.link/r/1-804-61668-0

Your review is important to us and the tech community and will help us make sure we're delivering excellent quality content.

Download a free PDF copy of this book

Thanks for purchasing this book!

Do you like to read on the go but are unable to carry your print books everywhere?

Is your eBook purchase not compatible with the device of your choice?

Don't worry, now with every Packt book you get a DRM-free PDF version of that book at no cost.

Read anywhere, any place, on any device. Search, copy, and paste code from your favorite technical books directly into your application.

The perks don't stop there, you can get exclusive access to discounts, newsletters, and great free content in your inbox daily

Follow these simple steps to get the benefits:

1. Scan the QR code or visit the link below

   `https://packt.link/free-ebook/9781804616680`

2. Submit your proof of purchase
3. That's it! We'll send your free PDF and other benefits to your email directly

Part 1: Diving into Amazon EC2 Fundamentals

The objective of this part is to establish a solid foundation in Amazon EC2 fundamentals, familiarizing you with its benefits, core components, instance types, network connectivity, and security best practices.

This part has the following chapters:

- Chapter 1, Introduction to Amazon EC2 and Its Benefits
- Chapter 2, Understanding Core Components of Amazon EC2
- Chapter 3, Creating and Managing Amazon Machine Images (AMI)
- Chapter 4, Choosing the Right Amazon EC2 Instance Type and Size
- Chapter 5, Networking and Connectivity in Amazon EC2
- Chapter 6, Implementing Security Best Practices in Amazon EC2

1
Introduction to Amazon EC2 and Its Benefits

This chapter forms the foundational bedrock of your understanding of Amazon EC2. We begin by unraveling the concepts of cloud computing and how Amazon EC2 stands as a pioneering solution in this domain. This chapter also highlights the distinctive advantages of what Amazon EC2 brings to businesses—from scalability to cost-effectiveness—and outlines real-world use cases that further underline its practical applications. We will also explore how EC2 stacks up against traditional hosting methods. Through the lens of this chapter, you will not only grasp the importance of EC2 in today's tech-centric world but also start shaping your path toward mastering its use cases.

The following topics will be covered in this chapter:

- Unveiling Amazon Web Services and EC2
- Benefits of EC2
- Amazon EC2 versus traditional hosting
- EC2 use cases
- Amazon EC2's standout features compared to other cloud platforms

Unveiling Amazon Web Services and EC2

Amazon Web Services (**AWS**) is a comprehensive cloud computing platform that provides an extensive suite of provisioned services such as computing power, storage, and databases to businesses, developers, and researchers across the globe. With its formidable infrastructure, unparalleled scalability, and economical pricing model, AWS has become the go-to choice for millions of customers, including startups, established enterprises, and organizations within the public sector.

At the heart of AWS lies one of its core services: **Amazon Elastic Compute Cloud (EC2)**. Amazon EC2 is a web service that allows users to lease virtual servers, known as instances, for running workloads and applications within the AWS ecosystem. The scaling of EC2 instances can be easily adjusted to meet fluctuating demand, with users being charged purely for the resources they utilize. This flexibility, combined with the wide variety of instances and configurations, renders EC2 an ideal solution for virtually any computational requirement.

Amazon EC2 has been instrumental in the transformation of computing. By significantly reducing the complexities of handling physical servers, EC2 allows developers to very much concentrate on writing code and creating innovative solutions without worrying about the underlying infrastructure. Moreover, the on-demand characteristic of EC2 allows businesses to react quickly to changing market conditions, scaling their computing resources as needed to stay competitive and efficient.

We will be diving deeper into the world of EC2 in the upcoming chapters, where you will be exploring its features, benefits, and best practices. This book aims to provide you the valuable insights and practical guidance to make the most of Amazon EC2, which will allow you to unlock the full potential of cloud computing. Without any more waiting, let's embark on this learning journey together and unlock the full potential of Amazon EC2!

Benefits of EC2

Amazon EC2 offers many advantages, making it a popular choice for businesses and developers alike. In this section, we will be discussing the key benefits of Amazon EC2 and its merits to understand how it can transform your application and revolutionize the way you build, deploy, and scale in the cloud.

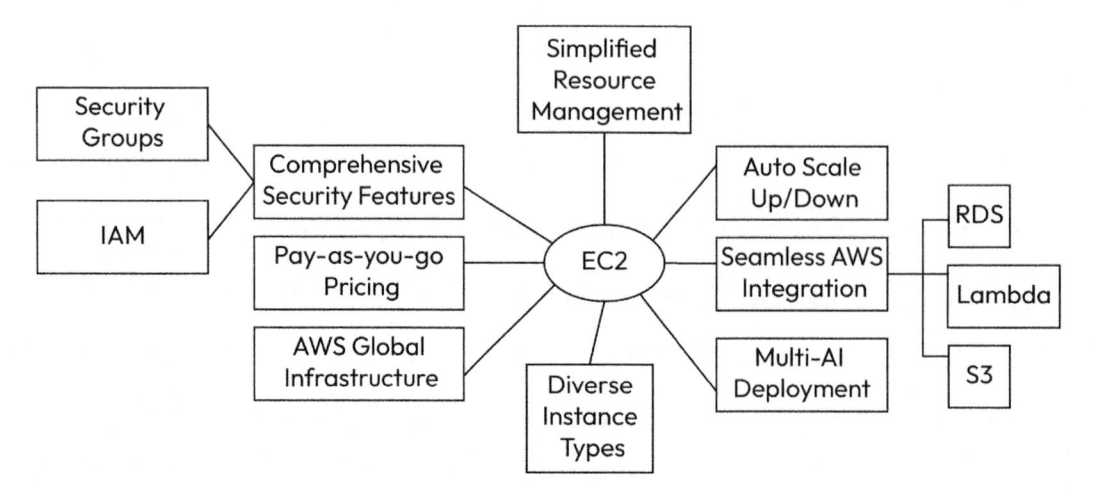

Figure 1.1 – Benefits of EC2

- **Cost efficiency**: One of the most compelling benefits of EC2 is the cost efficiency. With a pay-as-you-go pricing model, users only pay for the computing resources they use, eliminating the need for upfront investments in hardware or long-term commitments. This model simply allows organizations to adjust their computing resource flexibly to match their actual demand without pre-planning extensively, as is required for purchasing traditional servers. Additionally, Amazon EC2 offers several pricing options such as On-Demand Instances, Reserved Instances, and Spot Instances, each with its own set of advantages and use cases. On-Demand Instances allow you to pay for an hour or second, with no long-term commitments, while Reserved Instances let you reserve an instance for a specific period (say, one or three years) at a discounted price. Spot Instances, on the other hand, enable you to bid for unused EC2 capacity and can provide significant cost savings for workloads that can tolerate interruptions.
- **Scalability and flexibility**: Another key advantage of Amazon EC2 is its ability to allow users to quickly scale their resources up or down based on demand. This benefit is particularly useful for businesses that experience fluctuating workloads or seasonal peaks in traffic. It enables them to handle these situations without overprovisioning or underutilizing resources.

  Amazon EC2 also offers a wide array of instance types, with each of them designed to cater to specific workload types, such as memory optimized or compute-intensive tasks. This makes it very flexible for users to choose the most suitable instances for their needs, ensuring optimal performance and cost efficiency.
- **High availability and reliability**: Amazon EC2 is built on top of a highly available infrastructure, ensuring a highly available and reliable computing environment for applications hosted in the cloud. Inside a region, there are multiple data centers clustered together to form an availability zone, and there are multiple availability zones in the region. This similar setup is spread across different geographic regions (see *AWS Global Infrastructure* at `https://aws.amazon.com/about-aws/global-infrastructure/`), enabling EC2 to provide redundancy and fault tolerance ensuring that your application remains up and running even in the face of hardware failures or other issues.

  Furthermore, Amazon EC2 also offers advanced features such as auto-scaling and Elastic Load Balancing, which help distribute incoming traffic and automatically scale instances based on predefined conditions. All these features not only improve the availability and reliability of your application but also help you maintain optimal performance as your workloads change.
- **Security**: Security is a top priority for EC2. The platform provides several built-in features and tools to help you safeguard your data and applications. For example, with Amazon VPC, you can create a private and isolated section of the AWS cloud. This allows you to launch EC2 inside the custom network with custom network access control lists.

Additionally, EC2 offers features, such as security groups, that allow you to control inbound and outbound traffic to your instances and securely access them using SSH or RDP. Furthermore, you can augment additional access control to your EC2 instances with AWS **identity and access management (IAM)** to ensure that only authorized personnel can access your EC2 resources. It is also important to recognize that AWS adopts a shared responsibility model for security. In this paradigm, AWS is responsible for securing the underlying cloud infrastructure that supports cloud services, including the physical security of data centers, networking, and the virtualization layer, while customers are responsible for protecting their data, identity and access policies, and application-specific security settings. This shared responsibility model basically allows AWS to lay the foundation for securing the cloud environment while customers have the flexibility and responsibility to enforce their security constraints for their cloud deployments.

- **Ease of management**: Amazon EC2 simplifies the management of your computing resources, allowing you to focus on your business tasks rather than spending time on maintaining your infrastructure. AWS offers a multitude of interfaces, such as the management console, CLIs, or SDKs, to easily monitor your instances, including launching, stopping, and terminating them as needed.

    Additionally, Amazon EC2 supports purpose-driven services such as Amazon CloudWatch for monitoring, which allows you to monitor your instances and set alarms based on specific metrics such as CPU utilization or freeable memory. These alarms can help you to proactively address performance issues or identify opportunities for optimization.

    Amazon EC2 also supports the automation of resource management through AWS services such as AWS CloudFormation. This allows you to define and manage your infrastructure as a code, making it easy to deploy, update, and version your resources. This automation also extends to patch management with the AWS **Systems Manager (SSM)**, which simplifies the process of applying patches and updates to your EC2 instances and other resources.

- **Integration with other AWS services**: Amazon EC2 seamlessly integrates with a wide array of other AWS services, providing you with a comprehensive and flexible ecosystem to support your applications. For example, you can store your application data on object storage services such as Amazon S3, block storage services such as Amazon EBS, or a relational database service such as Amazon RDS. Furthermore, you can leverage the superior kin of Amazon EC2, AWS Lambda, for serverless computing.

    Integration with other AWS services enables you to build powerful, end-to-end solutions that leverage the full potential of the AWS cloud. This can lead to increased productivity, reduced operational complexity, and lower costs.

- **Support for various operating systems and processor architectures**: Selecting the ideal operating system or processor architecture for an application can often be challenging, but not when using Amazon EC2, which offers an extensive list of options that cater directly to those needs. Well-known options such as Linux, macOS, and Windows and architectures such as x86 or ARM being available on the platform give users greater variety in choosing what best suits their requirements without worrying about modifying their entire application framework to meet specifications. This allows for smooth functionality with ease across all selections!

- **Support from global infrastructure**: Amazon EC2 is widely supported across multiple regions and availability zones (see *AWS Global Infrastructure* at https://aws.amazon.com/about-aws/global-infrastructure/). This broad geographical support allows you to deploy your applications in closer proximity to your end users. This closer proximity provides a better user experience by reducing latency when a user accesses your application, thereby increasing the overall customer satisfaction.

  Furthermore, when you deploy your application across multiple regions and availability zones, you build a very highly available and fault-tolerant system, ensuring that your service remains operational in the face of any infrastructure failures or other regional issues.

- **Robust security and compliance**: Security is a top priority for AWS, and Amazon EC2 is not an exception. The platform offers various features and tools that can help guard the security posture of your application and data. You can use Amazon VPC to create an isolated network in the cloud and host your application inside your network perimeter. This allows your application to remain accessible only to authorized users and systems. Additionally, you can further improve your instance security posture by configuring security groups and network access control lists to define granular access to your instances.

  Amazon EC2 also supports integration with AWS IAM, allowing you to further enhance access control to your EC2 resources by defining permissions and policies for the users and groups who are accessing your resources. You can apply the principle of least privilege with IAM, ensuring that your users have the minimum necessary access to perform their tasks on your EC2 resources.

  Furthermore, it also gives us enormous confidence that AWS will continuously monitor our infrastructure and services to maintain its compliance in accordance with industry standards and certifications such as GDPR, HIPAA, and PCI DSS. This allows us to build applications on EC2 that meet our organizations' regulatory requirements and maintain a strong security posture.

- **Continuous improvement**: Just subscribe to the AWS blog's RSS feed and you will be delightfully bombarded by the constant updates on exciting new features and new announcements every single day! Amazon EC2 greatly benefits from this continuous improvement effort by AWS and ensures its platform always stays up to date with the latest technologies and best practices. Specific to EC2, AWS regularly introduces new instance types and performance enhancements, allowing you to take advantage of them for your applications hosted inside EC2. For example, EC2 support for powerful instance types that leverage cutting-edge hardware such as ARM processors and GPUs enables you to run high-performance workloads, such as machine learning and scientific simulation, at a lower cost.

> **Note**
> More on ARM processors and GPUs will be covered in *Chapter 4, Choosing the Right Amazon EC2 Instance Type and Size*.

So, by choosing Amazon EC2 as your computing platform, your application can benefit from AWS's ongoing innovation and commitment to excellence, ensuring that your applications are running on a state-of-the-art platform that evolves with your needs.

In summary, the benefits we discussed highlight that EC2 is a powerful and flexible computing platform for businesses and developers, making it a compelling choice for building and deploying applications in the cloud. Embracing these benefits allows EC2 to help you unlock the full potential of cloud computing, driving more innovation and, of course, amplifying the IT transformation of your organization.

As we delve further into this chapter, we will dive deeper into why EC2 outshines traditional hosting solutions and what values it brings to your plate. Let's continue to explore how EC2 fundamentally reshapes the landscape of hosting services.

Amazon EC2 versus traditional hosting

In this modern digital world, it is imperative for businesses to establish and maintain a strong online presence to make their businesses more reachable by end users and to stay ahead of their competitors. As you envision a highly available and durable online presence, you will need to have reliable hosting solutions that can support your applications and websites. The choice between Amazon EC2 and traditional hosting can be your pivotal choice here. So, let's embark on a comparison journey between the two hosting alternatives.

The traditional hosting can be broadly categorized into three types:

- **Shared hosting**: In shared hosting, multiple applications will be residing on a single server sharing system resources such as CPU, memory, and storage. While this option is most cost-effective, on the flip side, it may potentially lead to performance bottlenecks if the neighboring sites experience high traffic or consume excessive system resources.
- **Virtual private servers**: In the virtual private servers hosting model, you will have more control and dedicated resources by allocating a virtual partition on a physical server. Nevertheless, the virtual partition still shares the underlying host with the other virtual private instances.
- **Dedicated servers**: Dedicated servers stand on the other side of the rope, offering the highest level of control, but they can be pricey and also demand substantial management efforts.

Enter Amazon EC2, a groundbreaking cloud computing service that has revolutionized the hosting landscape forever. EC2 provides virtual servers or instances operating on AWS's worldwide global infrastructure. EC2 offers a flexible, scalable, and cost-efficient alternative that makes it stand out clearly from traditional hosting solutions. Unlike shared hosting or virtual private servers, EC2 instances have more controlled resource allocation, which helps to greatly reduce the impact of the "noisy neighbor" problem that is quite prevalent in traditional shared hosting environments. In contrast to dedicated servers, EC2 delivers top performance with reduced management efforts and lower costs.

Let's take some important metrics for application hosting and compare them between Amazon EC2 and traditional hosting:

- **Scalability**: Traditional hosting often requires manual intervention to scale resources, such as upgrading hardware or adding additional servers. In contrast, EC2 enables you to scale resources on demand or even automatically through integration features such as auto-scaling and **Elastic Load Balancing**. This ensures that your application can effectively handle surges in traffic by automatically scaling the resources on demand.

- **Flexibility**: Traditional hosting often restricts you to specific software and hardware configurations, and switching to a different software or hardware configurations when needed involves great effort. This often constrains your ability to adapt to evolving business requirements. In contrast, EC2 offers a wide array of selection choices, granting you the freedom to choose the best match for your needs with just a push button configuration with very minimal downtime.

- **Reliability**: The vast majority of traditional hosting providers typically operate in a single data center, which can potentially be a single point of failure. In contrast, EC2 instances can be distributed across multiple availability zones within a region, and each of the availability zones comprises multiple independent data centers, ensuring high availability and fault tolerance. This means even if any of the data centers or availability zones are down or not accessible for any reason, the same or other availability zones will still be available as they are supported by many redundancies, and your application will continue to be up and running.

- **Automation**: Amazon EC2 allows you to automate tasks such as deploying applications and managing infrastructure by leveraging its APIs and lifecycle hooks. EC2 also provides natural integration support with other automation services such as CloudFormation and CodePipeline to automate infrastructure provisioning and application deployment. This allows you to save time and minimize your human effort, making your operations more efficient and dependable.

- **Total cost of ownership**: Traditional hosting typically requires a fixed fee for a predetermined set of resources, regardless of its usage. It often involves hidden costs such as hardware maintenance and software licensing. In contrast, EC2 offers a pay-as-you-go approach, charging only for the resources you utilize. In totality, when considering the total cost of ownership, including human effort, data center licensing, and infrastructure management, EC2 clearly emerges as the most cost-effective choice.

In conclusion, it is very easy for you to see how Amazon EC2 stands out over traditional hosting solutions by means of scalability, reliability, automation, and total cost of ownership. By opting for EC2, you stay ahead of the curve, ensuring that your applications can run smoothly, efficiently, and securely. So, it is high time you say goodbye to traditional hosting and welcome the power of the cloud with Amazon EC2.

Now, let's proceed to explore various EC2 use cases to understand how this cloud service can be applied in a multitude of scenarios.

EC2 use cases

In this section, we will be exploring three diverse Amazon EC2 use cases, showcasing its remarkable flexibility and adaptability. The highlighted use cases illustrate EC2's potential to be employed in various situations to enhance efficiency, scalability, and cost-effectiveness, meeting the needs of a broad range of audiences.

Web application hosting

One of the most popular use cases of Amazon EC2 is web application hosting. Businesses of all sizes, from startups to large enterprises, can harness the potential of EC2 to deploy and scale their applications with ease. Consider, for example, an e-commerce firm that currently relies on traditional hosting and is experiencing a sudden surge in traffic due to a successful marketing campaign for its Black Friday sale. In this case, the traditional hosting may struggle to handle the increased load because of the fixed system resources, ultimately leading to a slow website performance or even downtime, frustrating its potential customers.

Now, imagine hosting the e-commerce application in Amazon EC2. In this case, the e-commerce application can quickly scale its infrastructure on demand by adding more instances to meet additional demand. Well, you can obviously rely on auto-scaling to scale the instances on demand automatically, ensuring you always have an appropriate number of instances provisioned to handle the traffic efficiently. Moreover, you can combine EC2 with additional AWS services such as EBS or S3 for storage and RDS for database management to create a seamless and highly available infrastructure for your applications. This level of flexibility and simplicity in creating a resilient and durable application allows you to maintain optimal application performance even during peak times, fostering a positive customer experience and encouraging customer loyalty.

Big data processing and analytics

In today's data-driven world, companies dealing with large amounts of data can benefit from the power and flexibility of Amazon EC2 for big data processing and analytics. EC2 provides a platform for data analysts, scientists, and engineers to perform complex computations, run machine learning models, or process massive data in real time to unlock valuable insights and drive business growth.

Now, imagine a healthcare organization that wants to analyze vast amounts of patient data to improve patient outcomes and the overall productivity in the organization. By leveraging EC2 instances, the organization can quickly set up powerful clusters to process the data and derive actionable insights. They also have the ability to choose from a wide range of instance types optimized for different workloads, ensuring they use the right resources for their specific needs, leading to improved efficiency and cost savings.

Furthermore, Amazon EC2 also supports seamless integration with other AWS data-related services, such as Amazon EMR for running big data frameworks (such as Hadoop and Spark) or Amazon

Redshift for data warehousing and analytics. This powerful and comprehensive ecosystem of services empowers organizations to fully harness the potential of their data and drive business innovation and stay ahead of their competition.

A multitude of other use cases

Beyond web application hosting and big data processing, Amazon EC2 offers a versatile platform that caters to diverse needs and a wide array of use cases. EC2's flexibility and scalability allow organizations to tailor their cloud infrastructure to meet their unique needs, empowering business innovation and unlocking new business opportunities. Let us explore a few examples to understand how EC2 can be applied across different scenarios.

- **Media and content delivery**: Media and entertainment companies can leverage EC2 instances to handle business logic processing, storage, and the delivery of multimedia content such as images, video, and audio files. By utilizing EC2 instances with high computing power and low latency networking capabilities, organizations can deliver a seamless and engaging user experience even for high-resolution media content. Also, recall the power of the ecosystem I mentioned earlier. Now, combining EC2 with other services such as CloudFront (a global content delivery network service provided by Amazon) lets your content reach your end users instantaneously and reliably, regardless of their geographic location.

- **Disaster recovery and backup**: Amazon EC2 can play a vital role in an organization's disaster recovery and backup strategies. By provisioning instances across multiple availability zones or even across regions, businesses can build a highly resilient infrastructure that can withstand failures and minimize downtime, delivering a durable application. You can also rely on EC2 instances to store and manage backups, ensuring your critical data is always available when there is a need. By combining EC2 with features such as EBS snapshots, organizations can create point-in-time backups of their data, allowing them to quickly recover from failures in the event of disaster recovery or data loss.

- **High-performance computing (HPC)**: Organizations involved in research, engineering, and scientific simulations can benefit from EC2 for their high-performance computing tasks. Specialized instance types, such as GPU or instances with high memory and compute capacity, enable users to run compute-intensive workloads with ease. By leveraging the AWS infrastructure, researchers and engineers can virtually access unlimited resources, accelerate meeting their objectives, and push their boundaries of innovation.

These use cases we discussed so far merely scratch the surface of the vast possibility that Amazon EC2 offers. With its flexibility, scalability, and cost-effectiveness, EC2 has the potential to revolutionize the way organizations build and manage their IT infrastructure, driving business growth and fostering the culture of IT innovation.

Amazon EC2's standout features compared to other cloud platforms

In this section, we will discuss various standout features of Amazon EC2 in comparison to its major competitors, such as Microsoft Azure **virtual machines** (**VMs**) and Google Compute Engine. This comparison will allow you to understand the unique advantages and capabilities of Amazon EC2 and how it can be actively leveraged to cater to your organization's needs:

- **Instance variety**: One of the key strengths of Amazon EC2 is the extensive range of instance types and configurations it offers. This variety allows EC2 to accommodate a wide variety of workloads, making it an adaptable solution for organizations with diverse requirements. In comparison, Microsoft Azure VMs and Google compute engine also provide various instance types, but the selections available in comparison to EC2 are unparalleled.

- **Global infrastructure**: AWS supports running your workloads across a vast global infrastructure. Their extensive network of data centers and edge locations ensures low latency, high availability, and improved performance for the workloads, which are hosted in EC2. Although Microsoft Azure and Google Cloud also have significant global footprints, AWS infrastructure is more expansive, providing a competitive edge for EC2.

- **Integration with AWS Ecosystem**: Amazon EC2 benefits from seamless integration with other services in the broader AWS ecosystem. This means that EC2 instances can easily work in combination with other AWS services, such as storage, databases, and analytics, allowing you to create powerful and full-fledged solutions. On the other side, Microsoft Azure VM and Google Compute Engine also offer integration with their respective ecosystems, but the sheer breadth of services within the AWS ecosystem provides EC2 with a unique advantage.

- **Customizable pricing models**: Amazon EC2 supports a wide range of pricing models, including On-Demand Instances, Reserved Instances, and Spot Instances. This broad range of pricing models creates flexibility for users, allowing them to select optimal pricing models based on their usage patterns of their workloads. On the other side, Microsoft Azure and Google Cloud also provide various pricing options for their VMs and Compute Engine. However, in comparison, EC2's pricing model gives it an edge as it supports many different commitments to cater to a broader set of use cases.

- **Proven track record**: AWS is a pioneer, and Amazon EC2 has been in the market for a considerable amount of time and has a strong reputation for its reliability, durability, performance, and innovation. This proven track record allows users to confidently host their workloads on EC2. Comparably, Microsoft Azure VMs and Google Cloud Compute Engine also provide a reliable and durable hosting environment, but the EC2's longer market presence makes it comfortably established as a solid foundation.

In summary, Amazon EC2's standout features make it a very robust and reliable choice for organizations looking to leverage the power of cloud computing for their workloads.

Summary

Now that we have reached the end of this chapter, let's take a moment to understand what we have explored in this fascinating world of Amazon EC2. We started off this chapter by exploring the numerous benefits of EC2, such as scalability, flexibility, and cost-effectiveness. Following that, we explored traditional hosting solutions, what their key differences with EC2 are, and how EC2 can offer significant advantages to businesses. We then explored various business use cases, emphasizing EC2's wide applicability across industries. Finally, we concluded the chapter by exploring EC2's standout features against other cloud computing platforms, showing that it is a powerful choice for hosting our workloads.

In the next chapter, we will dive deeper into the essential building blocks of EC2. This will provide you with a comprehensive understanding of its core components, including EC2 instances, AMI, instance types and families, the **Elastic Block Store (EBS)**, **Elastic network interfaces (ENI)**, IP addresses, security groups, and key pairs.

2
Understanding Core Components of Amazon EC2

In this chapter, we will meticulously explore EC2's central components and equip you with a robust understanding of its foundational elements.

As we explore this chapter, our topics of focus will include an in-depth understanding of EC2's core components, shedding light on its significance in the computing domain. Following that, we will dive into the dynamic world of Amazon EC2 instances, delving into their various kinds, lifecycles, and the pivotal role of instance metadata and user data.

As our journey progresses, we will unlock the mysteries of **Amazon Machine Images** (**AMIs**), understand their foundation through components such as the root volume and the instance store and the nuances of software configuration. This exploration also paves the way to create, share, and manage custom AMIs. As we move forward, you will encounter various EC2 instance types and families, obtaining a thorough understanding of the instance types and families available. This chapter illuminates their specific use case and guides you through the various purchasing options, namely On-Demand, Reserved, and Spot Instances.

But EC2's expanse doesn't end here. In the subsequent sections, we will introduce you to **Elastic Block Store** (**EBS**), highlighting different volumes available, such as General Purpose SSD, Provisioned IOPS SSD, and Magnetic, while shedding light on the importance of EBS snapshots and backups. This chapter also navigates you through the functionalities of **elastic network interfaces** (**ENIs**) and IP addresses, giving you a detailed understanding of ENIs and IP addresses, along with the concepts of association and disassociation. Finally, with a keen eye on securing the EC2 environment, we will discuss security groups and key pairs, providing an overview of their role in securing EC2 access.

The following topics will be covered in this chapter:

- Introduction to core components
- Amazon EC2 instances
- Instance metadata and user data
- How to avoid impersonation attacks with instance identity documents
- Instance purchasing options – On-Demand, Spot, and Reserved Instances
- Amazon Machine Images (AMIs)
- ENIs – fundamentals, configuration, and use cases
- Enhanced networking – fundamentals, capabilities, and use cases
- **Elastic Fabric Adapter (EFA)** – fundamentals, capabilities, and use cases
- Security groups and key pairs

Now, with this understanding, let's dive into the *Introduction to Core Components* section to commence this chapter.

Introduction to core components

Core components are an integral part of EC2 in ensuring the overall functioning of the service. By understanding each of the core components, you can make more informed decisions about your configuration options and optimize instances to your specific needs. If you are a beginner exploring cloud computing or an advanced user looking at mastering EC2, understanding the importance of core components will help you maximize the potential of this powerful service.

Without any further ado, let's dive in and explore the fascinating world of Amazon EC2!

Amazon EC2 instances

Diving into the heart of Amazon EC2, we encounter the pivotal concept of **EC2 instances**, virtual servers that power cloud applications. We will now delve into and understand different EC2 instance types and sizes and equip you with insights to select the right one that fits your application needs.

Definition and types of instances

EC2 instances come in a variety of types and sizes, providing enough flexibility to cater to various types of workloads. Each of the instance families is designed to address specific workloads and requirements, with their support ranging from memory-intensive, storage-optimized, and compute-optimized tasks. Understanding instance types and their differences will allow you to select the most suitable one for your particular use case, providing optimal performance with cost efficiency.

The following is a brief overview of some of the primary instance families:

- **General-purpose instances (A, M, and T families)**: General-purpose instances come with balanced compute, memory, and networking resources. This delicate balance makes them an ideal choice for workloads such as web applications, microservices, and small-to-medium databases. Typical use cases include the following:

  - **Web servers and application servers**: Web applications with moderate traffic and varying resource demands can be perfectly handled by general-purpose instances.
  - **Development and testing environments**: Development and testing environments typically don't need any specialized system resources. Their balanced distribution of system resources aptly supports running development and testing workloads.
  - **Small-to-medium databases**: Databases with a need for moderate resource requirements can be effectively handled by a general-purpose instance. This approach is particularly suitable when specific customization, control, compliance, and compatibility with a legal application cannot be achieved with managed services such as **Relational Database Service (RDS)**.

- **Compute-optimized instances (C family)**: Compute-optimized instances are packed with top-tier high-performance processors, making them superbly suitable for compute-heavy workloads such as batch processing, media transcoding, scientific modeling, **high-performance computing** (HPC), and so on. Typical use cases include the following:

  - **HPC**: An ideal place for executing scientific simulations, weather forecasting, or financial modeling workloads.
  - **Batch processing**: A perfect place for running large-scale batch and data processing tasks such as video encoding, image encoding, data compression, and so on.
  - **Gaming servers**: An ideal place for multiplayer gaming servers where robust and high-performance compute resources are required.

- **Memory-optimized instances (R, X, and Z families)**: Memory-optimized instances are highly suited for memory-intensive workloads that demand substantial amounts of RAM for their operations. This includes in-memory databases, real-time big data analytics, high-performance caching systems, and so on. Typical use cases include the following:

  - **High-performance databases**: Supporting large-scale in-memory databases such as SAP HANA or Redis.
  - **In-memory caches**: Enhancing the performance of an application by storing recurrently accessed data in memory.
  - **Big data analytics**: Ideal for running workloads that require processing large datasets, such as Apache Spark or Apache Flink.

- **Storage-optimized instances (D, H, and I families)**: Storage-optimized instances are ideal for workloads that necessitate high sequential read and write operations on sizable local datasets. These instances are perfect for use cases such as data processing, data warehousing, and distributed filesystems. Typical use cases include the following:

  - **Data warehousing**: Support massive data storage and processing needs for applications such as Amazon Redshift.
  - **Log processing**: Very suitable for real-time analysis of log data generated by servers, applications, or networks.

- **GPU instances (F, G and P families)**: GPU instances are equipped with powerful graphics processing units, making them a go-to solution for **machine learning** (**ML**), video processing, graphics rendering, and other GPU-accelerated workloads. Typical use cases include the following:

  - **ML**: Training and seamless deployment of **deep learning** (**DL**) models via well-known frameworks such as PyTorch or TensorFlow.
  - **Graphics rendering**: Very suitable for producing high-definition images and video for visual effects, **virtual reality** (**VR**) applications, or gaming applications.
  - **Scientific simulations**: Very effective for executing complex simulations in the fields of genomics, oil and gas, or the quantum industry.

- **ARM-based instances (Graviton2- and Graviton3-powered families)**: ARM-based instances are backed by AWS's in-house Graviton processors. These instances offer considerable performance improvements and cost efficiency over x86-type instances. This instance type is well suited for workloads such as web servers, containerized microservices, and databases. The Graviton processor lineup includes both Graviton2 and Graviton3 (recommended, newer generation), which greatly enhances performance and efficiency for customers. Typical use cases include the following:

  - **Containerized applications**: Instances powered by Graviton3 and Graviton2 are ideal for operating containerized orchestration platforms such as Kubernetes or Amazon **Elastic Container Service** (**ECS**). In particular, their cost efficiency makes them a suitable choice for microservices-based architectures.
  - **Data analytics and processing**: Graviton3- and Graviton2-powered instances are a great fit for data analytics and processing. Their computational efficiency paired with cost effectiveness makes them a prime choice for intricate data transformation tasks. For businesses aiming to extract meaningful insights from vast datasets, these instances stand out as a beacon of performance and affordability.

To help you select the right instance type for your use case, you may consider following the simple flowchart shown here:

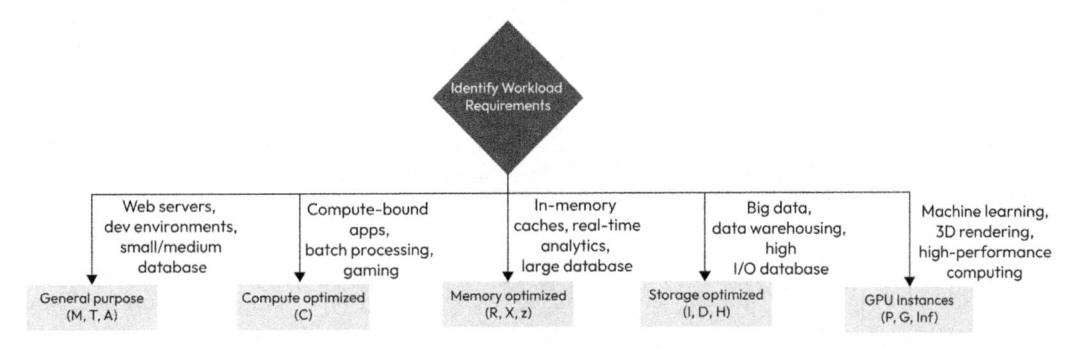

Figure 2.1 – Requirements for EC2 instance-type selection

By following the steps discussed earlier, you will gain a solid understanding of different types of EC2 instances, and that will further empower you to make informed decisions leading to peak performance and cost effectiveness for your specific application.

Instance lifecycle and instance states

When working with Amazon EC2 instances, it is essential to understand the instance lifecycle and its various instance states to effectively and optimally manage their availability. Their understanding and usage will provide you with control over instance costs by stopping or terminating them when they are no longer needed. Let's dive deeper to understand instance lifecycle transitions and their states further:

- **Launch**: The *launch* process is set in motion when you start a new EC2 instance. In this phase, AWS provisions necessary system resources such as computing capacity, storage, and networking based on the instance type and other configurations you have chosen. Subsequently, the instance then transitions to the *pending* state during its initialization process.

    - **State: Pending**: This transitional state occurs when the instance is launched but has not yet entered the *running* state. The instance is in the process of being set up during this state, and any interaction with it will remain unavailable until it is fully operational.

- **Start**: Once the initialization process is complete, the instance then advances to the *running* state. Here, you can establish a connection to the instance, perform required configurations or management tasks, deploy software applications, and so on. If the instance was previously stopped, then starting the instance will allow it to transition from the *stopped* state back to the *running* state.

  - **State: Running**: In this state, the instance is actively running and remains fully operational and accessible, allowing you to install or deploy applications and conduct any other management tasks.

- **Stop**: When you no longer require an instance but still need to retain its data and configuration, then you can stop it. Stopping an instance releases the associated compute resources, aiding you to control costs while preserving instance data that is stored in EBS volumes. When you stop the instance, it transitions from the *running* state to the *stopping* state and finally to the *stopped* state.

  - **States: Stopping and stopped**: The *stopping* state is a transient state marking instance transitions from the *running* to the *stopped* state. Upon reaching the *stopped* state, the instance will be inactive, and you will no longer be billed for computing resources. However, you will still incur charges for any EBS volumes and Elastic IP addresses that are attached to the instance.

- **Terminate**: If you no longer need an instance and want to permanently delete it, you can terminate it. Terminating an instance releases all associated resources, including EBS volumes, and deletes any data stored on the instance. The instance transitions from the *running* state to the *shutting down* state and finally to the *terminated* state.

  - **States: Shutting down and terminated**: The *shutting down* state is an intermediary state as the instance transitions from *running* to *terminated*. Once the instance reaches the *terminated* state, it is permanently deleted, eliminating any possibility of recovering its data or configuration.

Understanding instance lifecycles and instance states helps you ensure the effective management of EC2 instances. Also, by knowing when to start, stop, and terminate instances, you can ensure optimal performance and availability while minimizing costs.

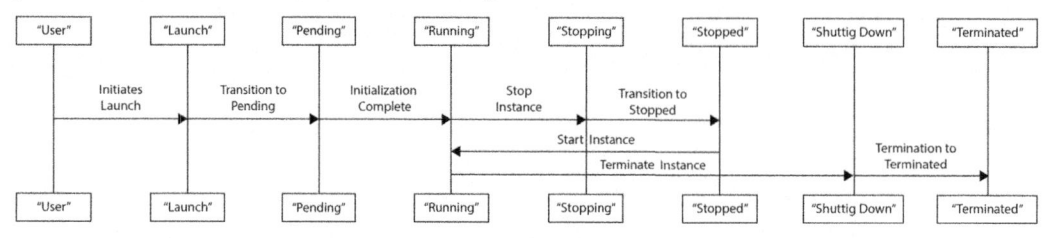

Figure 2.2 – EC2 instance state transition illustration

Instance state and instance lifecycle use cases for instance management

In this section, we will explore some practical use cases for instance states and instance lifecycles in relation to instance management. The relevance of this is quite significant across organizations regardless of their size or expertise:

- **Scheduled scaling**

    It is common for applications to experience predictable fluctuations in demand; for example, experiencing business traffic during business hours or specific days of the week. In such instances, you can configure *Amazon EC2 Auto Scaling policies* that can automatically launch and terminate instances at a predefined schedule. This ensures your infrastructure is precisely adapted to your demand patterns, optimizing resource utilization and costs.

> Note
>
> Stay tuned for *Chapter 7, Load Balancing and Auto Scaling with Elastic Load Balancer and Auto Scaling Groups*, where we will delve into the specifics of configuring EC2 Auto Scaling policies!

- **Development and testing environments**

    Very often, developers and testers require temporary instances for their tasks. These types of instances often contribute to unnecessary costs when they are left running outside business hours. By leveraging the instance states, you can automate start and stop actions for development and testing environments with AWS APIs to ensure they remain active only during business hours.

- **Disaster recovery (DR) and high availability (HA)**

    Instance lifecycles and instance states play an instrumental role in ensuring high application availability and resiliency in the event of failures and/or calamities. Monitoring instance states will allow you to automatically detect unhealthy instances and initiate failover processes such as launching new instances in different Availability Zones to allow your applications to remain available in the event of failures.

- **Infrastructure automation**

    As your infrastructure expands, managing individual instances becomes increasingly complex and time-consuming. By leveraging instance lifecycles and instance states as part of your automation strategy, you can streamline and automate routine tasks such as provisioning, monitoring, and improving your operational efficiency while also reducing the risk of human error.

With this understanding in place, let's move on to the next section. The next section will further expand your understanding, providing deeper insights into the effective management and operation of Amazon EC2 instances.

Instance metadata and user data

Amazon EC2 instances come with *extensive metadata* and *user-data features* that can help you manage your instances more effectively. In this section, we will delve into understanding instance metadata and user data, ways to access metadata, working with user data, differences between Instance Metadata Service version 1 (IMDSv1) and IMDSv2, instance identity documents, and several practical use cases for instance metadata and user data.

What is instance metadata and user data?

Instance metadata is data about your instance that you can use to configure or manage your running instance. Metadata includes *instance IDs*, *instance types*, *IP addresses*, *block device mappings*, and more. **User data**, on the other hand, is custom bootstrap data that you can provide while launching your instance. The user data is then executed at the time of bootstrapping your instance, which can be used to configure the instance or run as a script according to your use case at the time of instance startup.

How do you retrieve instance metadata?

You can access IMDS within a running instance by accessing the following URL: `http://169.254.169.254/latest/meta-data`. To query specific metadata information using IMDS, you can append the desired metadata item's path to the base URL. For example, to retrieve the instance ID using IMDS, you would use `http://169.254.169.254/latest/meta-data/instance-id`.

Working with user data

User data can be provided as a script or as plain text when launching an instance. With user data, you can perform common automated configuration tasks such as running scripts or installing software during the instance initialization process. Take note that user data is limited to 16 KB in size and is stored and accessible as a *Base64*-encoded string via IMDS by accessing the following URL: `http://169.254.169.254/latest/user-data`.

IMDSv1 versus IMDSv2

There are two versions of IMDS available: *IMDSv1* and *IMDSv2*. The original metadata service (IMDSv1) allows simple HTTP `GET` requests to retrieve metadata. In this version, there were concerns about potential security vulnerabilities, especially a type of attack called **server-side request forgery** (**SSRF**), whereby an attacker could trick an application into reaching out to IMDS, retrieve instance metadata such as **Identity and Access Management** (**IAM**) roles and other sensitive information, and exfiltrate that data. In the newer version, IMDSv2 introduces session-based authentication, which improves instance metadata security by mitigating issues such as SSRF attacks. IMDSv2 mitigates SSRF attacks with a two-step process: First, you create a session by sending a PUT request to the token endpoint with a unique token, `http://169.254.169.254/latest/api/token`. Second, you use the token in the header of subsequent requests to access metadata. It is highly recommended to use IMDSv2 for improved security.

Use cases for instance metadata and user data

Here are some use cases for instance metadata and user data:

- **Dynamic configuration**: IMDS allows you to configure applications running on the EC2 instance without the need for manual intervention. For example, if you are in need of an IP address and other metadata information, you can simply retrieve the information by hitting the metadata endpoint and configure your application to use it accordingly.
- **Automated deployment**: By leveraging instance user data, you can automate the deployment and configuration of an instance by passing scripts that get executed during the instance startup. This feature allows you to ensure that instances are automatically set up with the required application stack and configuration, reducing manual effort and the likelihood of human error.
- **Monitoring and logging**: Instance metadata can be leveraged to tag log files and other monitoring data generated by the instance. Leveraging instance metadata information makes it easier to efficiently manage and effectively analyze the data needed for troubleshooting. For example, you can include the instance ID in log filenames or log messages to assist you with easier and more seamless troubleshooting in distributed environments.

Through instance metadata and user data, we can dynamically configure applications, automate the deployment process, and enhance monitoring and logging mechanisms in EC2 instances.

In the next section, we will learn how to avoid instance impersonation attacks with instance identity documents to safeguard our instances effectively.

How to avoid instance impersonation attacks with instance identity documents

An **instance identity document** is a JSON-formatted document that provides cryptographically verifiable information about your instance. The document contains details including instance ID, account ID, and instance type, which can be used to verify instance authenticity and guard against instance impersonation attacks such as the following:

- **Instance ID spoofing**: In this attack, the attacker compromises an EC2 instance and alters the instance ID to match that of a legitimate EC2 instance. The attacker then takes advantage of the spoofed instance ID to manipulate other AWS services such as CloudWatch and **Elastic Load Balancing (ELB)** into treating the malicious EC2 instance as a legitimate one. By doing this, the attacker potentially gains unauthorized access to sensitive data or causes **denial-of-service (DoS)** attacks.

- **Unauthorized privilege escalation**: There is a possibility that an attacker may attempt to escalate privileges by associating an IAM role with higher privileges with the running EC2 instance. By leveraging an instance identity document, you can take control of the situation and enforce conditions in the IAM policy that restrict role association based on instance characteristics, which ultimately helps you to prevent unauthorized privilege escalation.

Example of an instance identity document

Before we dive deeper into understanding the steps involved in securing our instances, here is an example of an instance identity document to shed light on its importance and significance:

```
{
    "devpayProductCodes" : null,
    "availabilityZone" : "us-west-2a",
    "privateIp" : "10.0.0.19",
    "version" : "2017-09-30",
    "instanceId" : "i-1234567890abcdef0",
    "billingProducts" : null,
    "instanceType" : "t2.micro",
    "accountId" : "123456789012",
    "architecture" : "x86_64",
    "kernelId" : null,
    "ramdiskId" : null,
    "imageId" : "ami-5fb8c835",
    "pendingTime" : "2016-11-19T16:32:11Z",
    "region" : "us-west-2"
}
```

Steps to retrieving an instance identity document

Here are the steps to retrieve an instance identity document from an EC2 instance:

1. Request a session token from IMDS:

    ```
    TOKEN=$(curl -X PUT "http://169.254.169.254/latest/api/token" -H "X-aws-ec2-metadata-token-ttl-seconds: 21600")
    ```

    This command sends a PUT request to IMDSv2 and sets the token **time-to-live** (TTL) to 21600 seconds (6 hours). The token is stored in the TOKEN variable.

2. Retrieve the instance identity document:

    ```
    curl -H "X-aws-ec2-metadata-token: $TOKEN" http://169.254.169.254/latest/dynamic/instance-identity/document
    ```

This command sends a GET request to the IMDSv2 endpoint, using the token obtained in the previous step. The instance identity document will be returned in JSON format, as shown in the preceding example.

Now that we have gained clarity on instance identity documents and how to retrieve them, let's shift our focus toward understanding different types of purchasing options available for EC2 instances, where we will discuss how you can optimize your costs to cater to specific use cases. Let's dive in!

Instance purchasing options – On-Demand, Spot, and Reserved Instances

As we continue our exploration of Amazon EC2 instance types and families, it is essential for you to understand various purchasing options available to meet your specific needs and budget. EC2 offers five primary purchasing options: *On-Demand*, *Reserved*, *Spot*, *Savings Plans*, and *Dedicated* Instances. In this section, we will delve into each of the purchasing options, explaining their key features, benefits, and use cases to help to make informed decisions for your workloads:

- **On-Demand Instances**: On-Demand Instances offers the most straightforward and flexible pricing model. With this option, you pay for the compute capacity by hour or second, depending on the instance type, with no long-term commitments or upfront payments required. On-Demand Instances are ideal for users who want the following:

  - The ability to scale capacity up or down without any commitments.
  - The flexibility to test new applications or environments.
  - The option to handle variable workloads, such as development and testing, or short-term projects.

  While On-Demand Instances provide the greatest flexibility, they may not be the cost-effective choice for long-term, predictable workloads.

- **Reserved Instances (RIs)**: RIs are an excellent option for users with predictable workloads, offering significant cost savings compared to On-Demand Instances. By committing to a 1- or 3-year term, you can reserve EC2 instances and benefit from lower hourly rates. There are three types of RIs:

  - **Standard RIs**: These provide the most significant cost savings of up to 75% compared to On-Demand Instances and are best suited for steady-state workloads.
  - **Convertible RIs**: These offer up to 54% savings and provide the flexibility to change instance families, operating systems, and other attributes during the RI term.
  - **Scheduled RIs**: These are ideal for predictable, recurring workloads that only require capacity during specific time windows. These instances can be scheduled to be available during predefined timeframes.

RIs are the ideal choice for users with the following requirements:

- Have consistent workloads and want to commit to a long-term contract.
- Want to optimize cost for steady-state applications.
- Need capacity reservation for mission-critical workloads.

- **Savings Plans**: **Savings Plans** provides a flexible pricing model and offers significant cost savings over on-demand pricing. This can be considered similar to RIs but offers more flexibility. With Savings Plans, users can commit to a specific amount of compute usage (say, $10/hr) or commit to a 1- or 3-year term, and, in return, receive lower prices. This option is ideal for the following kinds of users:

  - Users with predictable usage that varies across instance types.
  - Users seeking savings over capacity reservations.
  - Users looking to simplify billing and cost management.

- **Dedicated Instances**: **Dedicated Servers/Instances** are EC2 instances with capacity dedicated to your full usage. This option can help you meet compliance requirements and reduce costs by allowing you to use your existing server-bound software licenses. This is ideal for users with the following requirements:

  - Have strict regulatory or compliance needs requiring physical isolation.
  - Wish to utilize existing software licenses compatible with Dedicated Hosts.
  - Need visibility and control over the placement of instances on a specific, physical server.

- **Spot Instances**: **Spot Instances** offer a cost-effective way to access unused EC2 capacity at significant discounts, up to 90% off the on-demand price. However, they come with the caveat that your instances can be terminated at short notice if capacity is needed by other users or if the spot price exceeds your maximum bid.

  Spot Instances are best suited for the following kinds of users:

  - Users who have flexible start and end times for their workloads.
  - Users who can handle interruptions or instance terminations gracefully.
  - Users who require large amounts of compute capacity for short durations, such as batch processing, data analytics, or scientific simulations.

Understanding the various EC2 purchasing options is crucial for optimizing costs and meeting your specific workload requirements. By evaluating the benefits and use cases of On-Demand, Reserved, and Spot Instances, you can choose the most suitable option for your organization and make the most of Amazon EC2 capabilities. With this foundational grasp on these purchasing options, let's transition to discussing another pivotal aspect of EC2: AMIs. We will dive deeper into the intricacies and importance of AMIs, providing you with insights for efficient EC2 usage.

Amazon Machine Images (AMIs)

AMIs are preconfigured/pre-built templates that enable you to streamline the launch of EC2 instances. An AMI encompasses all data required to initialize an instance. This includes the operating system, application server, and any additional software relevant to your requirements. By using AMIs, you can streamline your setup, minimize configuration errors, and guarantee a consistent environment across your instances. This overall process allows you to easily scale and manage your infrastructure.

Core components of AMIs

The following are the core components of AMIs:

- **Root volume**: The root volume serves as the principal storage device for an instance, housing the operating system, system files, and any other software required to launch and run the instance. The root volume can either be backed by EBS or instance store volumes. EBS-backed volumes offer increased durability, adaptability, and snapshot abilities, whereas instance store volumes offer low latency and high storage performance suitable for temporary data and other specific use cases.

- **Instance store volumes**: In addition to the root volume, an AMI may consist of multiple instance store volumes, which are ephemeral storage devices directly connected to the host hardware of the instance. Instance store volumes are ideal for temporary storage requirements offering excellent I/O performance with reduced latency. However, data stored on instance store volumes is not persistent, which means the data will be lost when the instance is terminated and in other failure scenarios.

- **Software configuration settings**: An AMI includes various software configuration settings, such as launch permissions, compatible instance types, and user-data scripts. These configurations ensure that the instance is launched with correct permissions and any other custom scripts required for your unique use case.

- **Metadata**: AMIs include metadata such as AMI ID, name, description, and ownership details. This information allows you to seamlessly identify, manage, and share your customized AMIs with others. It also aids you in version control of your AMIs and helps you ensure you are launching instances with up-to-date and secure configurations.

- **Security settings**: AMIs can be launched with security groups, key pairs, and IAM roles, allowing you to control your instances and secure your infrastructure. These settings are essential for maintaining a secure environment and complying with industry best practices and regulatory requirements.

AMIs serve as the blueprint for an EC2 instance, encompassing the root volume, additional storage with instance store volumes, essential software configurations, and vital security settings. With the foundation on AMI set, let's now delve into the significance of EBS and understand its significance within EC2.

> **Note**
> Please note that more on AMI will be covered in the next chapter.

EBS

As we continue our journey through the core components of Amazon EC2, we now turn our attention to EBS, a vital service that provides persistent block-level storage for your EC2 instances. **EBS** offers high-performance durable storage solutions that can grow with your needs, making it easier to handle your storage as your workloads change.

EBS volumes are designed to be highly available and reliable, ensuring that your data remains safe and accessible with minimal failures each and every year. Your EBS volumes are automatically replicated within the same Availability Zone. So, in the event of any hardware or underlying storage failure, your data storage is still protected. EBS volumes can also be easily attached or detached from EC2 instances, allowing you to move your data between instances seamlessly as needed. This convenience makes it easier for you to manage your storage needs on Amazon EC2.

EBS volumes are created independently of EC2 instances, which means your volumes can persist independently even after an instance is terminated. This feature is critical for preserving data and ensuring data is not lost when instances are stopped or terminated.

In addition to this flexibility and reliability, EBS offers various volume types to cater to support a broad spectrum of use cases, from general-purpose workloads to high-performance, I/O-intensive applications. In the next section, we will discuss different types of EBS volumes and understand the differences to select the most suitable EBS volume type for your type of workload, ensuring that your storage resources are optimized for both performance and cost.

Key benefits of EBS include the following:

- **Performance**: EBS offers faster response time and quick data transfers. This ensures that EBS meets performance delivery requirements for rigorous applications and tasks.
- **Durability**: EBS volumes possess an annual failure rate as low as 0.1 to 0.2%. This makes EBS a highly reliable and dependable partner for safeguarding your data.

- **Scalability**: EBS allows you to adjust your storage size up or down dynamically, providing greater flexibility to handle your storage needs effortlessly.
- **Data encryption**: EBS ensures your data stays protected both at rest and in transit. This allows you to ensure your data security and meet your business regulatory requirements.

Types of EBS volumes

As we continue our exploration of EBS, in this section, we will discuss different types of EBS volumes available for your usage and their respective use cases:

- **General Purpose SSD**: General Purpose SSD volumes, also known as gp2 or gp3 volumes, are designed to provide a balance between performance and cost. These volumes offer a baseline performance of 3 **input/output operations per second per gigabyte (IOPS)** and can burst up to 16,000 IOPS for gp3, depending on the volume size. General Purpose SSD volumes are suitable for a wide range of workloads, including the following:

  - Boot volumes for EC2 instances
  - **Content management systems (CMS)**
  - Small-to-medium-sized databases

  The main advantage of General Purpose SSD volumes is their ability to deliver consistent and predictable performance at an alternative cost. They are an excellent choice for most applications that require moderate IOPS and throughput levels.

- **Provisioned IOPS SSD**: Provisioned IOPS SSD volumes, also known as *io1* or *io2* volumes, are designed for I/O intensive workloads that require high IOPS and low-latency storage performance. Provisioned IOPS SSD volumes allow you to specify the number the IOPS you need while provisioning, and you can specify up to a maximum of 64000 IOPS for both io1 and io2 volumes. Provisioned IOPS SSD volumes are well suited for the following:

  - Large databases such as **online transaction processing (OLTP)** systems
  - HPC applications
  - Real-time analytics and data processing

  The main advantage of Provisioned IOPS SSD volumes is their consistency in delivering low-latency and high-throughput performance, making them ideal for I/O-intensive applications. However, this performance comes at a higher cost when compared to General Purpose SSD volumes.

- **Throughput Optimized HDD volumes (st1)**: Throughput Optimized HDD volumes, also known as *st1* volumes, are designed for workloads that require high throughput performance with support for large sequential I/O operations. These volumes provide cost-effective storage with a base throughput of 40 **mebibytes per second per tebibyte (MiB/s per TiB)**. Also, they offer support for burst capacity, with the potential to burst up to 500MiB/s. Throughput Optimized HDD volumes are ideal for the following:

  - Data warehousing
  - Log processing
  - Big data analytics

  In comparison with other SSD volumes, Throughput Optimized HDD volumes deliver a high throughput at a lower cost per GB. However, if an application demands low latency access or higher IOPS, then they are not suitable.

- **Cold HDD volumes (sc1)**: Cold HDD volumes are also known as *sc1* volumes, They are designed for workloads with large amounts of data, but you only need to access them in very rare situations. This is a cheaper storage option, available for you when you intend to prioritize cost over performance. These volumes offer a baseline throughput of 12 MiB/ s per TiB and can burst up to 80 MiB/s. Cold HDD volumes are well suited for the following:

  - Long-term backup storage
  - Archival storage
  - Infrequently accessed large datasets

  Cold HDD volumes come as an attractive option for scenarios where cost efficiency is higher than performance. However, sc1 volumes are not recommended for applications that require high IOPS or low-latency access.

Here's a simple flowchart to help you decide what kinds of storage volumes to use depending on your workload requirements:

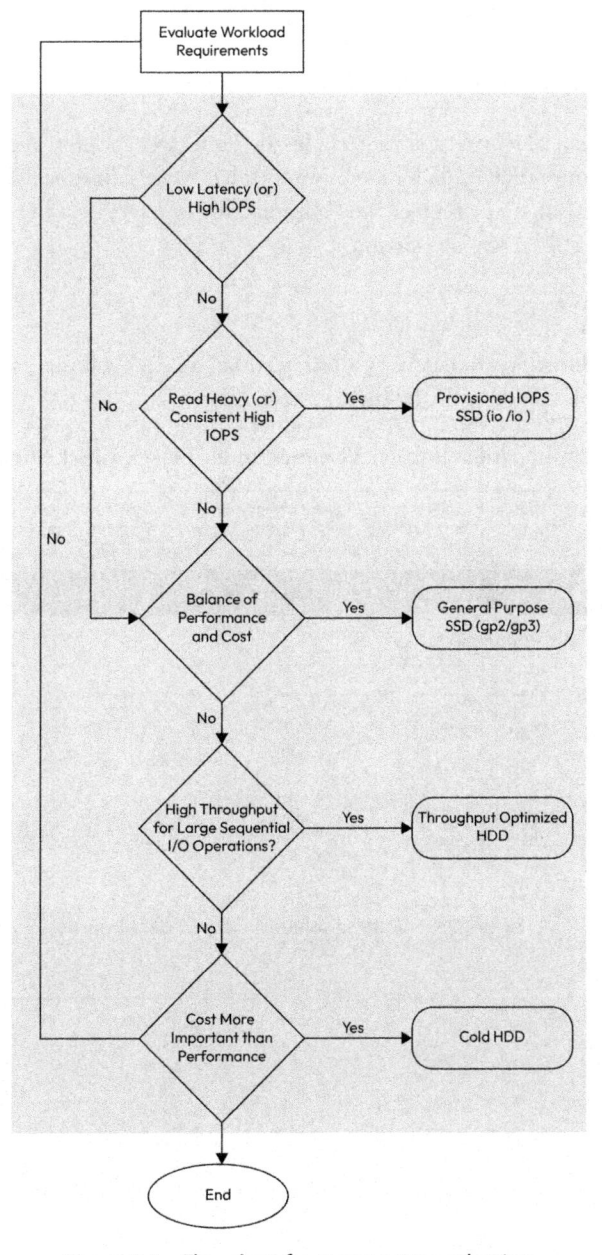

Figure 2.3 – Flowchart for storage-type selection

In summary, choosing the right EBS volume type is crucial based on your application demands, cost considerations, and performance needs. Now, let's dive into the EBS snapshots and backups to understand how to effectively safeguard and manage your data.

EBS snapshots and backups

EBS snapshots play a crucial role in capturing a **Point-in-Time (PIT)** backup of EBS volumes. Snapshots allow you to recover your crucial data for any storage or hardware failure scenarios. Snapshots can be created, deleted, copied, shared, archived, and automated. Now, let's dive in and explore each of the activities involved in the lifecycle of a snapshot.

Creating snapshots

Creating a snapshot allows you to capture a PIT backup of an EBS volume, as mentioned earlier. To create an EBS snapshot, complete the following steps:

1. Go to the EC2 dashboard and select **Volumes** under **Elastic Block Store**:

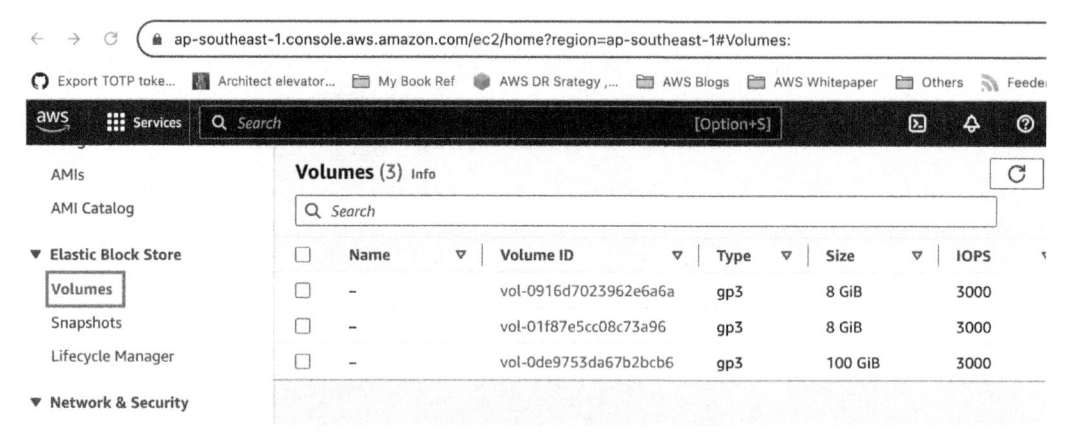

Figure 2.4 – Volume selection in EC2 dashboard

2. Choose the volume you want to snapshot and click on **Create snapshot** from the **Actions** menu:

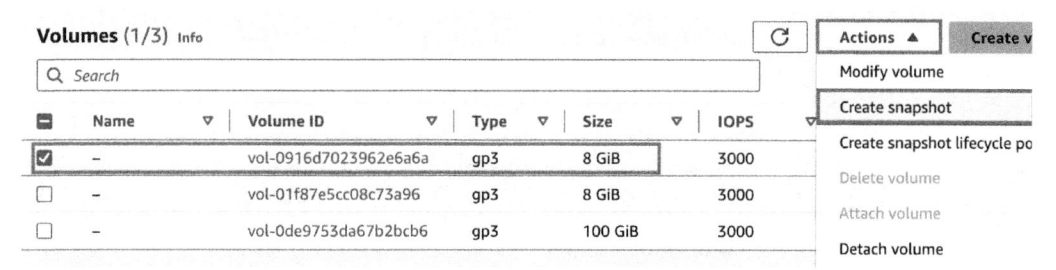

Figure 2.5 – Action to configure snapshot

3. Provide a description and, optionally, tags for your snapshot, and then click **Create snapshot**:

Figure 2.6 – Action to create a snapshot

Deleting snapshots

You may wish to delete your snapshot when it is no longer in use. To delete an EBS snapshot, you will need to follow these steps:

1. Go to the EC2 dashboard and select **Snapshots** under **Elastic Block Store**:

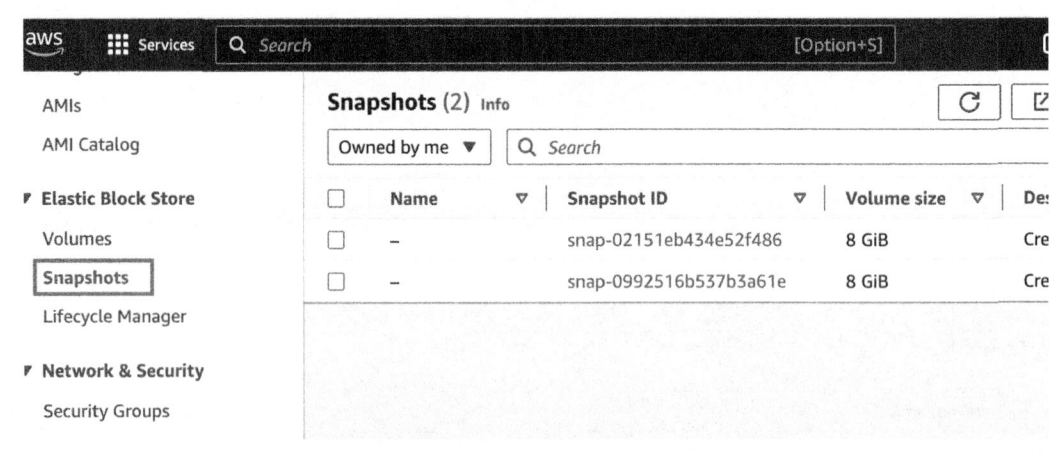

Figure 2.7 – Selecting Snapshots

2. Select the snapshot you wish to delete, click **Actions**, and then choose **Delete snapshot**. Confirm the deletion by clicking **Yes, delete**:

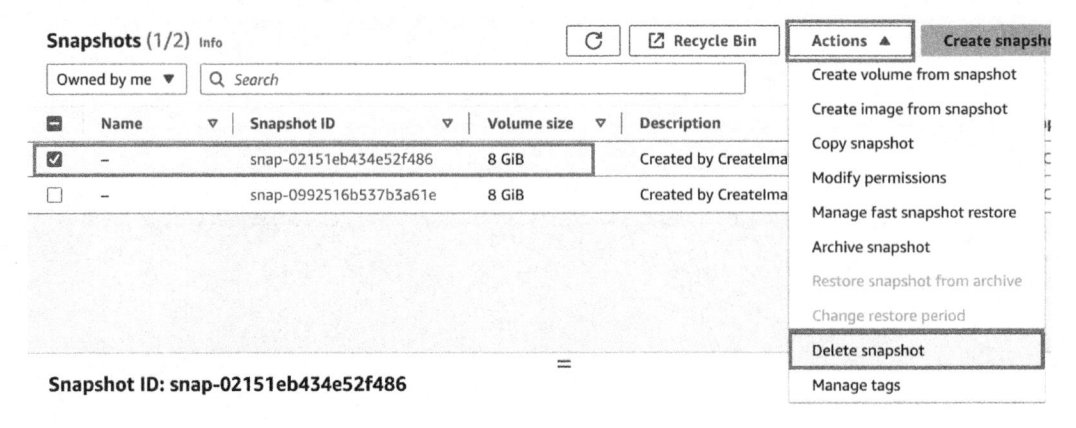

Figure 2.8 – Action to delete snapshot

Copying snapshots

Copying snapshots allows you to create an identical replica of an existing snapshot within the same or different AWS region. To copy a snapshot, follow these steps:

1. Select a snapshot from the **Snapshots** menu under **Elastic Block Store** in the EC2 dashboard:

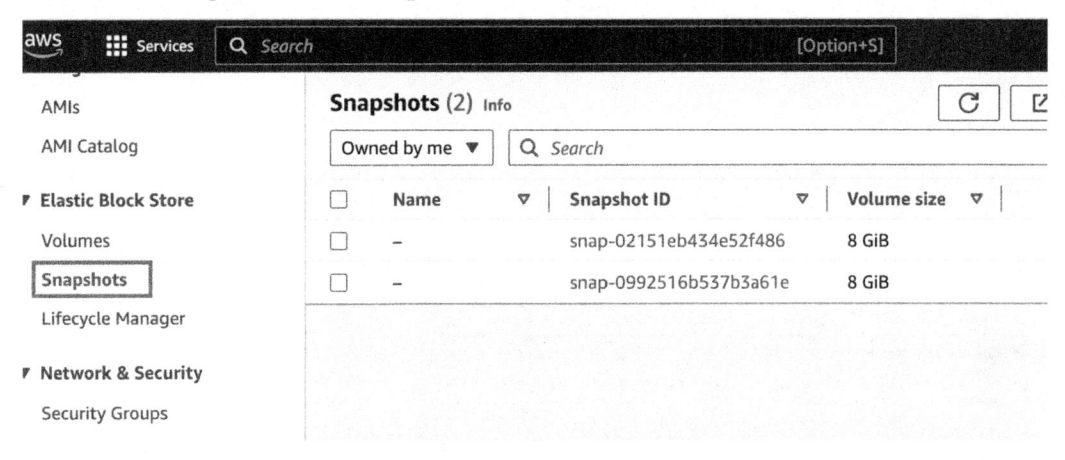

Figure 2.9 – Selecting Snapshots

2. Click **Actions**, then choose **Copy snapshot**:

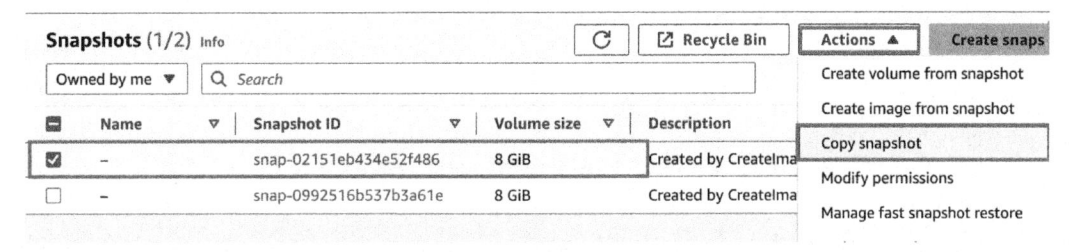

Figure 2.10 – Action to configure snapshot details

3. Select a destination region, provide a description, and add tags if necessary, then click **Copy snapshot**:

Description
A description for the snapshot copy.

[Copied snap-02151eb434e52f486 from ap-southeast-1] Created by Cı

255 characters maximum.

Destination Region
The Region in which to create the snapshot copy.

ap-southeast-1 ▼

Encryption Info
Use Amazon EBS encryption as an encryption solution for your EBS resources.
☐ Encrypt this snapshot

Tags - *optional* Info
A tag is a label that you assign to an AWS resource. Each tag consists of a key and an optional value. You can use tags to search and filter your resources or track your AWS costs.

No tags associated with the resource.

Add tag

You can add 50 more tags.

Cancel   **Copy snapshot**

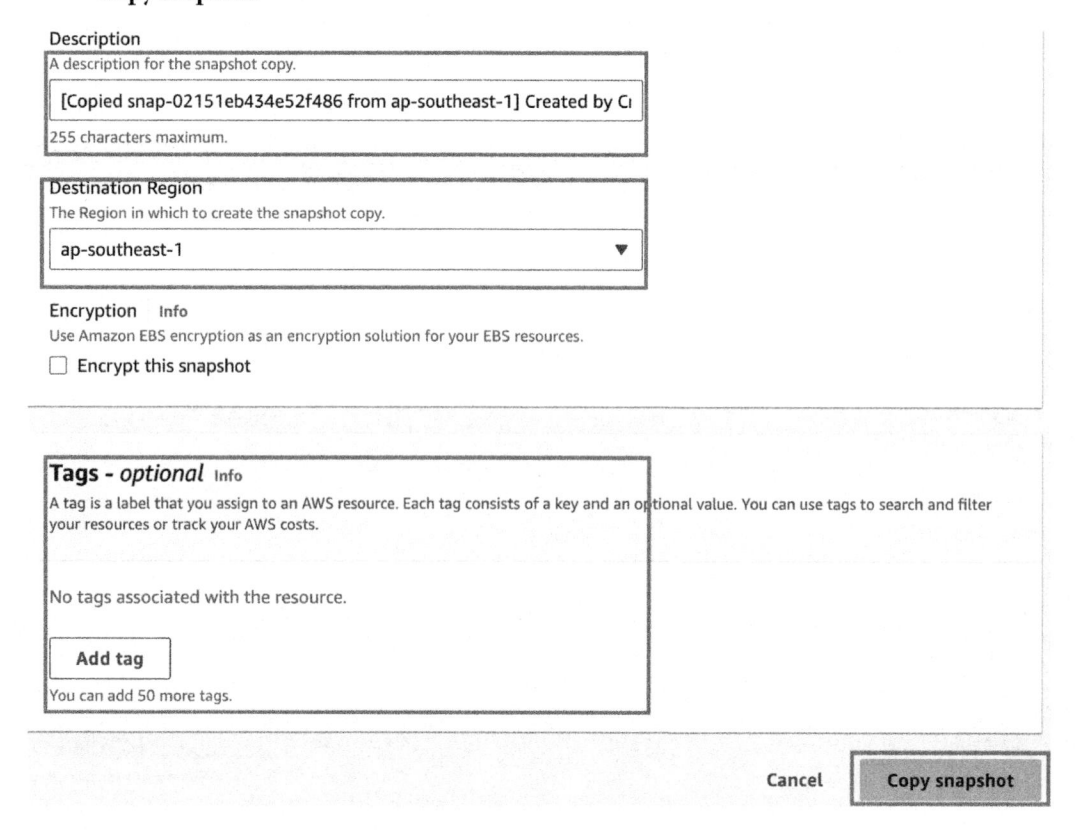

Figure 2.11 – Action to copy snapshot

Sharing snapshots

Sharing snapshots allows you to grant access to other AWS accounts. To share a snapshot, follow these steps:

1. Go to the EC2 dashboard and select **Snapshots** under **Elastic Block Store**:

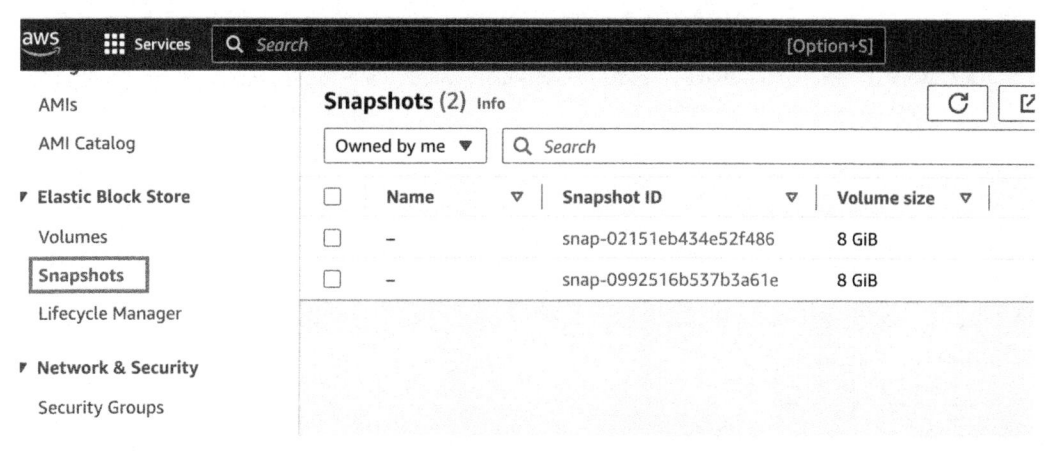

Figure 2.12 – Selecting Snapshots

2. Choose the snapshot you want to share, click **Actions**, and then select **Modify permissions**:

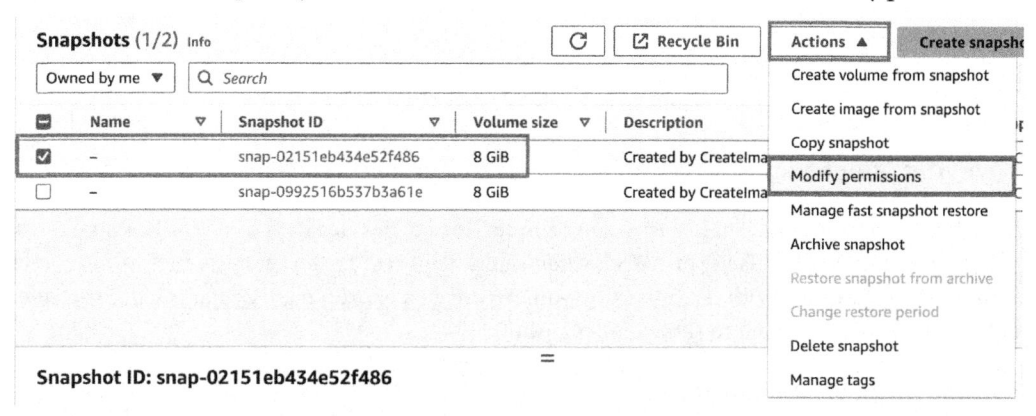

Figure 2.13 – Action to modify snapshot permissions

3. You can then add the AWS account ID of the user you wish to share the snapshot with or make it publicly accessible. Click **Save** to apply the changes:

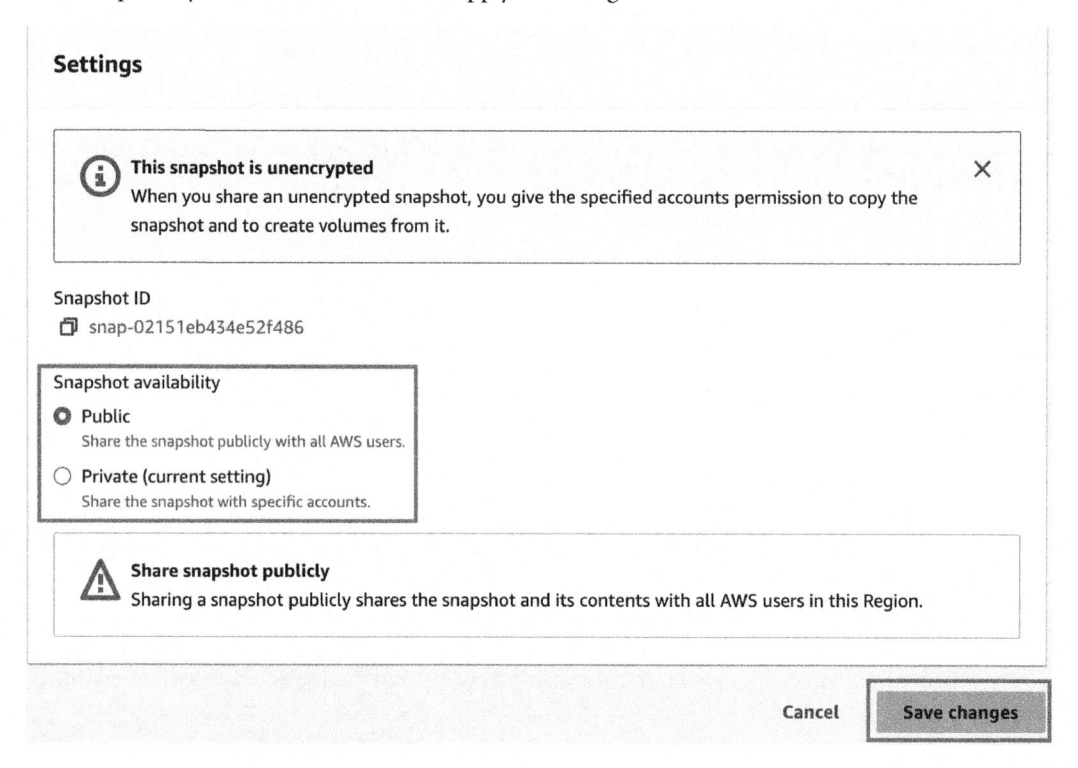

Figure 2.14 – Action to share a snapshot

Archiving snapshots

To archive snapshots, you can use Amazon **Simple Storage Service** (**S3**) or AWS Backup. Storing snapshots in Amazon S3 Glacier or AWS Backup vaults helps reduce storage costs and provides long-term retention options. With AWS Backup, you can create a backup plan, configure lifecycle rules, and specify the backup vault to store your snapshots.

Automating the snapshot lifecycle

AWS provides several options for automating the snapshot lifecycle, such as AWS Backup, Amazon **Data Lifecycle Manager** (**DLM**), or custom scripts using AWS SDKs. AWS Backup allows you to create a backup plan with a schedule, while Amazon DLM enables you to create lifecycle policies to automate snapshot creation, retention, and deletion.

With a clear understanding of EBS snapshots and backups, we now pivot our focus to the network aspect of our EC2 instances. In the upcoming section, we will delve into ENIs, exploring their fundamentals, configurations, and diverse use cases.

ENIs – fundamentals, configuration, and use cases

An **ENI** is a virtual network interface that you can attach to an EC2 instance hosted within a **virtual private cloud** (**VPC**). ENIs provide you great flexibility with the network configuration of your EC2 instances. The flexible configuration allows you to scale your EC2 instances to support advanced use cases such as network appliances or multi-homed instances. In this section, we will dive deeper and explore understanding ENIs, their properties, and configuration options such as attaching, detaching, and managing them. We will also touch upon and explore security and performance implications associated with ENIs and conclude by examining their use cases.

Understanding ENIs, their properties, and configuration options

An ENI consists of several properties, including the following:

- Primary private IPV4 address
- One or more secondary private IPv4 addresses
- One Elastic IP address per private IPv4 address
- One public IPv4 address
- One or more IPv6 addresses
- MAC address
- Security groups
- Source/destination check flag

These properties enable you to configure an ENI to suit your specific networking requirements. For example, you can associate multiple private IP addresses with an ENI to host multiple websites on the same instance or assign an Elastic IP to a secondary private IP address to achieve a failover configuration.

Attaching, detaching, and managing ENIs

ENIs provide you the flexibility to attach and detach from an EC2 while it is running or when it is in a stopped state (i.e. the instance). This flexibility can be achieved without compromising the availability of your EC2 instance, thus modifying the network configurations of your EC2 instances can be achieved on demand without any hassle. However, it is important to note that some instance types have a limit on the number of ENIs they can support, and this may affect your configuration options.

Security and performance implications

ENIs are associated with security groups, which control the inbound and outbound traffic for an instance. By attaching multiple ENIs to an instance, you can create fine-grained network access control policies for different applications or services running on the same instance. Additionally, the network performance of an instance is shared among its ENIs, so attaching multiple ENIs can provide additional bandwidth for high-traffic applications.

Use cases for multiple ENIs

There are several use cases for multiple ENIs with Amazon EC2 instances, including the following:

- **Multi-homed instances**: Instances with multiple ENIs can be configured to serve different network segments of VPCs, enabling you to isolate network traffic for different applications or environments
- **Network appliances**: Instances acting as network applications, such as firewalls, proxies, or load balancers, can benefit from multiple ENIs to manage traffic between different network segments or VPCs
- **HA and failover**: By using multiple ENIs with different IP addresses, you can create a failover configuration to maintain availability if one IP address becomes unreachable
- **Monitoring and operations management**: Instances can use a dedicated ENI for operations management and monitoring traffic, separating this traffic from application data

Having explored the intricacies of ENIs, let's now shift our focus to enhanced networking, a distinct feature that offers a unique set of capabilities and advantages over traditional ENIs.

Enhanced networking – fundamentals, capabilities, and use cases

Enhanced networking for EC2 is delivered through *supported EC2 instance types*. The **Elastic Network Adapter** (**ENA**) provides high-performance networking capabilities with improved networking performance by reducing latency, jitter, and packet loss, leading to better throughput, lower CPU utilization, and more consistent performance compared to traditional networking.

Enhanced networking leverages hardware and software optimizations to achieve these improvements. The optimizations include the usage of custom drivers and **single root I/O virtualization** (**SR-IOV**), which allows instances to communicate directly with the network hardware, bypassing the hypervisor layer, thus ultimately reducing CPU overhead and latency.

The benefits of enhanced networking include the following:

- **Higher throughput**: Enhanced networking can deliver significantly higher throughput compared to traditional networking, enabling instances to process more network traffic
- **Lower latency**: By reducing the time it takes for network packets to travel between instances, enhanced networking can decrease latency, improving the performance of latency-sensitive applications
- **Reduced jitter**: Enhanced networking provided more consistent network performance, with reduced packet loss and jitter, which is particularly important for real-time applications such as voice and video streaming
- **Lower CPU utilization**: By offloading network processing tasks to dedicated hardware, enhanced networking can free up CPU resources, allowing instances to focus on their primary tasks

Supported instance types and enabling enhanced networking

Enhanced networking is supported with many EC2 instance types, including recent-generation families such as C5, R5, M5, and others. If you are using Amazon or Windows AMIs, enhanced networking is often enabled by default. For other AMIs, you may need to install the required drivers and configure the settings manually. To understand if enhanced networking is available on your EC2 instance type, you can refer to the EC2 documentation (`https://docs.aws.amazon.com/AWSEC2/latest/UserGuide/enhanced-networking.html`).

Some significant features of ENA include the following:

- **High throughput**: ENA delivers up to 100 Gbps network throughput for data-intensive workloads on supported instances
- **Low latency**: ENA uses SR-IOV for direct communication with network hardware, reducing latency and improving application performance
- **Scalability**: ENA supports higher bandwidth and more virtual interfaces, allowing flexible networking configurations for changing workloads
- **Dynamic device queue allocation**: ENA optimizes performance by distributing network processing tasks across multiple CPU cores
- **Enhanced security**: ENA supports advanced security features, helping protect instances from network attacks

ENA use cases

In this subsection, we will explore various use cases and understand how ENA can enhance your networking capabilities and optimize the performance of your workloads. Let's dive into the details of ENA use cases:

- **HPC**: Instances supporting HPC workloads demand low latency and high throughput network requirements as this involves a rapid data exchange between them. ENA can be the right fit here, delivering optimal performance for HPC instances, and can significantly improve inter-node communication, resulting in faster computation times.
- **Big data and analytics**: Applications such as Apache Hadoop and Apache Spark supporting big data and analytics use cases often require high network bandwidth to efficiently process large datasets. ENA comes as a right fit, delivering optimal performance for data-intensive workloads through their high-throughput and low-latency networking.
- **Real-time applications**: Real-time applications, such as video streaming, online gaming, and **Voice Over IP** (**VoIP**), demand consistent network performance and low latency. ENA's reduced jitter and low latency can provide a more seamless experience for users, minimizing buffer and lag.
- **ML and artificial intelligence**: ML and AI workloads often involve transferring large volumes of data between instances for training and inference. ENA's high throughput can help speed up data transfers, reducing the time it takes to train and deploy ML models.

As we wrap up our in-depth exploration of enhanced networking, we have grasped its pivotal role and its immense contribution to AWS networking. However, for more specialized requirements, AWS offers another powerful tool: EFA. Let's dive into its fundamentals, capabilities, and the unique use cases it addresses.

EFA – fundamentals, capabilities, and use cases

Amazon EC2's **EFA** is a networking innovation specifically designed to meet the evolving requirements of HPC and ML workloads on AWS. EFA is designed to overcome the limitations of traditional network interfaces by providing lower latency and higher throughput. EFA delivers consistent latency, higher network throughput, and better scalability than traditional network interfaces. It achieves this superior performance and reduces overall communication overhead by bypassing the OS kernel, providing a direct path for communication between instances and the network adapter.

In this section, we will explore the purpose and use cases of EFA, as well as discuss supported instance types and some significant features of it.

Supported instance types

EFA is available on a variety of Amazon EC2 instance types, catering to diverse workloads and performance needs. These include the R5 and R5d families, which are optimized for memory instance applications; the C5, C5n, and C5d families, designed for compute-heavy workloads; the M5 and M5d families, offering a balanced mix of compute, memory, and networking resources; the G4 family, tailored for graphics-intensive and ML workloads; and the P3dn family, specifically designed for high-performance ML and HPC applications.

Significant features of EFA

EFA stands out as one of AWS's exceptional networking tools, packed with robust features tailored for modern workloads. Let's dissect some of its standout capabilities:

- **OS bypass**: EFA features an operating system bypass mechanism that provides a direct communication path between instances and network adapters. This bypass reduces communication overhead and latency, enabling faster and more efficient inter-node, making it an appropriate fit for HPC and ML workloads.

- **Enhanced security**: EFA is designed to operate within Amazon **Virtual Private Cloud** (**VPC**), ensuring that your workloads are isolated and secure. Additionally, EFA integration with AWS IAM enables you to control access to EFA resources, further strengthening your applications.

- **Seamless integration with popular frameworks**: EFA is designed to seamlessly work with popular HPC and ML frameworks such as Open MPI, **NVIDIA Collective Communication Libraries** (**NCCL**), and AWS ParallelCluster. This compatibility allows developers to easily incorporate EFA into their existing workflows and take advantage of its performance benefits without significant modifications to their applications.

Here's a simple flowchart to help you decide which adapter to choose among an ENI, ENA, and EFA:

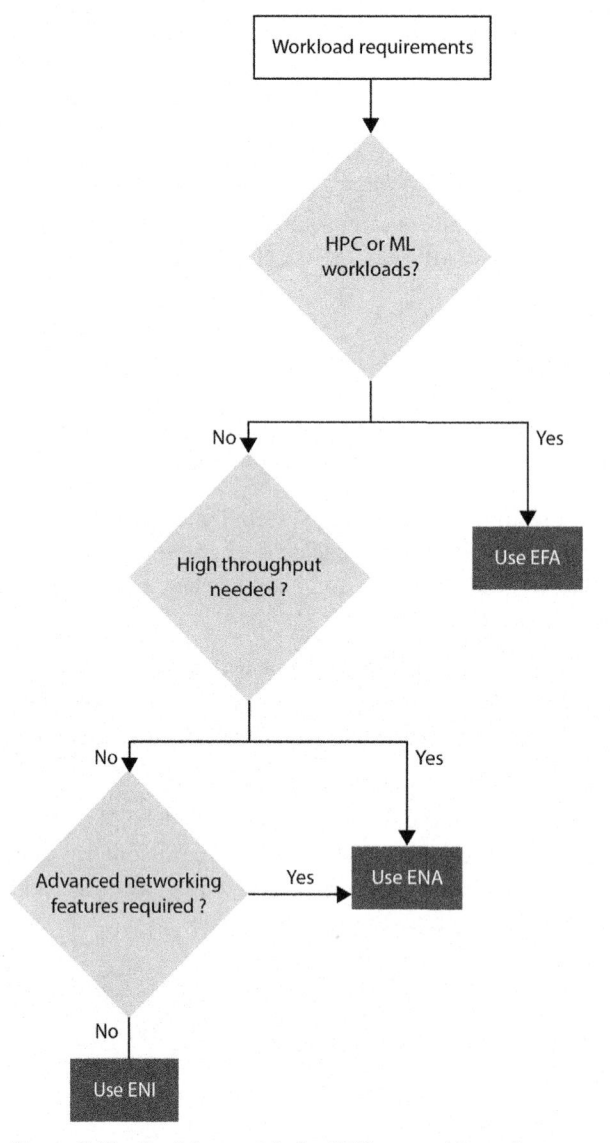

Figure 2.15 – Decision matrix for AWS networking adapters

As we wrap up our deep dive into the EFA, we have garnered a comprehensive understanding of its importance in Amazon EC2's ecosystem. Now, let's pivot to another pivotal aspect of EC2: security groups and key pairs. In the upcoming section, we will delve into the core security features of EC2 and understand their role in providing safety for Amazon EC2.

Security groups and key pairs

Security groups and **key pairs** are essential components of Amazon EC2 that help ensure the security of your instances. This section will provide an overview of these security features, explaining their role, how they work, and best practices for their use.

Security groups – virtual firewalls for your instances

Security groups act as virtual firewalls that control inbound and outbound traffic to your Amazon EC2 instances. They provide a crucial layer of security by allowing you to specify which traffic is permitted to your instances. Here's what you need to know about security groups:

- **Default and custom security groups**: When you create an instance, it's automatically associated with a default security group, which allows only outbound traffic. To customize your security settings, you can create your own security groups with specific rules.
- **Stateful rules**: Security group rules are stateful, meaning that if you allow incoming traffic for a specific port, the corresponding outgoing traffic is automatically allowed and vice versa.
- **Multi-layer security**: You can associate multiple security groups with a single instance, allowing for multi-layer security and increased flexibility in defining security rules.

Key pairs – secure authentication for your instances

Key pairs are used for secure authentication when you connect to your Amazon EC2 instances. They consist of a public key and private key and provide a more secure alternative to password-based authentication. Key pairs play an essential role in ensuring the security of your instances:

- **Public and private keys**: The public key is stored on the instance, while the private key is securely stored by the user. When you connect to an instance, the private key is used to verify your identity and grant you access.
- **Key-pair generation and management**: You can generate a new key pair using the AWS Management Console, the AWS CLI, or SDKs. Be sure to store your private key in a secure location, as it cannot be retrieved if lost.
- **Instance association**: When launching an instance, you can select an existing key pair or create a new one. The public key is then associated with the instance, allowing you to connect securely.

Best practices for security groups and key pairs

As we navigate the intricacies of AWS, it is imperative to observe best practices for security groups and key pairs to fortify your infrastructure. Here is a rundown of this pivotal process:

- **Implement the principle of least privilege (PoLP)**: Limit access to your instances by only allowing necessary traffic and removing any unnecessary rules from your security groups.
- **Use descriptive names and tags**: Assign meaningful names and tags to your security groups and key pairs to make it easier to identify their purpose and manage them.
- **Regularly review and update rules**: Periodically review and update rules in your security groups to ensure that they remain relevant and secure.
- **Rotate key pairs**: Regularly rotate your key pairs to reduce the risk of unauthorized access. Be sure to revoke old key pairs and update your instances with new ones.

With this, we have come to the end of the chapter.

Summary

We have just completed discussing the core components of Amazon EC2, diving into topics such as instance types, EBS, and ENIs, including essential security measures with security groups and key pairs. This knowledge serves as a backbone for utilizing EC2 effectively. We will now shift our focus to AMIs.

In the next chapter, we will understand the pivotal role AMIs play in EC2, explore the various types, learn about custom AMI creation and effective management, and dive deeper into best practices and troubleshooting.

3
Creating and Managing Amazon Machine Images (AMI)

In this chapter, we will expand beyond the basics and dive deeper into the captivating world of AMIs. We will discuss the creation and management of AMIs, the strategies for choosing the right AMI based on your specific use case, and the essential security best practices associated with managing your AMIs. We will also explore various ways to share and deregister AMIs and provide a well-rounded understanding of AMI life cycle management. By the end of this chapter, you will be better equipped to use AMIs efficiently and effectively in your AWS journey.

The following topics will be covered in this chapter:

- Exploring AMI virtualization – types, boot modes, and user-provided kernels
- Types of AMIs – an in-depth look
- Creating and sharing custom AMIs
- Launching EC2 instances from AMIs
- Best practices and cautions while creating custom AMIs

Exploring AMI virtualization – types, boot modes, and user-provided kernels

In this section, we are going to dive deeper into the critical aspects of AMIs that govern their functionality and performance. This will include exploring AMI virtualization types, understanding the importance of AMI boot modes, and navigating the concept of user-provided kernels.

AMI virtualization and its types

At the core of AMI is the virtualization type. Just like how the role of a skilled weaver is important in crafting a beautiful tapestry, the **virtualization** type plays a similarly important role in the fabric of your EC2 instances. There are primarily two virtualization types available in AWS – **hardware virtual machines** (**HVMs**) and **paravirtual** (**PV**) instances. They both have their unique advantages and use cases and understanding their merits and differences will allow you to make informed decisions and optimize your instance's performance.

In HVM, the guest operating system runs on the fully virtualized set of hardware as if it directly runs on the host hardware offering better performance and enhanced security. It also supports a wider range of instance types. It is recommended that you use current generation instance types and HVM AMIs when you launch your instances.

On the other hand, PV instances come with lightweight virtualization, thus offering us low virtualization overhead, faster boot times, and easier migration between the host systems. However, PV instances lack some advanced features found in HVM instances, such as support for GPU. As you explore the world of AMIs, understanding the key differences will help you select the appropriate choice for your use case and make a significant impact on your instance performance, resource utilization, and compatibility with other workloads.

When launching your EC2 instance, you have the opportunity to choose the AMI that aligns with your desired virtualization type. This can be seen in the following screenshot:

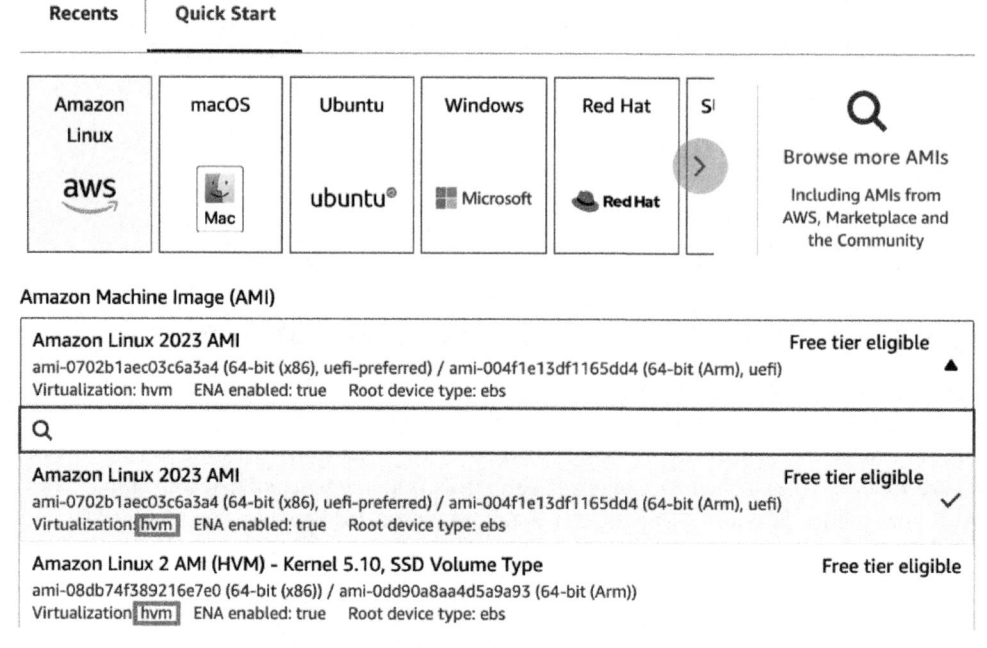

Figure 3.1 – Selecting an AMI virtualization type

AMI boot modes

The next important thing in the AMI is the **boot mode**. Just like how a mysterious incantation of a spell triggers a magical effect on a person or objects, the boot modes in EC2 govern the process of bootstrapping your instances. There are two primary boot modes available – **BIOS** and **Unified Extensible Firmware Interface (UEFI)**. BIOS is the traditional boot mode and has been in use for decades, while UEFI is a more modern and feature-rich alternative. Also, AWS offers you the additional flexibility of specifying **UEFI-PREFERRED** boot mode, under which when you set the boot mode to **UEFI-PREFERRED**. If the instance types support **UEFI**, then the instance is launched using **UEFI**; otherwise, the instance is launched on **Legacy BIOS**.

The modern UEFI boot mode offers several advantages over BIOS, such as *rapid boot times*, *improved security*, and *support for larger storage devices*. However, take note that BIOS boot modes are quite prevalent where legacy systems and applications exist. As you explore the world of AMIs, understanding boot modes will help you make the right choice for your instances to ensure optimal performance and compatibility.

Here is a table that illustrates the key differences between the different boot modes:

Feature	UEFI	BIOS
Boot process	Supports the secure boot process and prevents any malware by ensuring only the trusted software is loaded	Lacks the secure boot process and makes it more susceptible to boot time malware.
Partitioning support	Supports GUID Partition Table (GPT), allowing for larger disk sizes and more partitions	Supports Master Boot Record (MBR), limiting disk size to 2 TB and four primary partitions
Interface	GUI options are available for making configuration changes more user-friendly	Text-based interface, which can be less intuitive
Boot time	Potentially faster boot times due to optimized boot management	Generally slower boot times compared to UEFI due to older methods of hardware initialization.
Storage	Supports booting from larger storage devices (over 2 TB)	Limited to booting from storage devices up to 2 TB in size

Table 3.1 – Key differences between the boot modes

User-provided kernel

As you further navigate the world of AMIs, you will discover the flexibility and customization that they bring you by allowing you to provide user-defined kernels. The custom kernel option will be very helpful when you wish to tailor your operating system's core functionality so that it fits your use case. By configuring a custom kernel, you'll have more control over the operating system's behavior and performance.

User-provided kernels are not a prevalent option and are rather considered for some specialized use cases, such as high-frequency trading, where you may need a custom kernel option to make some low-level system adjustments to enhance security, improve performance, or introduce new features.

Keep in mind that this flexibility comes with additional responsibility, where you will be responsible for managing kernel patches and upgrades, as well as applying security fixes. You will require additional effort and expertise. So, you must weigh up the potential benefits against the operations responsibilities before embracing the user-provided kernels.

Let us now have an in-depth look at the different types of AMIs in the next section.

Types of AMIs – an in-depth look

In this section, we will explore two primary types of AMIs – **EBS-backed AMIs** and **instance store-backed AMIs**. We will compare their characteristics, such as boot time, root device volume, the size limit of the root device, data persistence, and charges, and their use cases.

EBS-backed AMIs – the Flexible and Durable options

The **Flexible** and **Durable** options of EBS-backed AMIs use Amazon **Elastic Block Store** (**EBS**) volumes for their root device storage. These types of AMIs offer several advantages over instance-store-backed AMIs:

- **Boot time**: The bootup time for EBS-backed instances is comparably faster than instance store-backed instances. Depending on the size of the EBS volume and instance, the boot times can vary between a few seconds to minutes.

- **Size limit of root device**: The storage size of EBS-backed instances can range between 1 GiB to 1 6Tib, thus providing greater flexibility for various workloads and use cases.

- **Root device volume**: As the root devices of EBS-backed AMIs are EBS volumes themselves, this enables us to make use of EBS features such as snapshots, encryption, and volume resizing.

- **Data persistence**: Data stored in the EBS volume continues to persist even when the instance is stopped or restarted. So, it allows you to persist the data across the instance restarts or terminations. Those applications that require data durability and consistency will benefit from this.

- **Charges**: The charges for the EBS-backed AMI include the EBS volumes attached to your EC2 instances. This includes root volumes and any additional EBS volumes.

- **States**: The instance states are important to the operations of EC2 instances. The EBS-backed instances can transition the instance between the *running*, *stopped*, and *terminated* states. You can make use of these states to start/stop instances so that you can manage your running costs.

Use cases for EBS-backed AMIs

EBS-backed AMIs provide a versatile and robust solution for various business and technical needs. Whether it's the ability to stop instances without data loss, handle dynamic workloads with flexible volume sizes, or offer consistent data durability, EBS-backed AMIs are crucial for diverse applications. Let's explore some specific use cases where these advantages come into play:

- Stopping instances without losing their data – for example, a web application with a large dataset stored on its root device volume
- Workloads that need flexible root volume sizes and enhanced performance – for example, a database server that experiences varying loads throughout the day
- Applications requiring data durability and data persistence – for example, an e-commerce platform that processes orders and maintains a record set of customer transactions

Instance store-backed AMIs – the high-performance choice

Instance store-backed AMIs utilize ephemeral storage that is directly attached to the instance host hardware for their root device storage. This type of AMI has the following unique set of characteristics:

- **Boot time**: Instance store-backed instances can take longer to boot than EBS-backed instances as their AMI must be fetched from Amazon S3 and loaded into the instance store before the instance can start.
- **Size limit of root device**: The root device size for instance store-backed instances is determined by the instance type and cannot be modified.
- **Root device volume**: Instance-backed AMIs rely on the instance store volumes for their root devices, offering low latency and high I/O performance.
- **Data persistence**: Data stored in the instance store volumes is ephemeral, meaning it is lost when an instance is stopped, terminated, or experiences a hardware failure. This makes instance store-backed AMIs suitable for temporary storage and specific use cases where data persistence isn't critical.
- **Charges**: In instance store-backed AMIs, the cost of the instance store volumes is already included in the instance pricing, so you are not required to spend additional charges for storage separately.
- **States**: In comparison to EBS-backed instances, instance store-backed instances can only transition between the *running* and *terminated* states. So, when the instance is terminated, the data stored on the instance store volume is evicted too.

Use cases for instance store-backed AMIs

Instance store-backed AMIs provide specific advantages for workloads where temporary storage, high I/O performance, and data loss can be tolerated. From serving static content to meeting the demands of high-performance applications, instance store-backed AMIs prove essential. Let's take a closer look at the scenarios where this type of AMI can be particularly effective:

- Data loss is acceptable for your workloads or can be mitigated through replication – for example, a stateless web server that serves static content where the static itself can be reproduced from the source
- Workloads where high I/O performance and low latency are needed – for example, a high-performance application that requires rapid access to the data stored in volumes to process large datasets
- Applications needing temporary storage needs, such as caches and buffers – for example, a video streaming service makes use of caches to store and deliver content to end users

With this comprehensive understanding of various types of AMIs and their specific applications, we are well prepared to dive into the next essential aspect of our journey – that is, creating and sharing custom AMIs.

Creating and sharing custom AMIs

Creating custom AMIs for custom needs can significantly streamline your instance provisioning process. By building custom AMIs, you greatly reduce the time and effort needed in configuring instances. Also, it helps ensure consistency across your infrastructure. In this section, we will explore creating custom AMIs and how you can leverage the EC2 image pipeline to simplify your AMI management process.

Creating custom AMIs

Creating a custom AMI is a straightforward process that can be accomplished using the Amazon EC2 management console. Here is a step-by-step guide to help you get started:

1. Navigate to the EC2 management console and select **Instances** from the left-hand menu:

Creating and sharing custom AMIs   53

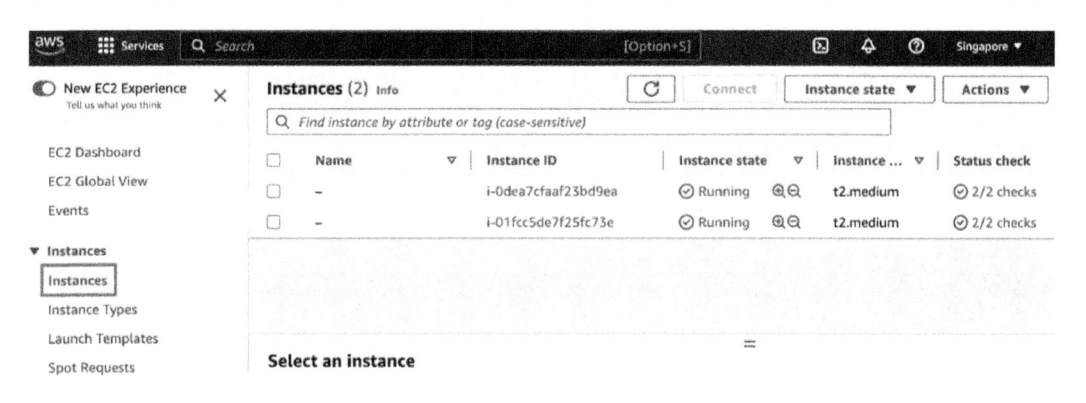

Figure 3.2 – EC2 instance landing page

2. Choose the instance you'd like to create an AMI from and ensure it's in a running state:

Figure 3.3 – EC2 instance selection

3. Click on the respective instance and then click **Actions**, under which select **Images and templates** and then **Create image**. This will open a new window where you can fill in the AMI details:

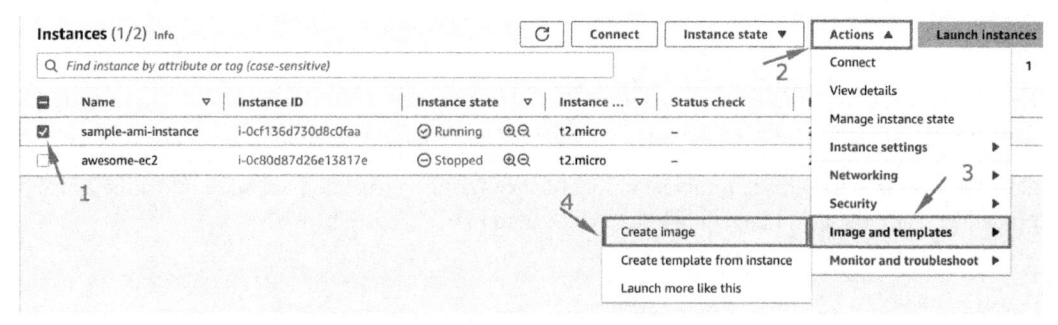

Figure 3.4 – Creating an image

4. Enter a unique name and description for your new AMI and configure any additional settings as required. Click **Create Image** to initiate the AMI creation process:

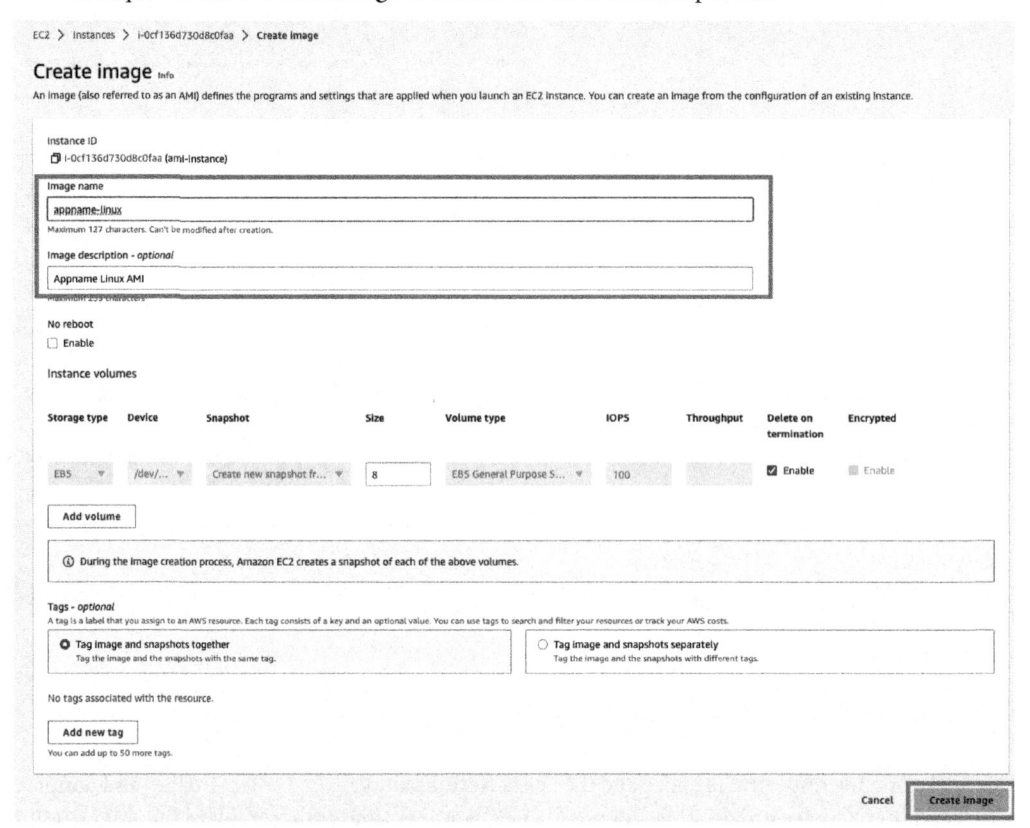

Figure 3.5 – Creating an image

Once the process is complete, your custom AMI will be available in the **AMIs** section of the EC2 management console, ready for you to launch the new instances.

Now, you are ready to take your understanding further. In the next section, we will explore the efficient process of using the EC2 image pipeline to create and manage custom AMIs.

Leveraging the EC2 image pipeline to create custom AMIs

The EC2 image pipeline offers you an automation framework to create, maintain, and share your custom AMIs. The image pipeline allows you to automate the creation of secure and up-to-date AMIs and make them consistent across your AWS infrastructure. So, by leveraging the EC2 image pipeline, you can do the following:

- Automate the creation of custom AMIs based on some events or through a predefined schedule
- Ensure the AMIs are up to date with the latest security patches and software updates
- Simplify sharing your AMIs with other AWS accounts or with an AWS organization

To get started with the EC2 image pipeline, navigate to the EC2 management console and select **Image pipeline** from the left-hand menu. On this page, click **Create image pipeline**, configure the necessary settings, and define the required pipeline actions for your image creation process:

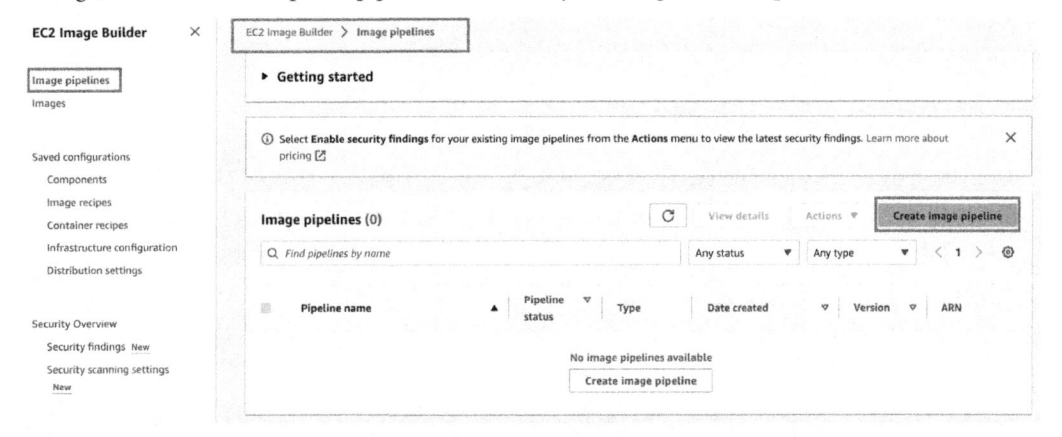

Figure 3.6 – Create image pipeline

Now that we have created a custom AMI, we will explore the use cases of creating a custom AMI.

Use cases for creating custom AMIs

Creating custom AMIs can be beneficial for several use cases:

- Preinstalling and configuring software packages as needed for the applications to be hosted on top of it
- Eliminating or reducing the manual configurations by automating and streamlining the instance provisioning process

- Ensuring the instance configurations remain consistent by using a standard custom image across your fleet of instances
- Reducing the risk of configuration drifting by maintaining version-controlled and up-to-date AMIs
- Tailoring custom AMIs to incorporate enhanced security hardening measures to meet the compliance requirements and regulatory standards of the financial services industry
- Optimized custom AMIs can achieve faster boot times by including only necessary software, improving responsiveness and scaling efficiency

Sharing custom AMIs

Once you have your custom AMI, the next step is to share it with others for broader distribution or collaborative development. You can share it with others in two ways – by specifying individual AWS account IDs or through AWS Organizations.

Sharing AMIs with individual AWS accounts

The steps to complete this are as follows:

1. Navigate to the EC2 management console and select **AMIs** from the left-hand menu.
2. On the **AMIs** page, locate your desired custom AMI. Then, right-click and select **Edit AMI Permissions**:

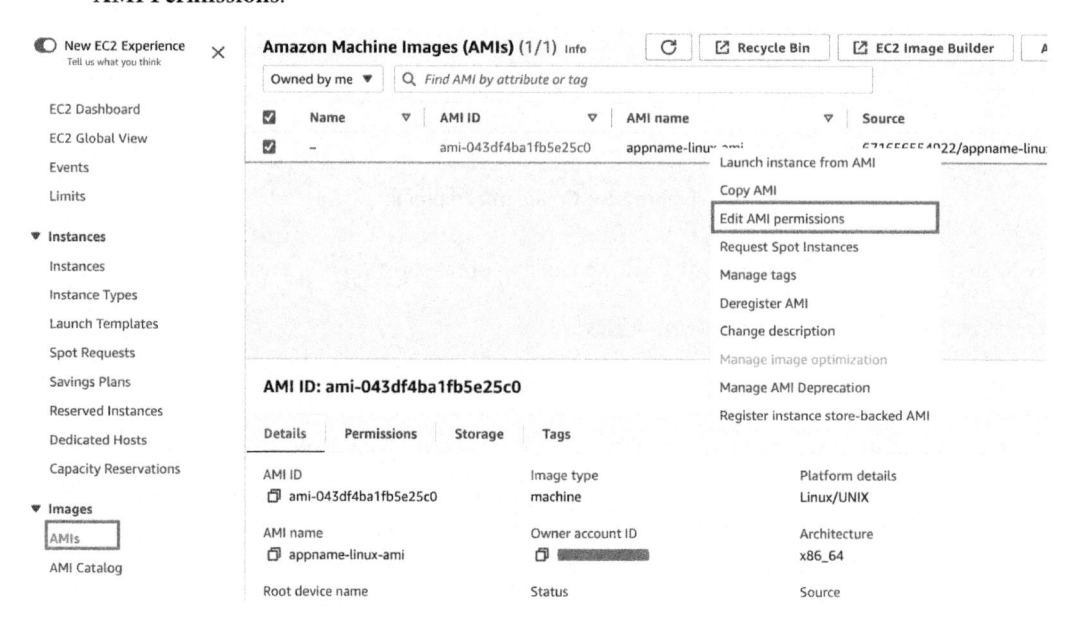

Figure 3.7 – Updating EC2's AMI permissions

3. Enter the desired AWS account ID you would like to share the AMI with and then click **Add permissions**:

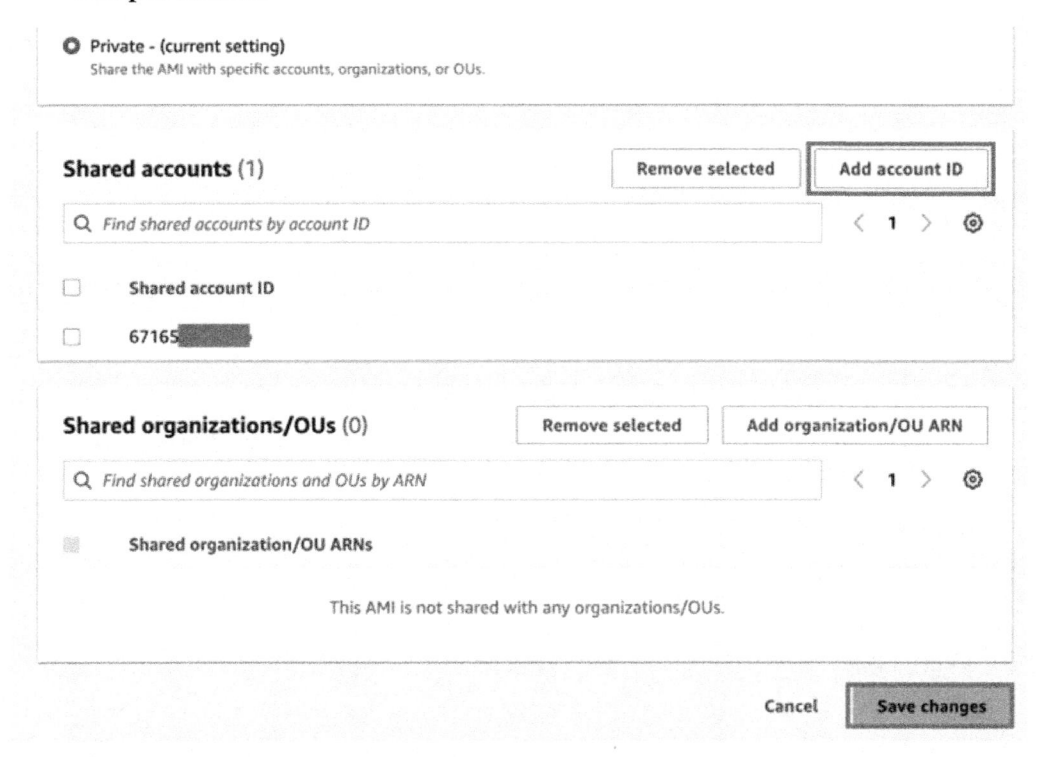

Figure 3.8 – Sharing the EC2 AMI with others

4. Click **Save changes** to apply your changes.

Sharing AMIs using AWS Organizations

AWS Organizations allows you to manage your organization's AWS accounts centrally. By leveraging AWS Organizations, you can share your custom AMIs with a bunch of AWS accounts grouped under an **organization unit** (**OU**) without having to specify individual account IDs.

To share your AMI using AWS Organizations, you will need to create a **Resource Access Manager** (**RAM**). Here is a step-by-step guide you can follow to share your custom AMI with an OU:

1. Navigate to the AWS RAM console.
2. Click **Create resource share** to start the sharing process:

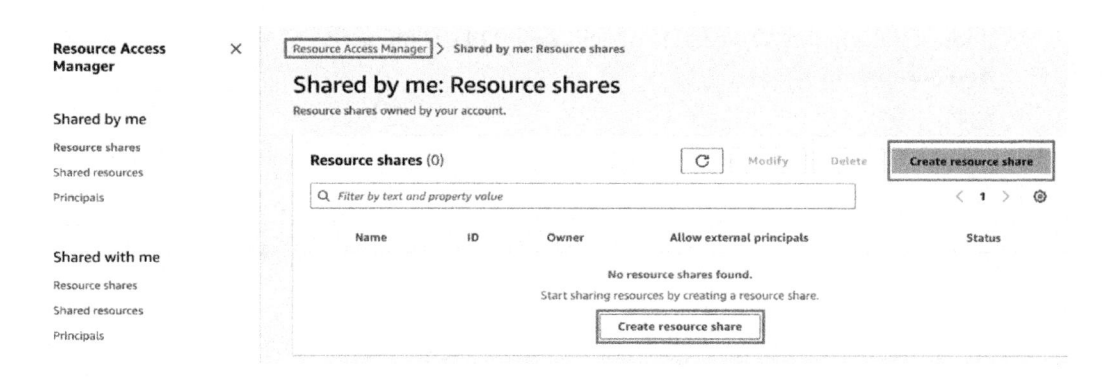

Figure 3.9 – Create resource share

3. Enter a name and description for your resource share.
4. In the **Resources** section, click **Select Resource Type** and select **Image Builder Images**:

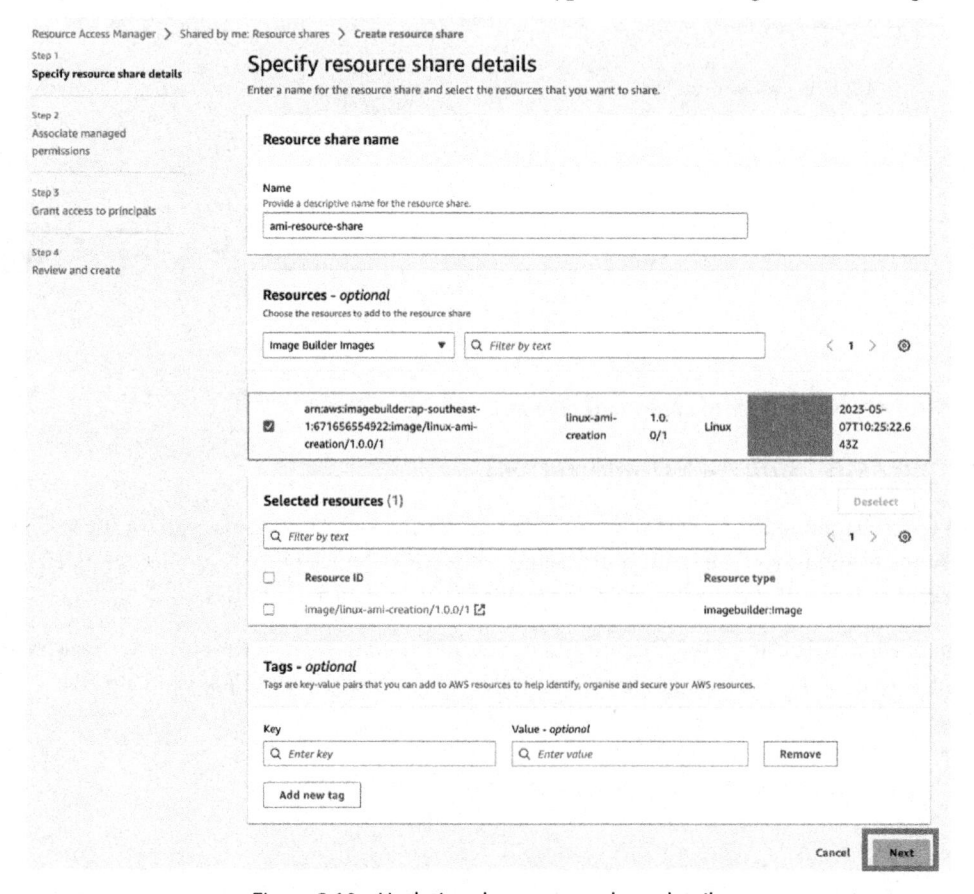

Figure 3.10 – Updating the resource share details

5. In the **Principals** section, select **Display organization structure** and then **Organization Units (OUs)** from the tree. Locate the OU you would like to share the AMI with and check the box next to it:

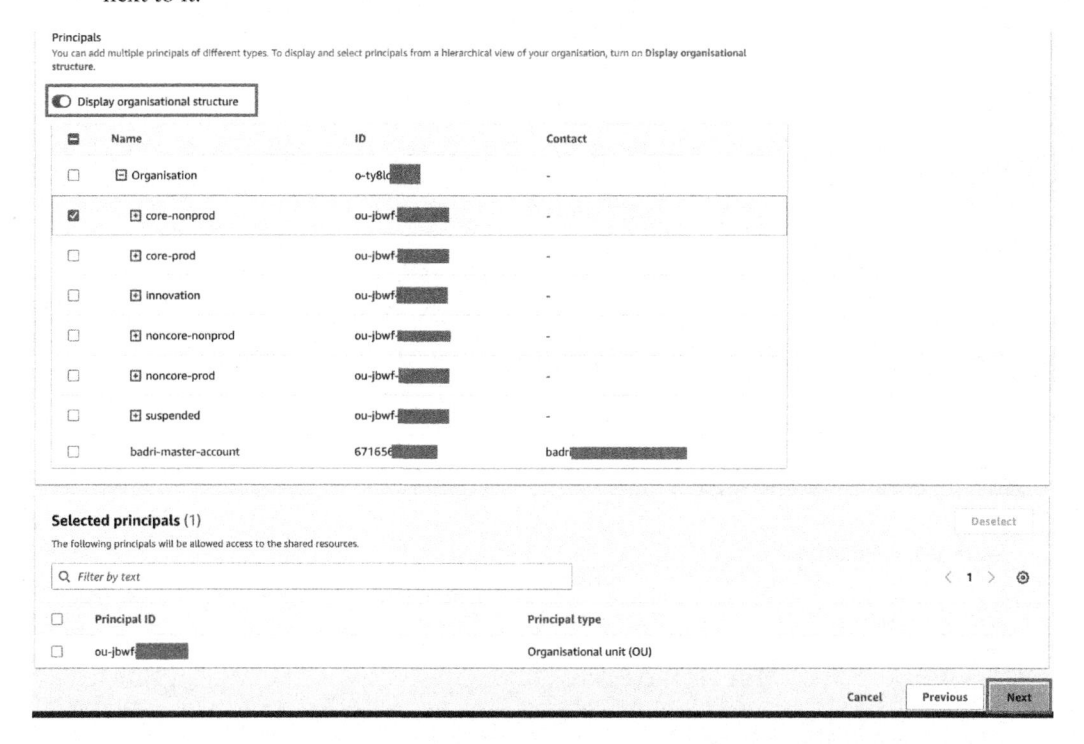

Figure 3.11 – Target resource share principals

6. Review your settings and click **Create resource share** to finalize the process:

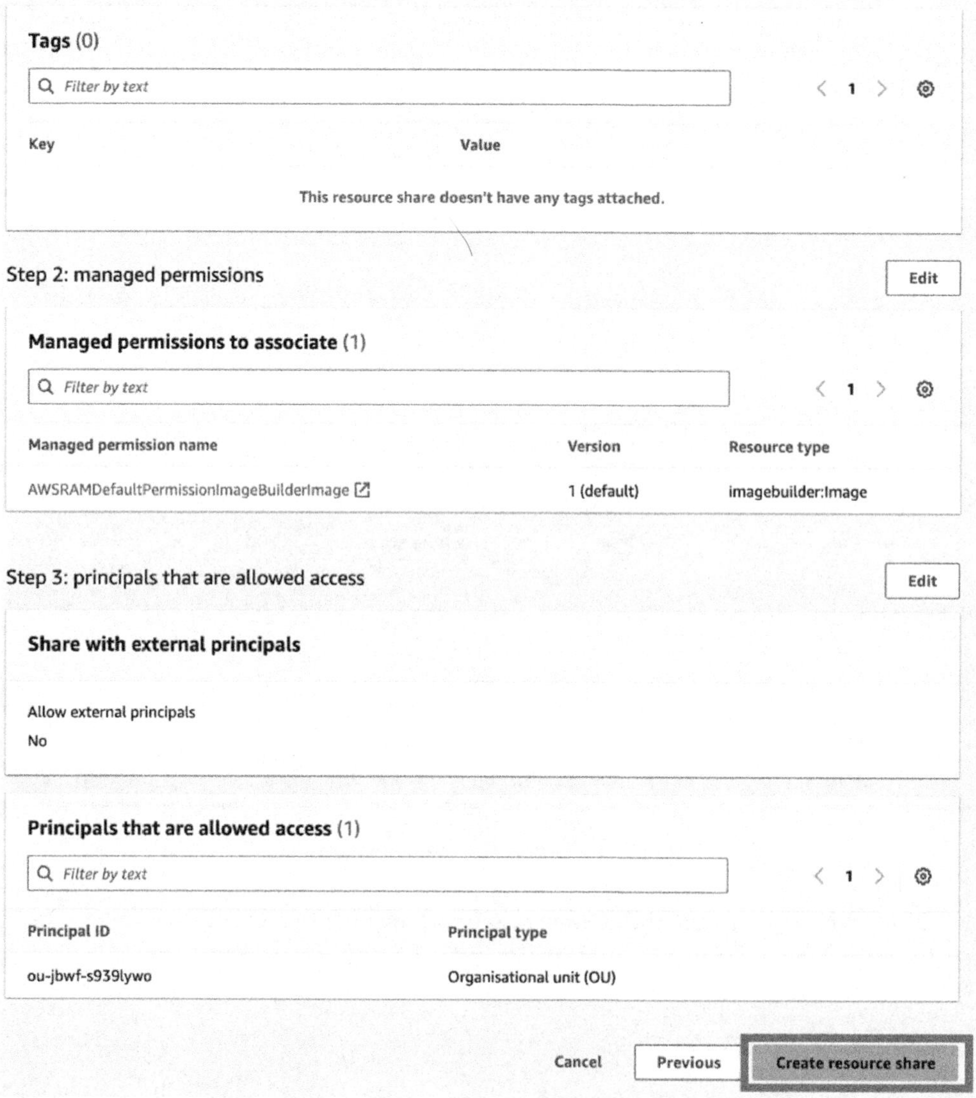

Figure 3.12 – Finishing the resource-sharing process

Your custom AMI is now shared with the specified OU, and all AWS accounts within that OU can launch instances based on the shared AMI.

With a solid understanding of creating and sharing an AMI, we are now ready to explore the next step in leveraging their potential to launch an EC2 instance. In the next section, we will delve into the details of this process to equip you with the knowledge needed to effectively utilize AMIs in your EC2 environment.

Launching EC2 instances from AMIs

In this section, we will learn the process of launching EC2 instances from AMIs. We will begin by selecting an appropriate AMI that fits your specific needs, after which we will discuss the details of configuring instance details during launch. Finally, we will discuss the process of reviewing and launching instances.

Selecting an appropriate AMI

Choosing the right AMI is like selecting the right ingredients for the recipe you wish to make. You are looking for the perfect blend of software, configuration, and resources that will help you achieve your desired outcome. Just like how choosing fresh, high-quality ingredients can greatly enhance the final dish, selecting an appropriate AMI very much determines the performance, security, and other capabilities of an EC2 instance.

In selecting an appropriate AMI, the first question you should ask yourself is, *"What is my instance going to do?"* The answer to this question will determine your choice. Say, for example, if you are launching a web server, then you might select an AMI that comes with the pre-installed Apache or Nginx. Likewise, if you are setting up a database server, you might choose an AMI that comes with MySQL or PostgreSQL. So, understanding your use case is the crucial first step that will help you in this selection journey.

Upon determining your use case, think about selecting the operating system. EC2 AMIs come with support for a variety of operating systems, including Amazon Linux, Ubuntu, Windows, and many others. You can make your choice based on your application requirements and, more importantly, team skills in managing the operating system.

Next, think about the processor architecture and its support for the instance type you plan to use. The processor architecture is compatible with certain instance types. For example, ARM-based AMIs can only be used with ARM-based instance types. So, make sure the AMI you choose is compatible with the instance types you wish to use.

Finally, consider the source of the AMI. Including its own, Amazon supports many AMIs from its marketplace vendors and partner ecosystems. So, it's important to choose an AMI from a trusted source to ensure the security of your instances.

Remember, selecting an AMI is not a one-size-fits-all decision. So, be clear with your needs and evaluate the various available options. Also, as your familiarity with AWS grows, so too will your skill in selecting the perfect AMI for your tasks.

Configuring instance details during launch

Once you have identified the perfect AMI, the next step in this process is to have your instance details configured. This is an opportunity for you to tailor your EC2 instance to the specific needs of your application. Follow these steps to set this up:

1. **Choose an instance type**: Determine your workload requirements to select the best instance type. For example, let's assume you are launching a web application that processes large amounts of data. In this case, choosing a compute-optimized instance type, such as a C5 instance, can benefit your use case as it offers a high ratio of compute resources to memory and comes as an ideal choice for compute-heavy applications:

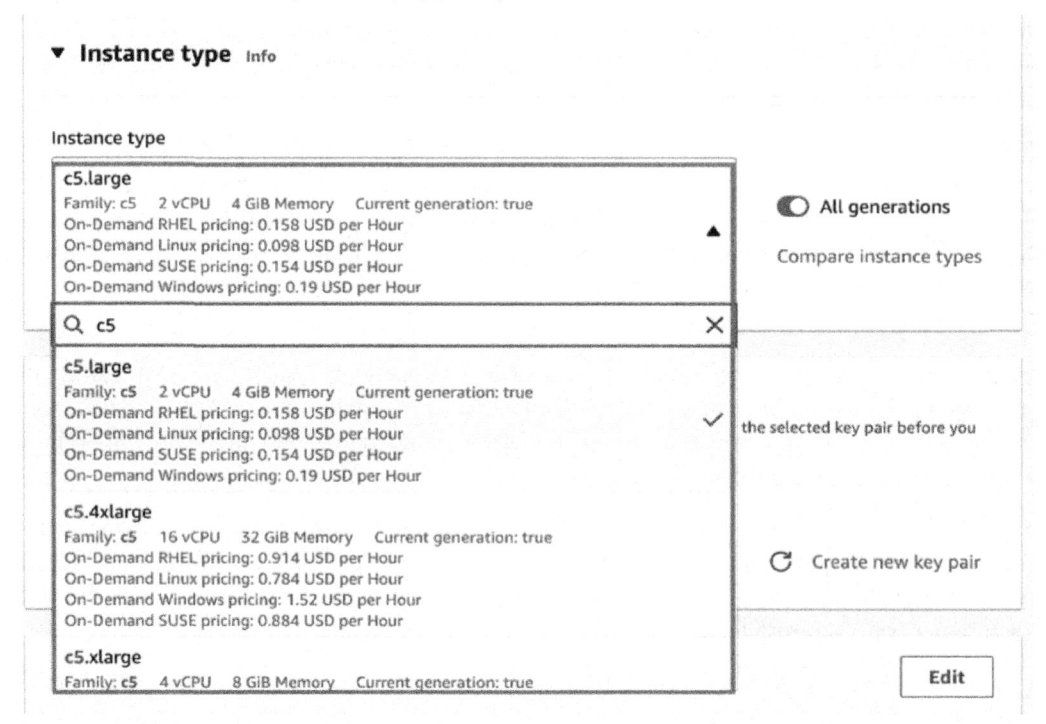

Figure: 3.13 – Choosing an instance type

2. **Configure the instance**: In this phase, you specify the number of instances to launch and choose the VPC and the subnet within a VPC. You can also assign a public IP address to your instance if needed. For example, most enterprise cloud-hosted applications are hosted inside the VPC for better isolation and security:

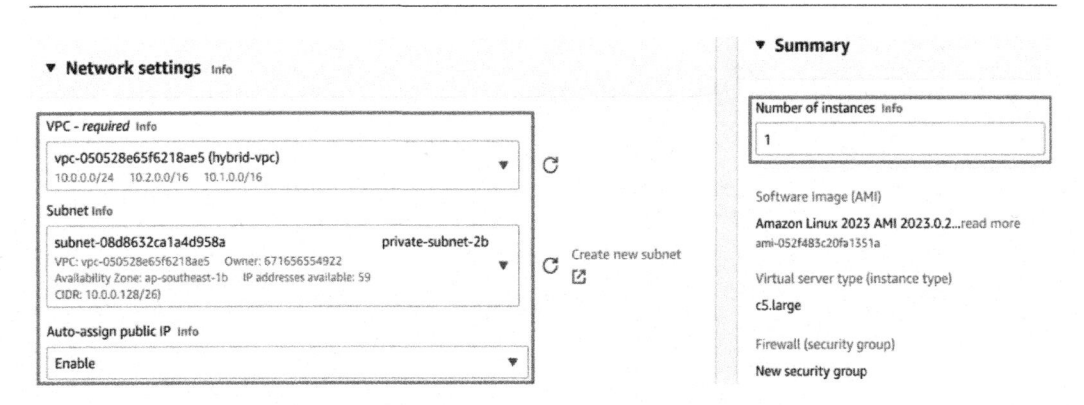

Figure 3.14 – Configuring the instance with network connectivity

3. **Add storage**: The AMI you select determines the root device volume, which contains the operating system image that will be used to boot the instance. While configuring storage, you can modify the size of the root volume or add additional EBS volumes or instance store volumes. For example, if your application requires a large database, then you might add an additional EBS volume and configure it for high IOPS to ensure fast and consistent performance. You can also dedicate this secondary volume to database storage:

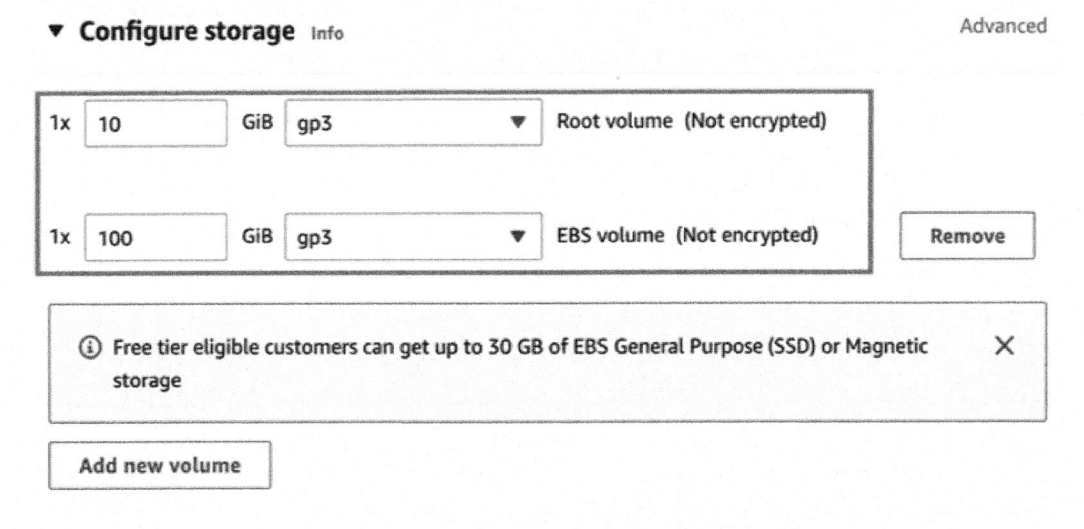

Figure 3.15 – Configuring the instance with storage

4. **Configure the security group**: Security groups act as a virtual firewall for your instance. Here, you must explicitly define security rules on top of the security group to allow only specific traffic to reach your instances. For example, if you are setting up a web server in your EC2 instance, then you can define security group rules that allow the inbound traffic on port **80** (HTTP) and port **443** (HTTPS):

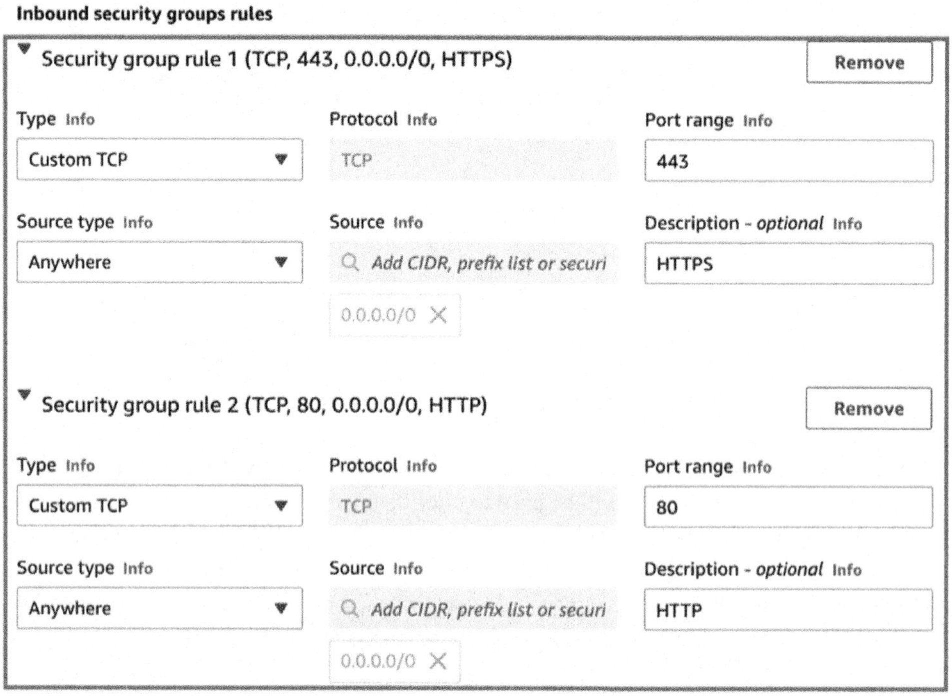

Inbound security groups rules

Security group rule 1 (TCP, 443, 0.0.0.0/0, HTTPS) [Remove]

Type Info	Protocol Info	Port range Info
Custom TCP	TCP	443

Source type Info	Source Info	Description - *optional* Info
Anywhere	Add CIDR, prefix list or securi... 0.0.0.0/0 ✕	HTTPS

Security group rule 2 (TCP, 80, 0.0.0.0/0, HTTP) [Remove]

Type Info	Protocol Info	Port range Info
Custom TCP	TCP	80

Source type Info	Source Info	Description - *optional* Info
Anywhere	Add CIDR, prefix list or securi... 0.0.0.0/0 ✕	HTTP

Figure 3.16 – Configuring the instance with a security group

Before launching your instance, you will be prompted to select and associate a key pair with your instance. The public key of the associated key pair will be retained while your instance is launched and the key pair can be used by the end user to establish a secure connection to the instance through SSH:

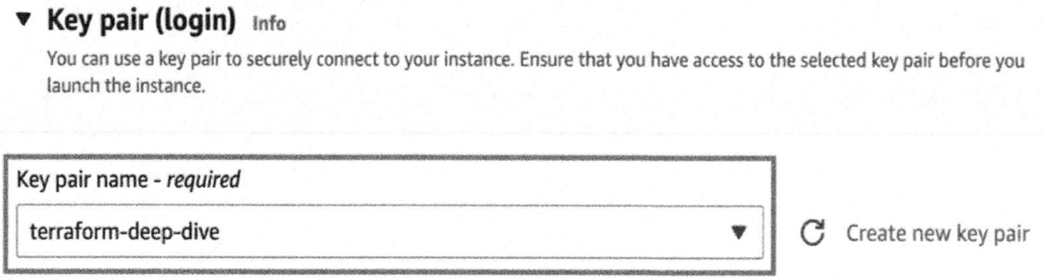

▼ **Key pair (login)** Info

You can use a key pair to securely connect to your instance. Ensure that you have access to the selected key pair before you launch the instance.

Key pair name - *required*

terraform-deep-dive ▼   ↻ Create new key pair

Figure 3.17 – Configuring the instance with a key pair

5. **Add tags**: Finally, adding tags will allow you to categorize your AWS resources in different ways – for example, by purpose or owner or by environment. This is a best practice that will help you identify your instances later:

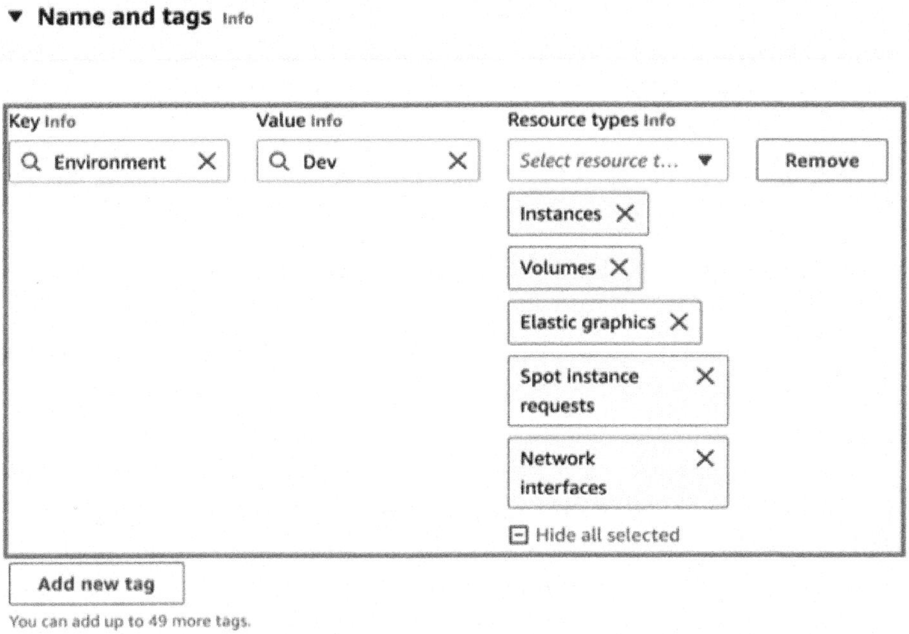

Figure 3.18 – Configuring the instance with tags

Each of these steps will allow you to customize your instance based on your specific need and will shape the functional and non-functional aspects of your instance.

Remember that a wide variety of configuration options are offered by AWS. So, you must be clear with your requirements and be specific with your selection as much as you can. Of course, don't fear missing out on any configurations as you always have the opportunity to reconfigure and relaunch your instance as your needs diverge.

Reviewing and launching instances

After configuring your instance details and before you launch your instance, you will have the opportunity to review your configuration settings and ensure everything is set up as intended. This will also serve you as an opportunity to update any configuration details before your instance goes live.

To review your instance configuration, navigate to the **Summary** section in the EC2 management console (*for visual guidance, see the screenshot provided at the end of this section*). This section will provide you with a comprehensive yet summarized version of your instance type, security group, storage settings, and more. Thoroughly review each of the sections while paying special attention to the following aspects:

- **Instance type**: Verify that you have chosen the right instance type for your needs. Remember that this choice affects the performance of your instance in terms of CPU, memory, storage, and network capacity.
- **Security groups**: Verify and confirm that the inbound and outbound rules in your security group align with your security policy. The rules in your security group must be explicitly defined to allow the type of traffic that can reach your instance. So, ensure the security group is configured in a least privileged manner, allowing necessary connections while blocking all the unnecessary traffic.
- **Key pair**: Verify that the key pair has been selected as intended. The associated key pair will allow you to securely connect to your instance once it is running.
- **Storage**: Check and ensure the storage volumes are configured as per your application needs. A couple of things you could do here is confirm the root volume associate is of the right type and size. Also, if you need to attach any additional volumes, then ensure they have been added correctly.
- **Tags**: Check and ensure that the instance is tagged correctly. Tags are essential for resource tracking and management, especially in larger environments:

Figure 3.19 – Summary of instance configuration

Once you've finished reviewing the configuration details, you can launch your instance by clicking the **Launch instance** button. At this stage, you will receive a final prompt to associate the key pair with your EC2 instance before the instance initialization begins.

In any case, remember that at any point in time, you will have full control of your EC2 instance. If you need to change your instance configuration, you can always stop, modify, and restart your instance with the updated configurations.

Now that you have mastered the process of launching EC2 instances from AMIs, we are ready to delve into understanding the best practices while creating custom AMIs. This knowledge will empower you to utilize your AMIs effectively, ensuring both efficiency and security in your operations.

Best practices and cautions while creating custom AMIs

There are best practices and cautions to consider while creating custom AMIs to ensure you are creating a secure, efficient, and consistent environment for your EC2 instances.

Best practices while creating custom AMIs

You can follow the practices described here to gain a great level of confidence in ensuring that launching and managing your EC2 instances is a robust process:

- **Update and patch**: Before you begin creating your custom AMI, always start by ensuring that your underlying operating system is up to date with the latest patches and security updates. This will allow you to ensure your custom AMI is free from any security and operational issues.

- **Minimize AMI size**: You can improvise your instance launch times by minimizing the size of your custom AMI. Always ensure you are removing any unnecessary files, temporary data, and other cached content before generating your AMI. Also, where possible, compress the files to further reduce your AMI size.

- **Use a base AMI**: Ensure the base AMI in use comes in from your organization or a trusted third party. This will ensure that you have a reliable foundation to build on top of.

- **Secure your AMI**: Ensure that your custom AMI has thorough security measures put in place, such as access controls, authorized user accounts, firewall rules, and so on. Also, remove any unnecessary services and follow the principle of least privilege to secure your AMI.

- **Regularly review and update**: Establish operational hygiene to ensure you are removing any unused AMIs to minimize your storage costs and avoid instances being launched with outdated ones.

- **Version control**: Ensure implementing a versioning strategy to scale your adaptation of custom AMIs. Following the versioning strategy lets you ensure you keep track of the AMI changes and roll back to a previous version if necessary. You can either make use of tags or AMI naming conventions to identify different versions of your AMIs.

What to watch for while creating custom AMIs

As you delve into the creation of custom AMIs, it is important to be mindful of certain considerations that can greatly influence the process. The following pointers will help ensure you safeguard against security risks while ensuring the proper functioning of your AMIs:

- Be cautious when sharing your custom AMIs with others. Make sure your AMI doesn't retain any sensitive data or credentials and be specific about updating permissions while sharing your AMI with other AWS accounts within your organization.

- Validate the source of your AMIs and ensure they can be trusted and meet your requirements. Check for AMI release notes or any other documentation from the provider to understand what's there inside your AMI to minimize potential security risks.

By following these practices, you can ensure your custom AMIs are securely built, efficient, and easy to manage.

Troubleshooting common AMI issues

AMIs are an integral part of EC2, acting as a brain and providing necessary information to configure and launch EC2 instances. However, in the world of technology, issues are inevitable and EC2 is no exception. Issues can sometimes occur with AMIs. Let's discuss some of the most common issues and their potential solutions.

Permission errors

Imagine launching an EC2 instance from a shared AMI, only to be surprised by a permission error. This error typically occurs when the requestor lacks permission to access the specified AMI. This issue can occur for many reasons, with the AMI owner revoking your permission or not providing your permission to the AMI in the first place.

In such an instance, ensure that the AMI owner has explicitly granted you launch permissions. Perhaps, if you are the owner yourself, then ensure you have correctly configured the permission in the first place.

Storage space issues

Imagine launching an EC2 instance from an AMI with the root device backed by an EBS snapshot that is larger than the specified EBS volume. In such a case, the process of launching an EC2 instance will ultimately fail as the instance cannot accommodate your data because of insufficient storage space.

To fix these issues, you can simply increase the size of your EBS volume or consider trimming your data and creating a new snapshot. You can also consider making use of other storage options with AWS, such as AWS S3 and EFS, to offload some of your data to keep the root device lean.

Inaccessible AMIs

You may encounter an issue where the AMI can be inaccessible. This can happen for many reasons, with AMIs being deregistered and deleted or the snapshot associated with the AMI being no longer available.

In such a case, as a first step, verify the status of the AMI in the management console. If the AMI is indeed deregistered or if the snapshot is deleted, you will have to recreate the AMI or restore the snapshot if possible. If the accessibility issues are because AMI is marked as private, then ensure you carry the necessary permissions to access it.

Launch failures

You may encounter a launch failure issue when launching an instance. This is particularly frustrating, especially when the cause of the failure isn't clear. This issue can happen for several reasons, such as an incompatible instance type, insufficient resource limits, or potential misconfigurations in the launch template.

To fix this issue, verify the error messages for any potential clues. Secondly, verify and ensure the instance type is compatible with the AMI selected. Finally, review your launch configurations for any potential mistakes.

> Note
> Remember to stay patient and follow a systematic approach while troubleshooting the issue. Make the most use of the resources available, such as AWS documentation and forums, to aid your troubleshooting. Following this process not only aids your troubleshooting and resolves your issue but also empowers you with a deeper understanding of EC2 and makes you a proficient cloud navigator!

Summary

By completing this chapter, you have learned how to create, share, and launch EC2 instances from AMIs, explored the best practices, and uncovered solutions for common issues. You also gained the ability to construct custom AMIs by leveraging the EC2 image pipeline to customize EC2 instances so that they match your specific requirements.

In the next chapter, we will explore the critical process of selecting the appropriate EC2 instance type and size and discuss how to ensure the selection matches the needs of your use case.

Further reading

To continue expanding your knowledge of AMI and Amazon EC2, consider exploring the following resources:

- Amazon EC2 user guide: https://docs.aws.amazon.com/AWSEC2/latest/UserGuide/concepts.html
- Amazon EC2 AMI documentation: https://docs.aws.amazon.com/AWSEC2/latest/UserGuide/AMIs.html

4
Choosing the Right Amazon EC2 Instance Type and Size

In this chapter, we will be specifically discussing the selection factors for deciding the appropriate EC2 instance type and size. Selecting the right EC2 instance type and size for your application can be considered a significant decision part of your implementation plan. Also, as I mentioned in *Chapter 3, Creating and Managing Amazon Machine Images (AMI)*, Amazon EC2 offers a diverse range of instance types with each having its own combination of CPU, memory, storage, and networking capabilities. So, as we delve further into this subject, we will not only revisit the concepts but also shed light on why making an informed choice is fundamental to the successful use of Amazon EC2.

In this chapter, we will begin by recapping various instance types and sizes available for EC2 instance provisioning, Subsequently, we will look into understanding your workload requirements and discuss how these prerequisites directly influence your EC2 instance selection.

We will then explore various purchase options available for EC2 instances, such as On-Demand, Reserved Instances, and Savings Plans, while also comparing their cost benefits and use cases. Following that, we will examine benchmarking and performance testing and discuss the importance of these activities in determining optimal instance type and size.

As we continue further, we will discuss the necessity of rightsizing your instance with the appropriate instance type and size to align with your business needs. Finally, we will round off this chapter by discussing some of the best practices for instance selection. Each of the sections aims to equip you with a well-rounded understanding of how to best choose your EC2 instance type and size.

The following topics will be covered in this chapter:

- Quick recap of EC2 instance types and sizes
- Understanding workload requirements
- EC2 instance purchasing options
- Benchmarking and performance testing

Quick recap of EC2 instance types and sizes

First, let's quickly recap what I mean by instance types and sizes. In AWS, each EC2 instance type represents a specific hardware configuration with a unique blend of CPU, memory, storage, and network resources. The types are then grouped into families that share common traits, making them well-suited for certain types of application workloads.

For example, **C-family instances** are *compute-optimized* and are ideal for CPU-intensive tasks, whereas **R-family instances** are *memory-optimized*, making them ideal for memory-intensive applications. Within each instance family type, the size (such as micro, small, medium, and large) represents the proportion of resources to be allocated to the respective instance.

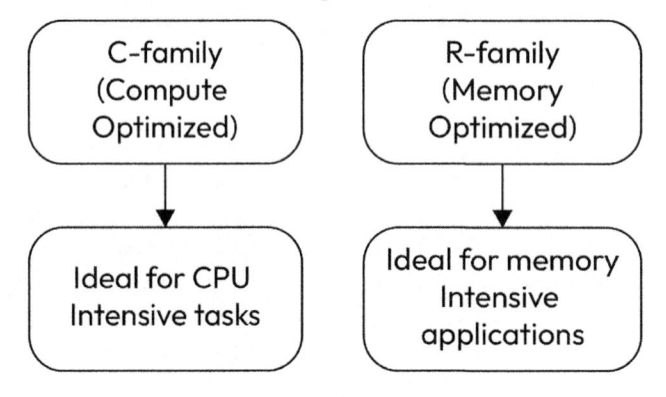

Figure 4.1 – Illustration of instance types

So, here's why the choice of instance type and size is so pivotal:

- **Performance**: Choosing the instance type directly impacts the performance of your application. Whether you need heavy computational power, a large amount of memory, high-speed storage, or robust networking capabilities, a well-chosen instance type meeting the characteristics of your application can provide you with the resources that your application needs and allow you to operate smoothly and efficiently.

- **Cost efficiency**: Selecting the right instance type allows you to optimize costs by closely aligning resource allocation to your actual application requirements. As AWS operates on a pay-as-you-go model, this means you only pay for what you use and it is in your best interest to use only what you need.

- **Scalability**: As your application demand and your user base grow, you will need to scale your application resources to meet the increased demand. The instance type you choose can directly influence your application's ability to meet the needs of your application demand and also how seamlessly you can scale.

- **Resource optimization**: The beauty of Amazon EC2 lies in its versatility. There is an instance type catering to just about any type of workload. This versatility allows you to choose the right instance type that best fits each component of your application, allowing you to optimize your overall resource utilization.
- **Future-proofing**: It is very likely that your current needs for your application may not be the same as your future needs. By choosing a versatile instance type, you can accommodate the evolving demands of your application in future-proofing your operations.

In this quick recap, we have refreshed our understanding of the various EC2 instance types and sizes with the details of why it is so pivotal to your application needs. Now, armed with this understanding, we are ready to delve into the next critical factor in our decision-making process to understand the workload requirements and how it will take us a step closer to making a well-informed selection of an EC2 instance.

Understanding workload requirements

An understanding of workload requirements plays a significant role in optimizing your resource utilization and ensuring high performance for your application. This understanding is very much required to strike a balance in achieving robust system performance in a cost-effective manner. If this is not done right, you risk over-provisioning or under-provisioning resources and risking your overall application performance. Now, let's begin the journey to deep dive into various factors of consideration and unlock their relevance in choosing the right instance type and size.

Analyzing CPU, memory, and storage needs

The CPU is like the brain of your EC2 instance. It carries out the instructions of the computer program by performing basic arithmetic, logic, input/output, and other control operations. The choice of instance type with the appropriate amount of CPU depends heavily on the computation needs of your application. For example, use cases such as machine learning, gaming servers, and scientific modeling are computation-intensive workloads and may require high CPU power for operations.

The memory, also known as RAM, holds the instance data in memory that is actively in use. This allows faster data access for the CPU. Use cases such as real-time big data analytics, in-memory caches, and high-performance databases require a high memory-to-CPU ratio.

Storage plays a critical role in holding the data persistently, and the choice is between instance storage (which provides transient storage but with high-performance disks) and elastic block storage (persistent storage that can be fine-tuned for performance). For use cases that require high speed and low latency, instance storage might be a better fit, and for use cases where long-term data durability and less frequent data access are important, then EBS may be more suitable.

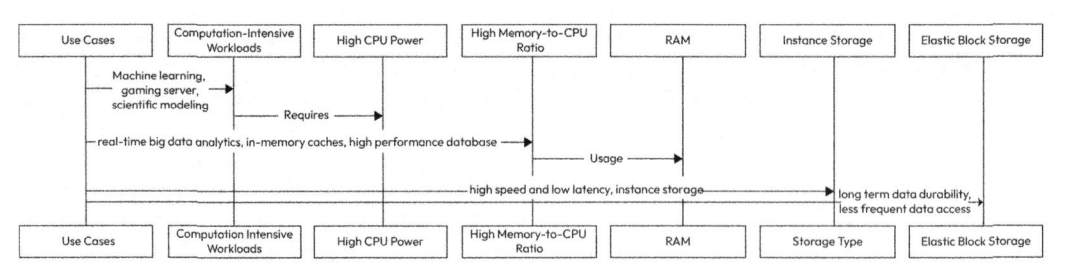

Figure 4.2 – Understanding workload requirements – CPU, memory, and storage

Networking and performance requirements

Networking and performance are two additional critical factors in choosing the right instance type and size. **Networking** involves the process of transmitting data between your instances and the rest of your infrastructure. It plays an important role in determining how well your application can serve its users. Amazon EC2 offers instances optimized for varying degrees of network performance defined by the number of packets per second, the maximum bandwidth, and typical network latency.

For example, workloads such as high-frequency trading, data warehousing, or massively multiplayer online games often require instances offering high network performance. On the other hand, workloads with moderate network demands such as development environments may function optimally on instances with lower network performance.

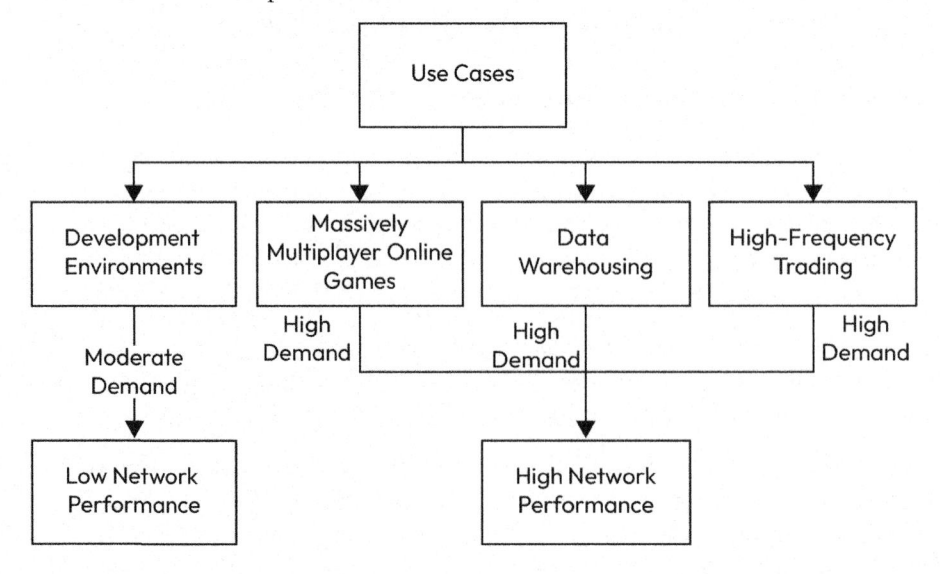

Figure 4.3 – Understanding workload requirements – network performance

Performance, in the context of an EC2 instance, typically refers to how efficiently an instance can execute your workload. The efficiency of the instance is not solely dependent on compute, storage, or memory; it is also influenced by other factors such as network latency and throughput, the speed of the storage attached to the instance, and other software optimizations.

You can gauge the performance of your EC2 instance by conducting real-world testing as appropriate to your nature of workload. Conducting this exercise will allow you to understand how the instance will perform under specific application demands, which, in turn, enables you to make an informed choice.

Application and infrastructure resiliency

Application and infrastructure resiliency are crucial considerations in ensuring seamless functioning of your systems and applications. Let's understand some key related factors and their influence on selecting the right instance type and size.

Application resiliency refers to the ability of an application to remain functional even when certain components fail under it. In AWS, it can be achieved through provisioning multiple EC2 instances with the load balancer and auto-scaling to meet variable demand. Selecting the appropriate instance type plays a pivotal role here. For example, compute-optimized instances are ideal for the computationally intensive workloads of your application, whereas memory-optimized instances are suitable for workloads needing large amounts of memory.

Infrastructure resiliency pertains to the durability and availability of your overall cloud infrastructure. It involves analyzing aspects such as physical servers, network connection, power supply, and even the geographical location of the data centers. So, when selecting the instance type, it is important to consider the regions where the instances are offered, as this can impact the resiliency of your infrastructure. For example, distributing your application across multiple Availability Zones can protect you from zonal-level failures.

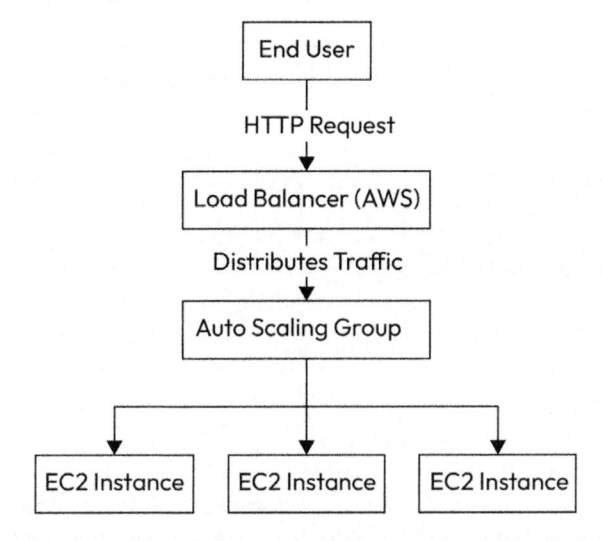

Figure 4.4 – Illustration of application resiliency with AWS EC2

EC2 instance purchasing options

As we continue our journey to optimize EC2 instance selection, in this section, we will turn our attention to discussing various EC2 instance purchasing options available. Selecting the right purchasing option is as important as selecting the right instance type and size as it can significantly influence the cost effectiveness of your cloud operations. We will start by exploring various distinct attributes of On-Demand Instances, Reserved Instances, Spot Instances, and Savings Plans. We will compare the cost benefits and highlight the use cases for which each option is suitable. So, without any further ado, let's embark on this exploration!

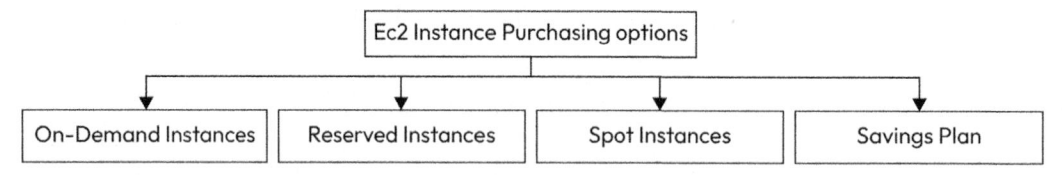

Figure 4.5 – EC2 instance purchasing options

On-Demand instances

Amazon EC2 **On-Demand Instances** offer a flexible, pay-as-you-go approach for running your applications in AWS Cloud. With On-Demand Instances, you are charged for per-second usage, which gives you an accurate alignment of costs with your resource consumption. This flexibility is particularly advantageous for short-term, sporadic workloads that can't be interrupted, allowing you to modify your EC2 usage in response to changing demands without making a long-term commitment.

Furthermore, the breadth of the available On-Demand instance types allows you to have customization of resource allocation according to your application's specific needs. Whether you require high CPU, memory, storage, or network performance, there's an On-Demand Instance tailored to meet these requirements. The On-Demand billing model is based on per-second usage with a minimum of 60 seconds, providing granular cost control, so you pay only for the exact duration of use.

However, it is important to note that On-Demand Instances are generally costlier than other EC2 instance purchasing options, such as Reserved Instances or Spot Instances, for long-term or predictable workloads. So, understanding your workload requirement is essential in choosing the most cost-effective instance purchasing option.

Reserved Instances

Reserved Instances (**RIs**) in Amazon EC2 offer a significant cost advantage for predictable and steady-state workloads. When you purchase an RI, you commit to 1 or 3 years of usage in exchange for a substantial discount, compared to On-Demand pricing. This makes RIs ideal for long-term projects where usage is guaranteed for the foreseeable future and is unlikely to be interrupted.

RIs are available in three types: *Standard*, *Convertible*, and *Scheduled*. Among these RIs, **Convertible RIs** offer a low discount but give you the flexibility to change instance family, operating system, tenancy, or even Availability Zone during the term. **Standard RIs**, on the other hand, are suitable for workloads running on a regular schedule such as office hour applications or batch processing tasks. Lastly, **Scheduled RIs** come into play when you have workloads running on a specific timetable, such as batch processing tasks or dev environments running only during business hours.

It is important to take note that the RIs are not cancellable or transferable. So, despite the cost-saving potential, it requires a careful analysis of your workload pattern for long-term commitment.

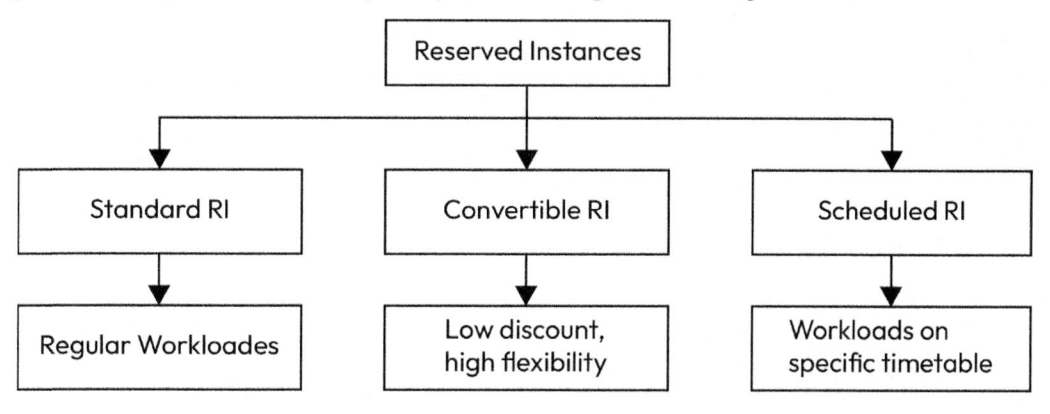

Figure 4.6 – RI types

Spot Instances

Spot Instances are an excellent way to achieve considerable cost savings on Amazon EC2. The idea behind Spot Instances is to make use of spare Amazon EC2 instance computing capacity and offer customers up to a 90% discount compared with On-Demand prices. However, Spot Instances fluctuate based on supply and demand, which requires some flexibility and adaptability in your application design.

Fault-tolerant applications with flexible start and end times can make use of Spot Instances at a significant discount. They are ideal for data analysis, batch jobs, background processing, and other tasks where it's okay if an instance gets interrupted. This caveat of unpredictability means that your instances can be reclaimed by AWS with just a two-minute warning if there is a higher demand.

So, despite their potential cost savings, Spot Instances may not be suitable for all types of applications. Using them effectively includes a clear understanding of your workload requirements and a readiness to manage unpredictable availability.

Savings Plans

Savings Plans are a cost-saving feature that offers flexibility and potential discounts for EC2, Fargate, and Lambda usage. Savings Plans can deliver up to 72% in savings, similar to RIs, but this comes with additional flexibility as they can apply to any instance family, size, availability zone, OS, or tenancy.

In essence, with a savings plan, you will commit to using a specific amount of computing power, measured in terms of dollars per hour, over a term of 1 or 3 years. This commitment is not specific to EC2 but can be applied to other services such as Fargate, Lambda, and SageMaker. So, the Savings Plan basically provides a flexible model where we can enjoy significant cost reduction without the need to commit to specific instance configurations.

Nevertheless, before engaging in a Savings Plan, conduct proper planning and analysis to understand your long-term workload requirements. This allows you to ensure your usage aligns with your forecasted commitment. Otherwise, the savings plan will be ineffective.

Comparing costs and use cases for each option

In choosing the right EC2 instance purchasing option, it is important for you to understand the use cases and the costs associated with each. This understanding will allow you to balance resource allocation, optimize costs, and fully leverage the potential of the AWS platform:

- **On-Demand Instances**: These provide great flexibility and are perfect for short-term sporadic workloads that cannot be interrupted. On-Demand Instances are priced per hour or second with no upfront cost. This makes them a good option for workloads with unpredictable bursts of activity. However, they are considered more expensive compared to other purchasing options, especially if you are running continuously for a longer period.

- **Reserved Instances**: These provide a significant discount compared to On-Demand pricing and are recommended for predictable steady-state usage. This purchasing option requires an upfront commitment of 1 or 3 years. So, be certain of your needs, otherwise, this can be a significant drawback for projects with uncertain future needs. The cost savings, however, will be substantial for long-term sustained workloads.

- **Savings plan**: This option provides a flexible pricing model while also offering significant savings on AWS compute usage. In this model, you have the flexibility to change the instance type, sizes, and Availability Zones across computer services, such as EC2, Lambda, Fargate, and SageMaker. In a savings plan, you will be committing to a specific amount of compute usage measured in dollars per hour for a term of 1 or 3 years.

- **Spot Instances**: Here, you take advantage of unused EC2 capacity in the AWS cloud at steep discounts. Spot Instances are ideal for workloads having flexible start and end times or fault-tolerant applications. Spot Instances come with no guarantee of availability of compute resources, which could be a major drawback for critical applications.

EC2 instance purchasing options   79

```
                    EC2 Instance Purchasing Options
         ┌──────────────┬──────────────────┬──────────────┐
    On-Demand        Reserved          Savings         Spot
    Instances        Instances          Plan         Instances
         │              │                 │              │
   Flexible, no    Upfront commitment, Flexible model, Unused capacity
   upfront costs   substantial long-term measured in $/hr at discounts, no
                   savings                             availability guarantee
         │              │                 │              │
    Flexibility     Steady State      Cost Savings   Steep Discounts
                      Usage
```

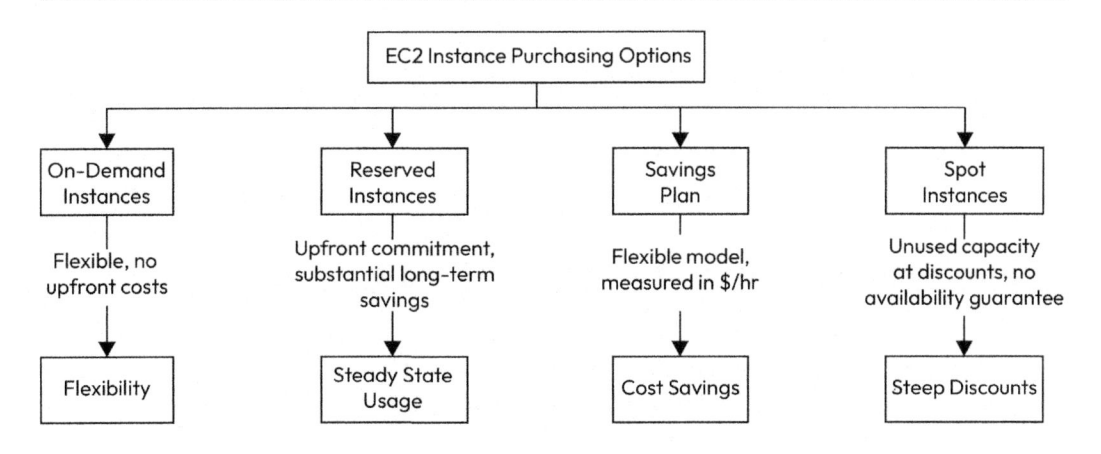

Figure 4.7 – Illustration of EC2 instance purchasing options

The following table serves as a concise summary, encapsulating the use cases, cost-effectiveness, and flexibility of each purchasing option discussed earlier, offering you a clear and comparative insight.

Purchasing Option	Use cases	Flexibility	Cost	Downsides
On-Demand	Short-term, irregular workloads, testing new applications (e.g., a temporary marketing website for a new product launch)	High	High (per hour/second)	Costliest for long-term; no sustained use discounts
Reserved Instances	Predictable, steady-state usage (e.g., a database server with consistent usage over a year)	Medium (long-term commitment)	Lower (upfront cost)	Upfront payment; less flexibility for instance changes
Savings Plans	Dynamic and evolving needs (e.g., a growing start-up scaling its services over time)	High	Lower (commitment per hour)	Spending commitment; management overhead
Spot Instances	Flexible, fault-tolerant, non-critical applications (e.g., a data analysis program that can be paused and resumed)	High	Lowest (availability not guaranteed)	Potential interruptions; loss of temporary data or processing

Table 4.1 – EC2 instance purchasing options

In summary, each purchasing option comes with its own advantages, and your selection should reflect your individual requirements and usage patterns. Regularly review your instance usage and take advantage of AWS Cost Explorer to make informed decisions about your EC2 purchasing strategy.

As we move forward, we will delve into the importance of benchmarking and performance testing and discuss the key role they play in choosing the right EC2 instance type and size for your application needs.

Benchmarking and performance testing

Benchmarking is similar to test-driving a car before buying it. In this process, you will be running a series of tests in an EC2 instance to measure its performance and the suitability of your workload. By benchmarking, you can understand the limits of an instance, assess how it performs under different conditions, and determine whether it meets your specific needs.

One key reason why benchmarking is essential in an EC2 environment is that EC2 instances can perform differently based on their configuration, even if they are from the same instance family. This is due to a variety of factors including the host's underlying hardware, network performance, and the nature of other workloads running on the same underlying host. So, by benchmarking you can avoid unpleasant surprises once the instance is deployed into production.

Furthermore, benchmarking also supports you in optimizing cost. We are often inclined to choose a larger, more expensive instance assuming that it would deliver higher performance. But in many cases, smaller or cheaper instances can suffice for your workload. So, benchmarking allows you to identify these opportunities and select the most cost-effective instance.

Tools and techniques for performance testing

There is an array of tools and techniques available to conduct performance testing. By conducting the performance testing, you can understand the capability of your EC2 instance, and by making use of these tools effectively, you can gain crucial insights by simulating load and optimizing your workload.

To start with, AWS CloudWatch is a powerful observability service in the AWS ecosystem. It collects and tracks metrics (log files) and sets the alarm. This allows you to monitor the performance in real time and initiate actions such as auto-scaling based on predefined thresholds. Furthermore, AWS Compute Optimizer stands out as a recommendation engine to suggest optimal EC2 instances based on historical utilization metrics. This AI-powered tool can predict optimal configurations, helping you balance cost and performance effectively.

Beyond AWS-native tools, you can make use of open source software such as Apache JMeter to stress test by simulating a heavy load on servers and networks to gauge performance under different load types. Also, tools such as Gatling can be leveraged for continuous load testing and support integration with development pipelines, making them ideal for DevOps environments.

Choosing the right tool or combination of tools largely depends on your specific needs. For example, you might choose AWS Compute Optimizer for rightsizing instances but Apache JMeter to stress test your application under heavy load scenarios. By understanding and applying these tools and techniques, you gain a powerful lever to steer your performance testing and, ultimately, make an informed decision about the right EC2 instances for your workload.

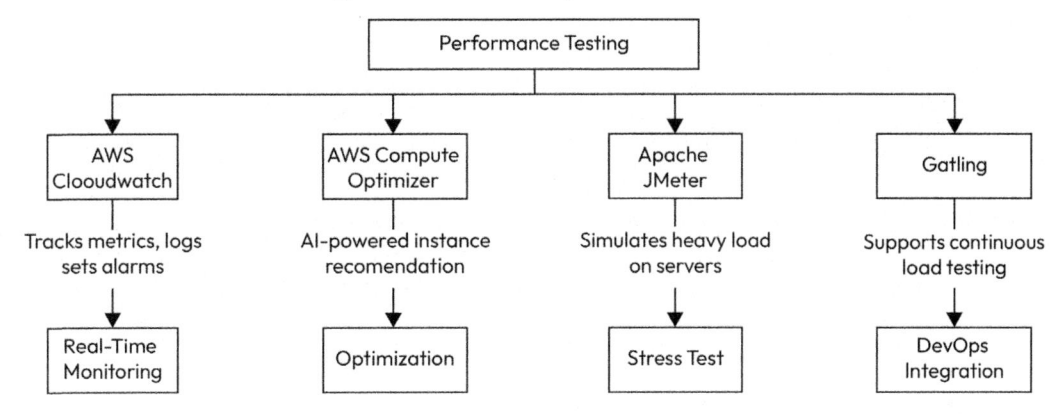

Figure 4.8 – Illustration of tools and techniques for performance testing

Rightsizing your instances

Rightsizing your EC2 instances is an essential process in aligning your workload requirements with the most efficient EC2 instance type and size. This process allows you to mitigate the risk of overprovisioning leading to excess costs or provisioning leading to subpar performance.

Make use of tools such as AWS Cost Explorer and Compute Optimizer to rightsize your instance. The tools take into consideration your historical usage data, provide recommendations for the ideal instance type, and help you identify whether the instances are under-utilized or over-utilized. Through its machine learning capabilities, AWS Compute Optimizer can recommend the optimal instance factoring in CPU, memory, and network utilization.

The outcome of benchmarking and performance testing is also integral to rightsizing your instance. Benchmarking allows you to determine which instances can deliver the optimal performance in the most cost-effective way, while performance testing can reveal whether a smaller instance type might suffice or a larger one is required, helping you steer clear of both underprovisioning and overprovisioning.

Also, consider the rightsizing process as an ongoing exercise. As your workload requirements change, it is important to reassess rightsizing your instances.

Best practices for instance selection

As we conclude this chapter, it is critical to reinforce the best practices for selecting an instance. The selection process is not a one-size-fits-all approach and it requires a deep understanding of your workload, budget, and other variety of options that EC2 provides. Let's begin by exploring the details of best practices:

1. To begin with, identify your workload requirements. This includes understanding the nature of your workload (whether it is compute-intensive, memory-intensive, or I/O-intensive) and computational requirements such as CPU, GPU, memory, and storage that your application needs. This awareness will allow you to map your requirements to the instance family.

2. Next, determine your workload patterns. If your application has a variable CPU usage, then burstable performance instances (T family) can be a good fit. If your usage pattern is steady and predictable, then Reserved Instances or Savings Plan could be a more cost-effective choice. Furthermore, if your workload can tolerate interruptions and isn't time-sensitive, then Spot Instances could provide substantial savings.

3. Your workload changes over time. Establish a regular review ritual and make use of tools such as Cost Explorer and Compute Optimizer to help monitor your resource utilization to identify opportunities for rightsizing. Benchmarking and performance testing cannot be overlooked too, and it is important you benchmark your application on different instance types and see which ones provide the best performance.

4. Finally, stay up to date with the AWS innovations. AWS is never out of an idea, and you will notice constant innovation and desire from AWS to introduce new instance types. So, keeping up with their innovations can help you find better ways to run applications and manage costs.

With this, we have come to the end of the chapter.

Summary

By completing this chapter, you have gained a deep understanding of how to evaluate workload requirements, navigate EC2 instance purchasing options, implement benchmarking and performance testing, and right-size your EC2 instances. This understanding will empower you to make well-informed decisions when selecting EC2 instances and aligning your choices with the specific needs and demands.

Up next, we will delve into networking and connectivity in EC2, where we will explore the essential aspects of networking within the EC2 ecosystem.

5
Networking and Connectivity in Amazon EC2

This chapter will look into the intricacies of Amazon VPC and its pivotal role in the EC2 ecosystem. It is important to understand that the success of your implementation is not only determined by selecting the right EC2 instance type and size, but is also significantly impacted by how well you navigate the networking landscape within Amazon EC2.

In this chapter, we will begin by familiarizing ourselves with the fundamental concepts of Amazon VPC, highlighting its importance in establishing a secure, customizable, and efficient networking environment for your EC2 instances. We will then dive into the hands-on aspect of creating, managing, and fine-tuning VPC to gain exposure to setting up and tailoring the networking infrastructure for your needs.

We will then unravel the specifics of subnets, CIDR blocks, route tables, and their roles in VPC, including their impact on EC2 networking. Also, security being a paramount concern, we will delve into the detailed discussion on security groups and network ACLs and guide you toward creating a robust and secure network defense for your environment.

Further, we will explore the functionality and use cases of elastic IPs and elastic network interface along with other integral elements in ensuring seamless network connectivity for your EC2 instances. As we progress, we will discuss VPC peering and other connectivity options such as Direct Connect, VPNs, and VPC endpoints.

Finally, we round off this chapter by instilling the design principles for networking in EC2, aiming to guide you toward a secure, efficient, and cost-effective EC2 networking environment. The goal of this chapter is to equip you with the comprehensive knowledge of networking in EC2 to allow you to build a secure, efficient, and robust networking environment for your EC2 environment.

The following topics will be covered in this chapter:

- Overview of VPC
- Significance of networking in EC2
- Creating and managing a VPC
- Subnets and route tables
- Security groups and network ACLs
- Elastic IPs and Elastic network interfaces
- VPC peering and connectivity options
- AWS Direct Connect and VPNs
- VPC endpoints and their use cases
- VPC design principles

Overview of VPC

Amazon **Virtual Private Cloud** (**VPC**) is a core service within the AWS ecosystem that allows users to provision a logically isolated section of AWS cloud by way of defining their own virtual network. Users can launch AWS resources inside the virtual network they define.

The essence of VPC lies in its ability to offer a robust combination of security, scalability, and customization in the realm of cloud computing.

Importance of AWS VPC

AWS VPC stands as a foundational element in the heart of AWS's vast ecosystem, bridging the gap between traditional networking and cloud innovation. Here are some important significances of AWS VPC:

- **Architecture and flexibility**: This virtual network closely resembles a traditional network that you would operate in your own data center with the additional benefits of utilizing the scalable infrastructure of AWS. The VPC comes with the flexibility to customize the network configuration that fits your specific needs, such as selecting your own IP address range, creating subnets, configuring route tables, internet gateways, and so on.

- **Security and control**: Amazon VPC offers robust security capabilities such as security groups and network access control lists, empowering users to apply inbound and outbound filters at both the instance and subnet levels for enhanced security measures. In addition to this, you can create a VPN or Direct Connect connection between your data center and your VPC. Doing this will effectively extend your corporate data center into the cloud.

- **Connectivity options**: Multiple connectivity options exist within Amazon VPC. These include VPC peering, which allows for direct network routing between different VPCs within the same AWS account or different AWS accounts. There's also AWS Direct Connect, which provides a dedicated, private connection from a remote network to your VPC. Similar to Direct Connect, you have VPN providing a private connectivity over the internet with a remote network to your VPC. Furthermore, you can use AWS Transit Gateway to interconnect thousands of VPCs and your on-premises networks to create highly scalable and manageable global network architecture.
- **Service integration**: Amazon VPC is tightly integrated with numerous other AWS services. For instance, you can host your relational database with Amazon RDS, deploy a web application on Amazon EC2, and even access the data from Amazon S3, still within VPC. This integration allows users to create sophisticated applications that leverage the security, scalability, and performance benefits of AWS.

Having navigated through the intricacies of VPC, it is clear how pivotal it is within the AWS's infrastructure. With VPC at its core, EC2 networking becomes more adaptable, efficient, and secure. In the next section, we will further demystify how these foundational concepts interact and elevate the AWS ecosystem.

Significance of networking in EC2

Networking plays a crucial role in Amazon EC2 by acting as a backbone that facilitates various forms of communication, security features, and more. Understanding the importance of networking in EC2 can significantly enhance the security, efficiency, and scalability of your cloud operations.

Let's delve deeper into these pillars of EC2 networking:

- **Connectivity**: Networking forms the backbone of EC2 instances. It facilitates communication between them, with other AWS services, and with external systems over the internet. Without networking, EC2 instances will practically be isolated and not usable.
- **Security**: Networking in EC2 supports a broad range of security features, helping you to protect the instances from unauthorized access. By making use of the security features such as security group and network access control lists, you can basically control the inbound and outbound traffic to your instances. Additionally, by leveraging VPC subnet settings, you can technically isolate your instances and control the flow of data, ensuring that your EC2 environment always aligns with the security best practices.
- **Performance**: Networking also heavily impacts the performance of your EC2 instances. With enhanced networking, you can achieve higher bandwidth, lower latencies, and greater packet-per-second performance. Selecting the networking option based on your workload can significantly impact the overall performance of your applications.
- **Scalability and redundancy**: Networking in EC2 supports scalability and redundancy by relying on features such as auto scaling groups and load balancing to distribute the incoming traffic across multiple instances and ensuring the application remains available to meet new demands coming in from unexpected spikes.

In conclusion, networking is vital in the EC2 ecosystem, not just as a functional component but as a tool that provides security, performance, and operational benefits. With this foundation in mind, it is important to understand how to effectively establish this backbone within AWS. So, let's begin by creating and managing your VPC.

Creating and managing a VPC

Creating a VPC allows you to establish the networking backbone for your applications. VPC provides you with secure and logical isolation for your resources in the cloud, while also offering a scalable and flexible environment akin to operating your own data center. The creation of VPC can be considered as a foundation step to launch and manage your resources in AWS.

Before diving into the creation process, it is important to note that every VPC has to be associated with an IP address range (CIDR block). The **CIDR range** specified during the creation of VPC cannot be changed afterward. The CIDR block can be anywhere from `/28` (16 IP addresses) to `/16` (65,536 IP addresses). Remember to choose a size suitable for your anticipated scale of workloads.

To create a VPC, you will have to navigate to the VPC dashboard on the management console. From there, you can follow the high-level steps:

1. Click on **Your VPCs** and then **Create VPC**:

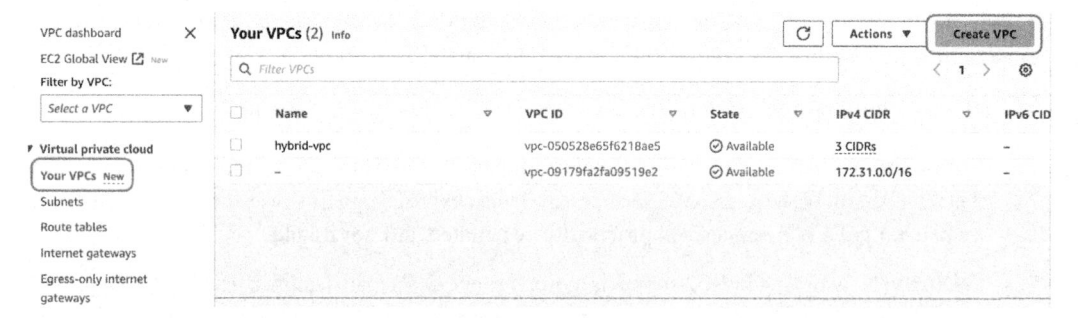

Figure 5.1 – Creating a VPC

2. Provide a name for your VPC for easy identification and management.
3. Specify the IPv4 CIDR block (e.g., *10.0.0.0/24*) based on your needs.
4. For **Tenancy**, select **Default** unless you have a specific need for a dedicated instance.
5. Add metadata to your VPC by way of including the **Tags**.
6. Click **Create**.

To further illustrate these steps, the following is the screenshot of the AWS console that details the configuration process for creating a VPC:

Create VPC Info

A VPC is an isolated portion of the AWS Cloud populated by AWS objects, such as Amazon EC2 instances.

VPC settings

Resources to create Info
Create only the VPC resource or the VPC and other networking resources.

- ● VPC only
- ○ VPC and more

Name tag - *optional*
Creates a tag with a key of 'Name' and a value that you specify.

    private-vpc

IPv4 CIDR block Info
- ● IPv4 CIDR manual input
- ○ IPAM-allocated IPv4 CIDR block

IPv4 CIDR

    10.0.0.0/24

IPv6 CIDR block Info
- ● No IPv6 CIDR block
- ○ IPAM-allocated IPv6 CIDR block
- ○ Amazon-provided IPv6 CIDR block
- ○ IPv6 CIDR owned by me

Tenancy Info

    Default ▼

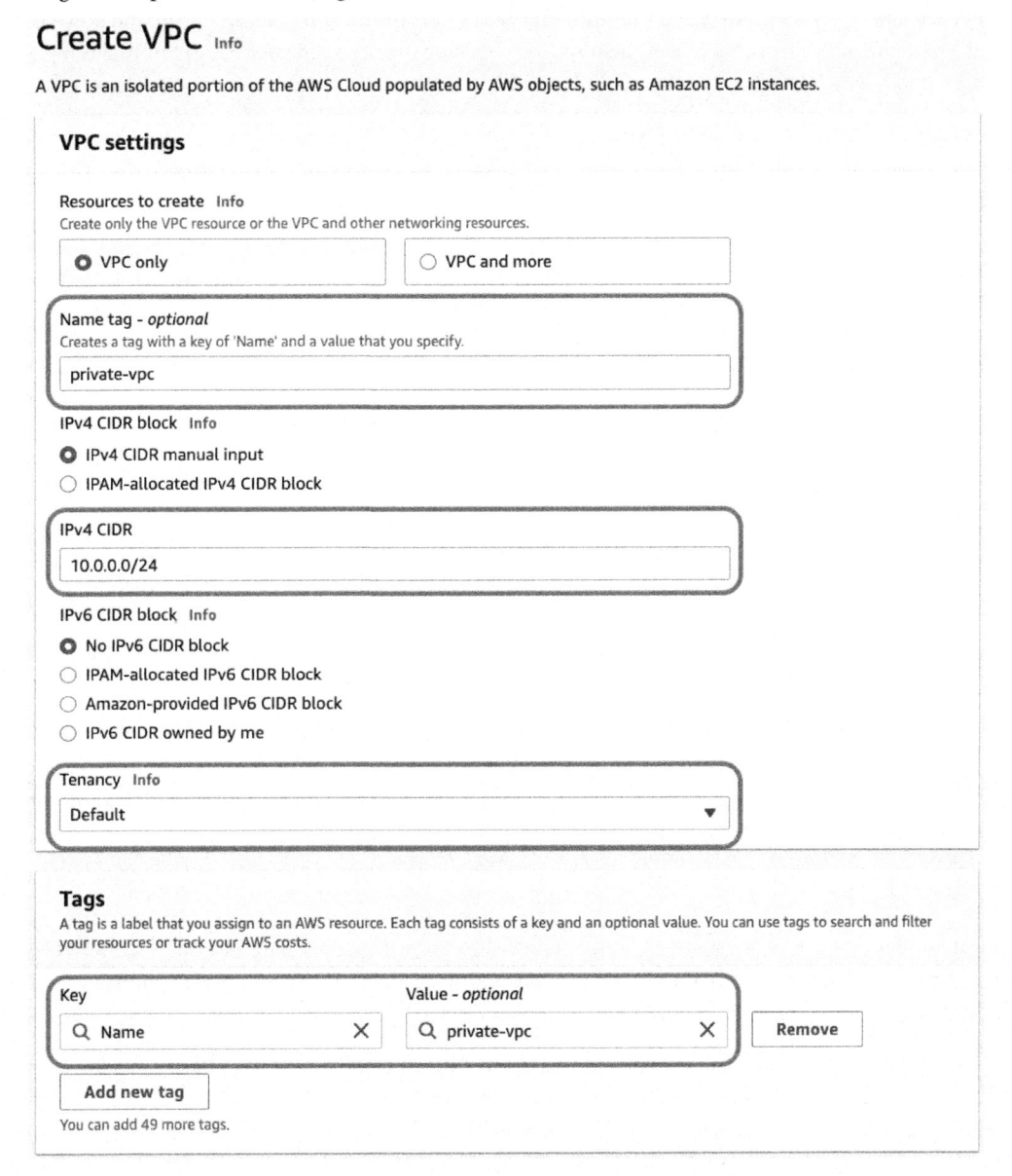

Tags

A tag is a label that you assign to an AWS resource. Each tag consists of a key and an optional value. You can use tags to search and filter your resources or track your AWS costs.

Key	Value - *optional*	
Name ✕	private-vpc ✕	Remove

Add new tag

You can add 49 more tags.

Figure 5.2 – Configuration details for VPC creation

At this stage, you've successfully created a VPC. This bare-bones VPC includes a **main route table**, a **default network access control list** (**ACL**), and a default security group.

In a very typical scenario, you would have to create new subnets inside the VPC, and each subnet you create will have its own IP address range within your VPC's CIDR block. The subnets inside your VPC also allow you to control the inbound and outbound traffic at the subnet level. Furthermore, you can make your resources hosted inside VPC available over the internet by way of including the **internet gateway (IGW)**.

Creating a VPC is just the beginning; there are numerous settings and components to consider such as NAT gateways, route tables, VPC peering, and more. Also, remember that creating VPC sets up the playground, but how you play the game depends on your application-specific needs and architecture.

VPC settings and configuration options

In the previous section, we created a bare VPC, but in a real world scenario, you would be configuring the VPC with a variety of settings and options that control how your VPC interacts with your applications and other AWS services. In this section, we will be diving deeper into each of the configuration settings and options. As a practical example, we will use a multi-tiered web application deployment on AWS with a side-by-side demonstration of how to effectively implement and adjust each of those settings.

Subnets

Inside your VPC, you can create one or more **subnets**, each serving as a separate network segment with its own IP address range, smaller than the overall VPC CIDR block. Subnets can be public (having a route to the Internet) or private (not having a route to the Internet), providing granularity in security and resource distribution.

For example, imagine that the e-commerce application is logically divided into different tiers—a public-facing web server tier, a private application tier (handling business logic), and a private database tier. In such a case, a design to place each tier in its own respective subnet for better network and resource management will be effective.

Route tables

Route tables define how the network traffic flow is directed within your subnets. Each subnet in your VPC must be associated with a route table, and the rules defined in the route table control the flow of the traffic.

For example, in an e-commerce application use case, different route tables can be created to cater to the needs of different subnets. For instance, the route table for a public subnet can be configured to carry a route to the internet gateway, whereas the route table associated with the private subnet carries a route to direct traffic to a NAT gateway, facilitating internet access only for the outbound traffic.

Internet gateway

An **internet gateway** acts as a bridge between your VPC and the internet. Once the internet gateway is created and attached to your VPC, it facilitates providing internet access to your VPC.

For example, in an e-commerce application use case, an internet gateway associated with the VPC can be configured to have a route in a public subnet. A load balancer can then be hosted inside a public subnet to serve the requests coming in from the internet.

NAT gateways/instances

NAT gateways/instances allow instances in the private subnet to connect to the internet to receive updates and downloads while preventing inbound traffic.

For example, in an e-commerce application use case, the instances are hosted in the private subnet (say, application server or database server) to allow necessary outbound internet access for receiving software updates or patches while still maintaining inbound isolation from the internet.

Network access control lists (NACLs) and security groups

Network access control lists (**NACLs**) and security groups provide VPCs with multiple layers of security in controlling the inbound/outbound traffic at the subnet level and at the instance level (security group).

For example, in an e-commerce application use case, NACLs can be configured at the public subnet and private subnet to filter the inbound/traffic at the subnet level, whereas the security group can be configured at the instance to allow traffic only from specific sources. For example, security groups at the load balancer can be configured to accept traffic from the internet while the security group applied at the application server instances can be defined to receive traffic only from load balancers. Finally, for the data tier (i.e., database), the security group can be configured to receive traffic only from application server instances.

VPC peering

VPC peering allows private connectivity between two VPCs. The peering connection can be configured so that there are two VPCs in the same account or different accounts, even across different AWS regions.

For example, in an e-commerce application use case, imagine a data analytics VPC has been set up to analyze and process the customer and transaction data. In such a scenario, VPC peering can be established between application VPC and data analytics VPC to securely transfer the data for analysis.

VPN connections and Direct Connect

Both **VPNs** and **Direct Connect** support secure private connectivity between your on-premises network and your VPC. The nature of connectivity, however, is different for both of them. We will be discussing this in more detail in a later section of this chapter.

For example, for an e-commerce application use case, it is natural for a company to have an on-premises data center. It can leverage VPNs or Direct Connect to securely establish private connectivity between its VPC and data center.

DHCP option set

A **DHCP option set** can be created for your VPC to associate custom DNS servers, NTP servers, etc., for the instances hosted inside the VPC.

For example, in an e-commerce application use case, you can associate `ecommerce.com` with all the instances, along with custom DNS servers, for such requirements.

Endpoints and endpoint services

VPC endpoints allow private connectivity between your resources hosted inside the VPC to the supported AWS services that are outside VPC. This nature of connectivity does not require an internet gateway, NAT, VPN, or Direct Connect.

For example, for an e-commerce application use case, you can leverage S3 for storing product images and DynamoDB for persisting shopping cart details. Product images and shopping cart details can be accessed privately by the resources hosted inside VPC leveraging VPC endpoints.

VPC Flow Logs

VPC Flow Logs allow you to monitor and troubleshoot the traffic that flows through your VPC. By configuring flow logs, you can gather insights about your network performance and security by understanding the traffic accepted/rejected by your VPC.

For example, for an e-commerce application use case, VPC Flow Logs can be configured to keep track of the network traffic, detect any anomalies, or identify any unauthorized network access attempts.

Modifying and deleting VPCs

As businesses evolve, so do their technological requirements. AWS VPC addresses this ever changing landscape by offering great adaptability. The standout advantages of using Amazon VPC are the flexibility to modify them to meet the evolving business needs and technology requirements. In this section, we will explore how to modify a specific configuration of VPC and also the steps and precautions to consider while deleting a VPC.

Modifying a VPC

AWS provides a range of options to modify your VPC configurations, but not every attribute of the VPC can be modified. It is important for you to understand what can/cannot be modified and carefully play around with constraints to meet your evolving needs:

- **IP address range**: The primary IP address range (CIDR block) of a VPC cannot be changed once set, but you can add a secondary IP range. This is useful for extending your network without creating a new VPC.

- **DHCP option set**: A VPC can be associated with one DHCP option set at a time. However, you can still create a new one to alter the DNS server, NTP, and domain name for the instances in your VPC.
- **VPC peering**: You can create or remove VPC peering connections to allow instances in different VPCs to communicate with each other like they are inside the same network.
- **VPC endpoints**: VPC endpoints can be added or removed to allow the resources hosted inside your VPC to establish a private connection to the supported AWS services.
- **ClassicLink**: If you are using classic EC2 instances, you can still disable ClassicLink to facilitate communication between them with the resources hosted inside VPC.

Deleting a VPC

Take note that you cannot delete a VPC if it contains active resources. So, before deleting a VPC, you must delete all its dependent resources such as subnets, route tables, network ACLs, security groups and any associated instances to result in a successful deletion.

To delete a VPC, you need to do the following:

- Navigate to the VPC dashboard on the AWS management console.
- Select the VPC you wish to delete.
- Click on the **Actions** drop-down menu located in the top-right of the console.
- Choose **Delete VPC**.

Here is a screenshot that visually guides you through these steps in the AWS management console:

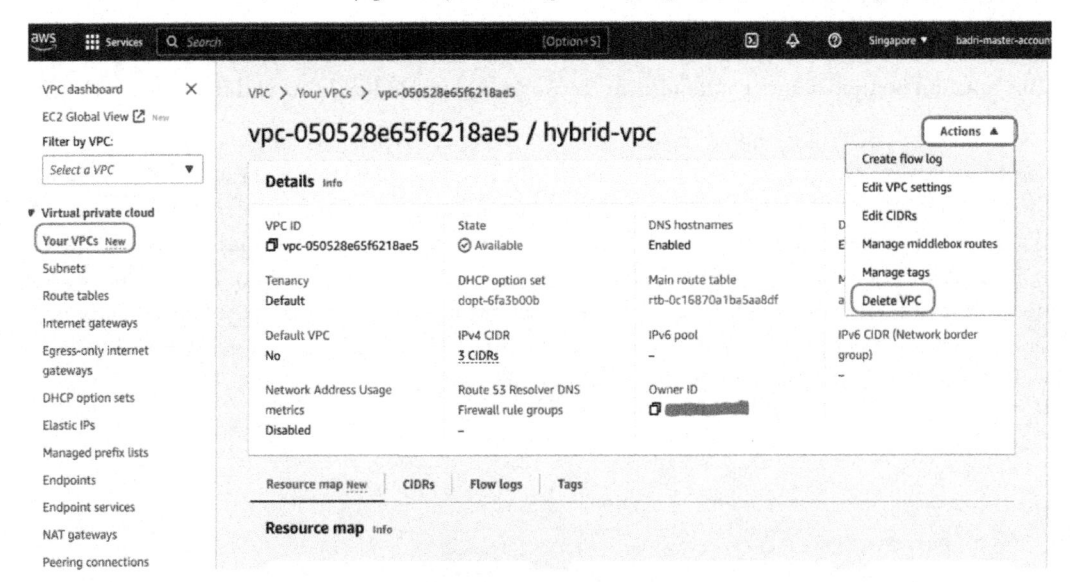

Figure 5.3 – Deleting a VPC

> **Note**
> Deleting a VPC is irreversible. So, once the deletion is made, none of its configurations and settings can be retrieved.

Subnets and route tables

The core foundation of VPC in AWS is built on top of three pivotal elements: subnets, CIDR blocks, and route tables. It is crucial to understand these components thoroughly to optimize your network architecture and ensure it aligns with your business needs.

Understanding subnets

A **subnet** is basically a logical subdivision of an IP network. In the context of AWS, a subnet resides in the single availability zone of your VPC. In other words, imagine a subnet as a unique compartment within your VPC where you can place your resources, such as EC2 instances, and isolate them between different compartments for security and administrative reasons.

A subnet can either be public or private and this is determined by whether they have a direct route to the internet. A public subnet has a route to an internet gateway, allowing instances within the subnet to reach the internet. In contrast, a private subnet does not carry a route to the internet and thereby restricts any form of inbound/outbound traffic, allowing you to enhance security posture for sensitive resources.

Understanding CIDR blocks

Classless Inter-Domain Routing (**CIDR**) blocks are a key component of IP addressing and subnetting. This notation method allows you to identify networks and individual hosts within the network.

For example, a CIDR block notation such as `10.0.0.0/16` represents an IP network and its size. The IP network is `10.0.0.0`, and `/16` specifies the number of bits that make up a network prefix. The `/16` indicates the first 16 bits (out of total 32 bits in Ipv4) used for network prefixes (i.e., `10.0` is a network prefix used for the network portion), leaving the remaining bits for host addresses (i.e., `0.0` is the host portion of the address. Here, we have 16 bits left, so we can have 2^{16} (65,536) unique host addresses. However, we typically subtract 2 from the total considering the fact that a typical subnet occupies a network address `10.0.0.0` and broadcast address `10.0.255.255`. This leaves us with `65,534` usable host addresses within that network.

We can sum this up in the following points:

- The /16 indicates that the first 16 bits are for the network portion
- This leaves us with 16 bits for the host addresses (since IPv4 addresses are 32 bits in total)
- The total number of addresses within this block is 2^16, which equals 65,536 addresses
- The number of usable addresses is typically 65,536 - 2 = 65,534, considering one address is used for the network and one is used for the broadcast

The following is illustration of CIDR calculation:

```
IP Address:    10          . 0         . 0         . 0
Binary:        00001010    . 00000000  . 00000000  . 00000000
Mask (/16):    11111111    . 11111111  . 00000000  . 00000000
               |---- Network Part ----| |-- Host Part --|
```

Figure 5.4 – Illustration of CIDR calculation

While creating a VPC, you assign it a CIDR block (the IP address range) which is the pool of IP addresses that your resources within the VPC can use. For example, if your VPC has a CIDR block of 10.0.0.0/16, then you can have up to 65,536 IP addresses (i.e., 10.0.0.0 to 10.0.255.255)

When you create a subnet, you choose a CIDR block from the IP address range within your VPC. This forms a subset of IP addresses within the VPC that can be used by the resources in the subnet. For instance, a subnet with the CIDR block 10.0.0.0/24 will have 256 IP addresses (10.0.0.0 to 10.0.0.255) available.

In summary, understanding the relationship between subnets and CIDR blocks is essential to design your VPC structure effectively.

Creating and managing Subnets

Once you have understood the relationship between subnets and CIDR blocks, you can go ahead and create subnets in your VPC. This is essential for establishing a secure, scalable, and efficient networking environment in AWS.

Creating a subnet

Creating a subnet involves the following steps:

1. **Create subnet**: Navigate to the VPC section in your AWS management console. Under that, select **Subnets** under **Virtual private cloud** on the left side of the screen. Then, click on **Create Subnet**:

Name	Subnet ID	State	VPC	IPv4 CIDR
private-subnet-2b	subnet-08d8632ca1a4d958a	⊘ Available	vpc-050528e65f6218ae5 | hy...	10.0.0.128/26
public-subnet-1a	subnet-0ca89c26c432091f9	⊘ Available	vpc-050528e65f6218ae5 | hy...	10.0.0.64/26
-	subnet-095c4a2cd2ee843d7	⊘ Available	vpc-09179fa2fa09519e2	172.31.0.0/20
public-subnet-2b	subnet-063c408c062bb8ebf	⊘ Available	vpc-050528e65f6218ae5 | hy...	10.0.0.192/26
-	subnet-092728f2ea03b66cd	⊘ Available	vpc-09179fa2fa09519e2	172.31.32.0/20
private-subnet-1a	subnet-0fc58855dc72fe89a	⊘ Available	vpc-050528e65f6218ae5 | hy...	10.0.0.0/26

Figure 5.5 – Creating a subnet

2. **Select your VPC**: Once you click on **Create Subnet**, you will be taken to a screen that displays Select your VPC ID, under which you will create the subnet:

VPC > Subnets > **Create subnet**

Create subnet Info

VPC

VPC ID
Create subnets in this VPC.

vpc-050528e65f6218ae5 (hybrid-vpc) ▼

Associated VPC CIDRs

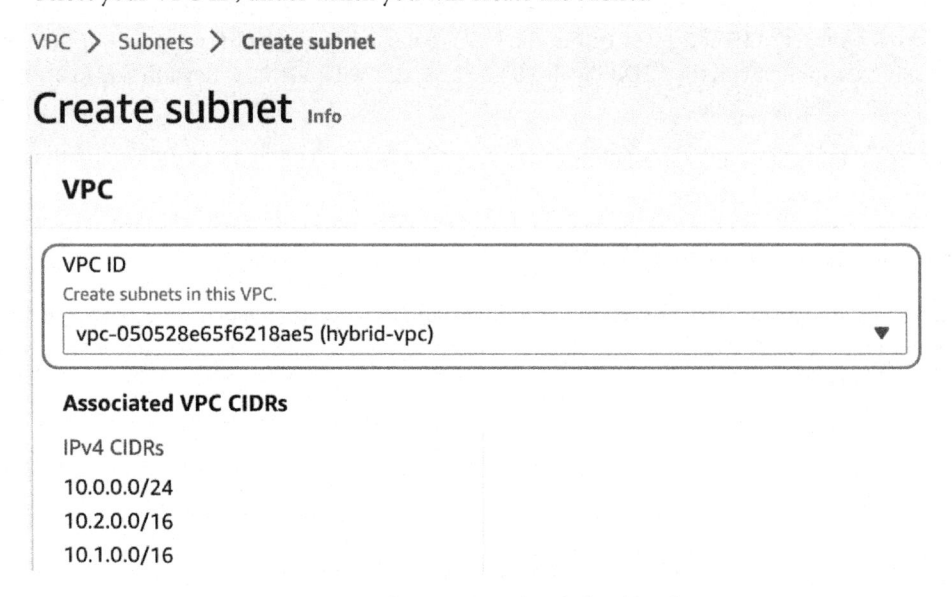

IPv4 CIDRs
10.0.0.0/24
10.2.0.0/16
10.1.0.0/16

Figure 5.6 – Configuring VPC details for the subnet

3. **Choose the availability zone and specify the CIDR block**: Next, you will have to Select the Availability Zone and Assign a CIDR block for your subnet. Take note that the CIDR block has to be unique between subnets. Choose the availability zone for your subnets to maximize availability and fault tolerance:

Subnet 1 of 1

Subnet name
Create a tag with a key of 'Name' and a value that you specify.

private-subnet-2c

The name can be up to 256 characters long.

Availability Zone Info
Choose the zone in which your subnet will reside, or let Amazon choose one for you.

Asia Pacific (Singapore) / ap-southeast-1c ▼

IPv4 CIDR block Info

🔍 10.2.0.0/24 ✕

Figure 5.7 – Configuring the availability zone for the subnet

4. **Define a name tag**: Defining tags is optional but recommended to organize and identify your AWS resources easily. Once this is done, click on Create **Subnet**:

▼ **Tags** - *optional*

Key	Value - *optional*	
🔍 Name ✕	🔍 private-subnet-2c ✕	Remove

Add new tag

You can add 49 more tags.

Remove

Add new subnet

Cancel   **Create subnet**

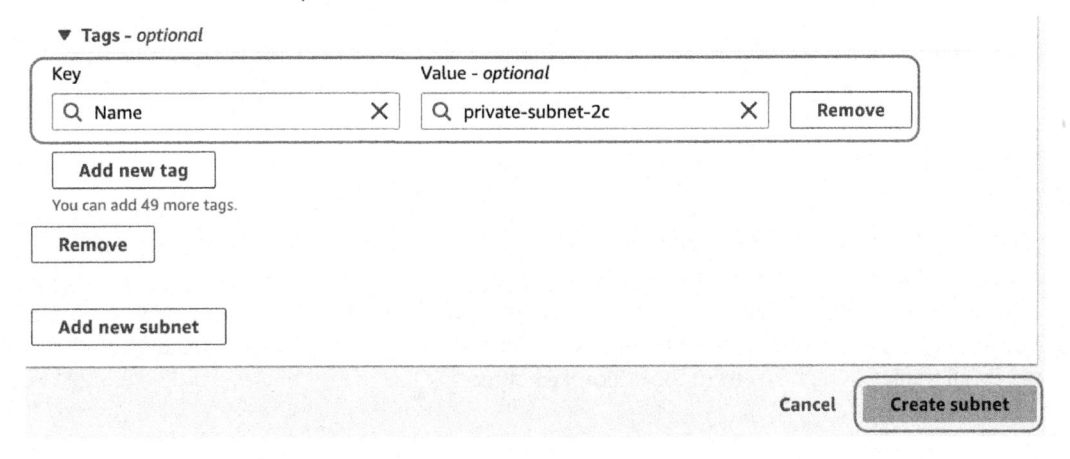

Figure 5.8 – Configuring tags for the subnet

Understanding the process of creating subnets in AWS is fundamental for your VPC design. By adhering to the steps outlined, you can establish an organized and secure subdivision within your network and lay the groundwork for efficient cloud operations.

Managing subnets

Managing the subnet involves the following activities:

- **Configuring route tables**: Route tables must be associated for each subnet to control and direct the traffic flow coming in and going out of the subnet
- **Network ACLs**: Network access control list comes as an additional layer of security for your subnets, allowing you to define a set of inbound and outbound rules to control the allowed traffic
- **Deleting subnets**: You can proceed to delete your subnet if that is no longer needed, but ensure it indeed does not carry any resources to avoid any disruptions

As we navigate from the nuances of subnet creation, we will delve into *Route table concepts and configuration*—a critical component that governs how the data moves within your VPC, ensuring seamless communication between resources.

Route table concepts and configuration

Imagine a route table as your traffic control center, helping you define routing for your network traffic and allowing you to determine where the network traffic is directed. A route table must be associated for each of the subnets in your VPC, and the rules inside the route table define the traffic routing for your subnets. Let's say you have a VPC CIDR block of `10.0.0.0/16` and two subnets, A and B, with the CIDR blocks `10.0.0.0/24` and `10.0.1.0/24`. To facilitate the network communication between these subnets, you will have to carry route tables with the rules facilitating the traffic movement between these subnets.

Route table concepts

Route tables carry a set of rules, called **routes**, that defines what network traffic should be routed to which target. Each routing rule in a route table includes a combination of a destination (specified in CIDR notation) and a target (where to route the traffic). The destination defines the desired IP addresses to be routed to network targets such as internet gateways, NAT gateways, and so on. For instance, if you want to direct all traffic from your subnet to the internet gateway, include a rule that targets all traffic (`0.0.0.0/0`) to the internet gateway.

Main and custom route tables

Each VPC comes with a main route table by default, which cannot be deleted. This main table is associated with all subnets in your VPC and is not explicitly associated with any other route table. You can basically create a custom route table with the rules fitting your network traffic needs. For instance, if you have a subnet that should not have access to the internet, you could create a custom route table without a route to an internet gateway and associate it with your desired subnet.

Routes

Routes are basically a combination of a destination and a target. The destination defines the IP address range of the traffic you wish to route, while the target defines where that traffic needs to be routed. The targets include an internet gateway to provide internet access, a virtual private gateway for VPN connections, or Direct Connect and network interfaces. For instance, imagine providing internet connectivity for the resources hosted inside your subnet; you can add a route with a destination of `0.0.0.0/0` pointing to the target of the internet gateway.

Route table configuration

AWS by default creates a local route in your route table, which allows the resources hosted inside the subnets to communicate with other subnets inside a VPC. Also, when you configure any additional custom routes, the more specific routes will take precedence for routing the desired network traffic to a target. For example, if your VPC CIDR range is `10.0.0.0/16`, a local route for `10.0.0.0/16` will be automatically added to your route table. Also, if you are carrying two routes—`0.0.0.0/0` pointing to internet gateway and a more specific route `10.0.2.0/24` pointing to NAT gateway—the more specific route will take precedence here.

Route table associations

Basically, the route table association is like the glue connecting your subnets to a broader network. As I mentioned in the *Main and custom route tables* section, by default, every subnet you create is associated with the main route table for the VPC. However, for more control over your network, you can associate a subnet with a custom route table.

Let's take an example to understand the use case for route table association. Imagine you have a VPC containing two route tables (main and custom) and two subnets, A and B. The main route table has a routing rule that allows a traffic flow to the internet, whereas the custom route table carries no such rule. Subnet A is associated with the main route table whereas subnet B is associated with a custom route table. You are now required to allow resources hosted inside Subnet B to have access to the internet, and in such case, you can simply change the route table association for subnet B to point to the main route table.

Here are the steps involved in updating the route table association for a subnet:

1. Navigate to the VPC dashboard in the AWS management console.
2. Under the **Subnets** section, select the subnet for which you want to change the route table association:

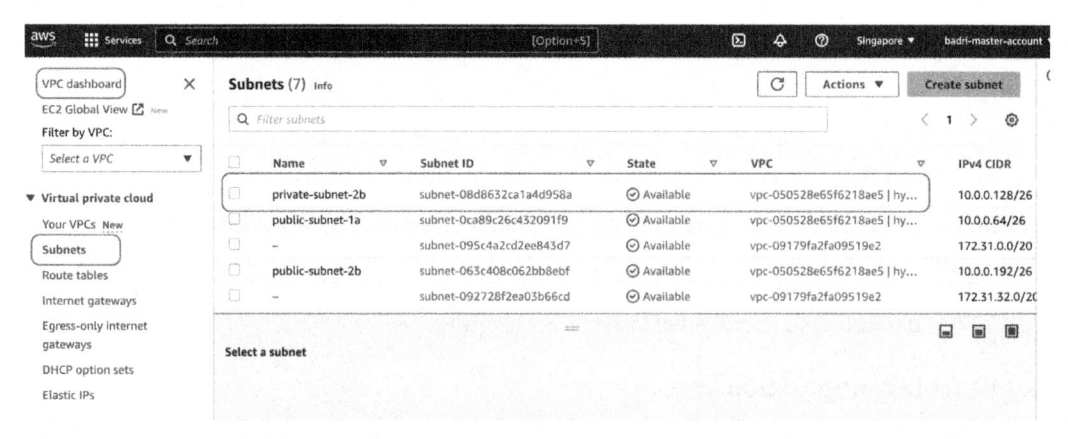

Figure 5.9 – Selecting a subnet for associating the route table

3. In the **Route Table** tab, select **Edit route table association**:

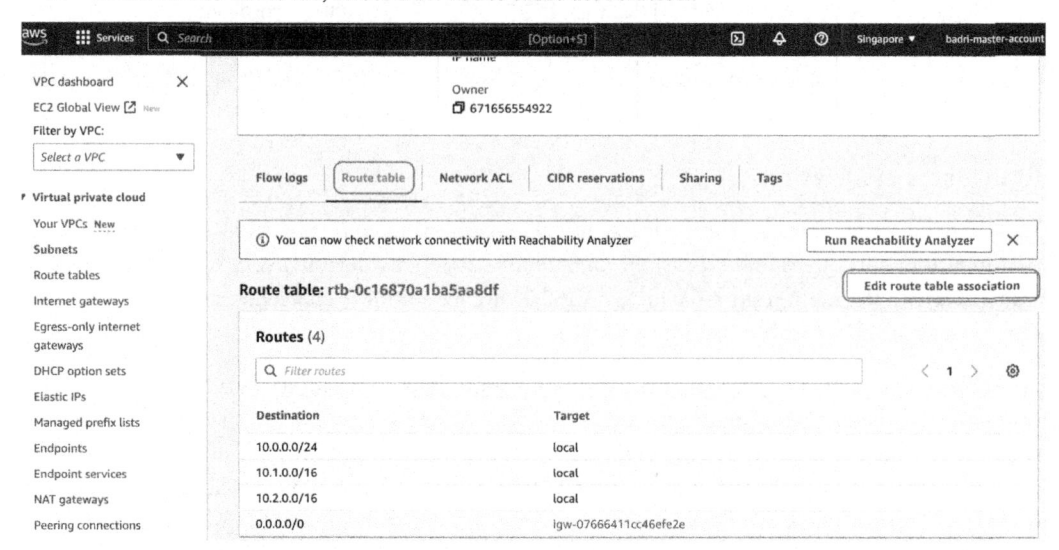

Figure 5.10 – Configuring route table association for a subnet

4. Choose the new route table to associate with the subnet and click **Save**:

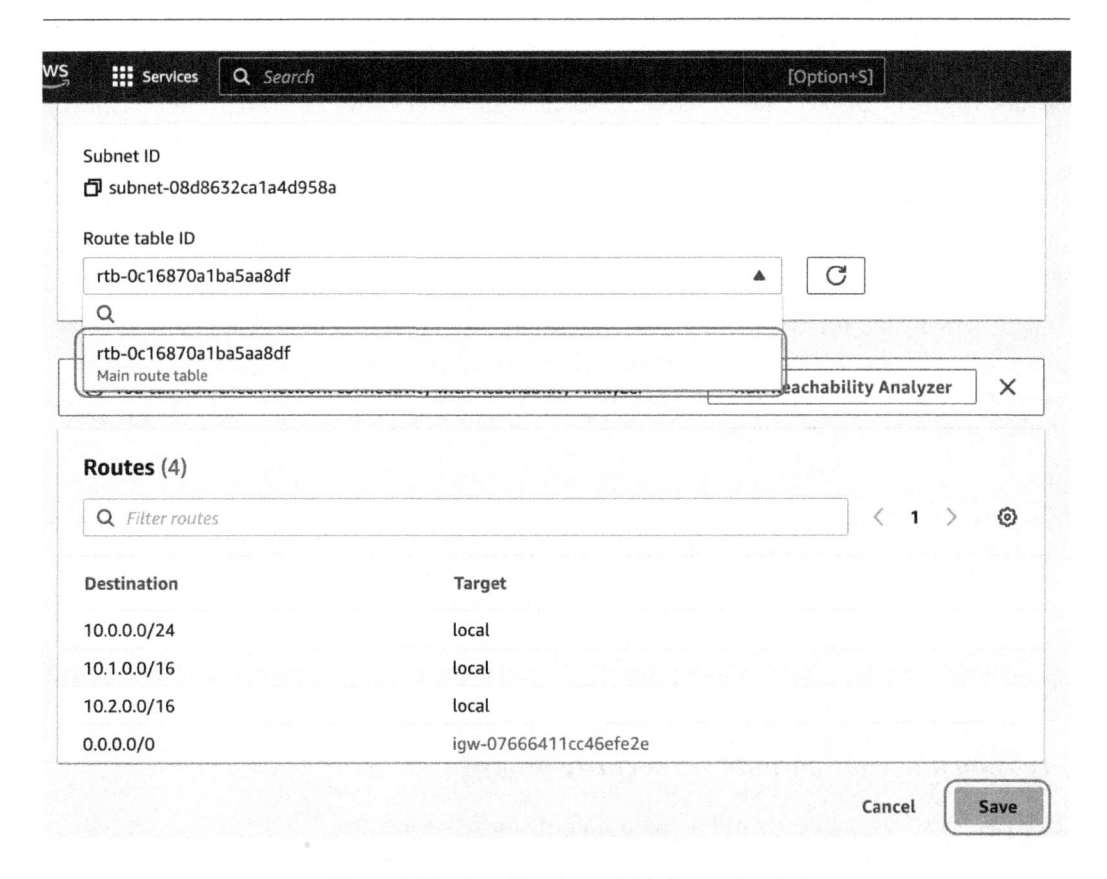

Figure 5.11 – Associate route table for a subnet

As we conclude this section, remember that a route table directs your VPC's traffic flow. Up next, we will explore how to keep our network safe by delving into the essential safety measures such as security groups and network ACLs.

Security groups and network ACLs

In this section, we will explore security groups and network ACLs and how these protective tools work to help us keep our AWS space safe. We will also explore how to set them up correctly and understand their key differences.

Introduction to security groups

Security groups are basically a virtual firewall for your EC2 instances, providing you with the control to regulate the inbound and outbound traffic at the instance level. Each security group is built with a set of rules that control the incoming and outgoing traffic of the associated EC2 instances, allowing you to refine and implement your firewall strategy with granular precision.

By design, security groups are stateful, which means that any traffic you permit to the EC2 instance is tracked and the corresponding outbound traffic is allowed to leave the instance automatically. The same is applied in the alternative direction too, i.e., if traffic is permitted by a security group to leave the instance, then the return traffic is automatically allowed inside the instance. This is a key principle that differentiates security groups from network access control lists, which are stateless, meaning the traffic is inspected in both directions without taking into consideration the allow/deny action permitted earlier.

You can specify one or more security groups for an EC2 instance, with up to five different security groups for each network interface. A security group can be associated with multiple EC2 instances, which facilitates applying a common set of rules to a group of instances effectively, simplifying the management of large infrastructures.

The default rules of a security group deny all inbound traffic while permitting all outbound traffic. This is a deliberate design by AWS to reinforce the security posture of your EC2 instances. However, the rules are entirely customizable, allowing you to modify the rules matching your requirements.

In terms of IP addressing, security groups support both Ipv4 and Ipv6, and the rules can either be defined as a CIDR block or reference another security group. Referencing a security group is particularly useful in scenarios where you want to allow traffic from all the instances associated with a particular security group.

Creating and configuring AWS security groups

To create a security group, you will need to complete the following steps:

1. Navigate to the VPC dashboard in the AWS management console.
2. Under the **Security groups** section, click **Create security group**:

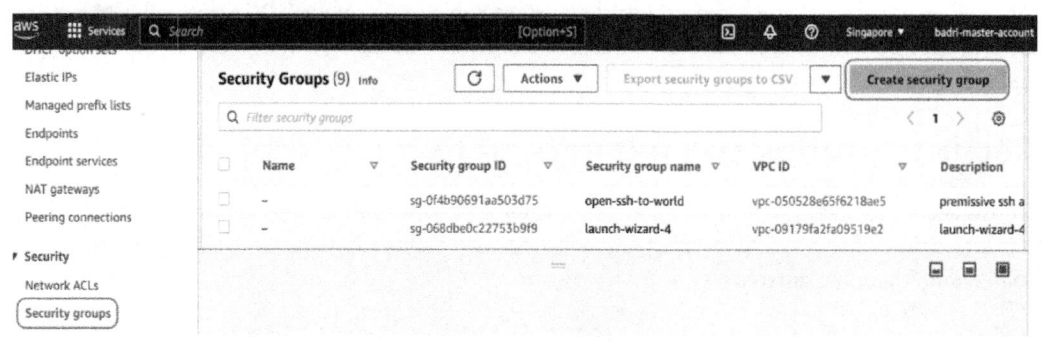

Figure 5.12 – Creating a security group

Security groups and network ACLs   101

3. Fill in the **Name** and **Description** and the **VPC** under which you will be creating the security group. As a general rule of thumb, make the name descriptive enough to understand the purpose of the security group you are creating:

Basic details

Security group name   Info

WebServerGroup

Name cannot be edited after creation.

Description   Info

Allow https access to internet

VPC   Info

vpc-09179fa2fa09519e2

Figure 5.13 – Configuring the security group name and description details

4. Fill in the **Inbound** and **Outbound** rules. For this instance, the rules allow HTTPS access from the internet and outbound access on port 80 and 443:

Inbound rules

Type	Protocol	Port range	Source	Description - optional	
HTTPS	TCP	443	Anywh... 0.0.0.0/0	Allow https from internet	Delete

Add rule

Outbound rules

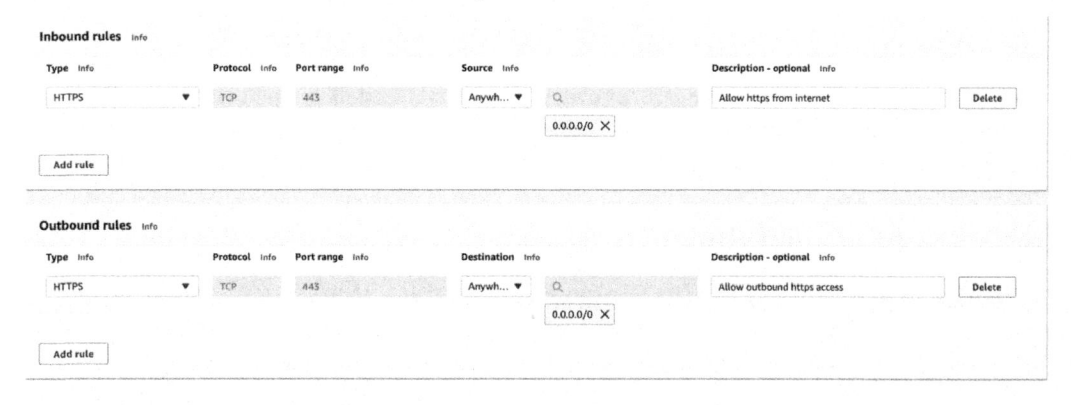

Type	Protocol	Port range	Destination	Description - optional	
HTTPS	TCP	443	Anywh... 0.0.0.0/0	Allow outbound https access	Delete

Add rule

Figure 5.14 – Configuring security group inbound and outbound rule details

5. Add **Tags** if required and click **Create security group**:

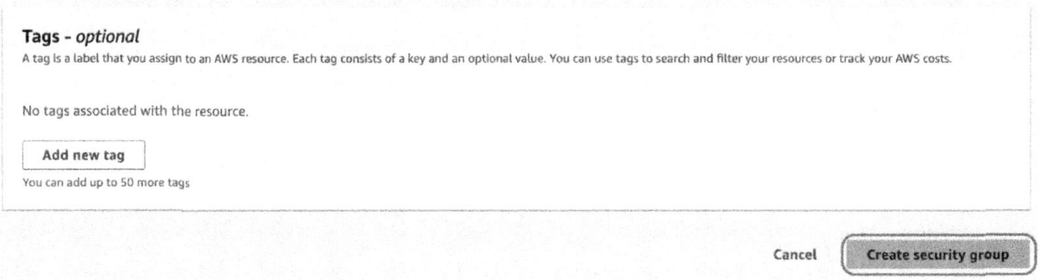

Figure 5.15 – Configuring the security group tag details

Let's dive a bit deeper into the rule conditions we defined to control the traffic flow. The rule conditions include the following information:

- **Type**: This refers to the kind of traffic for which the rule is defined, such as HTTP/HTTPS for web traffic or SSH for secure shell access.
- **Protocol**: This refers to the network protocol used for the traffic, such as UDP (or) TCP.
- **Port range**: This defines the range of network ports to which the specific rule will be applied.
- **Source (for inbound rules) or destination (for outbound rules)**: This indicates where the traffic originates (for inbound rules) or where it is heading to (for outbound rules). You can indicate a specific IP address, a range of IP addresses, or a security group.

You can still modify the rules of the security group after initial creation. In that case, the new rules are automatically applied to all the instances that are associated with the security group. This flexibility allows you to rapidly respond to the changing access requirements or potential security issues.

Network ACLs overview

Network access control lists (**NACLs**) are another pillar in the AWS security architecture. NACL functions as a firewall for controlling traffic in and out of a subnet within your VPC. Unlike security groups, NACLs are applied at the subnet level rather than the instance level.

The interesting differentiation of NACL from the security group is that NACLs are stateless (meaning they don't maintain the context of the connection) where each packet of the data is inspected independently. NACL contains separate lists for inbound and outbound rules, where each rule dictates the permitted or denied traffic. Each of the rules in NACL includes a rule number, type, protocol, port range, source (for inbound rules) or destination (for outbound rules), and an action of either allow or deny.

NACL scrutinizes the traffic entering and leaving the subnet, and its rules are evaluated in the order starting from the lowest number. As soon as the rule matches the traffic, it is applied regardless of any subsequent rules that may also match.

NACL can be associated with multiple subnets, but each subnet can only be associated with one NACL. By default, when you create a VPC, the default NACL is associated with each of the subnets inside the VPC, permitting all inbound and outbound traffic.

Creating and configuring network ACLs

To create a network ACL, you will need to complete the following steps:

1. Navigate to the VPC dashboard in the AWS management console:

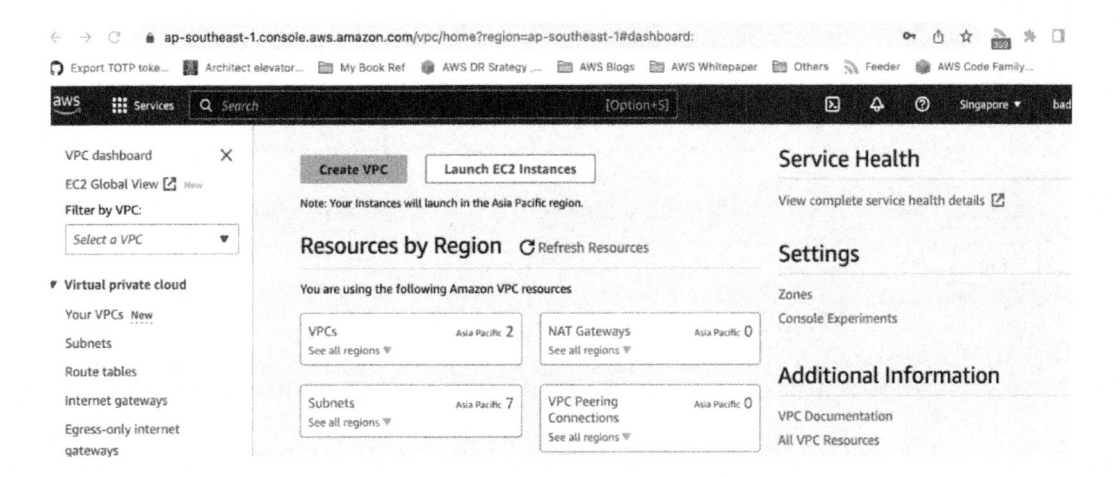

Figure 5.16 – VPC dashboard in AWS management console

2. Select **Network ACLs** from the sidebar and click **Create network ACL**:

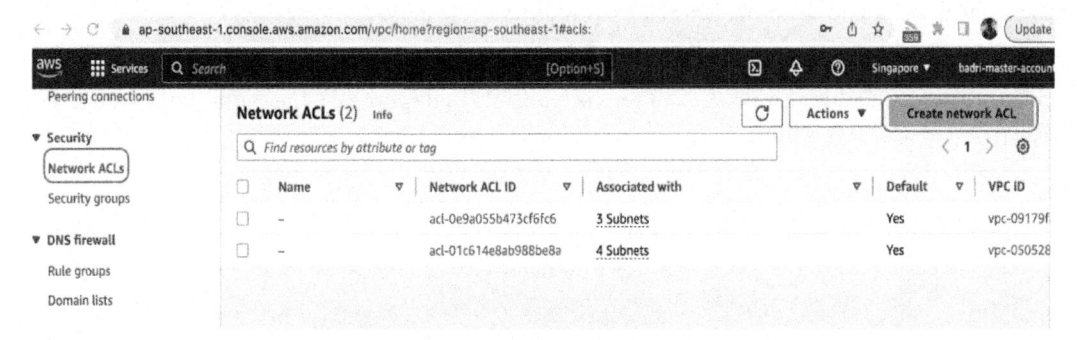

Figure 5.17 – Creating a network ACL

3. Specify a **Name** and select the **VPC** under which this network ACL will reside. Also, include the **Tags** necessary. Then, click **Create network ACL**:

Create network ACL Info

A network ACL is an optional layer of security that acts as a firewall for controlling traffic in and out of a subnet.

Network ACL settings

Name - *optional*
Creates a tag with a key of 'Name' and a value that you specify.

```
public-acl-01
```

VPC
VPC to use for this network ACL.

```
vpc-050528e65f6218ae5 (hybrid-vpc)
```

Tags
A tag is a label that you assign to an AWS resource. Each tag consists of a key and an optional value. You can use tags to search and filter your resources or track your AWS costs.

Key	Value - *optional*	
Name	public-acl-01	Remove tag

Add tag
You can add 49 more tags

Cancel | **Create network ACL**

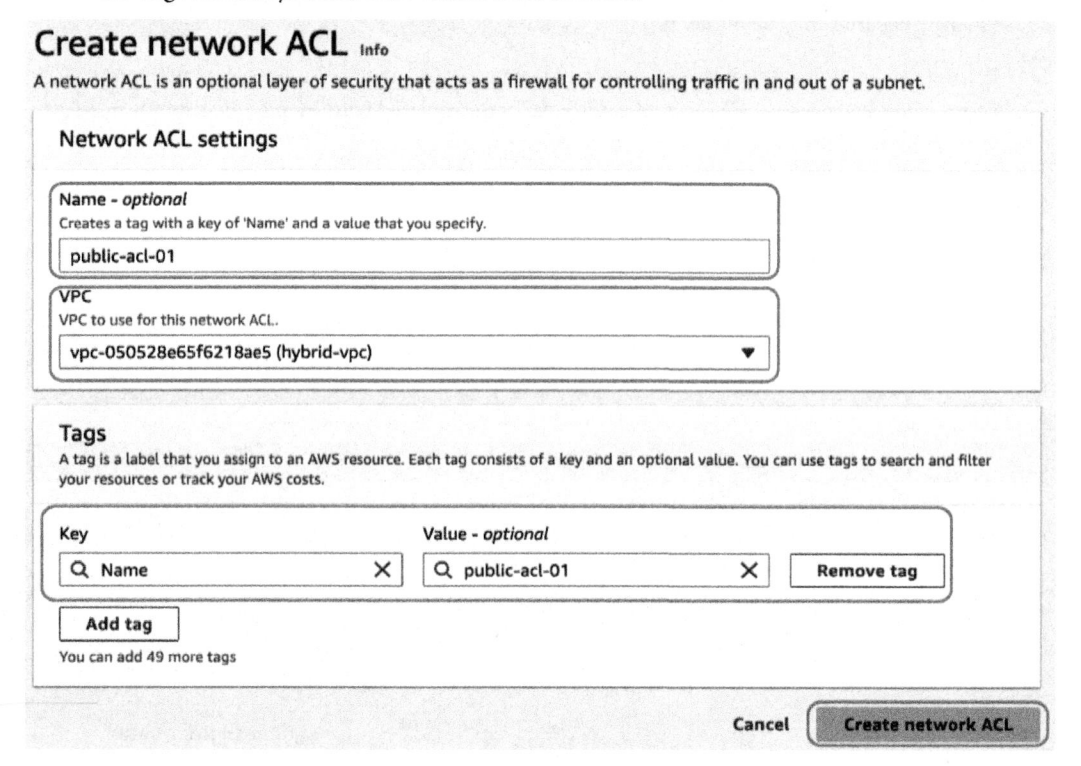

Figure 5.18 – Configuring network ACL details

Once the network ACL is created, the next task is to configure the rules. As I mentioned earlier, network ACLs have separate lists for inbound and outbound rules. When adding rules, you must specify a rule number, type (based on the IP protocol), port range, source/destination CIDR block, and rule action (allow or deny). Remember that the rules in the network access control list are processed in order of their rule number and the processing stops as soon as a rule matches the traffic.

Here is an example of allowing HTTP traffic to the subnet. In this case, you would create an inbound rule with a rule number (e.g., `100`) and set the type to HTTP (port `80`), the source to `0.0.0.0/0` (any IP), and action to **Allow**:

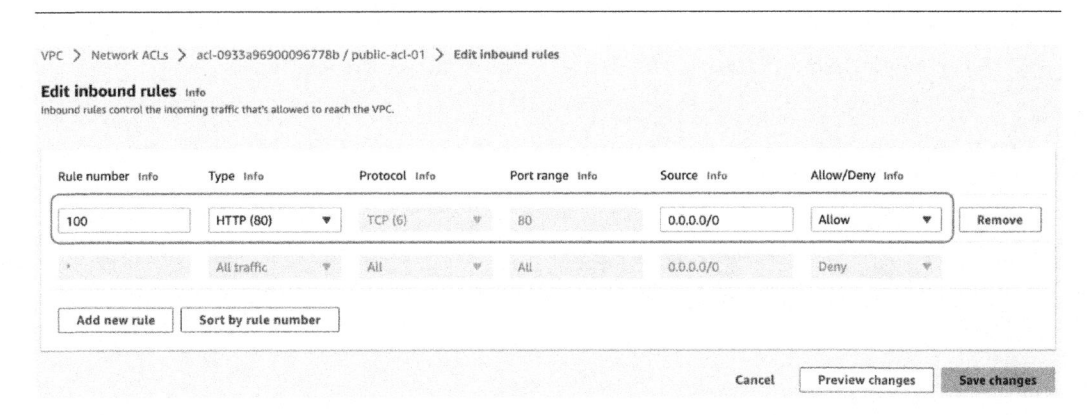

Figure 5.19 – Configuring the inbound rules for the network ACL

By default, a network ACL includes a rule numbered *, which is processed if no other rules match. This rule denies both inbound and outbound traffic.

Once the rules are defined, you need to associate the network ACL with the subnet to link the rules you have specified. You can associate the network ACL by following these steps:

1. Select your **Network ACL** from the sidebar under the VPC dashboard in the AWS management console:

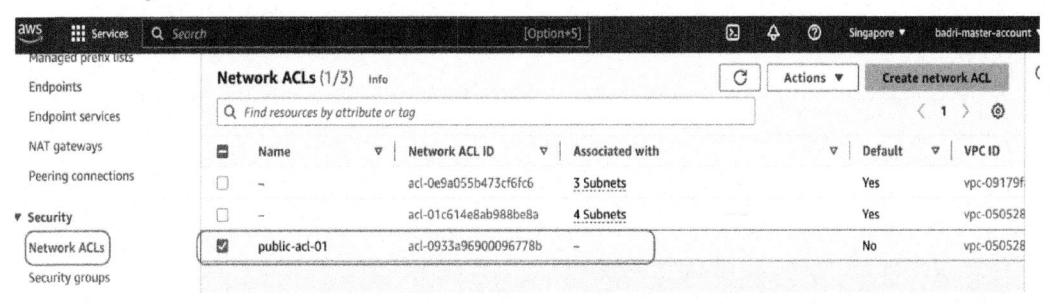

Figure 5.20 – Selecting a network ACL

2. Click on the desired **Network ACL** and select **Edit Subnet Associations**:

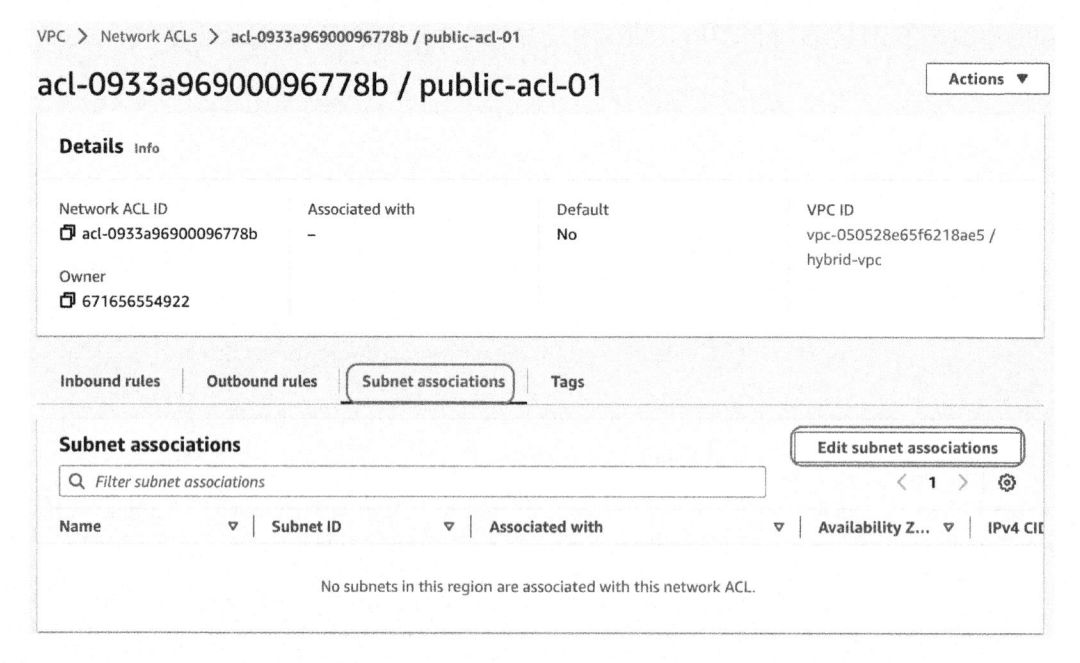

Figure 5.21 – Configuring the subnet association for network ACL

3. Associate the desired **Subnets** and click **Save changes** to associate the network ACL with the subnets:

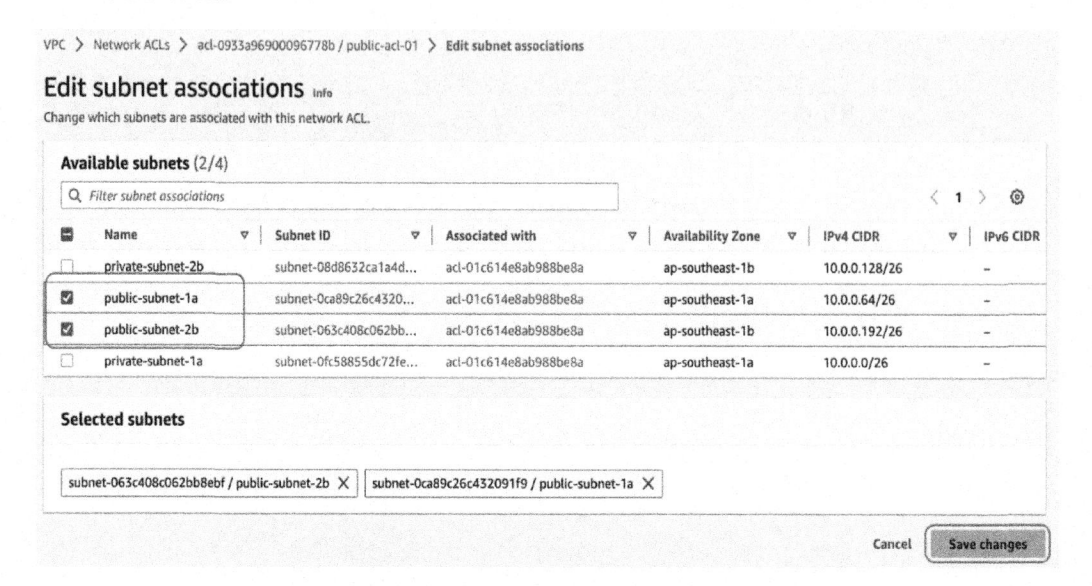

Figure 5.22 – Associating the subnet with the network ACL

Up next, we are going to explore *Elastic IPs and Elastic network interfaces*, where we will see how these parts make our AWS setup even better and more flexible.

Elastic IPs and Elastic network interfaces

Think of AWS as a digital neighborhood, where Elastic IPs are like those sturdy, unchanging address plates you put out in front of your house; even if you do a remodeling inside, the address plates remain the same, pointing to the remodeled house. On the other hand, Elastic network interfaces act like a road and pathways, connecting all these houses. Together, they exist to ensure the community remains well connected and reachable. Now, let's take a deeper dive and explore how they do this.

Understanding Elastic IPs and their use cases

Elastic IP is an innovative feature offered by AWS. The design of an Elastic IP provides static, public IPv4 addresses that you can dynamically assign to your AWS resources. Unlike the traditional public IP addresses, which can change due to events such as instance stop/start cycles (or) hardware failures, an Elastic IP address remains consistent.

One of the major use cases for Elastic IPs is to mask the failure of an underlying instance or software. In a scenario where you have a faulty instance, the design allows you to quickly remap the Elastic IP to another instance and ensure your service remains accessible. Another use case is around third-party software and licensing. Using Elastic IPs allows you to maintain the software license across the instance start/stop lifecycles or even if you need to replace the instance all together.

In spite of the numerous benefits offered by Elastic IP in allowing us to ensure operational resilience, they come with their considerations. For example, AWS charges for Elastic IP addresses that are not associated with a running instance or if they are associated with the unattached network interface. It is a deliberate design by AWS to encourage the efficient use of precious public IPv4 addresses.

Now, let's dive deeper into the practical steps, exploring how to allocate and associate Elastic IPs.

Allocating and associating Elastic IPs

As we embark on this hands-on journey, we will uncover the process of allocating and assigning an Elastic IP.

Allocation of Elastic IP

Allocating an Elastic IP address comes as a first step in using this service. The allocation allows you to reserve an address for your use. To allocate a new Elastic IP address, follow these steps:

1. Navigate to the EC2 dashboard in the AWS management console and click **Elastic IP**:

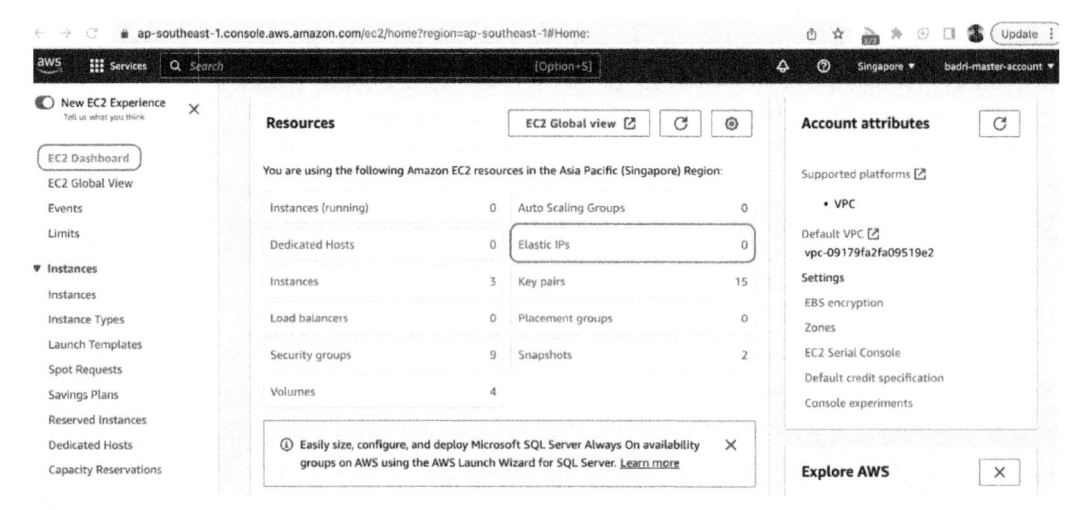

Figure 5.23 – Navigating to select an Elastic IP

2. Choose **Allocate new address**:

Figure 5.24 – Action to allocate an Elastic IP address

3. Persist the default actions and click **Allocate**:

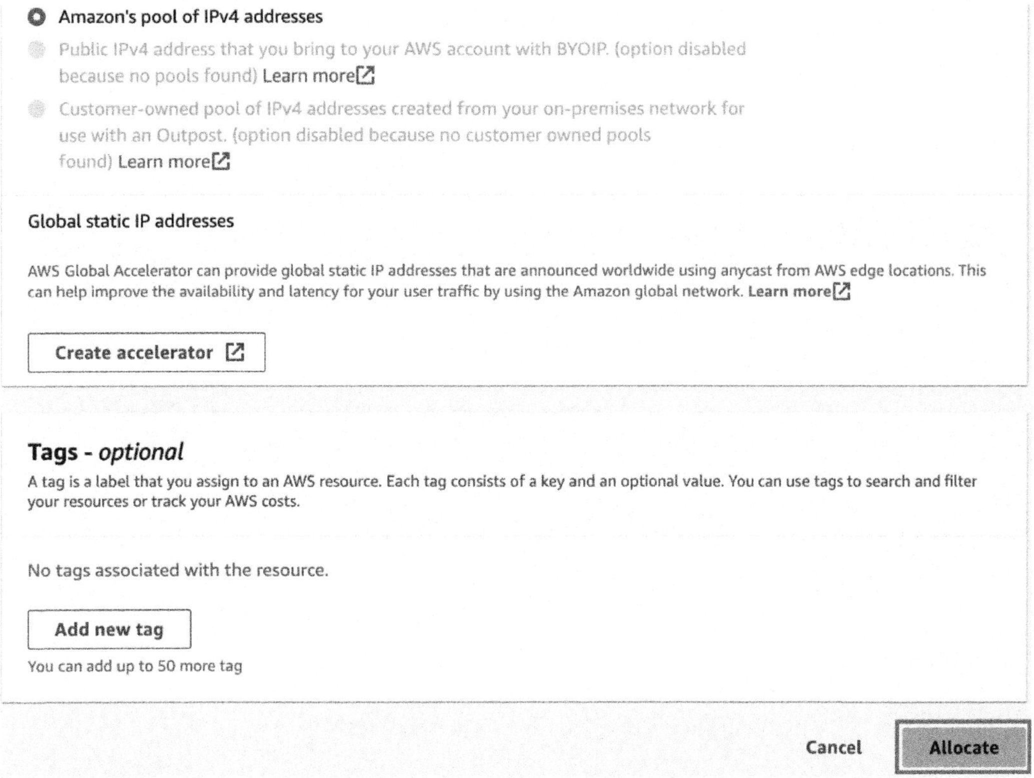

- ● Amazon's pool of IPv4 addresses
- ○ Public IPv4 address that you bring to your AWS account with BYOIP. (option disabled because no pools found) Learn more
- ○ Customer-owned pool of IPv4 addresses created from your on-premises network for use with an Outpost. (option disabled because no customer owned pools found) Learn more

Global static IP addresses

AWS Global Accelerator can provide global static IP addresses that are announced worldwide using anycast from AWS edge locations. This can help improve the availability and latency for your user traffic by using the Amazon global network. Learn more

[Create accelerator]

Tags - *optional*

A tag is a label that you assign to an AWS resource. Each tag consists of a key and an optional value. You can use tags to search and filter your resources or track your AWS costs.

No tags associated with the resource.

[Add new tag]

You can add up to 50 more tag

Cancel   **Allocate**

Figure 5.25 – Allocating an Elastic IP address

4. A new Elastic IP address is now allocated to your AWS account. Remember this is just an allocation and it is not associated with any instance yet.

Associating Elastic IP

Once an Elastic IP is allocated to your AWS account, you can associate it with an EC2 instance or a network interface. Complete the following steps to do so:

1. In the Amazon EC2 console, under **Network and Security**, choose **Elastic IPs** and select your desired Elastic IP:

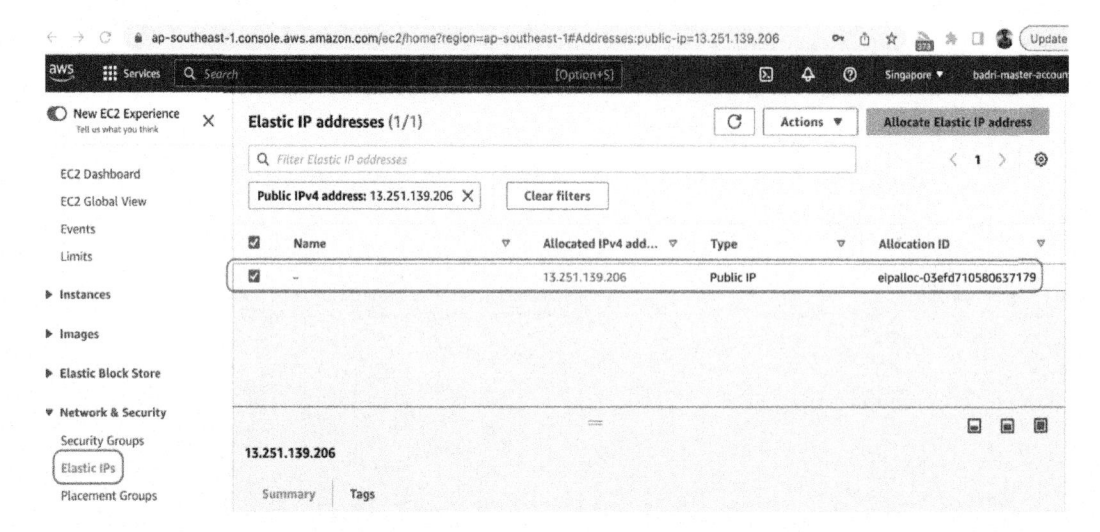

Figure 5.26 – Choosing the desired Elastic IP

2. After selecting your desired **Elastic IP**, click **Actions** then **Associate IP address**:

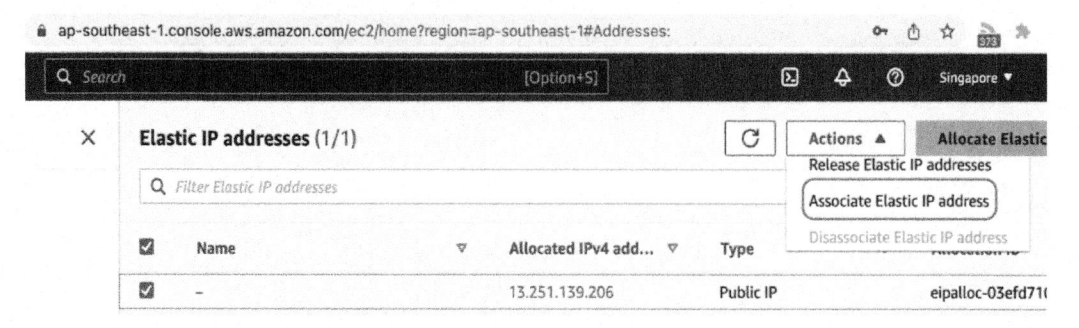

Figure 5.27 – Associating an Elastic IP address

3. In the **Associate Elastic IP address** dialog box, choose the instance or network interface to associate the Elastic IP address with and then choose **Associate**:

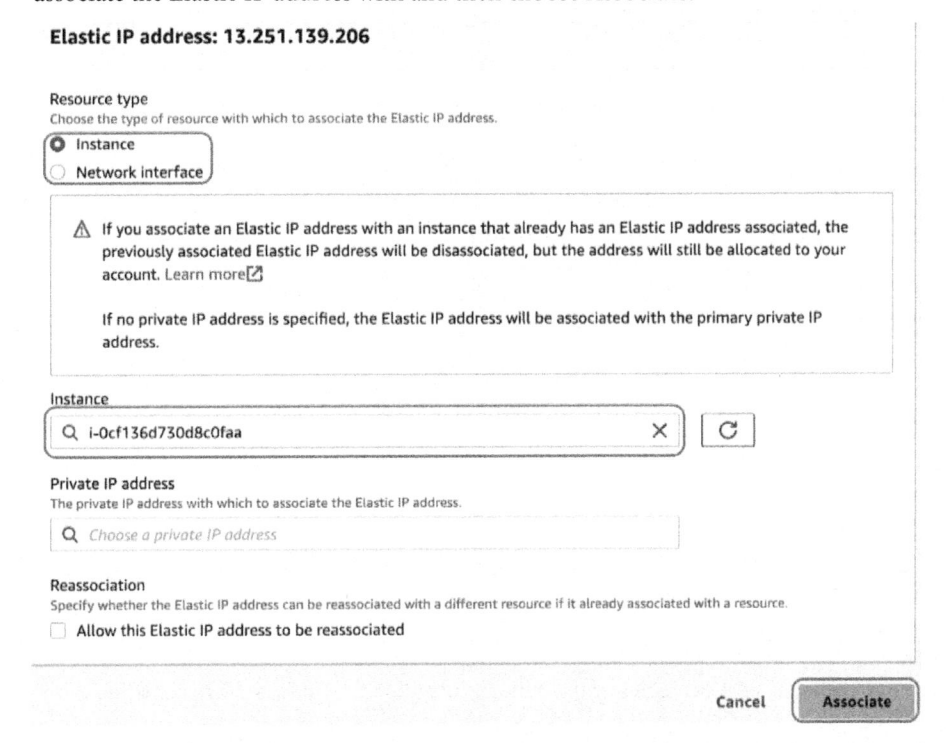

Figure 5.28 – Finalizing associating an Elastic IP address

> **Note**
> If an instance is already associated with the public IP address, associating the Elastic IP will replace the public IP address with Elastic IP address.

Also, take note that you will incur an additional charge (nominal in value) if the allocated Elastic IP is not actively associated with an instance or network interface.

Elastic network interfaces

An **Elastic network interface** (**ENI**) is a virtual networking component within Amazon VPC and is attached to an EC2 instance. An ENI allows the instance to communicate with other instances over the network. Let us explore the characteristics of an ENI in detail.

Characteristics of ENIs

Each ENI is equipped with the following properties.

- **Primary private IPv4 address**: This acts as a primary address that communicates with the network. This primary address will remain persistent throughout the lifetime of an ENI.
- **One or more secondary private IPv4 addresses**: Secondary addresses can be added to an ENI. They can be moved or reassigned to other ENIs or instances.
- **One Elastic IP (EIP) per private IPv4 address**: Each private IPv4 address can be associated with an Elastic IP address to facilitate the communication with internet.
- **One public IPv4 address**: One public IPv4 address (i.e., the address routable from the internet) can be associated with an ENI.
- **MAC address**: An ENI carries a unique MAC address that will be used to identify the network device.
- **Source/destination check flag**: An ENI carries a flag that decides if the EC2 instance should check the network packet's source and destination.
- **Security groups**: One or more security groups can be associated with an ENI.

Use cases of ENIs

ENIs can be tactically and strategically used in a multitude of scenarios. Here are some of them:

- **Management network**: A network interface can be created to isolate the management traffic from data traffic. This helps you to facilitate carrying out administrative activities and management tasks without disrupting the application traffic.
- **Network and security appliances**: Many third-party networks and security appliances, by design, require multiple network interfaces (one for management and one for data).

Creating and attaching Elastic network interfaces to an EC2 instance

Let's delve into creating and attaching Elastic network interfaces to an instance to facilitate seamless network communication.

Creating an ENI

Follow these steps to set up your own ENI and prepare it for receiving connection:

1. Navigate to the EC2 dashboard in the AWS management console:

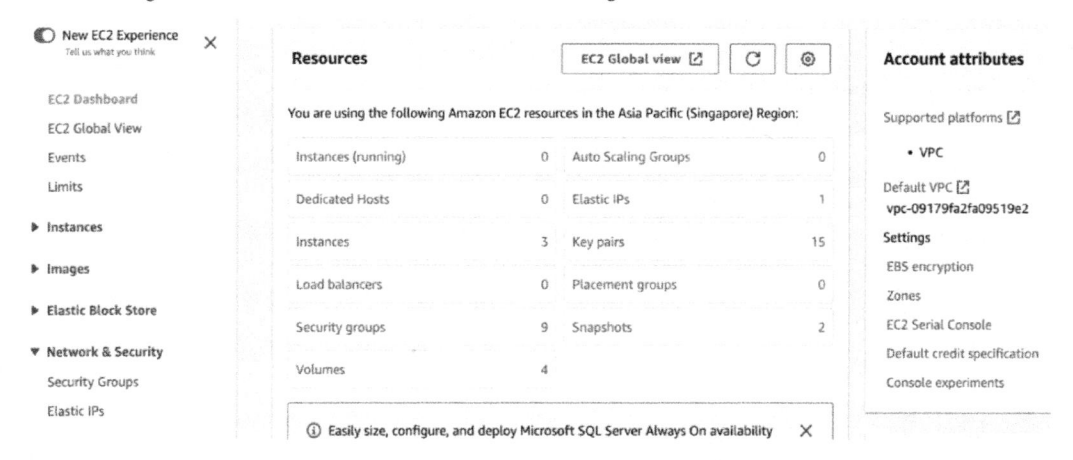

Figure 5.29 – EC2 dashboard in AWS management console

2. Select **Network Interfaces** from the sidebar in the EC2 dashboard. Then, click **Create Network Interface**:

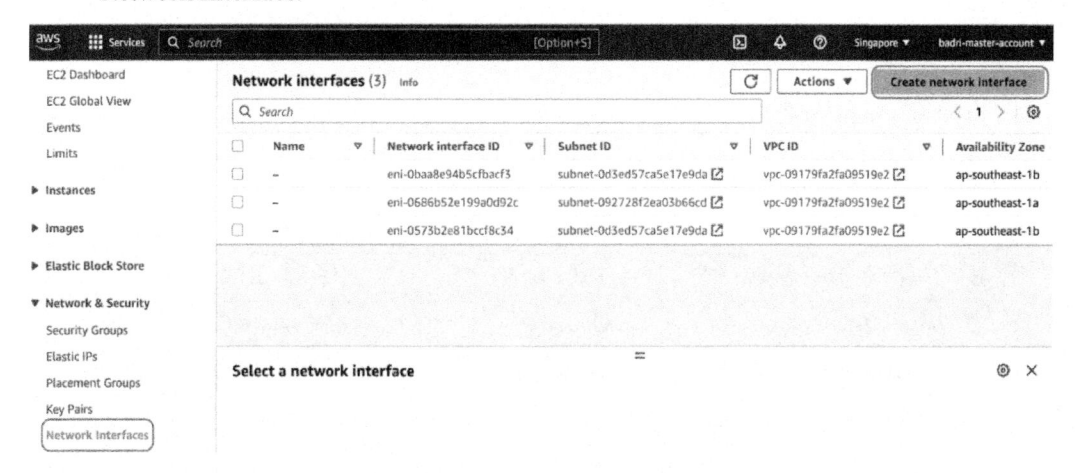

Figure 5.30 – Creating a network interface

3. In the **Create Network Interface** configuration wizard, input the necessary information, including the description, **Subnet**, **Security group**, and **Private IP**:

Description - *optional*
A descriptive name for the network interface.

web-app-eni

Subnet
The subnet in which to create the network interface.

subnet-08d8632ca1a4d958a

Private IPv4 address
The private IPv4 address to assign to the network interface.
- Auto-assign
- Custom

Elastic Fabric Adapter
- Enable

▼ **Advanced settings**

You can optionally set the IP prefix delegation

IPv4 prefix delegation
The IPv4 prefixes to assign to the network interface.
- Do not assign
- Auto-assign
- Custom

Security groups (1/4) Info

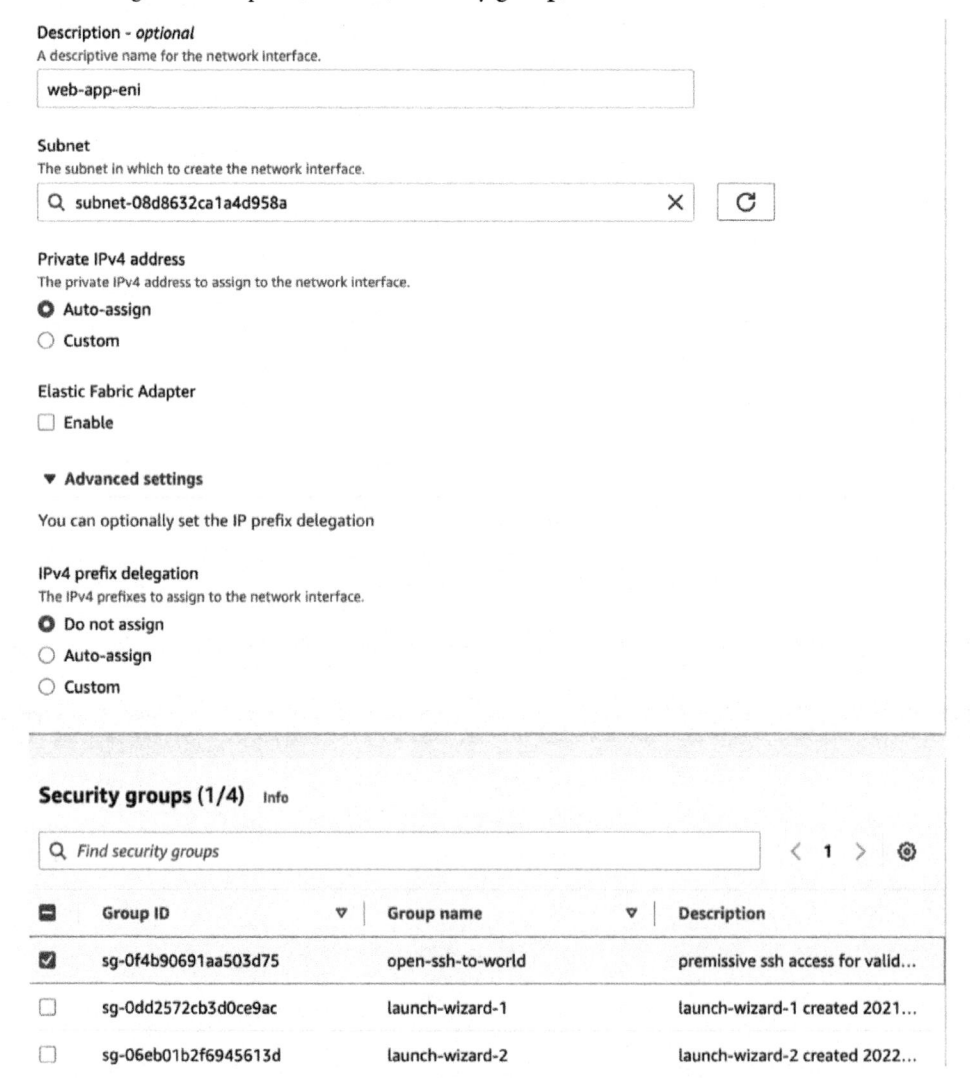

	Group ID	Group name	Description
☑	sg-0f4b90691aa503d75	open-ssh-to-world	premissive ssh access for valid...
☐	sg-0dd2572cb3d0ce9ac	launch-wizard-1	launch-wizard-1 created 2021...
☐	sg-06eb01b2f6945613d	launch-wizard-2	launch-wizard-2 created 2022...

Figure 5.31 – Configuring the network interface

4. Click **Create**.

Your ENI has now been created, but it is not associated with any instances.

Elastic IPs and Elastic network interfaces   115

Attaching an ENI to an instance

Now that we have created the ENI, let's walk through the steps involved in securely attaching an ENI to an EC2 instance to facilitate seamless communication:

1. Go back to the **Network Interfaces** section in the EC2 dashboard.
2. Select your **Desired ENI** you want to associate with an EC2 instance. Then, click **Attach**:

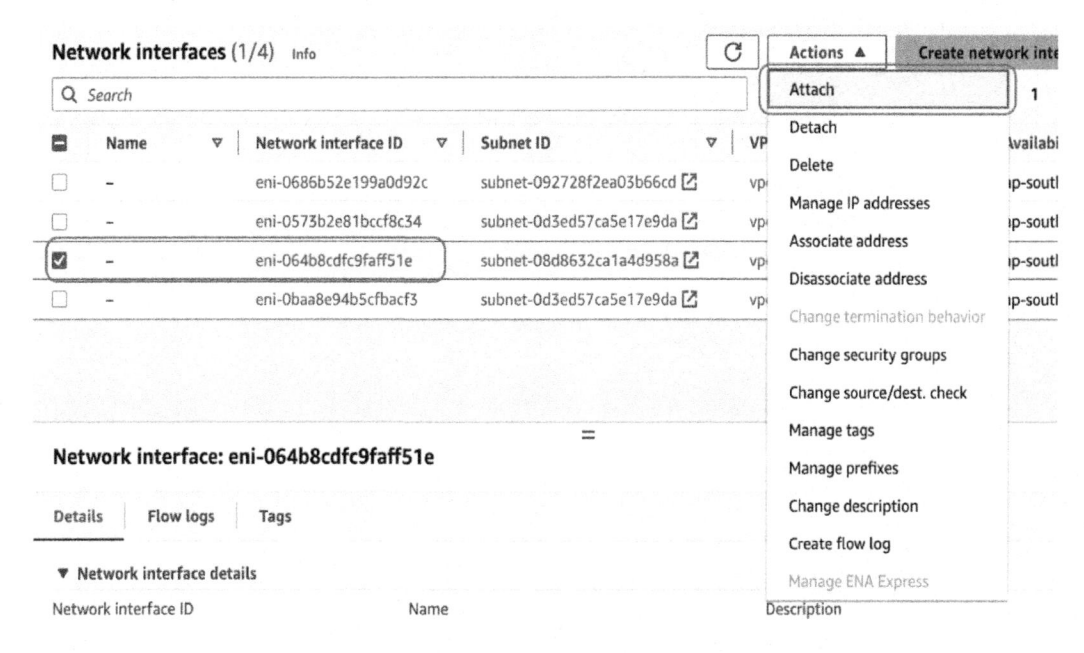

Figure 5.32 – Targeting an Elastic network interface for attachment

3. In the **Attach** network dialog box, select the instance you want to attach to the ENI. Then, click **Attach**:

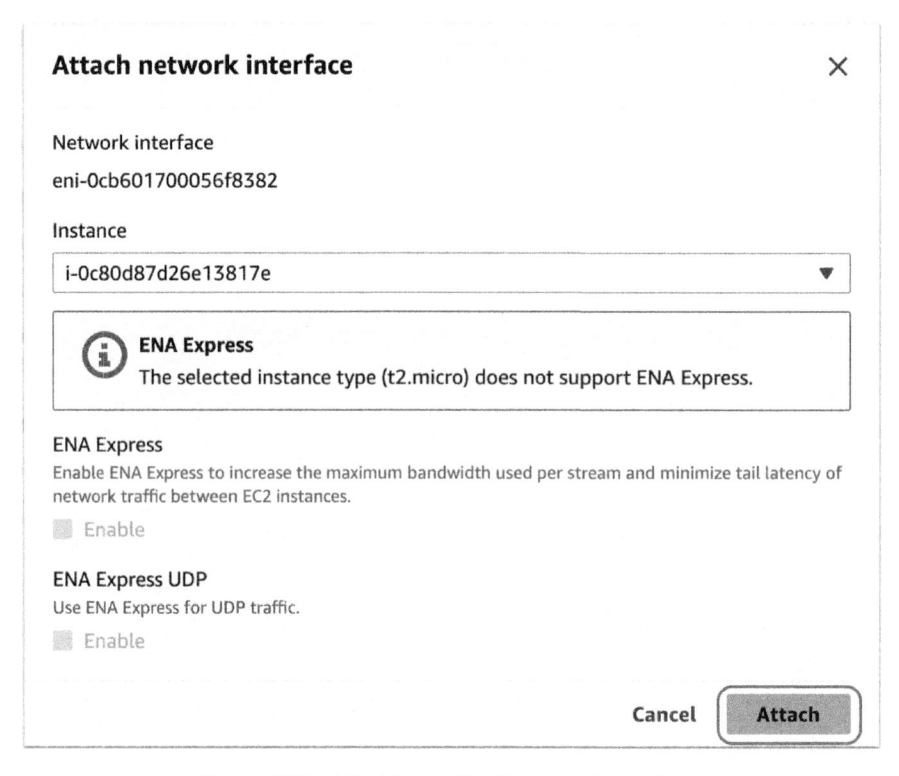

Figure 5.33 – Attaching an Elastic network interface

Your ENI is now attached to the specified EC2 instance. This basically means the instance can now send and receive traffic through the ENI. By doing this setup, you have enhanced the networking capabilities of your EC2 instance. Next, we will shift our focus to VPC peering and various other connectivity options, which further aim to enhance the networking capabilities within your EC2 environment.

VPC peering and connectivity options

Imagine two separate islands in a vast ocean. VPC peering is like building an exclusive bridge to connect these oceans directly to facilitate easier communication between them. In this section, we will explore how AWS lets these islands or VPCs connect and share information without the need for public internet.

VPC peering concepts and setup

VPC peering allows you to establish networking connectivity between two different VPCs. By creating VPC peering, you can create a route using each VPC private IP address as if they were in the same network. Peering connection can be established between VPCs in the same region or different regions inside the same AWS account or different AWS account.

Concepts of VPC peering

Let's understand the essential building blocks that underpin the mechanism of VPC peering:

- **IP addressing**: For the VPC peering to work, ensure the connecting VPCs do not have overlapping CIDR blocks. Each VPC must have a unique CIDR block to communicate with the others.
- **Transitive peering**: AWS VPC peering connections are non-transitive. Let's say you have three VPCs: A, B, and C. There is a peering connection established between A–B and B–C. This peering connection doesn't create an automatic routing from A to C, and you would still need to create a peering connection between A and C to have network connectivity between them.
- **Region consideration**: You are allowed to create a VPC peering connection between VPCs in different AWS regions. This peering type is otherwise called inter-region VPC peering. This peering connection is done in the same way as creating a VPC peering in the same region.
- **Security**: You can create and associate a security group the same way for the instances in the peered VPC as you would do so for the instance in the same VPC.

Setup

Let's dive into the process of establishing the VPC peering connection:

1. **Request VPC peering connection**:

    I. This step has to be executed from the requester VPC. Navigate to **VPC** in your AWS management console. Select **Peering Connections** from the left sidebar and click **Create Peering Connection**:

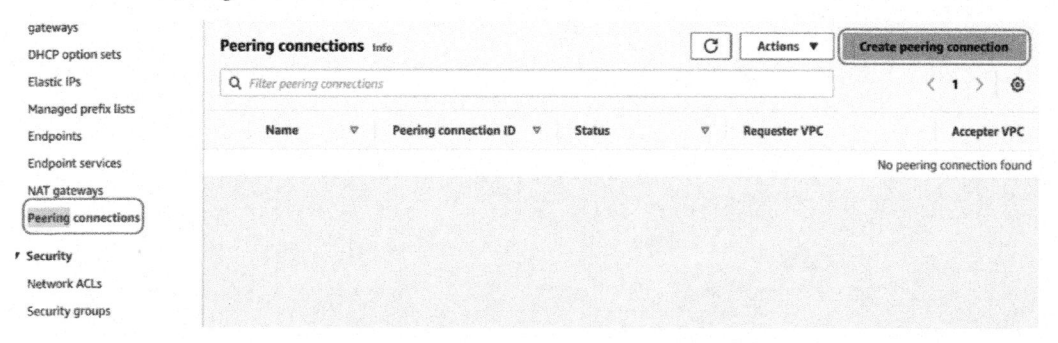

Figure 5.34 – Creating a VPC peering connection

II. Inside the **Create Peering Connection** dialog box, fill in the details for **Name** and **Source VPC**:

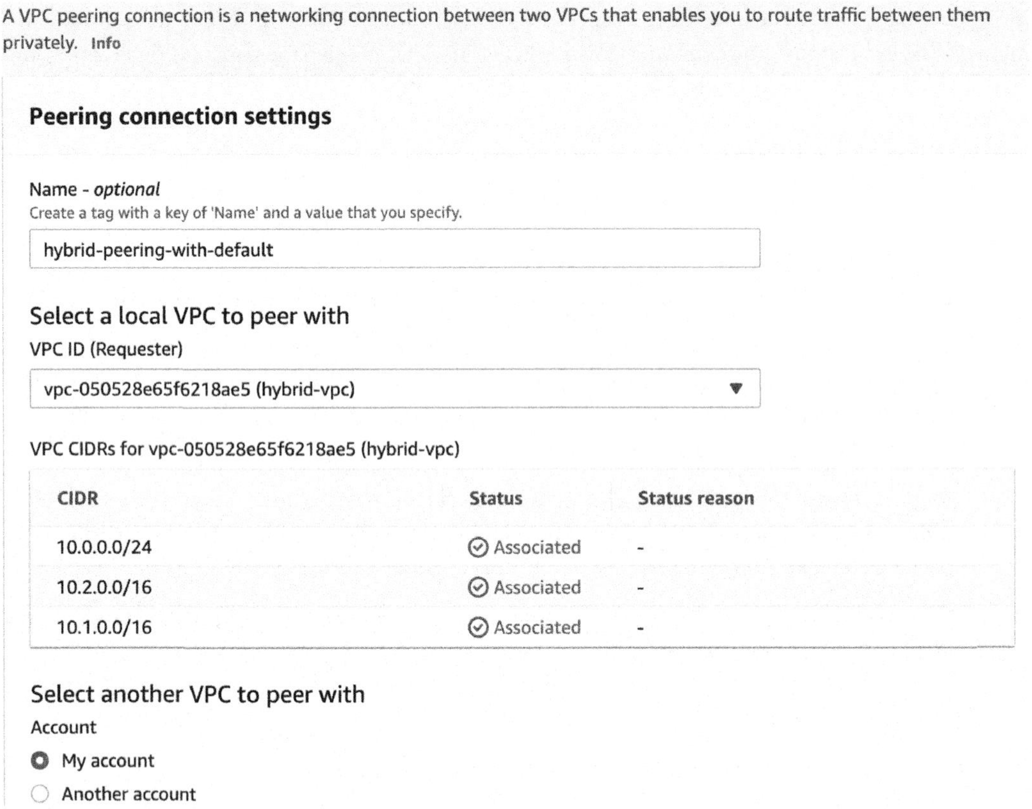

A VPC peering connection is a networking connection between two VPCs that enables you to route traffic between them privately. Info

Peering connection settings

Name - *optional*
Create a tag with a key of 'Name' and a value that you specify.

hybrid-peering-with-default

Select a local VPC to peer with

VPC ID (Requester)

vpc-050528e65f6218ae5 (hybrid-vpc)

VPC CIDRs for vpc-050528e65f6218ae5 (hybrid-vpc)

CIDR	Status	Status reason
10.0.0.0/24	⊘ Associated	-
10.2.0.0/16	⊘ Associated	-
10.1.0.0/16	⊘ Associated	-

Select another VPC to peer with

Account

● My account
○ Another account

Figure 5.35 – Configuring the name and source VPC for VPC peering

III. Inside the **Create Peering Connection** dialog box, fill in **Destination VPC & Tags**. Then, click **Create Peering Connection**:

Region
- ● This Region (ap-southeast-1)
- ○ Another Region

VPC ID (Accepter)

vpc-09179fa2fa09519e2

VPC CIDRs for vpc-09179fa2fa09519e2

CIDR	Status	Status reason
172.31.0.0/16	⊘ Associated	-

Tags

A tag is a label that you assign to an AWS resource. Each tag consists of a key and an optional value. You can use tags to search and filter your resources or track your AWS costs.

Key	Value - *optional*	
Q Name ✕	Q hybrid-peering-with-default ✕	Remove

Add new tag

You can add 49 more tags.

Cancel | **Create peering connection**

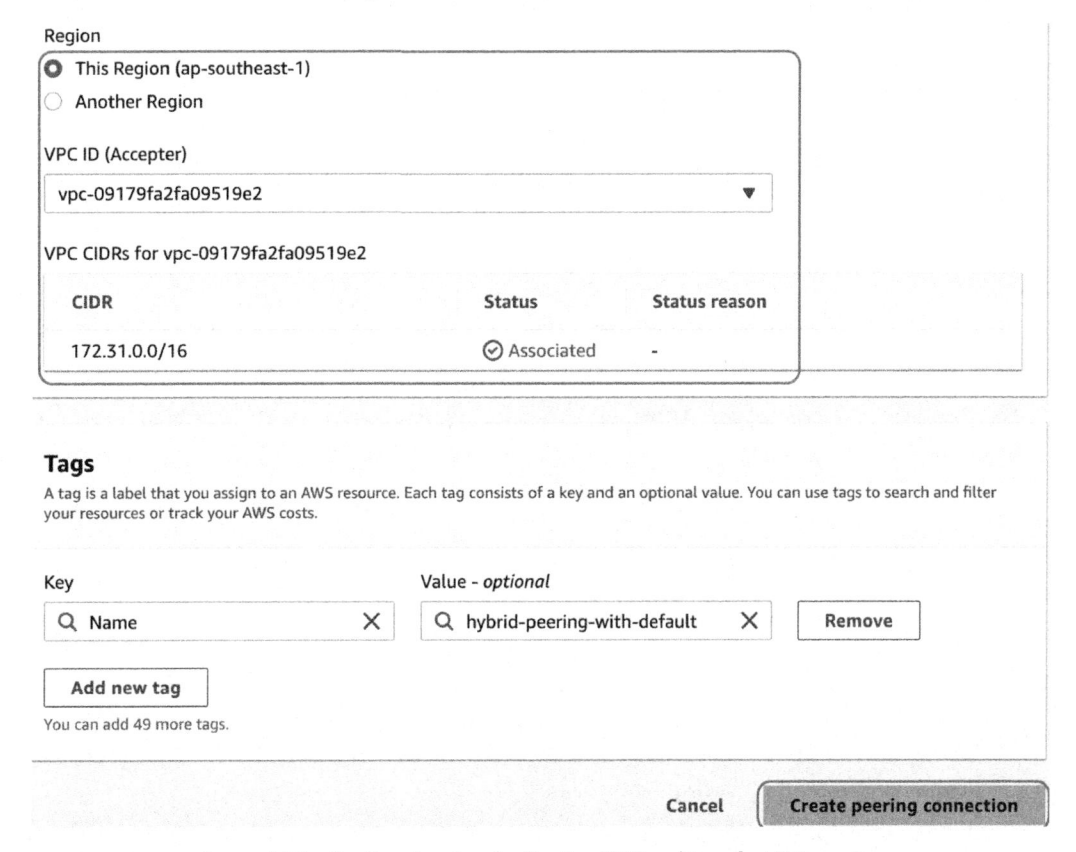

Figure 5.36 – Configuring the destination VPC and tags for VPC peering

2. **Accept the peering connection**: At this stage, you have successfully initiated the VPC peering request to the target VPC. Now, the owner of the target VPC must accept the peering connection request to activate it. This can be done from the **Peering connections** section of the VPC console:

120 Networking and Connectivity in Amazon EC2

VPC > Peering connections > pcx-02f0d40d9f11f378b

pcx-02f0d40d9f11f378b / hybrid-peering-with-default

Actions ▲
- Accept request
- Reject request
- Edit DNS settings
- Edit ClassicLink settings
- Manage tags
- Delete peering connection

ⓘ **Pending acceptance**
You can accept or reject this peering connection request using the 'Actions' menu. You have until Friday 20:17:13 GMT+8 to accept or reject the request, otherwise it expires.

Details Info

Requester owner ID
671656554922

Accepter owner ID
671656554922

VPC Peering connection ARN
arn:aws:ec2:ap-southeast-1:671656554922:vpc-peering-connection/pcx-02f0d40d9f11f378b

Peering connection ID
pcx-02f0d40d9f11f378b

Requester VPC
vpc-050528e65f6218ae5 / hybrid-vpc

Accepter VPC
vpc-09179fa2fa09519e2

Status
⏱ Pending Acceptance by 671656554922

Requester CIDRs
3 CIDRs

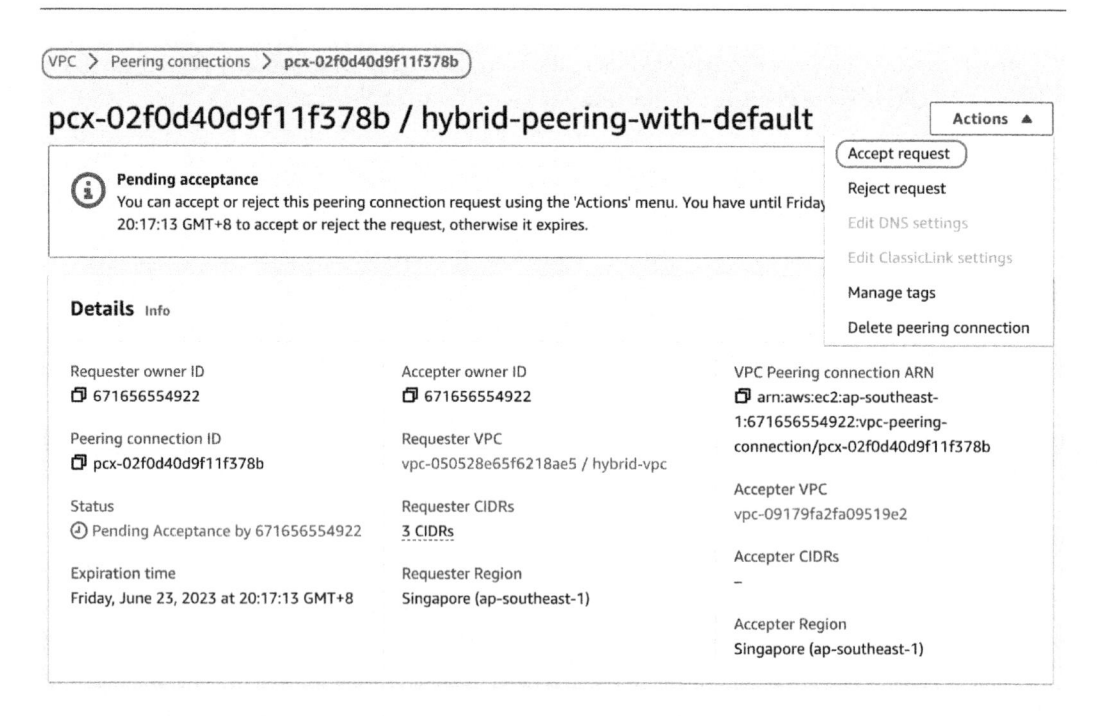

Accepter CIDRs
–

Expiration time
Friday, June 23, 2023 at 20:17:13 GMT+8

Requester Region
Singapore (ap-southeast-1)

Accepter Region
Singapore (ap-southeast-1)

Figure 5.37 – Accepting the VPC peering connection request

3. **Update the route table**: After the peering connection request is accepted by the owner of the target VPC, you need to add routes to the route table of each VPC to enable traffic flow. The destination for your route should include the CIDR block of the target VPC. The target will be the peering connection itself, as shown:

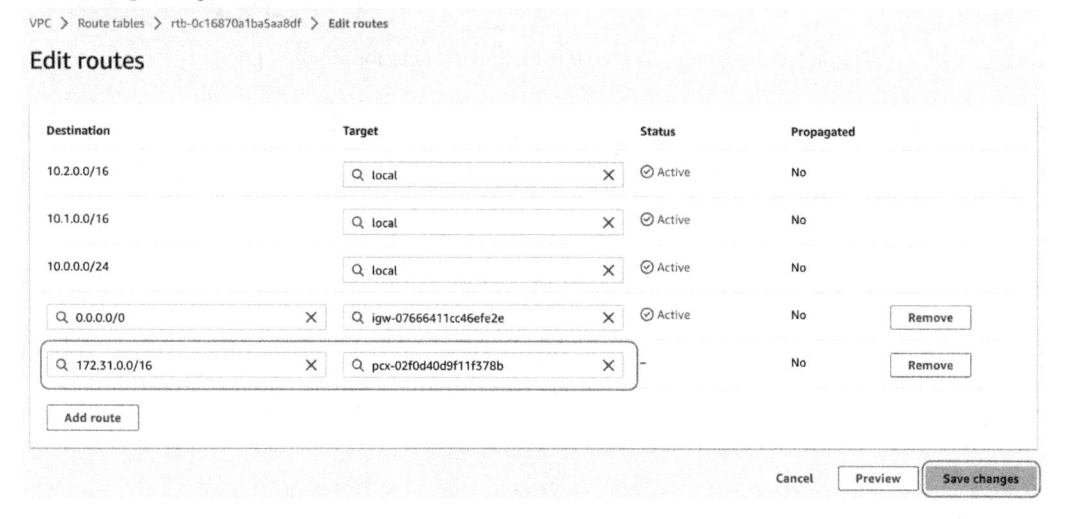

VPC > Route tables > rtb-0c16870a1ba5aa8df > Edit routes

Edit routes

Destination	Target	Status	Propagated	
10.2.0.0/16	local	⊘ Active	No	
10.1.0.0/16	local	⊘ Active	No	
10.0.0.0/24	local	⊘ Active	No	
0.0.0.0/0	igw-07666411cc46efe2e	⊘ Active	No	Remove
172.31.0.0/16	pcx-02f0d40d9f11f378b	–	No	Remove

Add route

Cancel | Preview | **Save changes**

Figure 5.38 – Configuring the routing details for the VPC peering connection

4. **Update security groups and NACLs**: Finally, update your security groups and network ACLs to ensure the necessary traffic is allowed between the peered VPCs.

As we venture forward, let's delve into another essential aspect of AWS networking—using Direct Connect and VPNs for establishing a dedicated and secure connection between AWS and data centers. It is much like creating a private bridge across a bustling river.

AWS Direct Connect and VPNs

AWS Direct Connect allows you to establish a dedicated network connection between your data center and AWS cloud environment. This dedicated network connection alleviates latency, variable performance, and security issues while providing a more consistent network experience with reduced latency, dedicated bandwidth, and reduced network costs. Direct Connect provides a more reliable alternative when compared to internet-based access to AWS resources.

The use cases for Direct Connect include hybrid cloud architectures, big data and analytics, disaster recovery, and migration. For example, a company may leverage Direct Connect to securely transfer sensitive information to the cloud without exposing it to the public internet or to connect their on-premises data centers to the cloud, thereby paving a way for seamless hybrid cloud architectures.

AWS VPNs, on the other hand, creates an encrypted tunnel and allows your traffic to securely flow through the internet or over Direct Connect. There are two types of VPN connections offered by AWS— site-to-site VPNs and client VPNs:

- Site-to-site VPNs offer secure IPsec connections from your on-premises network to your Amazon VPCs
- AWS Client VPN allows the end user to have secure access to AWS resources and on-premises networks from any location with their devices, such as laptops, desktops, and mobile devices

Both Direct Connect and VPN have their unique use cases and can also be combined to meet specific needs. For instance, you can create a secure, encrypted tunnel over the Direct Connect connection for an added layer of security.

By leveraging Direct Connect, VPN, or both, you can achieve your network connectivity needs with the right balance of cost, speed, and security

As we conclude exploring Direct Connect and VPN, we have understood the significance of how a dedicated network connection can bolster the communication between AWS and our infrastructure. As we move forward, we will delve into VPC endpoints and unravel how they can facilitate a specialized channel to interact with AWS services to streamline our access within the vast AWS ecosystem.

VPC endpoints and their user cases

VPC endpoints in AWS provide secure private connectivity between your VPC and supported AWS services. Once a VPC endpoint is created, it acts as a starting point for traffic, which is initiated against the respective AWS service. VPC endpoints come in two flavors:

- **Interface endpoints**: When an interface endpoint is created, an Elastic network interface with a private IP address from the IP address range of your subnet is allocated to an endpoint. The private IP address serves as an entry point for the traffic destined against the respective AWS service.

- **Gateway endpoints**: Unlike interface endpoints, gateway endpoints are associated with an entire VPC as opposed to individual subnets. A gateway endpoint creates a gateway and is added to the route table for the traffic destined to the respective AWS service. Gateway endpoints are currently only supported for S3 and DynamoDB.

VPC endpoints offer enhanced privacy since all the traffic between the VPC and supported AWS services does not leave your network.

Now, let us try to understand their use cases:

- **Accessing AWS services from isolated VPC**: If you have a VPC without an internet gateway or NAT gateway, you can use VPC endpoints to access the supported AWS service. Creating an endpoint doesn't require your traffic to traverse the public internet.

- **Improved network performance**: VPC endpoints offer low latency routes and improved network performance over internet-based connections. This is especially beneficial if your application transfers large amounts of data.

- **Security control**: Endpoints allows you to apply granular security policies to define who can access your service and what actions are allowed to be performed.

Overall, VPC endpoints act as an essential foundation block in building your AWS environment, providing enhanced security, improved network performance, and cost savings while accessing the supported AWS services from inside VPC.

VPC design principles

As we reach the conclusion of this chapter, it is apt that we dive into the design principles of VPC. When it comes to practicing network architecture in Amazon EC2, adhering to proven principles can guide you in creating an efficient, secure, and easily manageable networking environment:

- **Segregation and organization**: Consider segregating your VPC into multiple subnets, typically aligned with different layers in a multi-tier application architecture. For example, you might have separate subnets for your web servers, application servers, and database servers. This segregation and organization allows you to have a simplified security and access control, efficient traffic routing, and increased network performance.

- **Plan for scalability and flexibility**: Design your network architecture to support growth and changes over time. For instance, choose CIDR blocks wisely to allow for future expansion. Use Elastic IPs, which can be dynamically remapped between your workloads allowing you to quickly adapt to changes in your network. Also, ensure that your design allows for the addition of more subnets or scaling of resources within a subnet without major restructuring.
- **Automate network configuration**: Automate as much as possible. Utilize services such as AWS CloudFormation or Terraform for infrastructure as a code. Leveraging this type of automation allows you to automate your setup and teardown of environments, reduces manual effort, reduces errors, and can help enforce compliance and governance policies.
- **Implement security at all levels**: Security should not be an afterthought. Implement security at all levels, from security groups and network access control list to IAM policies for AWS service access. Also, consider encryption for sensitive data both at rest and in transit.
- **Enable monitoring and logging**: Enable CloudWatch for your networking components to monitor the performance and log your network activity. This monitoring will aid you in detecting unusual network patterns, security threats, and other network performance issues.

Summary

In this chapter, we have explored Amazon VPC and the pivotal role it plays in EC2 networking in great depth. We learned about VPC creation, subnets, CIDR blocks, and route tables. Following that, we explored security groups, network ACLs, and the principles of secure network design. Our journey also included Elastic IPs, network interfaces, VPC peering, and connectivity options such as Direct Connect and VPN.

As we transition to the next chapter, we shift our focus to security best practices for EC2 to create and operate a secure and efficient AWS environment.

6
Implementing Security Best Practices in Amazon EC2

As we continue exploring the world of Amazon EC2, we will turn our attention to implementing security best practices. We will start this chapter by providing a solid foundation of EC2 security, discussing the details of the relevance of security in the cloud and the shared responsibility model. Then, we will navigate the intricate terrain of IAM while putting special emphasis on roles, instance profiles, and policies. We will also discuss data encryption, both at rest and in transit, and touch base on other network security elements, such as security groups, network ACLs, and more. We will dive into areas such as operating system patch management and application-specific security considerations such as Amazon GuardDuty for threat detection, as well as AWS CloudTrail and CloudWatch, to aid you with auditing activities. The goal of this chapter is to arm you with a comprehensive toolset for ensuring EC2 security.

The following topics will be covered in this chapter:

- Introduction to Amazon EC2 security
- **Identity and access management (IAM)**
- Data encryption
- Network security
- Operating system and application security
- Advanced threat detection with GuardDuty

Introduction to Amazon EC2 security

Security plays an important role in the operation of organization assets in the cloud. Security in the cloud, including Amazon EC2, is not just critical but a foundational one. Although the cloud offers flexibility, scalability, and cost efficiency, it also presents a unique array of security considerations. Specifically, a service such as EC2 is susceptible to an extensive range of potential threats. A lapse in security measures can lead to catastrophic outcomes, as we have seen with incidents such as the Capital One breach (`https://www.capitalone.com/digital/facts2019/`), where a security exploit led to over 100 million customer records being accessed.

Ultimately, cloud security is a shared responsibility where Amazon embeds security into the core services to ensure the security of the cloud, while the customer is responsible for the security in the cloud. We'll discuss this shared responsibility in the next section.

Shared responsibility model

The shared responsibility model in AWS, as well as Amazon EC2, represents a cooperative approach to cloud security. Under the shared responsibility model, AWS ensures the *security of the cloud* – safeguarding the infrastructure that underpins its services – while the customer is tasked with the *security in the cloud* – essentially safeguarding the data they control within the AWS environment.

As a customer, your responsibilities include *data management, encryption, asset management*, and *authorization* for your resources with IAM, as well as implementing network security measures such as security groups and network ACLs. There are plenty of features available and it is solely the customer's responsibility to make use of them optimally to safeguard their needs.

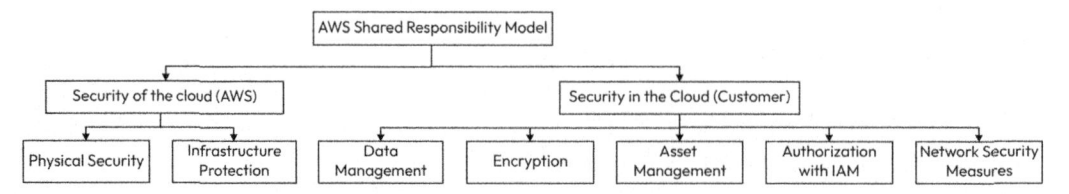

Figure 6.1 – Illustration of AWS's shared responsibility model

Now, let's discuss how shared responsibility works concerning Amazon EC2. In Amazon EC2, AWS is responsible for securing the underlying infrastructure that supports the EC2 services, including the hardware, server facilities, and host operating system. Meanwhile, the customer is responsible for securing the guest operating system. This includes operating system updates, security patches, and application software or utilities installed by the customer on the instances. A thorough understanding of this shared responsibility is essential in practicing and implementing security best practices in Amazon EC2.

With this foundational understanding in place, it's time we turn our attention to IAM to unravel its role in fortifying EC2 security.

IAM

AWS IAM is an essential service that enables granular control over access to AWS resources, including Amazon EC2. IAM facilitates secure management of users, groups, roles, and permissions, allowing you to define who can do what in your AWS environment. Users in IAM can be people or services interacting with AWS, while groups are a collection of users sharing the same set of permissions. IAM roles, on the other hand, are another kind of identity with defined permissions that can be assumed by users, applications, or services.

IAM in the context of Amazon EC2

IAM relevance in an EC2-specific context is immense. With IAM, you can define who can launch or terminate your EC2 instances, who can start or stop the instances, or to the level of who can modify your system attributes. For example, you can use IAM roles to grant permissions to applications running on your EC2 instances, allowing them to access other AWS services without the need to manage security credentials. Instance profiles, which are the containers for IAM roles, can be passed to the EC2 instance at the time of launch. This ability to securely delegate permissions is particularly crucial in a microservices architecture, where you might have different EC2 instances performing different tasks, each requiring different access levels to your resources.

Furthermore, with IAM, you can explicitly state what actions are allowed or denied. By attaching these policies to IAM identities, you can manage access to EC2 resources at a granular level. Also, with additional features such as identity federation and multi-factor authentication, IAM provides a robust and flexible approach to managing your EC2 resources to ensure a strong security posture within your EC2 environment.

Creating and managing IAM roles for EC2 instances

As we delve further into the world of AWS IAM, understanding how to create and manage IAM roles for EC2 instances becomes essential. IAM roles offer a secure way to grant permissions to your EC2 instances without the need to share access keys.

Creating an IAM role involves the following key steps:

1. Sign in to the AWS management console and navigate to the IAM dashboard:

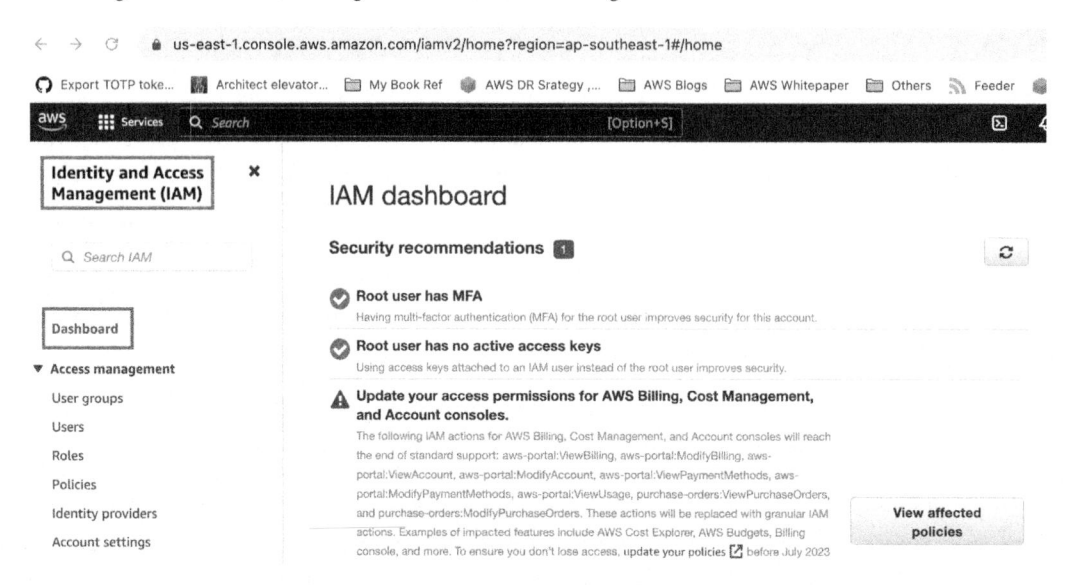

Figure 6.2 – IAM dashboard

2. Click **Roles**, then **Create role**:

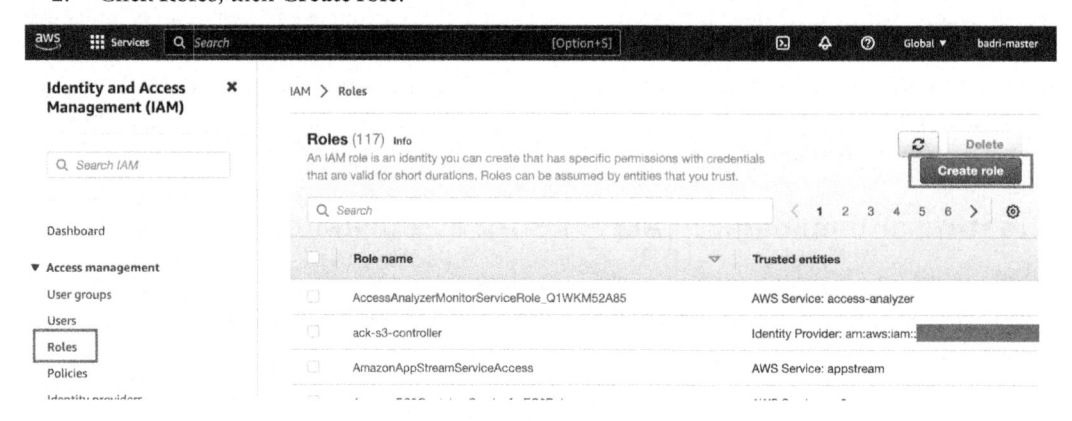

Figure 6.3 – Defining a new IAM role

IAM 129

3. Here, you will be asked to choose the type of trusted entity. In this context, we will select **AWS Service** and then **EC2**. Then, click **Next**:

Figure 6.4 – Selecting a trusted IAM entity

4. Upon clicking **Next**, you will be taken to the **Add permissions** policy page, where you can select the necessary AWS-managed or customer policy to attach to the role. Once you've done this, click **Next**:

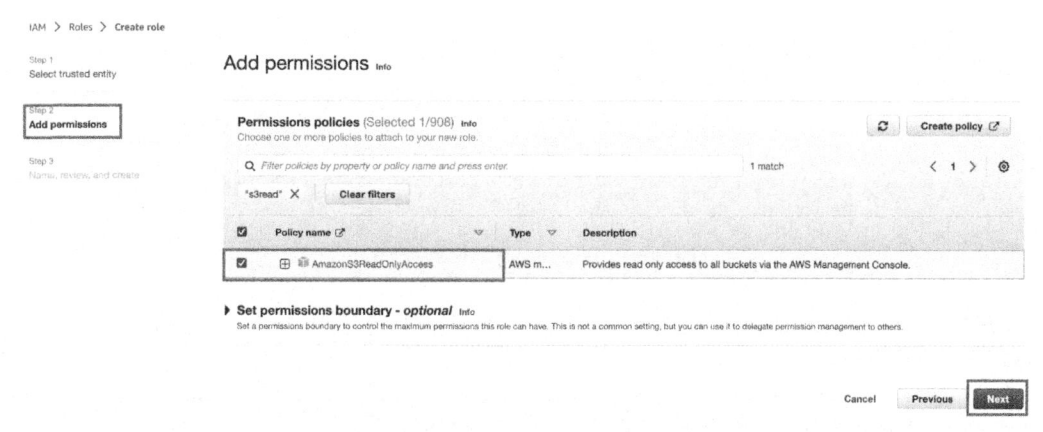

Figure 6.5 – Attaching the IAM policy

5. Once you have selected the necessary policies, review your *role's name*, *description*, and *policies*, and then click **Create role**:

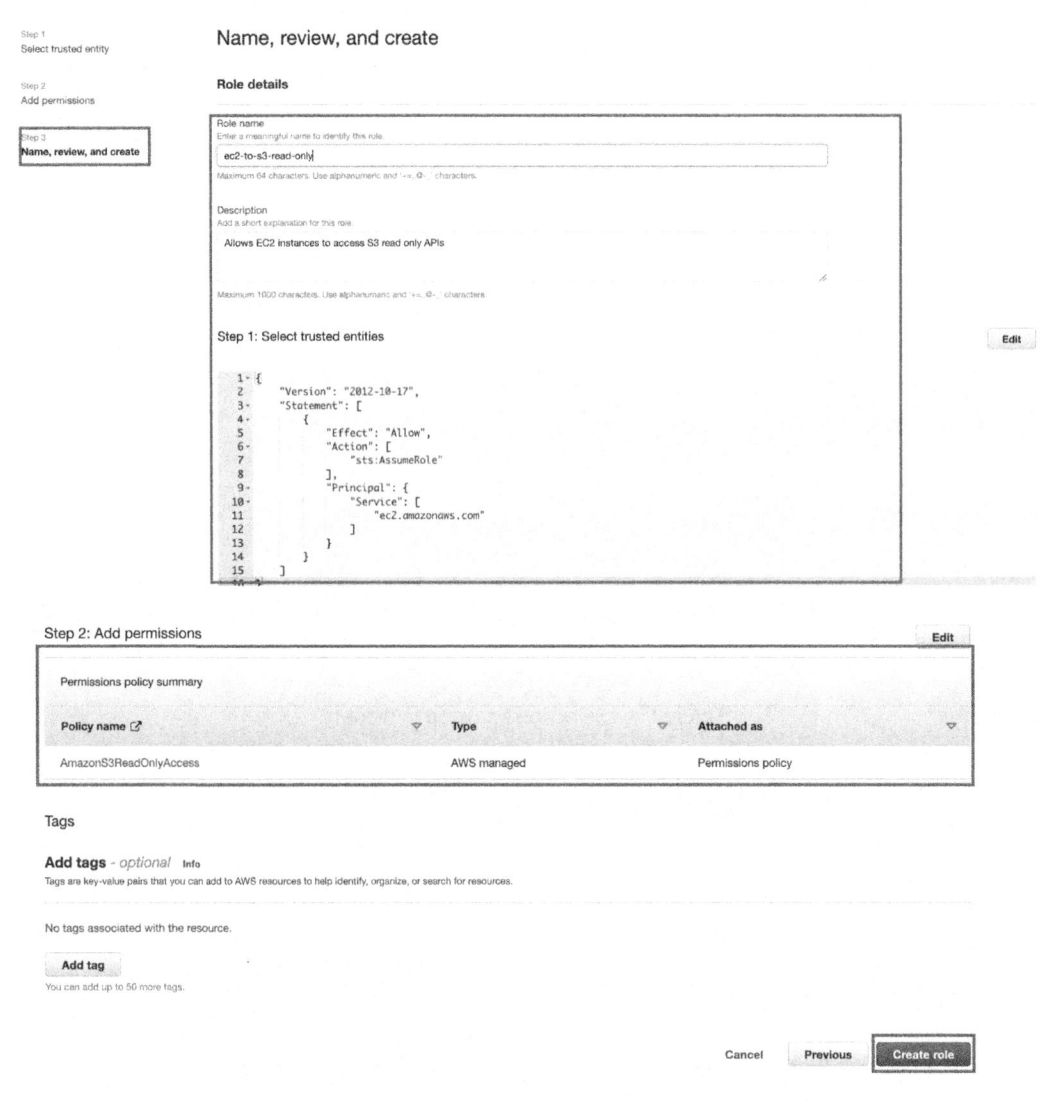

Figure 6.6 – Creating a new IAM role

Once you have created the role, you can associate it with an EC2 instance. Associating an IAM role can be done while launching an EC2 instance; you can even associate an existing instance without rebooting it. The IAM role associated with an EC2 instance enables the instance to make signed API requests to the AWS services allowed by the role permissions.

By associating the IAM roles, you help enhance the security of your EC2 instance by eliminating the need for developers to embed the AWS keys directly into the applications. Roles also eliminate the need for rotating the access keys manually by facilitating automatic key rotations. By leveraging IAM roles, you can achieve secure, scalable, and efficient management of permissions in your AWS environment.

Understanding instance profiles and policies

Instance profiles and policies are the important pillars that support the security and permission handling of your EC2 instances.

An **instance profile** acts as a container for an IAM role that we can use to pass permissions to an EC2 instance at launch time. In other words, the instance profile paves the way to attach an IAM role to the EC2 instance. When you specify an IAM role while launching an instance or when you associate it after launching an instance, AWS automatically creates an instance profile for the role and associates it with the instance. The applications running on the instance can then access AWS resources that the role has permission to use.

Moving on to IAM policies, they define a set of permissions that determine what actions are allowed and denied for an IAM entity (that is, user, group, or role). IAM policies are written in JSON format, which provides granular control over AWS resources. When a policy is attached to an IAM role that is associated with an EC2 instance, it determines what actions the applications or services running on that EC2 instance can perform on which resources and under what conditions.

For example, imagine a scenario where an application hosted inside the EC2 instance needs to read data from a specific S3 bucket. In this case, you need to create an IAM policy that allows the **S3:GetObject** action on the desired S3 bucket and include this policy inside the IAM role. At this point, you can assign the IAM role (this action automatically creates an instance profile) to the EC2 instance. This setup allows the application running inside the EC2 instance to read data from the specified S3 bucket.

> **Note:**
> Please ensure you are following least privilege permissioning while defining policies.

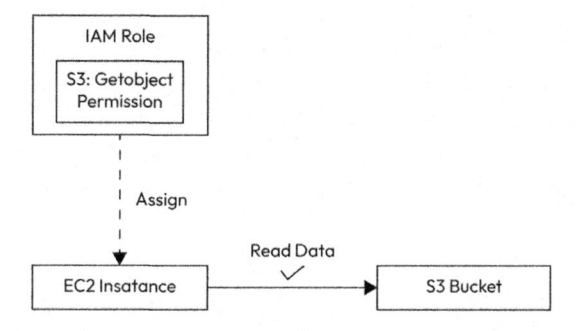

Figure 6.7 – Illustration of an EC2 instance profile

Next, we will shift our focus to data encryption, examining how to safeguard your EC2 instances using techniques such as encrypting your data at rest for EBS volumes and snapshots, performing data in transit using **transport layer security** (**TLS**)/**secure socket layer** (**SSL**), and managing encryption keys with AWS **Key Management Service** (**KMS**).

Data encryption

In this section, we will discuss another key topic of Amazon EC2 – **data encryption**. Here, we will explore topics that are specific to protecting and safeguarding data within the EC2 environment while covering two fundamental aspects:

- Data at rest encryption for EBS volumes and snapshots
- Data in transit encryption with TLS/SSL and key management with AWS KMS

Let's dive in and explore how data encryption practices contribute to creating a well-rounded secure EC2 environment.

Data at rest encryption for EBS volumes and snapshots

Encryption at rest plays a crucial role in protecting your data's confidentiality and integrity. In the context of Amazon EC2, this often involves leveraging data at rest encryption for EBS volumes and snapshots. Amazon EBS offers the ability to encrypt the data at rest seamlessly and also employs robust standards to secure the data at both the volume and snapshot levels. Encryption in EBS uses keys from AWS KMS, which offers transparent data encryption with little or no operational overhead.

Encryption for EBS volumes takes place on the servers hosting EC2 instances. This ensures that data is encrypted as it travels between EC2 instances and EBS storage. Upon creating an encrypted EBS volume and attaching it to a compatible EC2 instance type, the following occurs:

- Data at rest within the volume is encrypted
- Data in transit between the volume and instance is encrypted
- All snapshots derived from the EBS volume are encrypted

Snapshot encryption is another important feature. An EBS snapshot is a point-in-time copy of your data. If your EBS volumes are encrypted, then the EBS snapshots that are created out of the EBS volumes are also encrypted. Additionally, you can enforce encryption for your EBS snapshots by using AWS IAM policies to ensure that all your backups are encrypted and securely stored in your AWS environment.

Data in transit encryption with TLS/SSL

Both TLS and its predecessor, SSL, are cryptographic protocols that were created to facilitate secure communication between the client and the server over the network. TLS/SSL functions by establishing an encrypted tunnel between the client and server and transferring the data on top of it. This encrypted tunnel allows you to ensure the data remains private and secure at any point in time during the communication.

In the context of Amazon EC2, TLS/SSL facilitates the secure transfer of data between EC2 instances and other systems/services. When data is transferred out of an EC2 instance, it can be encrypted before it is transmitted. making it indecipherable to unauthorized individuals who might intercept it during its journey. Likewise, incoming data can be decrypted upon receipt by the EC2 instance.

Implementing TLS/SSL encryption requires a thorough understanding of how to manage and deploy SSL/TLS certificates. However, you can take advantage of services such as **AWS Certificate Manager** (**ACM**), which does the heavy lifting and simplifies your overall process of certificate management.

Key management with AWS KMS

A key management system is responsible for creating, storing, using, and retiring the encryption keys that are responsible for safeguarding your data.

AWS KMS comes in as a secure, scalable, and resilient managed service offering that provides seamless control over your cryptographic keys. AWS KMS allows you to create and manage cryptographic keys with ease and control their use across a wide range of AWS services in your applications. Here are some of the key features of AWS KMS:

- Centralized key management
- Auditing key usage with AWS CloudTrail
- Permissions management with AWS IAM
- Seamless encryption techniques with AWS services

In the context of Amazon EC2, KMS can be used for a variety of functions. For example, you can use KMS keys to encrypt your EBS volumes, and/or you can use KMS keys in conjunction with SSL/TLS for data in transit to have strong protection against unauthorized access.

Creating and managing cryptographic keys with KMS involves four steps:

1. **Key creation**: Start by creating a **customer master key** (**CMK**). Think of this as a logical representation of a key. The CMK can also be used directly to encrypt/decrypt data for data up to *4 KB* in size.

2. **Data key generation for large data**: For encrypting larger amounts of data, it is not feasible to use CMK directly. Instead, you must generate data keys using CMK. These data keys can be leveraged to encrypt more sizeable data.

3. **Implementation of access control**: Proper access control is important in managing cryptographic keys. You can prevent unauthorized access by associating IAM policies with key management.

4. **Automatic key rotation**: One of the important features of KMS is its ability to perform automatic key rotation while limiting the blast radius for unforeseen scenarios.

With these steps in place, you can ensure a robust and secure mechanism for key management with AWS. In the next section, we will dive deeper and explore the nuances of protecting network infrastructure within AWS.

Network security

In the context of Amazon EC2, the role of **security groups** and **network access control lists** (**NACLs**) plays an integral part in establishing the network security of Amazon EC2. The aspect of network security is of paramount importance and a careful balance between accessibility and security is needed while utilizing this layer of defense to enable system functionalities while minimizing your potential vulnerabilities.

Security groups are your primary defense mechanism for your EC2 instances. A security group acts as a virtual firewall for your EC2 instances in regulating the inbound and outbound traffic at the instance level. Each EC2 instance can be associated with one or more security groups with the rules defined to whitelist what traffic is allowed to reach or exit the instances. Importantly, security groups are stateful. This means that any inbound traffic that's allowed through will automatically enable the outbound traffic to flow through without any interruption and vice versa.

NACLs, on the other hand, function as a secondary layer of defense, providing an additional layer of security at the subnet level. Unlike security groups, NACLs are stateless, which means both inbound and outbound traffic must be explicitly allowed. NACLs can also allow/deny the traffic based on the IP protocol, service port, or source/destination IP address, offering granular control over your traffic flow.

By using them together, security groups offer a flexible instance-level firewall while NACLs offer broader subnet-level security, thus forming a comprehensive defense strategy for your EC2 instances.

Additional network security best practices

Several network security best practices can significantly enhance the security posture of your EC2 instance and make it harder for potential threats to penetrate your EC2 environment.

First, you should implement the principle of least privilege to reduce the potential network points for malicious activities to happen. The idea is to allow only the necessary traffic for your application to function and block everything else. For example, If you are running a web server in your EC2 instance, then typically, the only ports that need to be open are port 80 and port 443.

Secondly, you should segregate your network architecture inside **virtual private clouds** (**VPCs**) using subnets. By segregating your resources into different subnets, you can separate public-facing instances from internal-facing ones, thus adding an extra layer of defense to your network.

It is also beneficial to make use of VPC Flow Logs to visualize your network traffic. You can take advantage of flow logs to monitor and troubleshoot connectivity issues. Flow logs also assist you in identifying malicious activity, such as reconnaissance and unusual data transfer.

PrivateLink is also another tool that you can make use of to enhance your network security. This enables you to access services across different accounts and VPCs while keeping all your network traffic within the AWS network, thereby eliminating exposure to the public internet.

Finally, You can augment your network with AWS Shield to protect from **distributed denial of service** (**DDoS**) attacks. Shield provides automatic defenses to safeguard your applications running on AWS.

These strategies, when integrated, provide a robust network security strategy. Once you've finished establishing a defense against your network posture, you must address operating system hardening, patch management, and application-level security considerations. We will be delving into these crucial aspects of EC2 security in the upcoming section.

Operating system and application security

The operating system and application security are a crucial aspect in protecting your Amazon EC2 instances at the operating system and application layers. In this section, we will discuss the security best practices and strategies you can implement to fortify your instances and applications against potential cyber threats.

Operating system hardening is the process of tightening the exposure of the system to reduce its surface vulnerability. A hardened system is typically more secure than a default system as it has been configured to cease any unnecessary function, which helps to prevent possible attack vectors. In the context of Amazon EC2, operating system hardening plays a vital role in your overall security strategy.

When we practice operating system hardening in Amazon EC2, the primary focus is to enforce the principle of least privilege. This principle is based on the premise that any service or program should only be granted the bare minimum privileges of what is needed for it to function. For example, say you are running a web server in an EC2 instance. The purpose of the web server is to serve web pages to the end user. So, in this context, you can practice limiting the privileges for the web server to prevent any write access to the directories where the web pages are hosted on that server. By following this practice, you could potentially prevent any harmful damage done by an attacker exploiting the vulnerabilities in that server.

Securing user access to EC2 instances forms another critical aspect of operating system hardening. This includes creating appropriate user roles and permissions and ensuring that only authorized users have access to the instances. On top of the operating system, AWS IAM can be used to control user access to AWS EC2 services and resources.

The final yet critical aspect of operating system hardening is establishing a process to ensure continuous monitoring and managing ongoing updates. This process involves keeping a close eye on the system logs and executing timely security updates on the system to prevent any exploitation of system vulnerabilities. You can make use of various tools and services inside AWS, such as Systems Manager for patch updates, and automate the process to execute ongoing updates to the system. You can also rely on services such as CloudWatch to regularly monitor system logs.

Patch management and updates

Patch management is a critical task in the life cycle of Amazon EC2 instances. The essential aspect of patch management is to maintain the security and integrity of operating systems and applications. Patch management includes testing and installing patches on the administered computer system. Also, considering the dynamic nature of cyber security threats, timely application of patches is the top priority in maintaining the security and integrity of operating systems and applications running on Amazon EC2.

In AWS, you can make use of managed services such as Systems Manager and Patch Manager to simplify the process of patch management; you can make use of them to apply both security-related and other types of updates. With Patch Manager, you can control and automate how your instances are patched and thereby ensure compliance with your organization's patch policies. Patch baselines allow you to define a set of rules to determine which patches are approved or disapproved for an instance and thereby provide granular control over the patching process. For example, you can auto-approve all critical updates for patching while enforcing manual review for moderate updates. In addition to this, you can rely on Amazon EC2 Image Builder to create a custom AMI where you can meticulously pre-configure all the security measures, ensuring the AMI image is fully fortified for deployment with your EC2 instances.

In parallel to effective patch management, it is important to monitor your system behavior post-patching activities to ensure there are no anomalies and that even if they exist, they are handled properly. Amazon CloudWatch comes in handy for this, allowing you to visualize insightful metrics and set up alarms to narrow down unusual activities. Moreover, it is important to maintain a viable rollback strategy for patches as they can sometimes cause unexpected problems. AWS allows you to create an AMI as a backup, which can be deployed if a patch necessitates a rollback.

Application-level security considerations

Application-level security is a comprehensive strategy that considers the nuances of the application running the platform and handles them holistically. This ensures the applications and their processes and the data they manage are secured from both internal and external threats.

Practicing secure coding and enforcing strict access controls are essential in ensuring application-level security. AWS IAM can be combined with Amazon EC2 to associate granular permissions at the application level. AWS also provides AWS Shield, a managed DDoS protection service that safeguards applications on AWS. Another service that helps you guard application-level security is **Web Application Firewall** (**WAF**), which helps you protect your application from common web exploits that could affect your application availability or compromise security

Achieving effective application security also involves securing your application data both in transit and at rest. **AWS Certificate Manager** (**ACM**) can be used to deploy SSL/TLS certificates for your applications and KMS to create/manage your encryption keys for securing your data at rest. AWS also offers services such as Inspector for conducting automated security assessments on Amazon EC2 and Macie for data classification in the S3 bucket. By integrating all these services and practices, you can significantly boost your application-level security by mitigating risks at the application layer. But how do we proactively detect and prevent potential threats? That brings us to our next topic.

Introduction to Amazon GuardDuty for threat detection

Amazon GuardDuty is a powerful threat detection service that's designed to monitor your AWS account for malicious activities and unauthorized behavior. GuardDuty protects your AWS environment by leveraging powerful machine learning and anomaly detection techniques, including integrated threat intelligence mechanisms, to identify any potential threats. Let's discuss some integral parts of this process.

Logging with AWS CloudTrail and CloudWatch

In the context of GuardDuty and broader AWS security, AWS CloudWatch and CloudTrail play a critical role in terms of monitoring, logging, and observing activities within your AWS environment. **CloudTrail** captures all the API calls or events in your AWS environment and provides a detailed event history of your AWS account activity. This allows you to perform security analysis, resource change tracking, compliance auditing, and even troubleshooting. On the other hand, **CloudWatch**, though primarily used to observe operational health and performance, can be extended to collecting and monitoring log files, setting alarms, and reacting automatically to changes in your AWS resources.

CloudTrail plays an important role in your security setup. It captures information that is very important for security analysis, such as the following:

- The identity of the API caller
- The time of the API call
- The source IP address of the caller
- The request parameters
- The response elements returned by the AWS service

This logging aids your security analysis to monitor activity, track resource changes, and identify any unauthorized or unexpected activity. CloudWatch, on the other hand, allows you to customize your dashboard and stream logs so that you can monitor your resources in one place and set alarms based on the state of your resources and events to automate action on your behalf.

The combination of CloudTrail and CloudWatch provides you with a comprehensive and robust logging and monitoring system that reinforces the security of your Amazon EC2 environment.

Auditing and analysis techniques

GuardDuty is an intelligent threat detection service that continually monitors for malicious or unauthorized behavior to detect a security incident. By focusing on auditing and analysis techniques with GuardDuty, you can enhance your AWS security posture by effectively identifying potential threats before they escalate.

GuardDuty works by analyzing logs and events from various sources, namely VPC Flow Logs, DNS logs, and CloudTrail events, to identify any threatening activity in your AWS environment. However, understanding the results requires systematic auditing and analysis techniques.

First, you need to configure GuardDuty to generate findings where each of the findings is presented with a detailed description and recommended remediation actions. You can establish a routine to review and address these findings. You can also automate your remediation response for specific types of findings by integrating GuardDuty with CloudWatch Events and Lambda to isolate compromised instances or block suspicious IP addresses.

Secondly, you can leverage SecurityHub to aggregate your security events from GuardDuty and other services. **SecurityHub** provides you with a centralized and consolidated view of the security alerts to assist you with the analysis of compliance posture across your AWS environment. This centralized approach to audit findings enhances your ability to understand the nature and magnitude of threats across your AWS environment.

Finally, deeper analysis might be necessary to unveil complex threats. In such cases, you can export GuardDuty findings to an Amazon S3 bucket for further examination. On top of this S3 bucket, you can use tools such as Amazon Athena and Amazon QuickSight to query and visualize the data to understand more nuanced insights about the security state of your AWS environment.

Summary

In this chapter, we thoroughly examined the security best practices in Amazon EC2. We started with operating system hardening and its importance in minimizing vulnerabilities and attack surfaces. Then, we discussed the necessity of routine patch management updates to protect our systems from known threats. We also discussed the importance of ensuring proper configurations and establishing secure coding practices. Finally, we delved into GuardDuty, which we can use to take advantage of intelligent threat detection, and learned the techniques and processes involved in auditing and analysis.

In the next chapter, we will discuss how the security practices outlined here integrate with scalability and availability concepts.

Part 2: Building a Resilient Application on Amazon EC2

The objective of this part is to equip you to build resilient applications on Amazon EC2, covering load balancing, auto scaling, storage optimization, monitoring, logging, maintenance, and automation using various AWS services and their best practices.

This part has the following chapters:

- *Chapter 7, Load Balancing and Auto Scaling with Elastic Load Balancer and Auto Scaling Groups*
- *Chapter 8, Understanding Amazon EC2 Storage Options*
- *Chapter 9, Optimizing Performance with Amazon EC2 Placement Groups and Pricing Model*
- *Chapter 10, Monitoring, Logging, and Maintenance with Amazon CloudWatch, AWS CloudTrail, and Backup Strategies*
- *Chapter 11, Automating Amazon EC2 – AWS CloudFormation and Infrastructure as Code*

7

Load Balancing and Auto Scaling with Elastic Load Balancer and Auto Scaling Groups

In this chapter, we will look into load balancing and auto-scaling with **Elastic Load Balancer** (ELB) and Auto Scaling groups. We will unravel the essential components of managing web traffic and ensuring application availability. We will begin by delving into the world of load balancing and understanding its role in distributing incoming traffic efficiently across multiple targets. Then, we will explore the nitty-gritty details of setting up and fine-tuning load balancers. As we progress, you will become familiar with the world of Auto Scaling Groups, from their basic configurations to advanced management techniques. We will also shed light on the relationship between Auto Scaling groups and load balancing, emphasizing the best practices for joint utilization.

The following topics will be covered in this chapter:

- Introduction to elastic load balancing
- Setting up and configuring load balancers
- Load balancer best practices
- Introduction to Auto Scaling groups
- Configuring and managing Auto Scaling groups
- Integrating ELB with Auto Scaling groups
- Best practices for using ELB and Auto Scaling groups together

Introduction to ELB

Imagine a busy cop managing cars at a crowded crossroads. That's precisely the role AWS's **Elastic Load Balancer** (**ELB**) plays in the online world for web traffic. The role of ELB is to automatically distribute an application's incoming traffic across multiple targets, ensuring that no single server bears an undue burden:

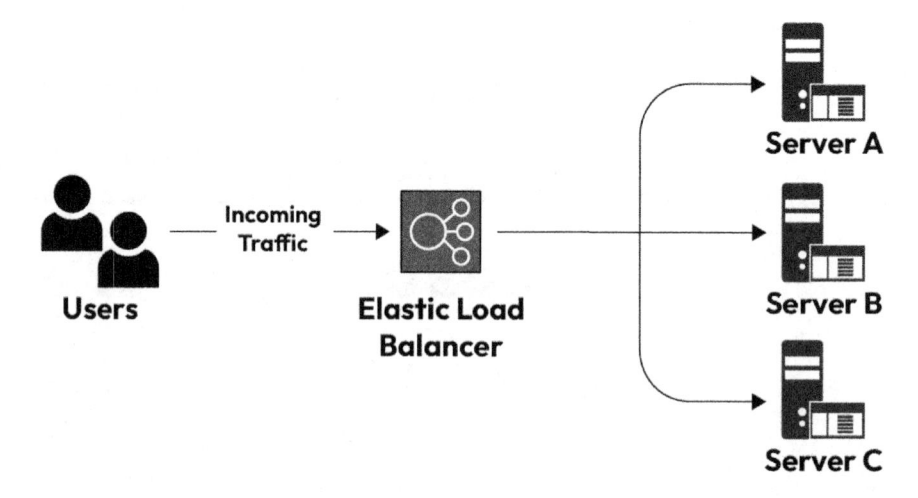

Figure 7.1 – ELB load distribution

Types of load balancers

Just like different intersections require different traffic strategies, AWS understands that different applications have unique demands. To cater to this diversity, AWS offers different types of load balancers, each fine-tuned for specific scenarios. Let's explore the details of the load balancer and demystify their roles and responsibilities.

The following are some of the different types of load balancers in AWS:

- **Application load balancer (ALB)**: An ALB is designed for HTTP and HTTPS web traffic, the different types of application traffic that are available. Unlike other load balancers, which focus on routing based on the source and destination, also known as *Layer 4* in the **Open System Interconnection** (**OSI**) model, ALB operates at the application layer of the OSI model, also known as *Layer 7*.

If you're wondering what these layers are in the OSI model, then it is important to know that the OSI model is divided into seven distinct layers, with each having a specific role in managing network communications:

- Physical
- Datalink
- Network
- Transport
- Session
- Presentation
- Application

Here, each layer is responsible for different aspects of data transmission and networking protocols. We will briefly look at Layer 4 and Layer 7, which are the layers ELB operates in. You can read more about the details of the other OSI layers here: `https://en.wikipedia.org/wiki/OSI_model`. Let's take a look:

- **Layer 7 (application layer)**: This layer dives deep into the message's content, such as the URLs or headers, to make intelligent routing decisions. If you had different services for different parts of your website, ALB could send requests for `/pathA` to one part of the service and `/pathB` to another.

- **Layer 4 (transport layer)**: While ALB focuses on Layer 7, it's worth understanding Layer 4 too. Layer 4, also known as the transport layer, routes data based purely on the IP address and port, without caring about the content.

- **Advanced routing**: ALB's superpower lies in its ability to make decisions based on content. For instance, if your site has different services for the web and mobile versions, the ALB can route users based on their device type, identified by headers in their requests.

- **Use case**: ALB is a perfect use case for microservices architectures or container-based applications. If your setup has different services, ALB helps route the traffic accurately.

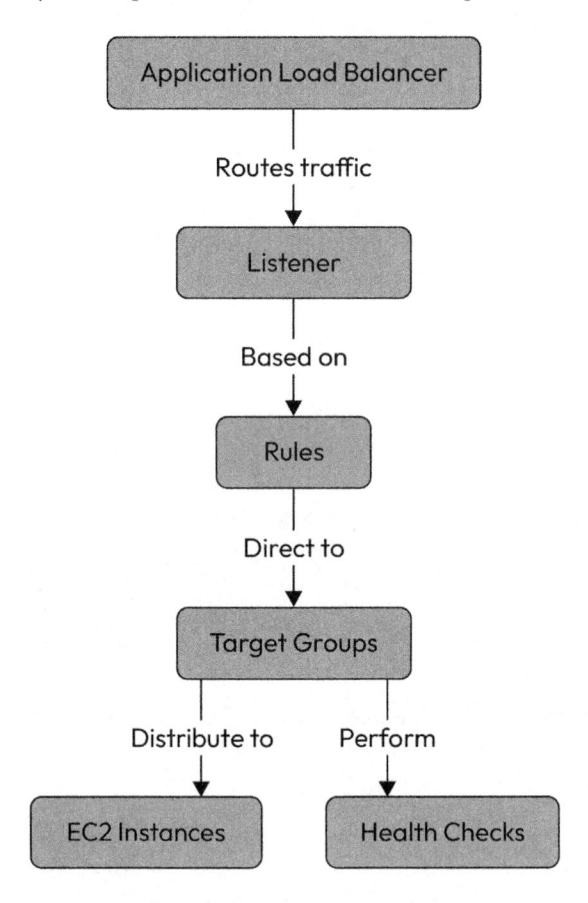

Figure 7.2 – Illustration of an ALB

- **Network load balancer (NLB)**: NLBs operate at the transport layer (Layer 4). This layer is also a no-nonsense layer as the traffic is directed purely based on IP protocol data, making the overall process very efficient.

    - **Performance**: NLBs are built for performance, and this is your go-to load balancer for an application that demands lightning-fast response times and has the requirement to process tens of thousands of requests per second.

- **Use case**: NLBs are ideal for ultra-fast web applications, real-time gaming applications, and other applications where performance matters in terms of microseconds:

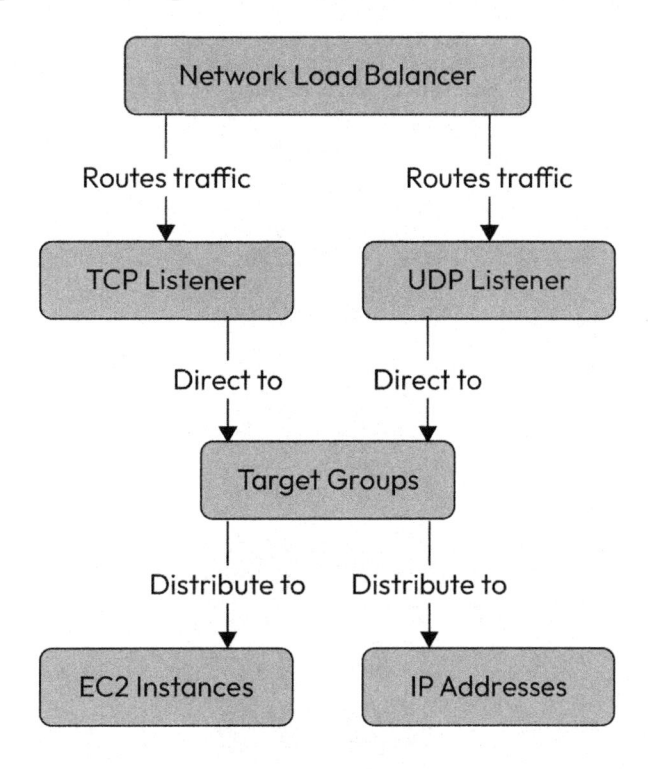

Figure 7.3 – Illustration of an NLB

- **Gateway load balancer (GWLB)**: A GWLB is a type of load balancer that is designed specifically for deploying, scaling, and managing third-party virtual appliances such as firewalls, intrusion prevention and detection systems, and deep packet inspections within your VPC:

    - **Transparent inspection**: The main advantage of GWLB is its ability to transparently inspect the traffic without changing it. This means they see the traffic exactly as it arrives, making the inspection more genuine and reliable.

- **Use case**: If your setup involves third-party tools that you need to get an unaltered view of, you can use a GWLB:

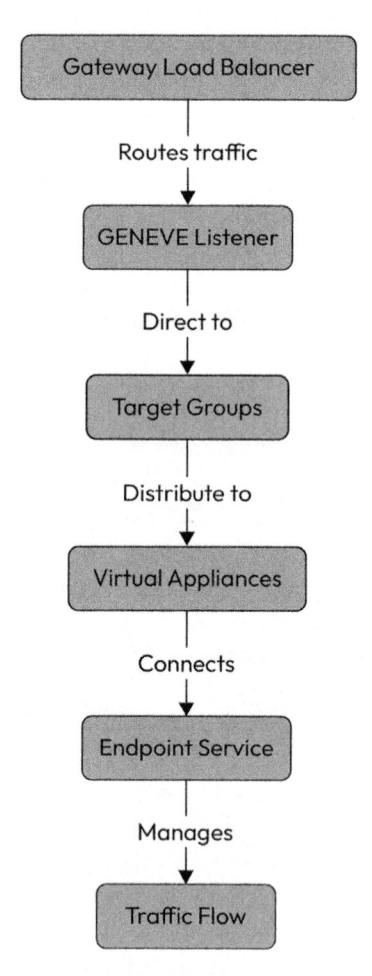

Figure 7.4 – Illustration of a GWLB

AWS ELB's beauty lies in its versatility. It offers a buffet of choices to suit any of your use cases, from serving simple web pages to running complex sets of microservices; there is a load balancer to keep things running smoothly. Understanding the range of choices is just the beginning. Now, let's delve deeper into how you can set up and tailor these load balancers to your specific needs.

Setting up and configuring an ELB

For a robust digital system, it is crucial to have a strong tool that skillfully manages the web traffic. ELB effectively serves as a reliable shield, making sure your apps stay quick and responsive, even when user activity spikes. While picking the right load balancer is the good first step, much of your success comes from the careful setup and detailed configuration of it. Also, it's worth noting that while the GWLB has its specialized use cases, our focus here will be on ALBs and NLBs. Let's dive in and understand the steps involved in setting up the most popular choice – the ALB.

ALB

In this section, we will look at the processes involved in setting up an ALB in AWS.

Creating and configuring listeners

Listeners are the heart of your ALB; they constantly check for connection requests. These requests are typically based on the port and protocol you have set. When creating a listener, you would specify a protocol (either HTTP or HTTPS), a port, and the associated actions (such as redirecting or forwarding a request) when a rule condition is met.

To configure a listener for ALB, you will need to do the following:

1. **Navigate to Load Balancers under EC2:** Navigate to the EC2 service and, under the **Load Balancing** section, select **Load balancers**:

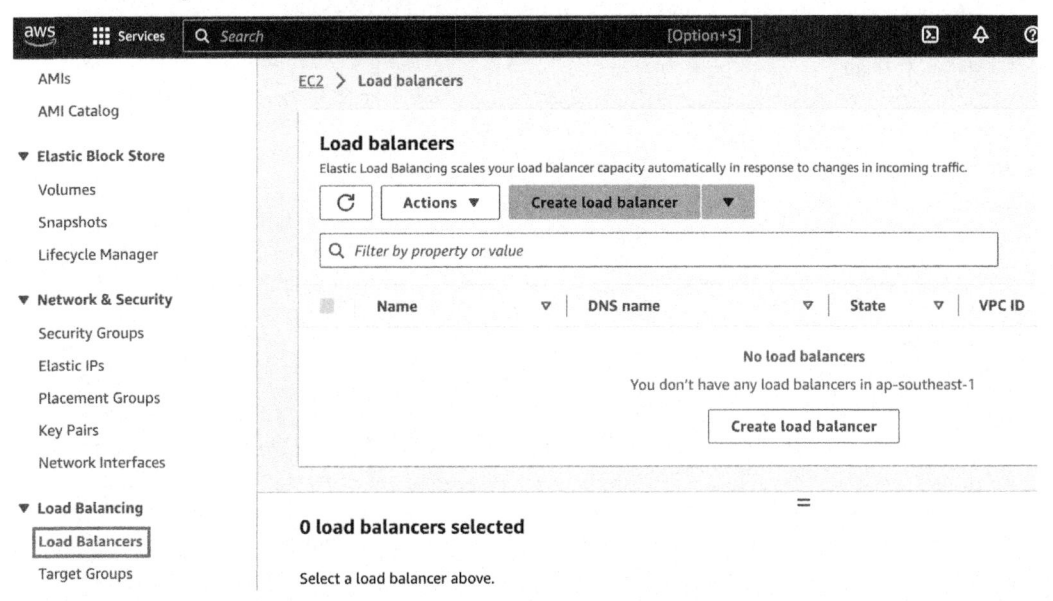

Figure 7.5 – EC2 Load balancers landing page

2. **Choose your ALB**: Select **Create load balancer** and opt for **Application Load Balancer**:

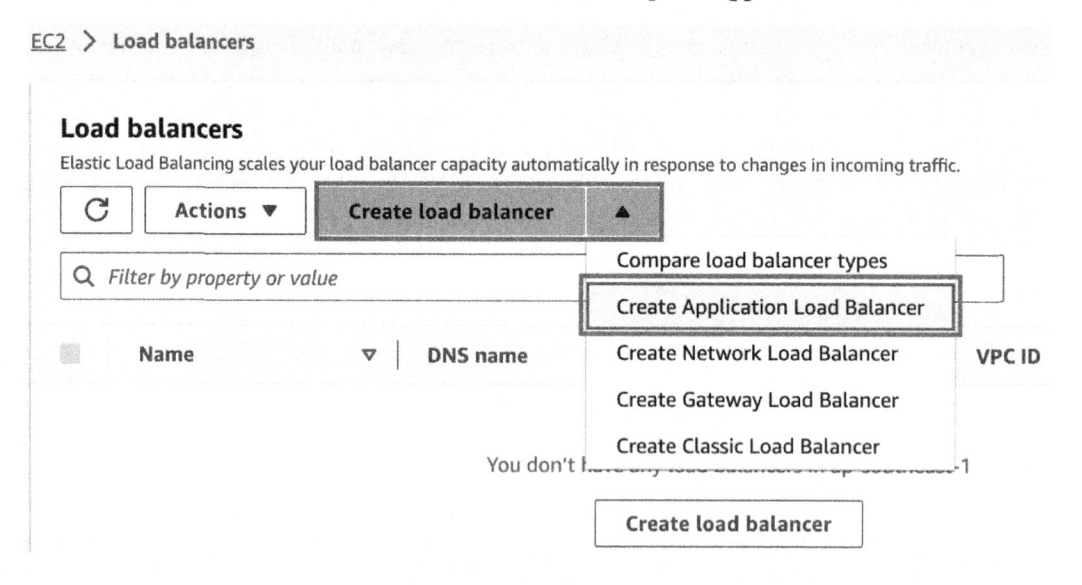

Figure 7.6 – Creating an ALB

3. **Define listener settings**: When creating or editing your ALB, you will be prompted to define listener settings. Specify the protocol (typically *HTTP/HTTPS*) and the port. The most common configurations are **HTTP** on **Port 80** and **HTTPS** on **Port 443**:

Figure 7.7 – Configuring the ALB protocol and port details

4. **Specify the default actions**: For every listener, you need to specify a default action, such as forward or redirect. Choose **Forward to** and then select your target group:

Figure 7.8 – Configuring the ALB listener's details

> **Note**
> Choose **Forward to** when you want to distribute the incoming traffic to specific target groups for load balancing across the servers. On the other hand, opt for **Redirect to** when you need to reroute the requests for purposes such as enforcing HTTPS or redirecting to a different domain.

5. **Additional rules (optional)**: You can create more rules for your listeners, such as redirecting HTTP requests to HTTPS.

Target groups

Behind every great listener is the **target group**, which does the heavy lifting. Once your listener rules have determined where to send the request, target groups come into play. A target group is a set of resources, such as EC2 instances or containers, that are poised to handle the incoming traffic.

To configure a target group, you will need to do the following:

1. **Go to Target Groups**: Within the EC2 dashboard, under **Load Balancing**, select **Target Groups**:

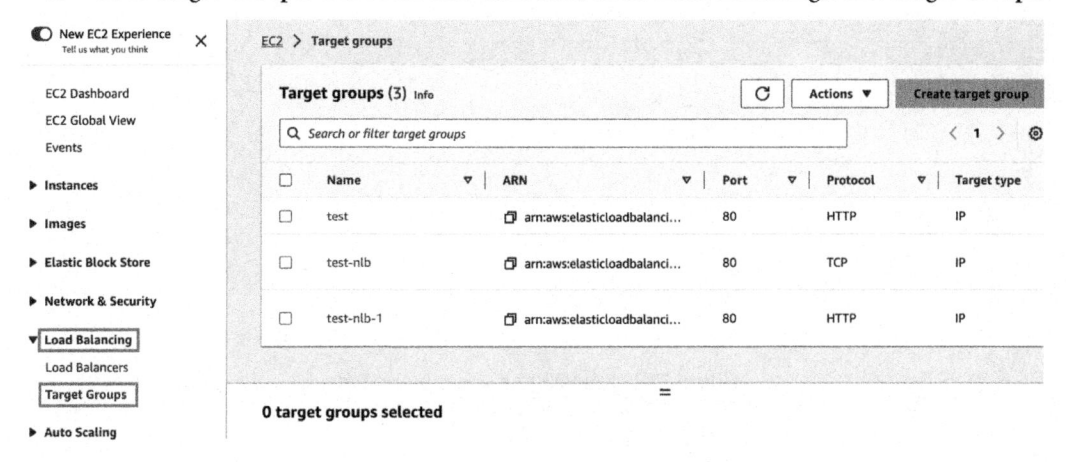

Figure 7.9 – The Target groups landing page

2. **Create a target group and define a protocol/port**: Click **Create target group** and provide a **Target group name** value. Then, define the **Protocol** and **Port** details. This should match your listener's details:

Target group name

hello-world-app

A maximum of 32 alphanumeric characters including hyphens are allowed, but the name must not begin or end with a hyphen.

Protocol | Port
HTTP ▼ : 80
1-65535

VPC

Figure 7.10 – Configuring the target group's details

3. **Target type selection**: Choose whether you want to route traffic to instances, IP addresses, Lambda functions, or another ALB:

Choose a target type

◉ **Instances**
- Supports load balancing to instances within a specific VPC.
- Facilitates the use of Amazon EC2 Auto Scaling ↗ to manage and scale your EC2 capacity.

○ **IP addresses**
- Supports load balancing to VPC and on-premises resources.
- Facilitates routing to multiple IP addresses and network interfaces on the same instance.
- Offers flexibility with microservice based architectures, simplifying inter-application communication.
- Supports IPv6 targets, enabling end-to-end IPv6 communication, and IPv4-to-IPv6 NAT.

○ **Lambda function**
- Facilitates routing to a single Lambda function.
- Accessible to Application Load Balancers only.

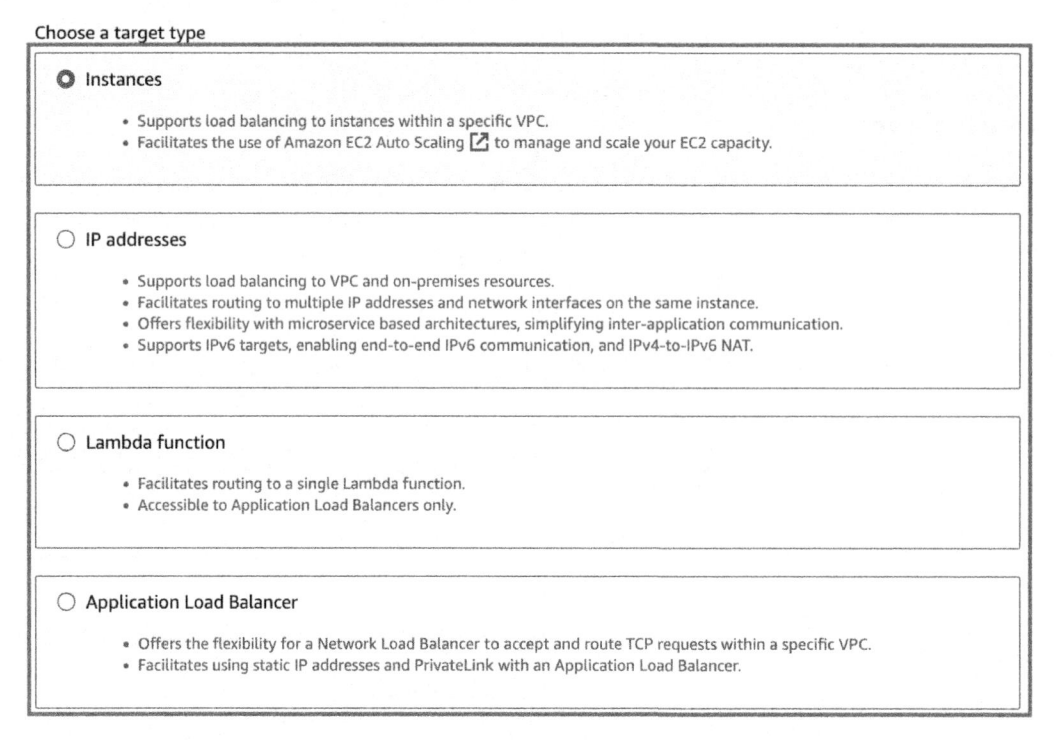

○ **Application Load Balancer**
- Offers the flexibility for a Network Load Balancer to accept and route TCP requests within a specific VPC.
- Facilitates using static IP addresses and PrivateLink with an Application Load Balancer.

Figure 7.11 – Choosing a target group type

4. **Advanced health check settings**: At this point, you can configure health checks in terms of their path, port, and more (we will explore this more in detail in the upcoming section):

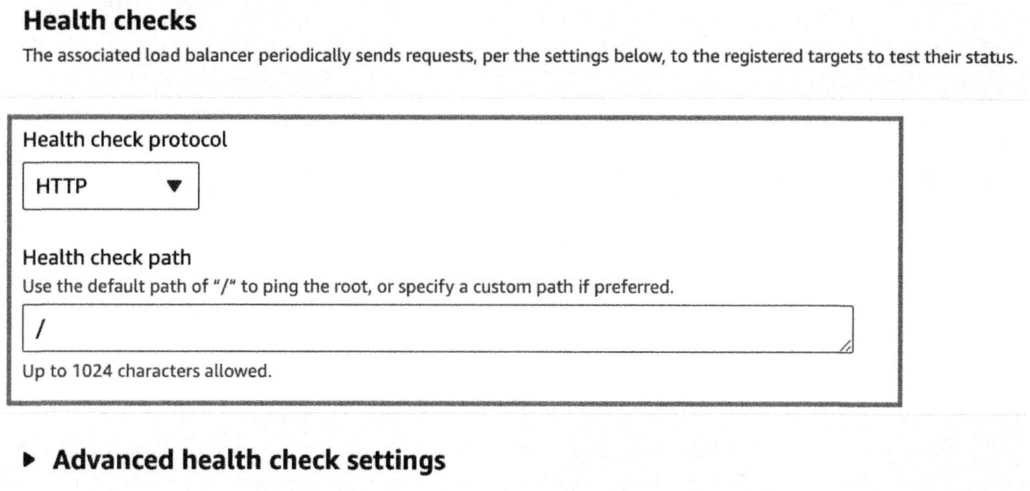

Health checks

The associated load balancer periodically sends requests, per the settings below, to the registered targets to test their status.

Health check protocol

[HTTP ▼]

Health check path
Use the default path of "/" to ping the root, or specify a custom path if preferred.

[/]

Up to 1024 characters allowed.

▶ **Advanced health check settings**

Figure 7.12 – Configuring the ALB's health check details

5. **Register targets**: Once your target group has been created, you can register targets, such as EC2 instances, with this group.

Health checks

It is paramount that you ensure your resources are up and running at all times. **Health checks** are the ALB's way of verifying if a resource in your target group is functioning optimally. Health checks are automated tests that are periodically sent to each target, testing for a successful response. If a target fails a specified number of consecutive health checks, then it is considered *unhealthy* and won't receive traffic until the health check becomes green.

To configure a health check, you will need to complete the following steps:

1. **Select your target group**: Navigate to the **Target Groups** section within **Load Balancing** and choose your desired target group:

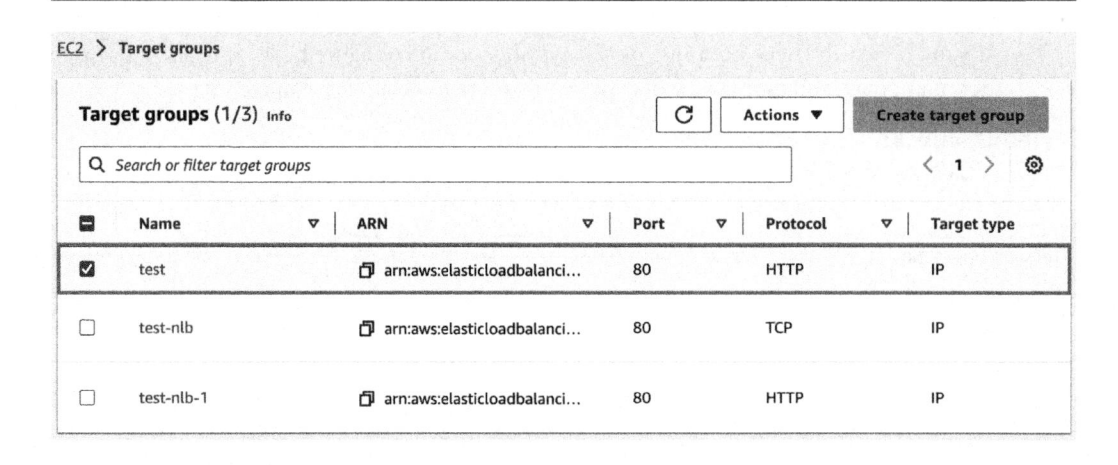

154 Load Balancing and Auto Scaling with Elastic Load Balancer and Auto Scaling Groups

Figure 7.13 – Selecting the desired target group

2. **Edit your health checks**: In the **Description** tab, you will see a section for **Health checks**. Click **Edit**:

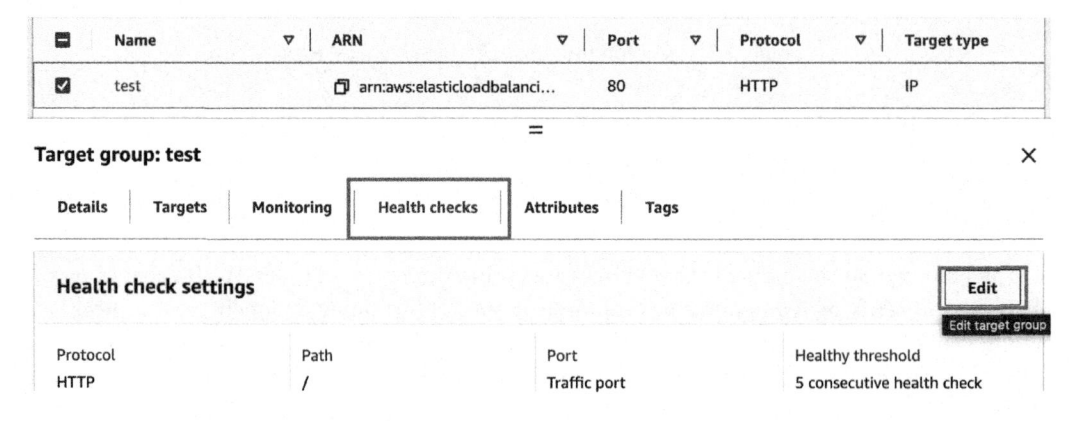

Figure 7.14 – Defining the target group's health check details

3. Configure the following health check settings:

   - **Protocol**: Typically HTTP/HTTPS
   - **Port**: The port on which the target responds
   - **Path**: The endpoint on which the system checks the health of the target.
   - **Advanced settings**: Here, you can configure intervals, timeout durations, and thresholds for healthy/unhealthy counts:

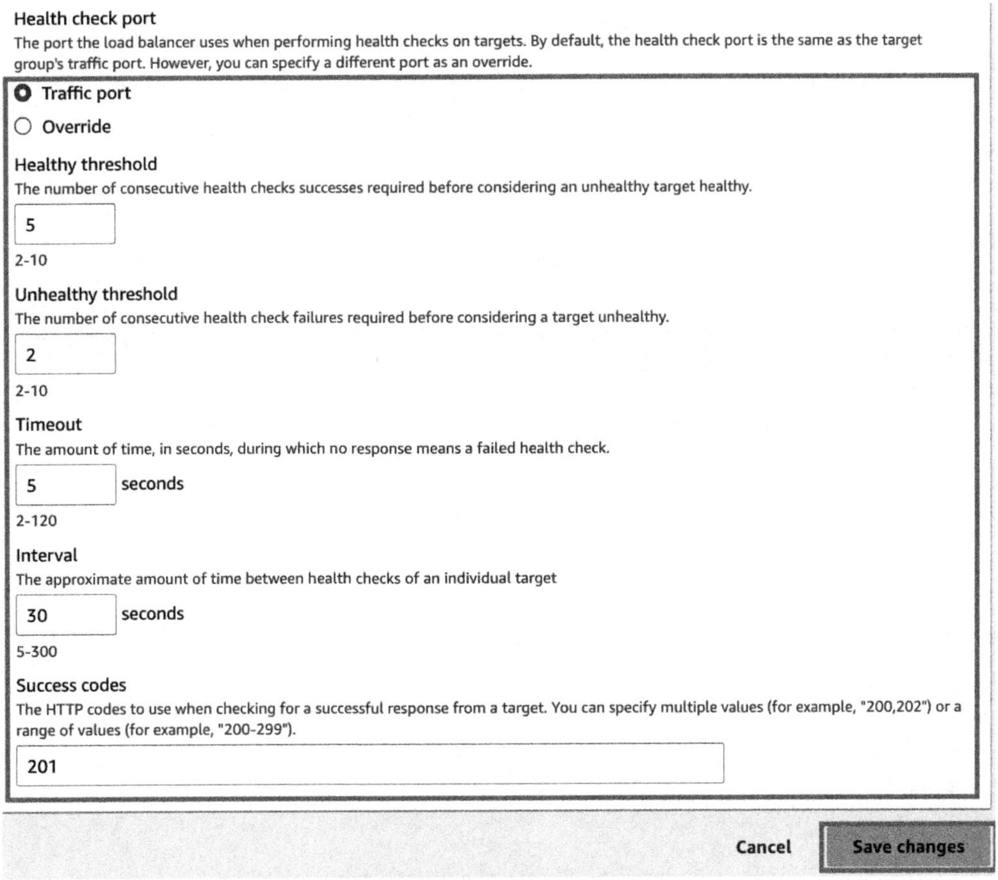

Setting up and configuring an NLB   155

Health check port
The port the load balancer uses when performing health checks on targets. By default, the health check port is the same as the target group's traffic port. However, you can specify a different port as an override.

● Traffic port
○ Override

Healthy threshold
The number of consecutive health checks successes required before considering an unhealthy target healthy.

`5`

2-10

Unhealthy threshold
The number of consecutive health check failures required before considering a target unhealthy.

`2`

2-10

Timeout
The amount of time, in seconds, during which no response means a failed health check.

`5` seconds

2-120

Interval
The approximate amount of time between health checks of an individual target

`30` seconds

5-300

Success codes
The HTTP codes to use when checking for a successful response from a target. You can specify multiple values (for example, "200,202") or a range of values (for example, "200-299").

`201`

Cancel   **Save changes**

Figure 7.15 – Configuring the target group's health check details

4. **Save changes**: After configuring, make sure you save your health check settings.

By carefully configuring listeners, target groups, and health checks, you can ensure optimal traffic distribution and maximum uptime for your applications. Next, we will learn how to configure an NLB.

Setting up and configuring an NLB

Now that you've become acquainted with the intricacies of ALBs, it's time we turn our attention to their high-performing counterparts: NLBs. An NLB is designed to handle millions of requests per second while maintaining ultra-low latencies. This ensures that your system remains resilient and rapid in responding to new demands. However, to truly unlock their potential, you have to ensure they are configured appropriately. In the following sections, you will understand the various steps involved in setting up an NLB. So, let's delve in and understand the process.

Creating and configuring listeners

Listeners are essential as they wait for new incoming connection requests from clients. They are configured with a protocol and a port for receiving new connections from clients and a destination protocol and port for targets.

Let's dive into the steps for configuration:

1. **Navigate to the Amazon EC2 dashboard**: From the AWS Management Console, open the Amazon EC2 dashboard:

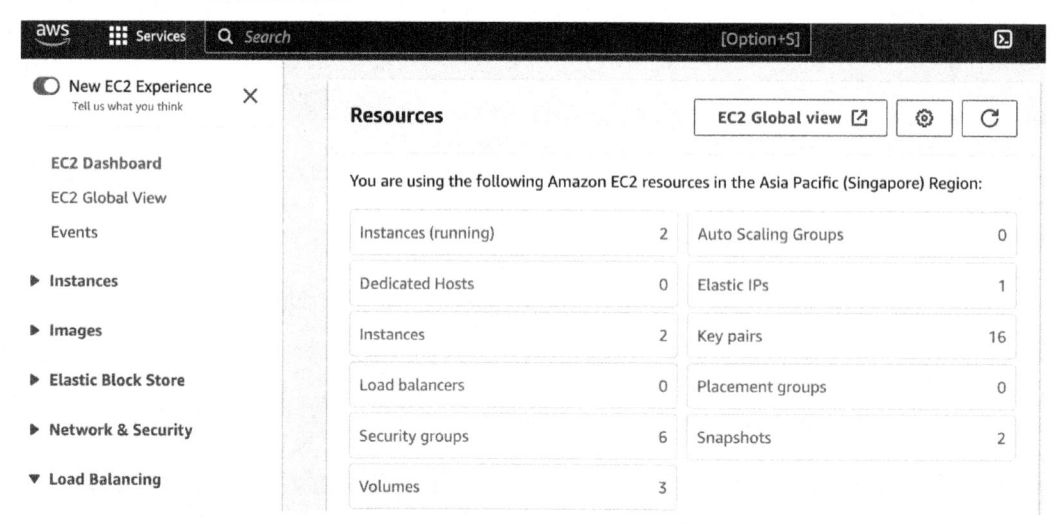

Figure 7.16 – EC2 dashboard landing page

2. **Access the available load balancers**: Under the **Load Balancing** section on the left pane, choose **Load balancers**:

Setting up and configuring an NLB   157

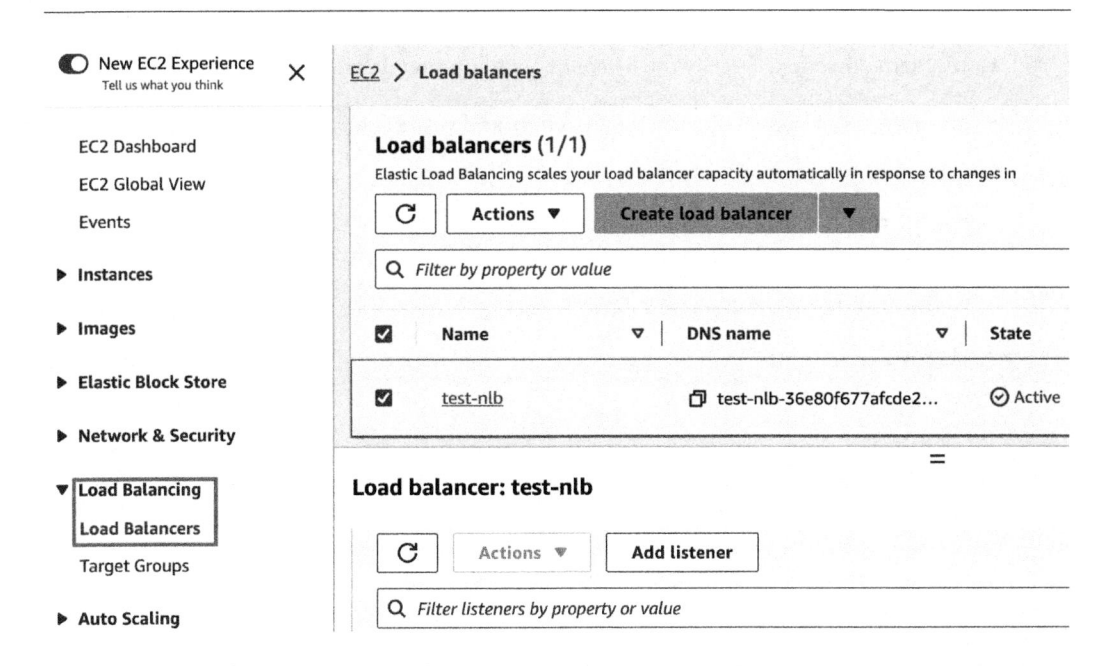

Figure 7.17 – EC2's Load balancers landing page

3. **Choose the NLB:** Click the drop-down icon next to **Create load balancer** and choose **Create Network Load Balancer**:

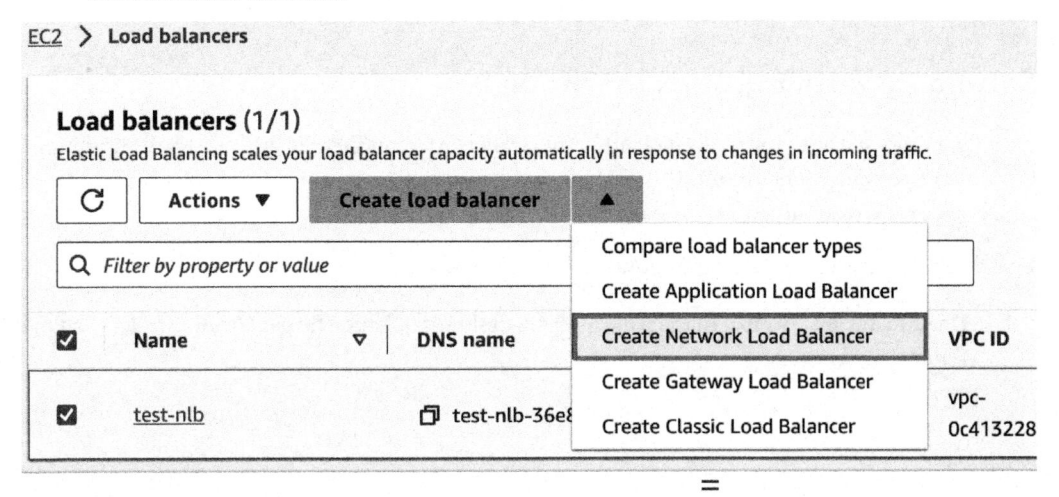

Figure 7.18 – Creating an NLB

4. **Configuring listeners**: Specify the listener's configuration details:

   - From the lower pane, switch to the **Listeners and routing** tab.
   - Click **Add Listener**.
   - For the new listener, select the desired protocol (typically **TCP/UDP** or **TLS**) and specify the port you want to use for client connections.
   - Confirm and save the configuration:

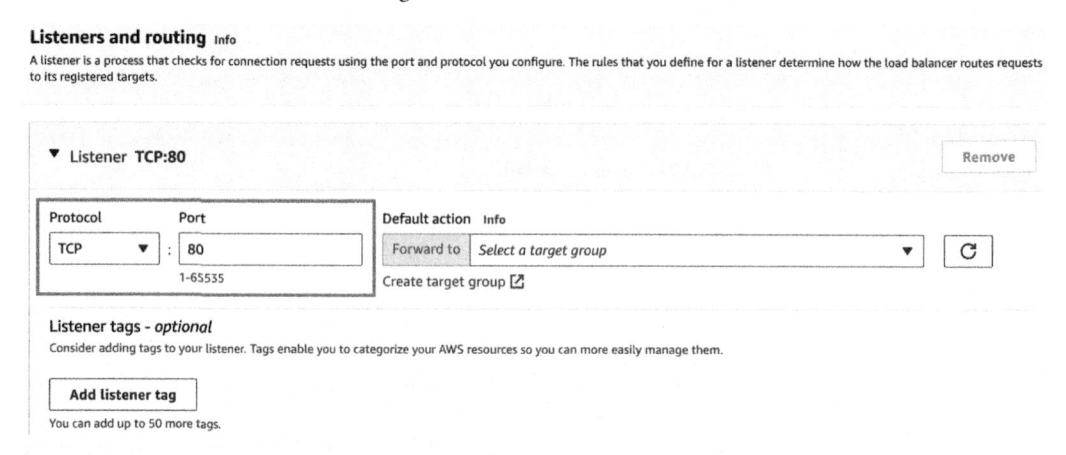

Figure 7.19 – Configuring the load balancer's listener details

Setting up target groups for the NLB

An NLB employs target groups to efficiently route traffic based on their health and availability. Target groups ensure your client's requests find their way to a functioning service, be it an EC2 instance, container, or microservice.

Let's dive into the steps for configuration:

1. **Head to Target Groups**: In the Amazon EC2 dashboard, locate **Target Groups** under the **Load Balancing** section:

Setting up and configuring an NLB   159

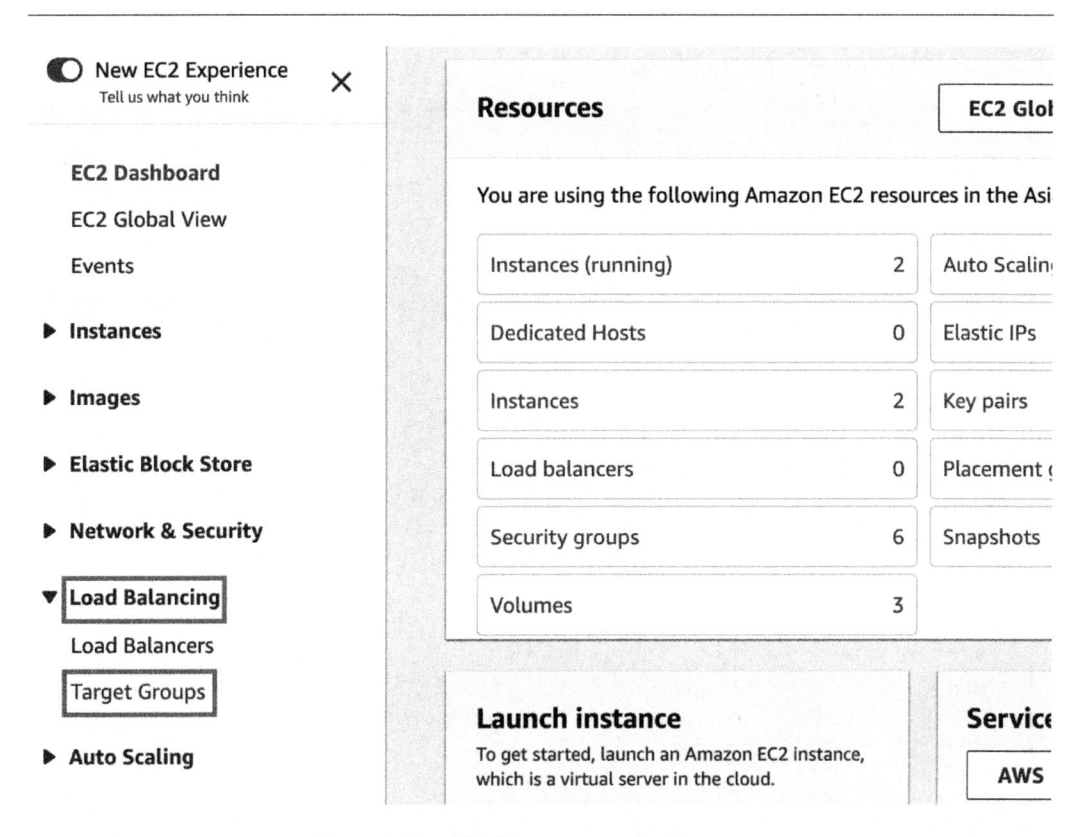

Figure 7.20 – EC2's Target groups landing page

2. **Initiate creation**: Click **Create target group**:

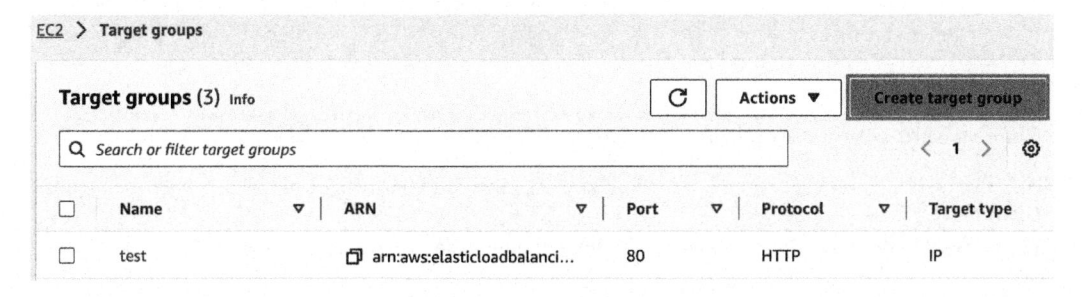

Figure 7.21 – Creating a target group

3. **Configuration**: Specify the necessary configuration details:

    I. Define the target group's name.

    II. Specify the necessary protocol, port, and VPC for your application's requirements.

III. Save the created target group:

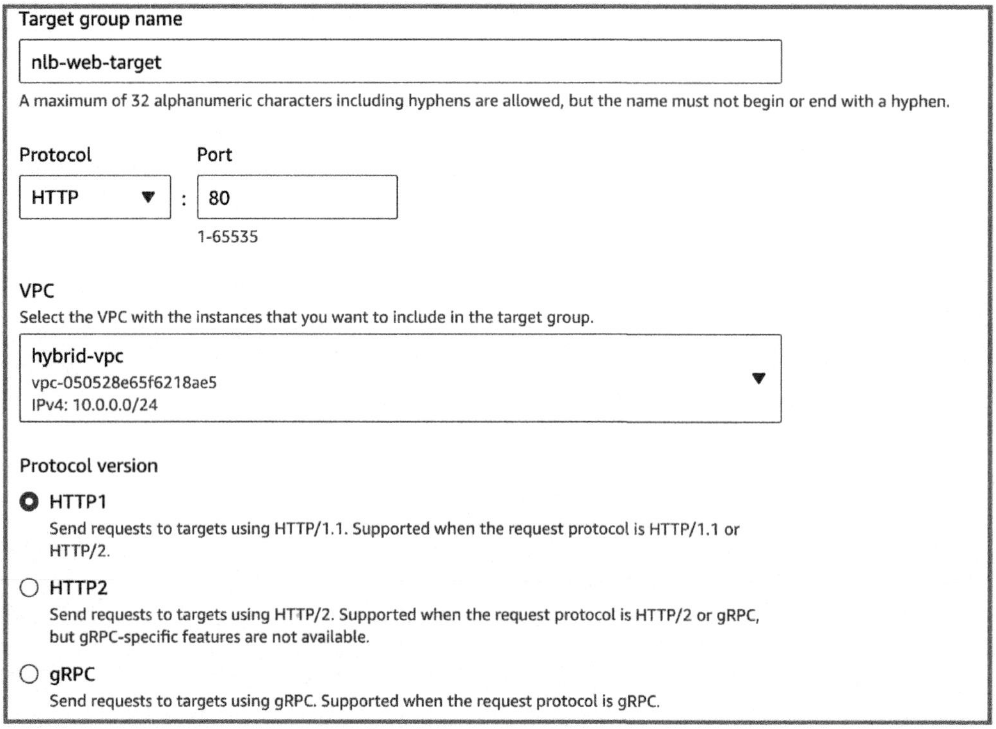

Target group name

nlb-web-target

A maximum of 32 alphanumeric characters including hyphens are allowed, but the name must not begin or end with a hyphen.

Protocol **Port**

HTTP ▼ : 80

1-65535

VPC
Select the VPC with the instances that you want to include in the target group.

hybrid-vpc
vpc-050528e65f6218ae5
IPv4: 10.0.0.0/24

Protocol version

● HTTP1
Send requests to targets using HTTP/1.1. Supported when the request protocol is HTTP/1.1 or HTTP/2.

○ HTTP2
Send requests to targets using HTTP/2. Supported when the request protocol is HTTP/2 or gRPC, but gRPC-specific features are not available.

○ gRPC
Send requests to targets using gRPC. Supported when the request protocol is gRPC.

Figure 7.22 – Configuring the target group's port and protocol details

4. **Association**: Link the target group you've created with the desired NLB by editing the NLB's listener settings:

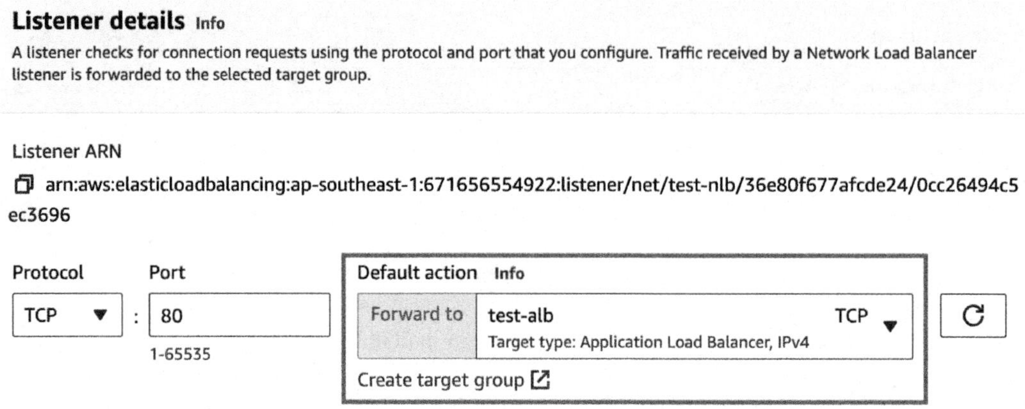

Listener details Info

A listener checks for connection requests using the protocol and port that you configure. Traffic received by a Network Load Balancer listener is forwarded to the selected target group.

Listener ARN

arn:aws:elasticloadbalancing:ap-southeast-1:671656554922:listener/net/test-nlb/36e80f677afcde24/0cc26494c5ec3696

Protocol **Port** **Default action** Info

TCP ▼ : 80   Forward to test-alb TCP ▼
1-65535   Target type: Application Load Balancer, IPv4

Create target group

Figure 7.23 – Configuring the target group's listener details

Configuring health checks for targets

NLB's effectiveness lies in its ability to only route traffic to health targets. Health checks play a pivotal role in determining the target's health and making sure your services remain available to clients.

Let's dive into the steps for configuration:

1. **Access your target group**: Inside the Amazon EC2 dashboard, go to your previously created target group:

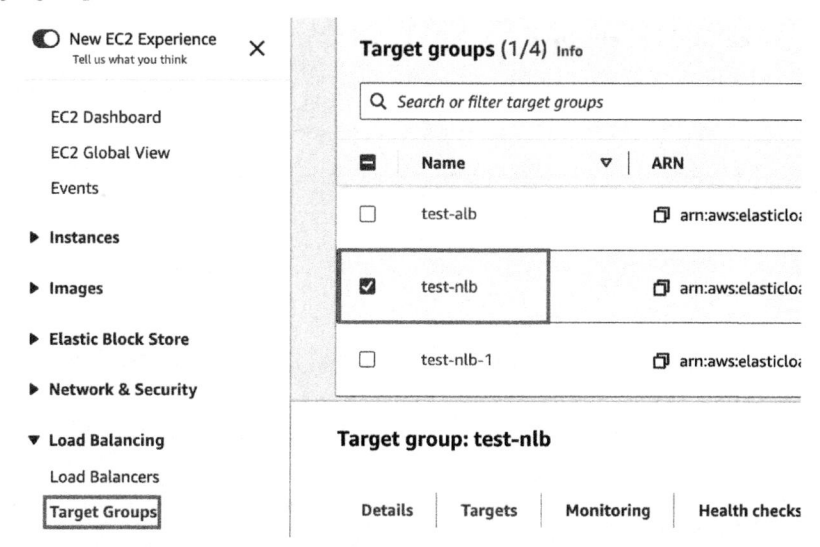

Figure 7.24 – EC2's Target groups landing page

2. **Adjust your health checks**: Specify the health check configuration details by following these steps:

    I. Navigate to the **Health checks** tab.
    II. Click **Edit**:

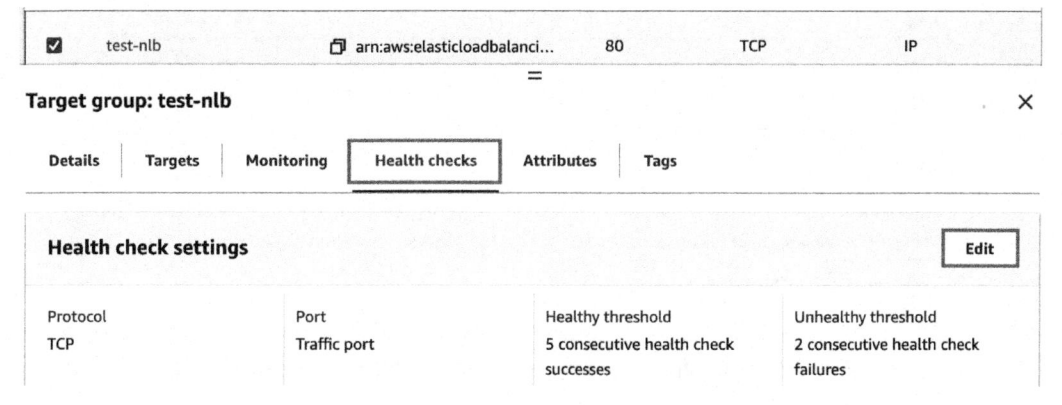

Figure 7.25 – Configuring health checks for the target group

III. Define the appropriate settings for your health checks. This usually includes specifying the protocol and port the NLB will use to verify the health of the registered targets:

Health checks

The associated load balancer periodically sends requests, per the settings below, to the registered targets to test their status.

Health check protocol

TCP ▲
TCP ✓
HTTP
HTTPS

Health check settings

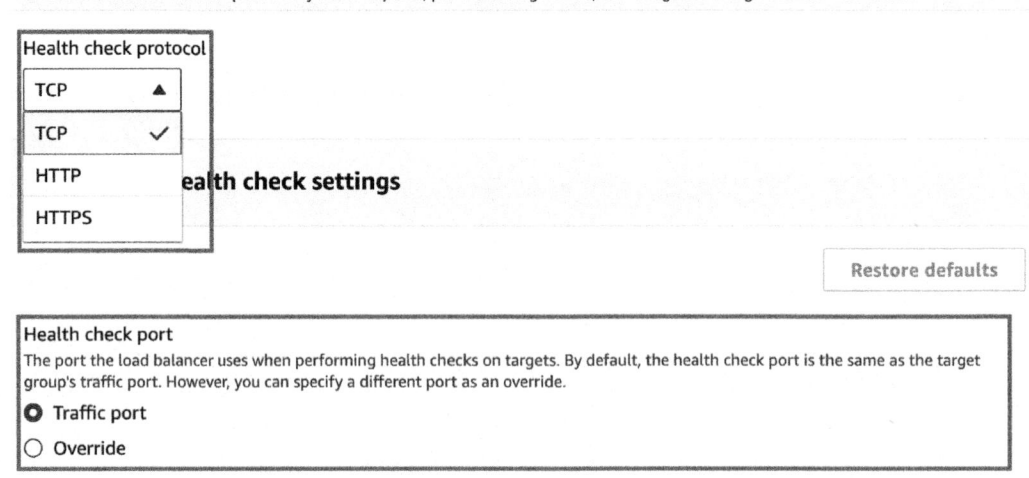

Restore defaults

Health check port
The port the load balancer uses when performing health checks on targets. By default, the health check port is the same as the target group's traffic port. However, you can specify a different port as an override.
● Traffic port
○ Override

Figure 7.26 – Configuring the target group's health check details

IV. Set your thresholds in determining healthy and unhealthy states. This helps the NLB make informed decisions about traffic routing:

Healthy threshold
The number of consecutive health checks successes required before considering an unhealthy target healthy.

5

2-10

Unhealthy threshold
The number of consecutive health check failures required before considering a target unhealthy.

2

2-10

Timeout
The amount of time, in seconds, during which no response means a failed health check.

10   seconds

2-120

Interval
The approximate amount of time between health checks of an individual target

30   seconds

5-300

Figure 7.27 – Configuring the target group's health check thresholds

V. Review your settings for accuracy and save your changes:

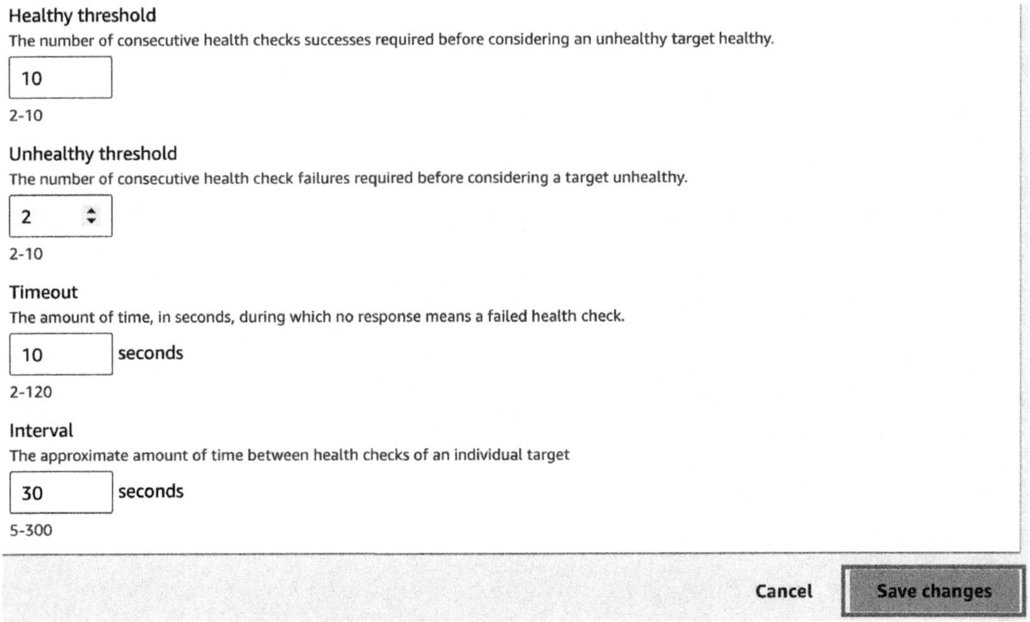

Healthy threshold
The number of consecutive health checks successes required before considering an unhealthy target healthy.

`10`

2-10

Unhealthy threshold
The number of consecutive health check failures required before considering a target unhealthy.

`2`

2-10

Timeout
The amount of time, in seconds, during which no response means a failed health check.

`10` seconds

2-120

Interval
The approximate amount of time between health checks of an individual target

`30` seconds

5-300

Cancel | **Save changes**

Figure 7.28 – Saving the target group's health checks

By carefully executing these steps, your NLB is positioned to efficiently handle and distribute incoming traffic, ensuring your application remains responsive and available. Setting up proper configuration is just another piece of the puzzle.

Load balancer best practices

Just having the right tools isn't enough in the constantly evolving digital landscape – the mastery lies in how you use them. The AWS ELB, for instance, isn't merely about distributing incoming traffic. When configured correctly and by implementing the best practices, it becomes a powerful shield, safeguarding your application's performance and resilience. Let's dive in and explore these practices that drive excellence.

Cross-zone load balancing

Cross-zone load balancing enables even distribution of incoming traffic across multiple Availability Zones, enhancing fault tolerance and application availability. Let's understand why it matters and how to implement using ELB.

Why it matters

Cross-zone load balancing facilitates distributing your application traffic evenly across all your backend instances. This will allow you to prevent overloading a single zone, ensuring that even if one of your zones experiences issues, your application remains available.

How to implement it

To implement this, you will need to do the following:

1. By default, ALBs have cross-zone load balancing enabled. For NLBs, however, you will need to modify this later upon creation:

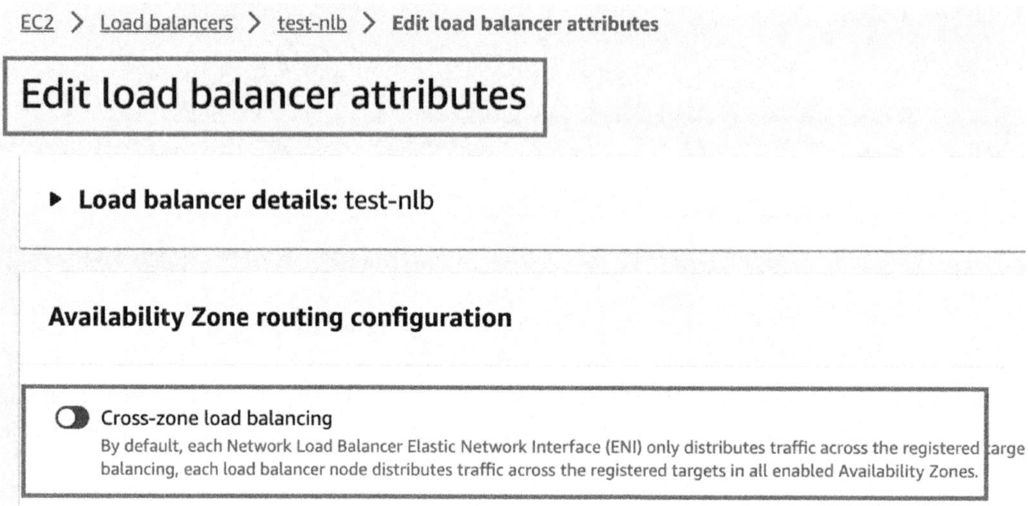

EC2 > Load balancers > test-nlb > **Edit load balancer attributes**

| **Edit load balancer attributes** |

▶ **Load balancer details:** test-nlb

Availability Zone routing configuration

◯ Cross-zone load balancing
By default, each Network Load Balancer Elastic Network Interface (ENI) only distributes traffic across the registered arge balancing, each load balancer node distributes traffic across the registered targets in all enabled Availability Zones.

Figure 7.29 – Configuring your load balancer's attributes

2. Ensure that your application instances are evenly distributed across Availability Zones to benefit from this.

SSL/TLS offloading

SSL offloading describes the process of delegating the process of encrypting/decrypting SSL traffic to a dedicated hardware/software unit. Let's understand why it matters to offload SSL/TLS via ELB and how to implement offloading it.

Why it matters

Securing your application traffic is non-negotiable, but why do you want to tax your backend servers with the computational overhead of encryption? You can simply offload this task to ELB to free up your backend servers to focus on delivering the content.

How to implement it

To implement, you will need to do the following:

1. Set up your listeners on your ELB to listen to HTTPS (secured) traffic:

Listener details

A listener checks for connection requests using the protocol and port that you configure. The default action and any additional rules that you create determine how the Application Load Balancer routes requests to its registered targets.

Listener ARN

arn:aws:elasticloadbalancing:ap-southeast-1:671656554922:listener/app/test-alb/5f3f7c3f1ed9a393/ff078733e3f520c4

Protocol : Port

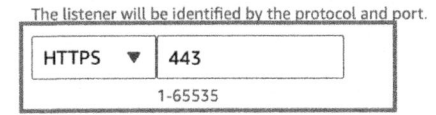

The listener will be identified by the protocol and port.

HTTPS ▼	443
	1-65535

Figure 7.30 – Configuring SSL termination for listeners

2. Upload your SSL/TLS certificates to AWS Certificate Manager and associate them with your load balancer:

Secure listener settings Info

Security policy

Your load balancer uses a Secure Socket Layer (SSL) negotiation configuration, known as a security policy, to negotiate SSL connections with clients.

ELBSecurityPolicy-TLS13-1-2-2021-06 (recommended) ▼

Compare security policies

Default SSL/TLS certificate

The certificate used if a client connects without SNI protocol, or if there are no matching certificates. This certificate will automatically be added to your listener certificate list.

| From ACM ▼ | Select a certificate ▼ | C |

Request new ACM certificate

Figure 7.31 – Configuring SSL certificates for listeners

3. Configure your backend instances so that they can handle unencrypted traffic while your ELB manages to secure external traffic.

Monitoring and logging

Monitoring and logging are crucial for tracking application performance, identifying potential issues, and ensuring optimal performance and security for your load-balanced applications. Let's understand why it matters and how to implement it in ELB.

Why it matters

In the vast digital landscape, it is easy to miss anomalies or potential issues. However, by keeping a vigilant eye on your traffic and ELB's performance, you can preemptively address the concerns before they escalate.

How to implement it

To implement it, you will need to do the following:

1. Make use of the available monitoring metrics from CloudWatch for your ELB, such as **RequestCount**, **UnHealthyCount**, and **HTTPCode_ELB_5XX**, to gain invaluable performance insights.
2. Edit your load balancer attributes to enable access logs for your load balancer. These logs provide detailed information about requests, helping you analyze traffic patterns and troubleshoot issues:

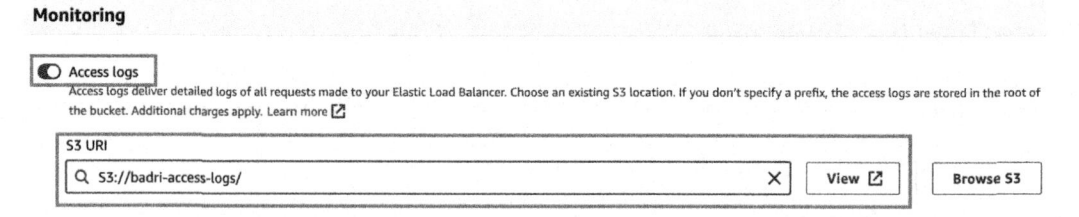

Figure 7.32 – Activating access logs for your load balancer

As we wrap up this section, remember that in the vast digital landscape, it is often fine-tuning that sets apart the good from the great. Adapt these practices and let your ELB stand as a testament to your commitment to excellence.

In the next section, we will look at Auto Scaling groups, which help ensure your resources scale and respond dynamically as per the demands of your applications.

Introduction to Auto Scaling groups

The dynamic nature of the internet requires our application to be as fluid as the tides, adjusting and adapting to ever-changing demands. This is where AWS's **Auto Scaling groups** (**ASG**) come into play. ASG seamlessly aligns with ELB to ensure that your application meets the ongoing demand without any hitches and makes your application grow or shrink based on demand. Let's dive deeper to understand these concepts.

Understanding the concept and components of ASG

Think of ASG as your digital traffic manager, automatically adjusting the number of EC2 instances you are running, based on real-time demand. Here's a bit more information on how it works:

- **Desired capacity**: This metric defines the number of EC2 instances that ASG should maintain at all times. If an instance fails, ASG brings up another one to take its place, keeping the overall capacity consistent.
- **Launch template/configurations**: This is a blueprint that ASG uses to launch EC2 instances. This blueprint contains information such as which AMI to use, the instance type, and the key pair.
- **Scaling policies**: These are the rules you set to allow ASG to decide when and how it should scale. For example, if CPU usage crosses the 80% threshold for 10 minutes, add two more instances.
- **Cooldown periods**: After the ASG initiates a scaling action, it waits a bit to let things stabilize. The duration of the *cooling period* determines how long ASG should wait to initiate another scaling action. This ensures ASG doesn't go on a scaling spree.
- **Health checks**: ASG continuously monitors the health of its scaling targets. If any of them fail, ASG replaces them automatically.

With these core components in play, ASG maintains a perfect balance of resources for your application.

Use cases and benefits

ASG doesn't provide simple scaling, but it does deliver smart scaling solutions. Here's why businesses rely on its usage:

- **Cost-efficiency**: Instead of over-provisioning and paying for unused resources, ASG lets you pay only for what you use. When the demand is low, ASG scales down the resources, cutting costs.
- **High availability**: If an instance goes down in one Availability Zone, ASG brings up another one seamlessly without your end users being aware of this.
- **Smooth deployments**: If you are planning to roll out new features, ASG can divert traffic to new instances while the old instances are updated, ensuring zero downtime.
- **Integration with load balancers**: ASG can be paired up with a load balancer. This ensures the traffic is distributed evenly across instances. As more instances are added or removed in ASG, ELB takes note of it and adjusts accordingly.

Here are some real-world scenarios for the usage of ASG:

- **e-commerce websites**: Imagine the traffic spikes on Black Friday or Cyber Monday sales. ASG can automatically scale up instances, ensuring that the website doesn't crash and transactions go smoothly.
- **Launch events or webinars**: When you are launching a new product or hosting a massive webinar, you can't always predict the traffic. ASG can be put in place to handle the ongoing demand seamlessly.

In essence, ASG keeps your apps and service like a well-oiled machine, irrespective of user load or any unforeseen hiccups. With a solid grasp of its concepts and benefits, let's delve into the nitty-gritty details of configuring and managing ASG.

Configuring and managing ASG

Now that we have grasped the fundamental concepts of AWS's ASG, it's high time we dive deep into its functionalities and learn how to configure and manage it for optimal performance. We will begin this journey by understanding the foundational building blocks, such as launch templates and scaling policies, and then progress into concepts such as life cycle hooks, logging, and monitoring.

Launch templates

Launch templates are the backbone of your EC2 instance deployment within ASG. They superseded the deprecated launch configurations, offering enhanced flexibility and versioning capabilities. Consider launch templates as blueprints, detailing the specifications for instances that will be automatically deployed by ASG.

With this understanding in context, let's explore the features of launch templates:

- **Versioning**: Launch templates allow us to create different versions. This feature comes in particularly handy when you want to update instance specifications without disturbing the currently deployed instances. With versioning, you can maintain legacy setups while rolling out new configurations simultaneously.
- **Override capability**: Launch templates offer a holistic configuration for instances. However, there are times when you will need to update certain parameters for a specific deployment. In such a case, you can still simply override the individual settings for that particular launch instead of creating a whole new template.
- **Simplified management**: As launch configurations have been deprecated, managing instances through launch templates streamlines the overall process of handling specifications and managing deployments.

Setting up launch templates

To set up launch templates, you will need to do the following:

1. **Access the AWS console**: Navigate to the Amazon EC2 dashboard and look for **Launch Templates** under **Instances**:

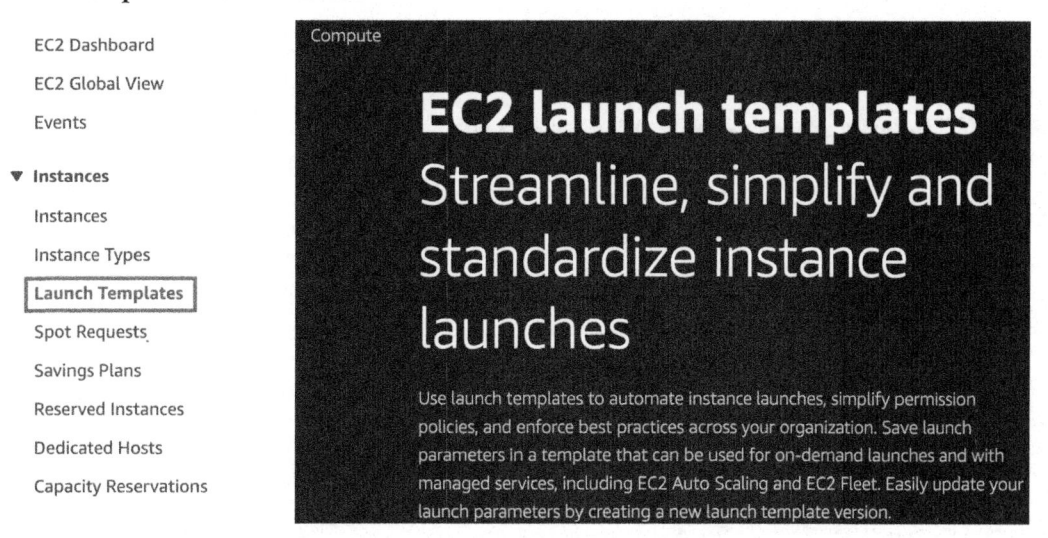

Figure 7.33 – EC2's Launch Templates landing page

2. **Begin the creation process**: Select **Create launch template**:

Figure 7.34 – Creating a launch template

3. Specify your instance details and click **Create launch template**:

- **AMI selection**: Choose the appropriate AMI that will act as the base for your instance.
- **Instance type**: Decide on the size and capability of your instance based on your application's needs.
- **Storage details**: Define how much and what type of storage should be attached to the instance.
- **IAM roles**: If your instance needs specific permissions, associate the appropriate IAM role.
- **Security groups**: Security groups act as a crucial feature in determining the accessibility of your instance. Set up security groups so that they act as a virtual firewall, allowing only permitted traffic to go in and out of your instance:

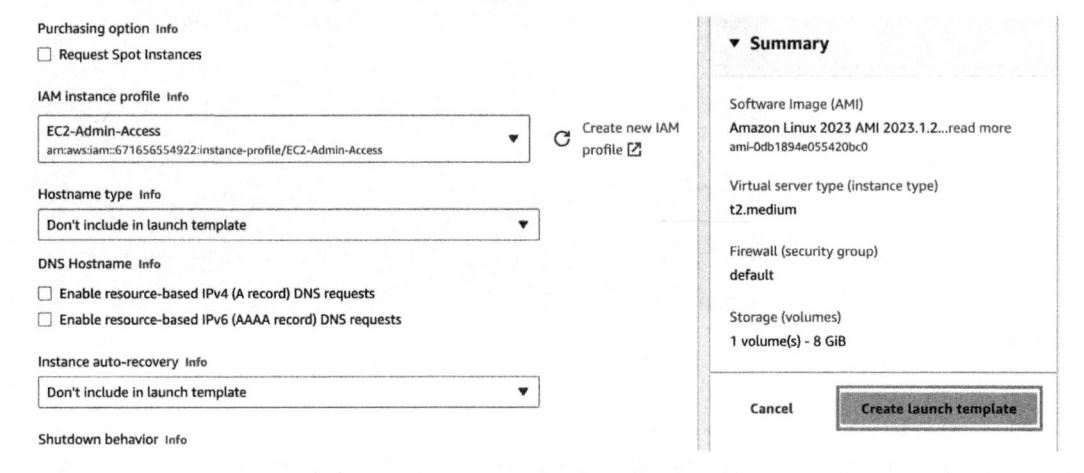

Figure 7.35 – Creating a launch template

- **Version management**: Upon creating the launch template, you will see the default version (that is, No:1). However, as you update or modify the template, ensure you are creating a new version. This way, the history and the progression of configurations remain traceable:

Launch template ID	Launch template name	Default version
lt-0be0c0e6626b60ab6	webapp-template	1

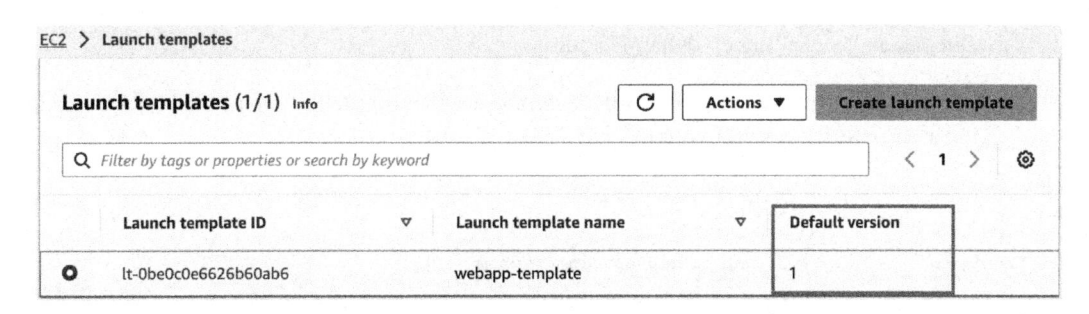

Figure 7.36 – Verifying the created launch template

With launch templates in place, you will set the foundation for automated and scalable deployments via ASG. As you confidently deploy instances tailored to your exact application specifications, it is essential to understand how scaling policies are made. Let's navigate to our next section, where we will discuss the scaling policies you can use to determine how your infrastructure adapts to varying demands.

Scaling policies

ASG, while automating deployments, also brings another level of sophistication in adapting to changing infrastructure demands. Having a predefined set of instances is rarely efficient as we can't predict user traffic against our application workloads in real time. Enter **scaling policies**. These policies ensure that you have the right number of instances available to handle the load for your application.

Now, how do you determine *the right number*? AWS offers three primary scaling policies to cater to varying needs: *dynamic scaling*, *predictive scaling*, and *scheduled scaling*. Each approach has its own distinct advantage and use case. Let's start with the most commonly used scheduling policy of the trio: dynamic scaling.

Dynamic scaling

The fundamental premise of **dynamic scaling** is *real-time responsiveness*. By monitoring specified CloudWatch metrics such as CPU utilization or network I/O, dynamic scaling automatically adjusts the number of instances based on real-time demand.

By defining thresholds, dynamic scaling automatically scales up (adding instances) and scales down (removing instances) instances and ensures that you are never over-provisioned during lulls or under-provisioned during spikes.

Let's dive in and explore setting up dynamic scaling:

1. **Access the AWS Management Console**: Begin by heading over to the Amazon EC2 dashboard. Under **Auto Scaling**, select your desired ASG:

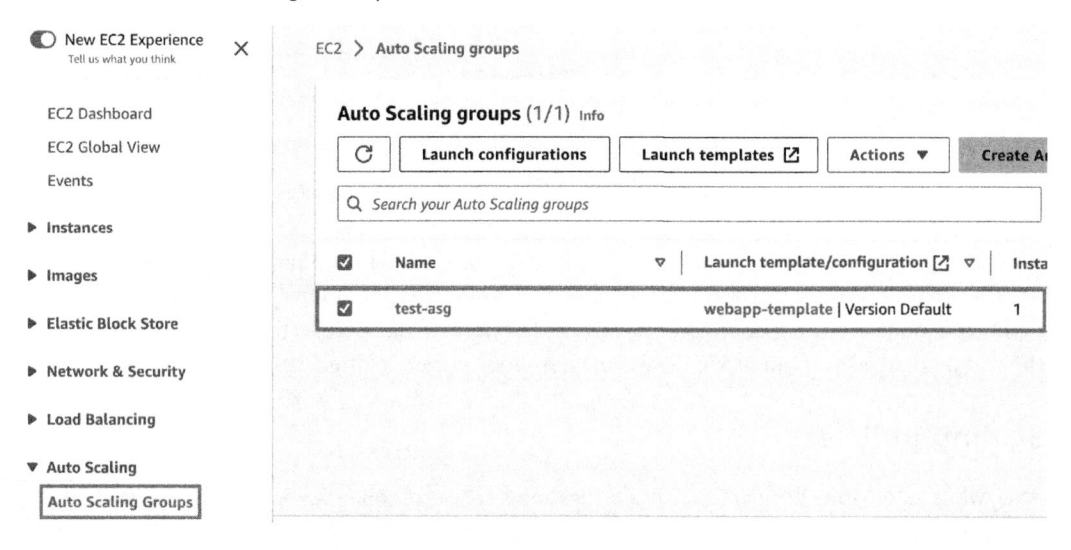

Figure 7.37 – EC2's ASG landing page

2. **Specify the scaling policy**: Click on the **Automatic Scaling** tab and select **Create dynamic scaling policy**:

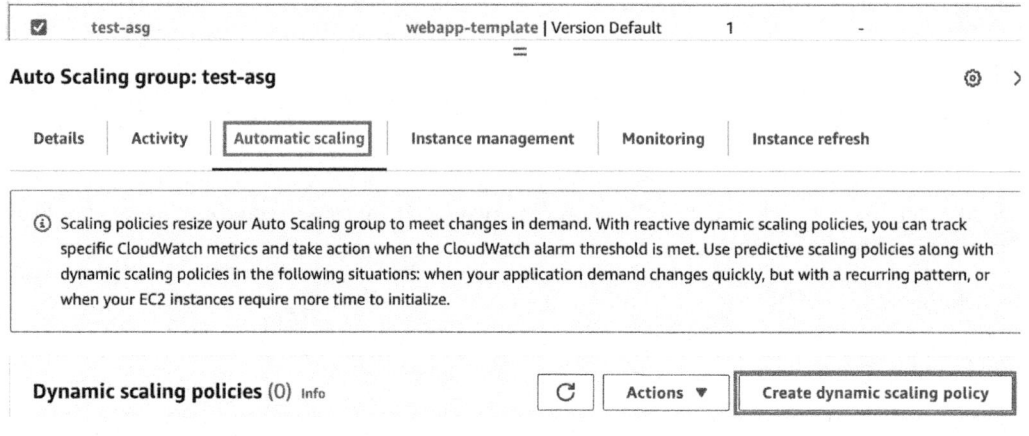

Figure 7.38 – Defining a dynamic scaling policy

3. **Choose a metric**: Opt for a CloudWatch metric. CPU utilization is a common starting point, but depending on your application, you might consider other metrics, such as network traffic or request count.

4. **Set thresholds**: Define thresholds to indicate when the scaling action should take place.
5. **Configure the warmup duration**: Optionally, specify the warmup duration in seconds to specify the number of seconds it takes for the newly launched instance to warm up.
6. **Review and implement**: Double-check your configuration, ensuring your thresholds make sense for your application. Once you are satisfied, confirm and implement the policy:

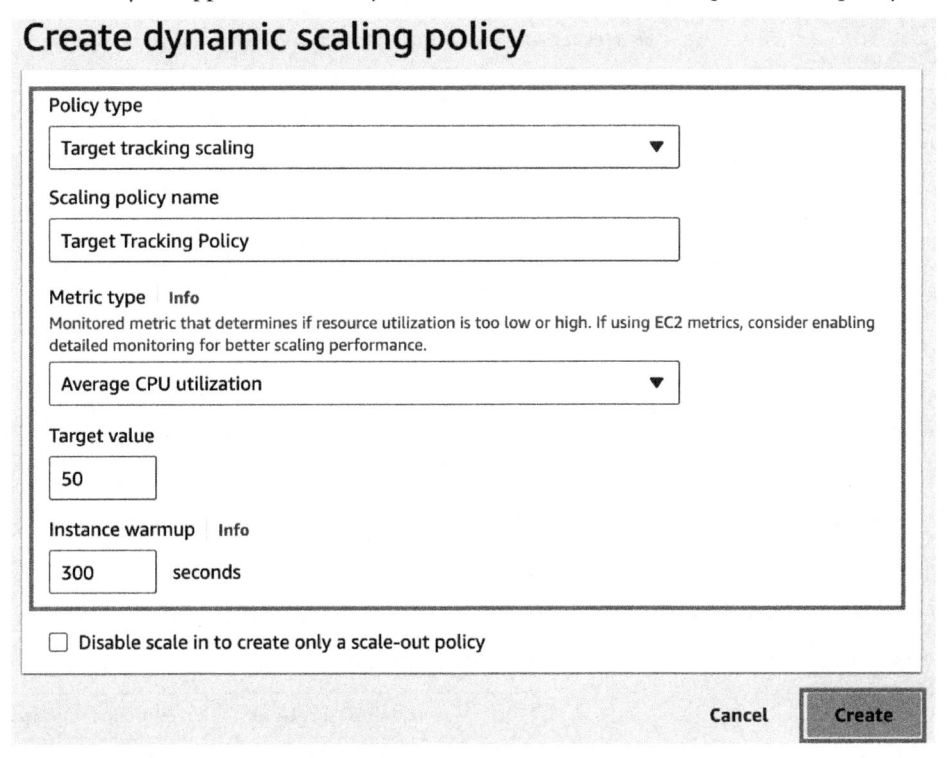

Figure 7.39 – Configuring the dynamic scaling policy

Dynamic scaling allows you to keep your infrastructure responsive. For a deeper dive, consider exploring step scaling and simple scaling policies as part of dynamic scaling. Next, let's see how predictive and scheduled scaling can forecast and plan for your demands.

Predictive scaling

In our digital age, traffic spikes don't always come as a surprise (for example, traffic demand on Black Friday sale for an e-commerce application). Thanks to the introduction of analytical tools and past data, we can now predict when they might occur. Enter **predictive scaling**, a mechanism that's designed to foresee your infrastructure's demand based on historical data, ensuring your resources are positioned and ready, even before the actual surge hits. It is like having a crystal ball in hand that allows your applications to seamlessly handle the incoming flood of requests, turning potential challenges into smooth operations.

Let's dive in and explore setting up predictive scaling:

1. **Access the AWS Management Console**: Head over to the EC2 service:

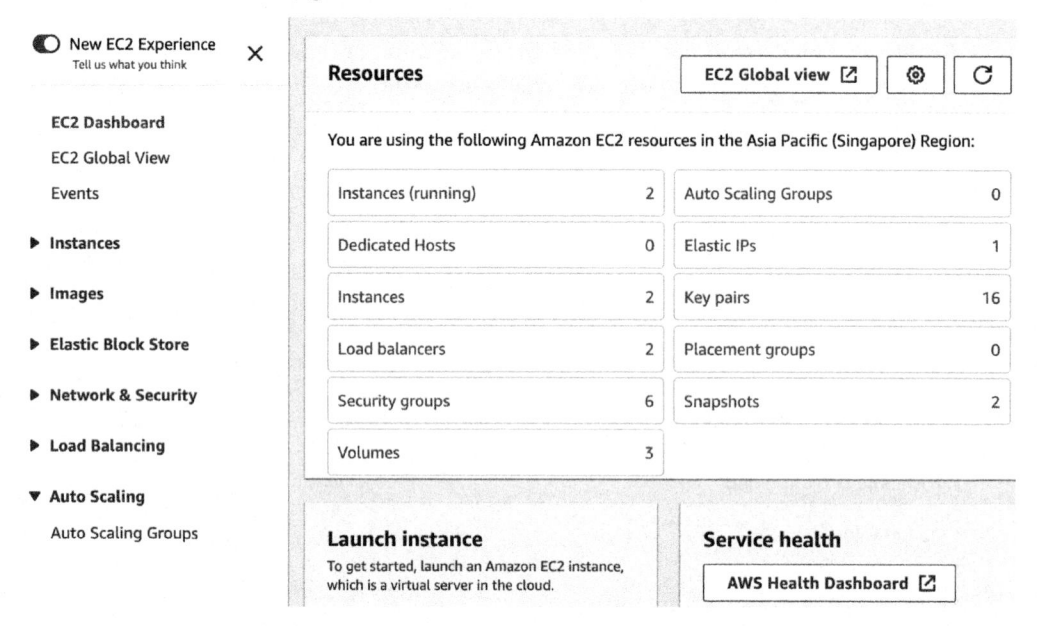

Figure 7.40 – The EC2 dashboard

2. **Navigate to ASG**: Find the ASG you want to apply predictive scaling:

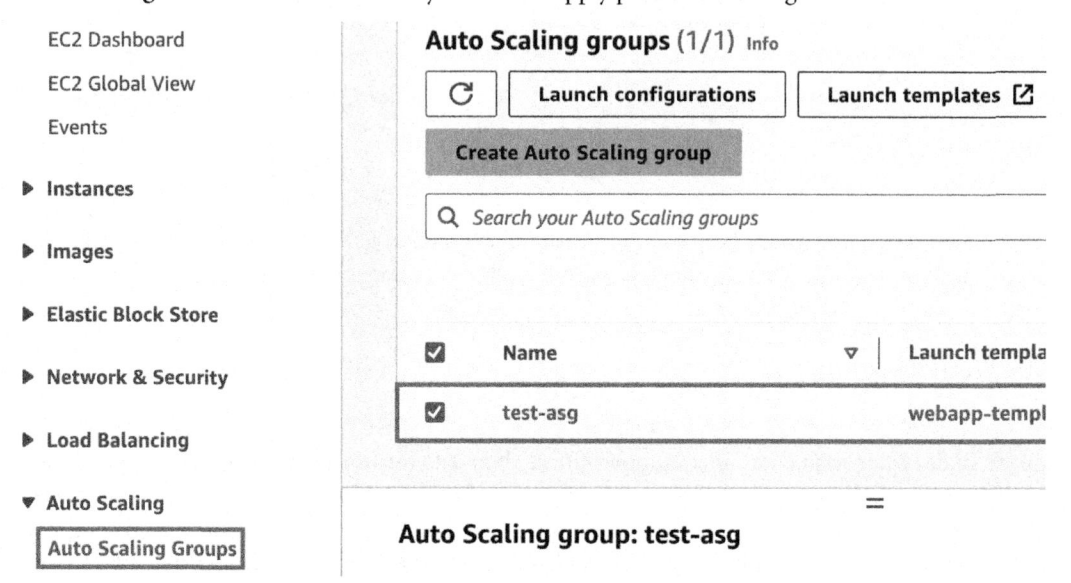

Figure 7.41 – EC2's ASG landing page

3. **Create a scaling policy**: Click on **Automatic Scaling** and choose **Create predictive scaling policy**:

☑	Name ▽	Launch template/configuration ▽	Instances ▽	Status ▽
☑	test-asg	webapp-template | Version Default	1	-

Auto Scaling group: test-asg

Predictive scaling policies (0) Info — Actions ▼ — Create predictive scaling policy

Evaluation period

Evaluation based on 2 days ▼

Name ▽	Metric pair	Forecast and scale ▽	Recommendation ▼

Figure 7.42 – Defining predictive scaling policy

4. **Define the metrics**: AWS uses CloudWatch to track and predict the required metrics. Make sure CloudWatch has been gathering data against your resources for some time to make accurate predictions:

Metrics and target utilization Info

Metrics

There are two metrics for predictive scaling. One metric tells the policy about the load your application has been under. The other metric and the target utilization determine the overall average utilization to target.

CPU utilization ▼

Target utilization

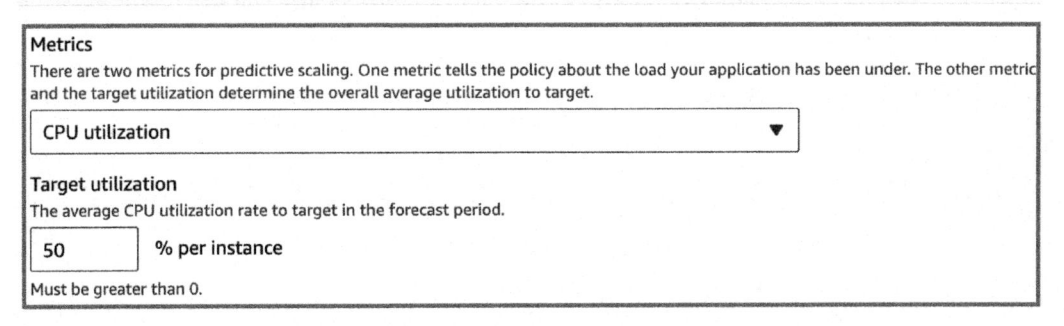

The average CPU utilization rate to target in the forecast period.

50   % per instance

Must be greater than 0.

Figure 7.43 – Configuring metrics for predictive scaling

5. **Adjust the forecasting parameters**: Specify how much in advance you want to scale (for example, 1 hour before the predicted traffic) and indicate if you want to buffer maximum capacity above the forecasted capacity:

Additional scaling settings - *optional*

Pre-launch instances   Info

Control the time when new instances are launched to ensure that they are ready to handle traffic. The scaling action will start earlier than the time in the hourly load forecast by this amount of time.

[5]   [minutes ▼]

Minimum: 0, Maximum: 60

Max capacity behavior   Info

Choose whether to override maximum capacity when the forecasted capacity is greater than maximum capacity.

☑ **Buffer maximum capacity above the forecasted capacity**

If the forecasted capacity is close to or exceeds the maximum capacity, allow predictive scaling to add capacity as needed beyond what is forecasted by up to the specified percentage. If set to 0, Amazon EC2 Auto Scaling may scale capacity higher than the maximum capacity to equal but not exceed forecast capacity.

[10]   %

Minimum: 0, Maximum: 100

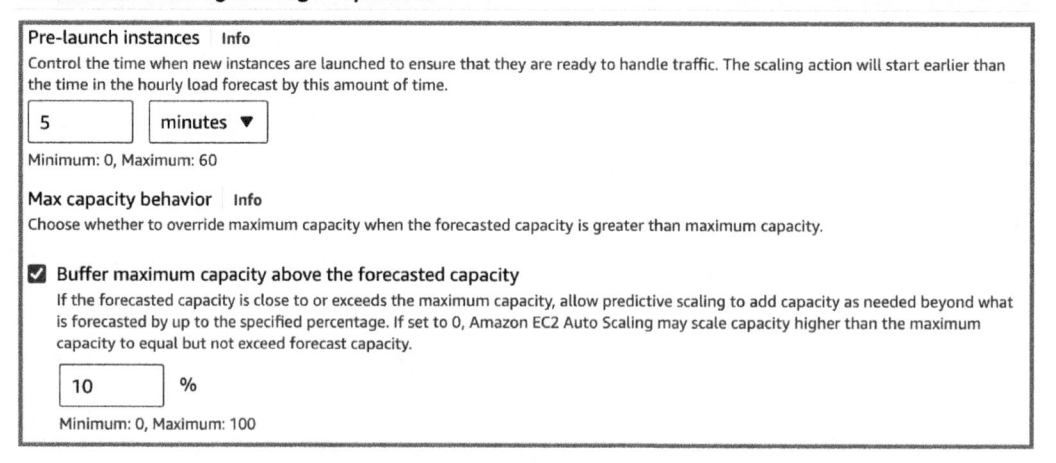

Figure 7.44 – Configuring instances for predictive scaling

6. **Review and implement**: Double-check your configurations. Once you're satisfied, save and apply the policy.

Remember, predictive scaling works best when it has a significant amount of past data to analyze. The more data it can access, the more accurately it can predict, making your infrastructure truly future-ready.

Next, let's explore how scheduled scaling can further refine your infrastructure's responsiveness, ensuring it aligns perfectly with known traffic patterns.

Scheduled scaling

Well, in the rhythm of business operations, some moments are very predictable, such as the rush that's experienced during holiday sales or the evening/weekend spikes observed on a streaming platform. With these patterns, which are more cyclical than random, **scheduled scaling** emerges as the right fit. It empowers businesses to pre-plan scaling activities based on known traffic patterns, ensuring you are always a step ahead and fully prepared for expected demand surges.

Let's dive in and learn how to set up scheduled scaling:

1. **Go to the AWS Management Console**: As usual, navigate to the EC2 service to begin this journey:

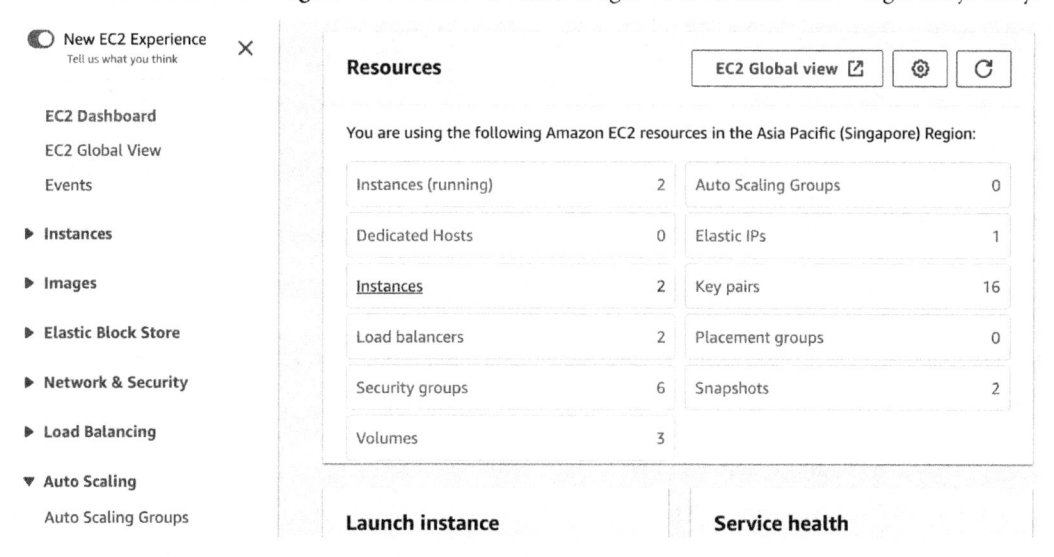

Figure 7.45 – The EC2 dashboard

2. **Navigate to ASG**: Find and select the ASG you wish to integrate with scheduled scaling:

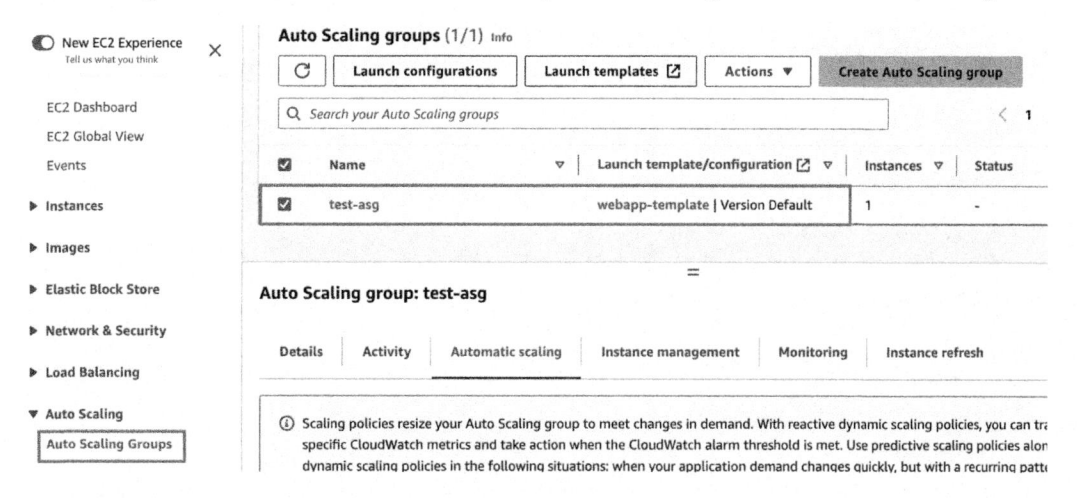

Figure 7.46 – EC2's ASG landing page

3. **Create a scaling policy**: Click on **Automatic Scaling** and select **Create scheduled action**:

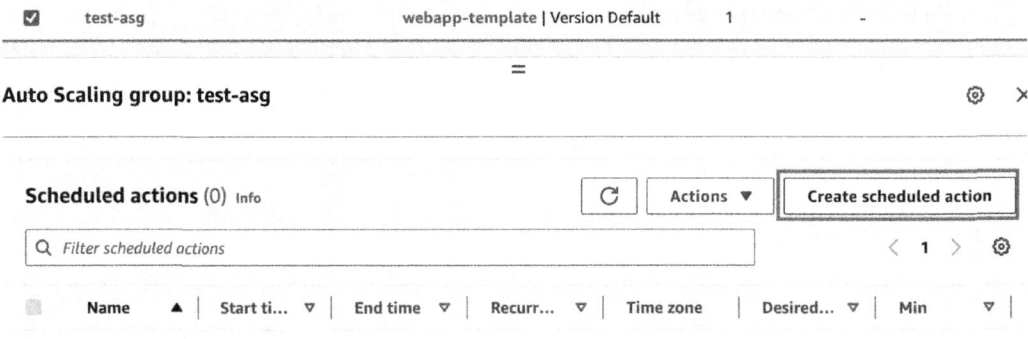

Figure 7.47 – Defining a scheduled scaling action

4. **Set your schedule**: This is where the magic happens. Specify the exact date and time you anticipate the traffic surge. For recurring events, you can even set up cron expressions.
5. **Determine capacity**: Based on your traffic predictions, adjust the desired, maximum, and minimum capacities for the scheduled period.
6. **Review and activate**: Review your settings to ensure everything is accurate. If all looks good, save the policy. With that, you're all set:

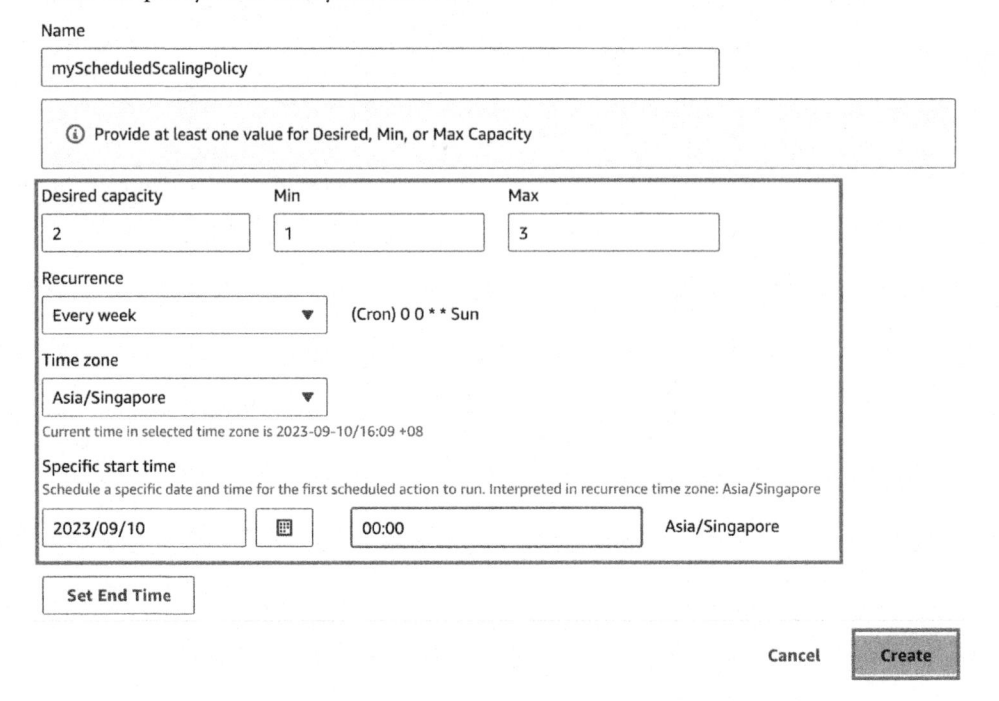

Figure 7.48 – Configuring instance capacity for a scheduled action

By harnessing the power of predictive scaling, you can transform predictions into proactive measures. This guarantees peak performance during crucial business movements.

As we pivot from these scaling strategies, it is crucial to understand the life cycle of instances and how life cycle hooks play an integral role in defining the Auto Scaling process. Let's dive in.

Life cycle hooks

Amid scaling up and down, ensuring each of the instances follows the choreography is vital. This is where the lifecycle hooks come in. **Life cycle hooks** ensure that instances seamlessly transition between states in the ASG, allowing you to execute precise actions at exact moments.

Let's delve deeper into the details of the life cycle hooks.

EC2 instance launching

This life cycle hook allows you to pause the EC2 instance as it's launched and gives you the time to perform custom actions or scripts before it's launched.

Setup

Let's learn how to set up this life cycle hook for an ASG:

1. Head over to the Amazon EC2 dashboard and select your desired ASG:

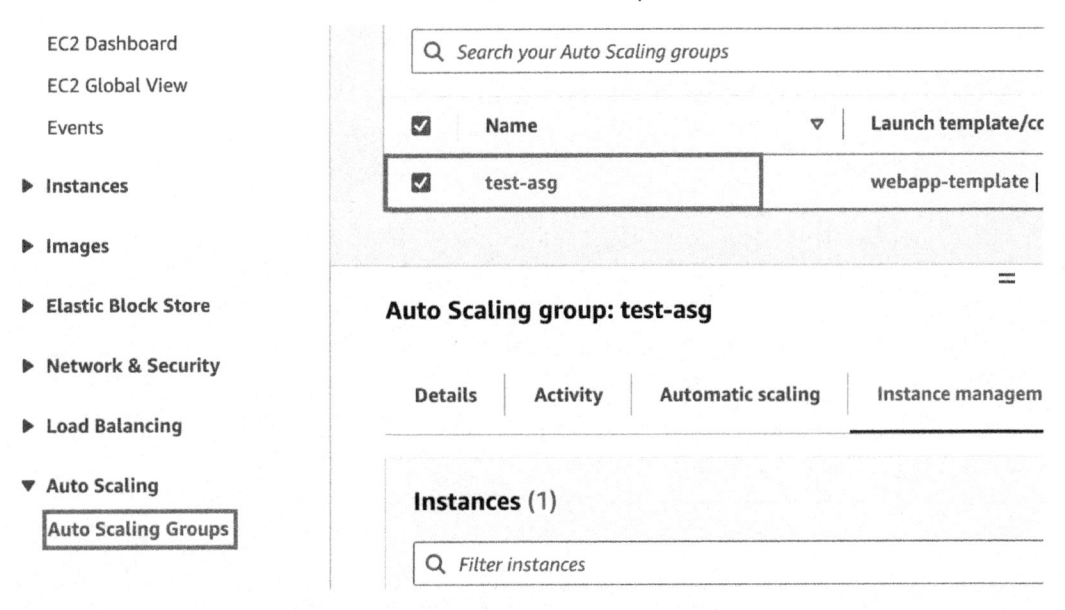

Figure 7.49 – EC2's Auto Scaling group landing page

2. Navigate to **Lifecycle hooks** under **Instance management** and click **Create lifecycle hook**:

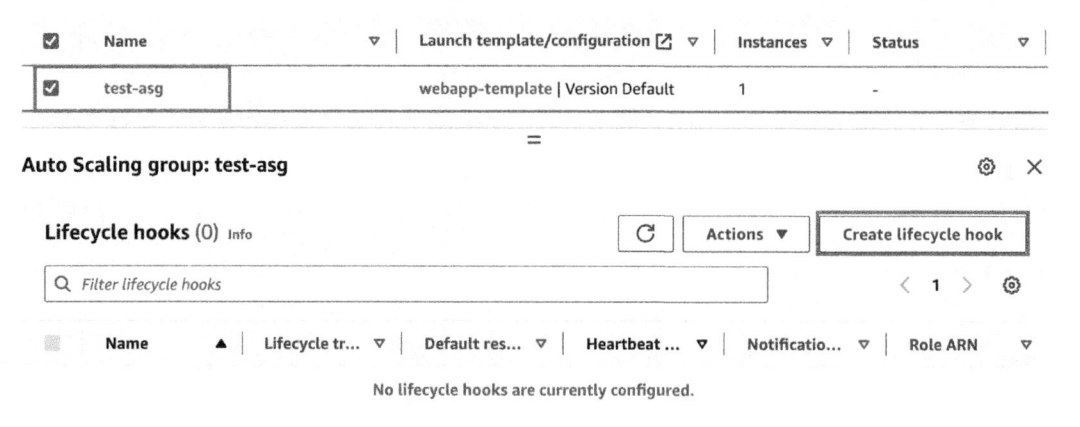

Figure 7.50 – Defining a life cycle hook

3. Define the hook for the **Instance Launch** transition, specify any notification option, and set the heartbeat timeout:

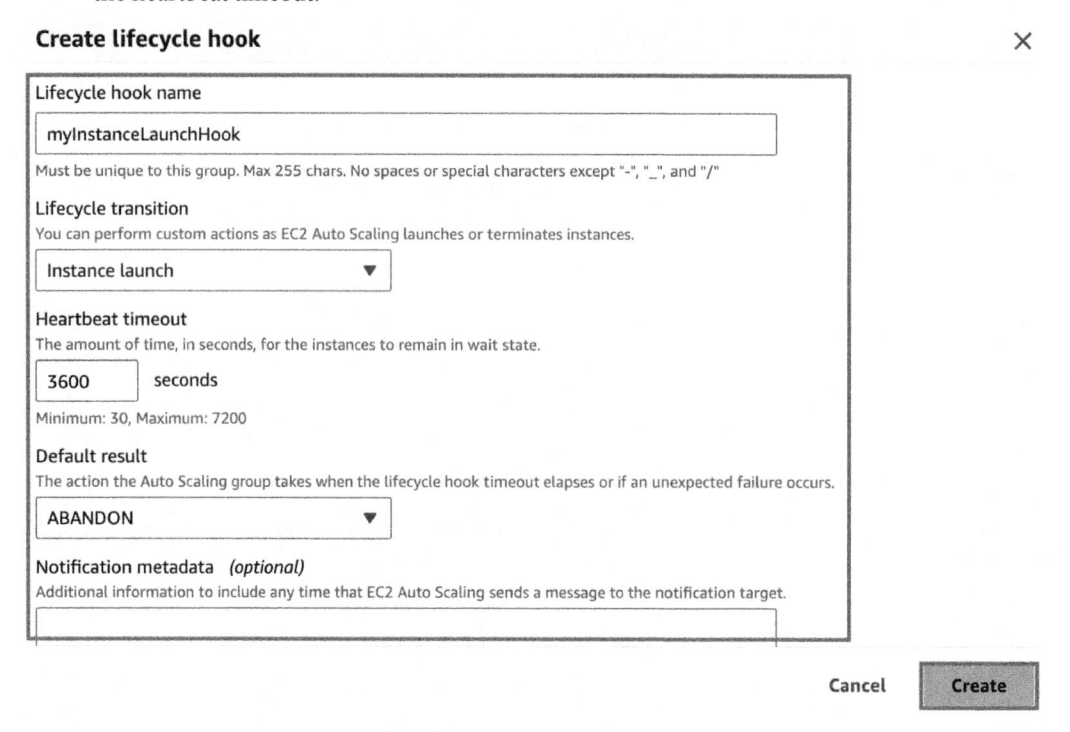

Figure 7.51 – Configuring the life cycle hook's details

EC2 instance terminating

The EC2 instance terminating life cycle hook enables you to pause the termination process of an EC2 instance, providing you with the opportunity to perform custom tasks or finalize operations before the instance is fully shut down.

Setup

Let's learn how to set up this life cycle hook:

1. Follow the same navigation described previously for the **EC2 Instance Launching** hook:

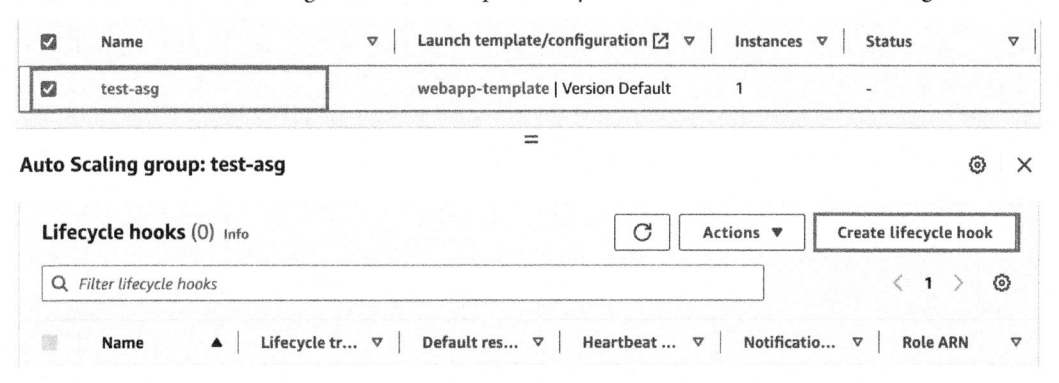

Figure 7.52 – Defining a life cycle hook

2. Configure this hook for the **Instance Terminate** transition, deciding on the notification settings and finalizing the heartbeat timeout:

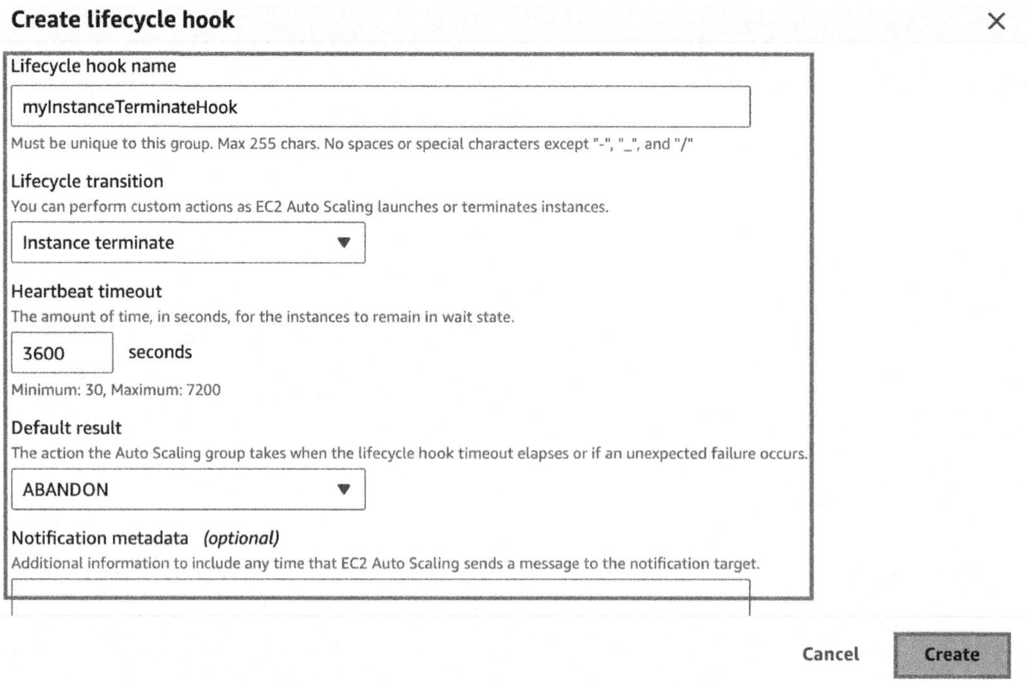

Figure 7.53 – Configuring the life cycle hook's details

Understanding the nuances of life cycle hooks will not only allow you to streamline ASG's operations but also ensure that no valuable action is missed in the rapid pace of scaling. As you gain mastery of launch templates, scaling policies, and life cycle hooks, the next pivotal step will be to harness the combined power of ELB with ASG. By delving into the intricacies of associating target groups, distributing traffic, and setting health checks, you are paving the way for establishing resilient and robust infrastructure. Let's dive in!

Integrating ELB with ASG

Merging the power of ELB with ASG is like creating a dynamic duo that can tackle traffic surges and optimize application performance. This blend not only ensures uninterrupted availability but also ensures fair distribution of traffic across distributed workloads. While the concept sounds intriguing, the real magic lies when you get to understand the nuts and bolts of this integration. So, let's begin our exploration of how to associate target groups with ASGs.

Associating target groups with ASGs

The core aspect of this integration is associating target groups with ASGs. By doing so, we can ensure that as the ASG scales, the newly launched instances are automatically registered with the load balancer and that when the instance gets terminated, they get deregistered automatically, thereby keeping the traffic routing updated and efficient.

Let's learn how to set this up:

1. **Access the AWS Management Console**: Begin by navigating to the Amazon EC2 dashboard. Then, under **Load Balancing**, opt for **Target Groups**:

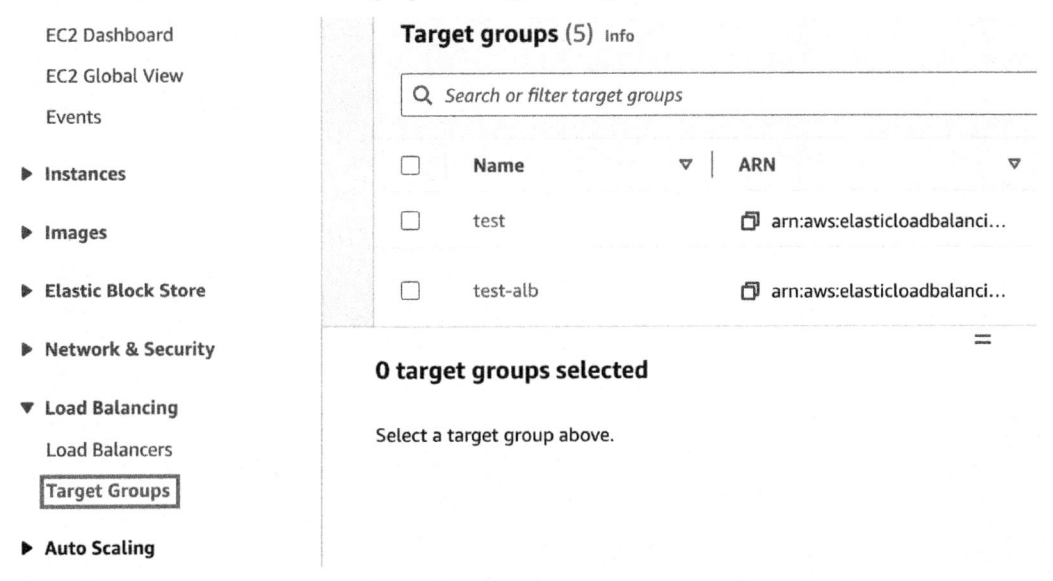

Figure 7.54 – EC2's Target groups landing page

2. **Create a target group**: If you haven't already, create a new target group and specify the protocol, port, and health check settings:

Protocol | Port
HTTP ▼ : 80
1-65535

VPC
Select the VPC with the instances that you want to include in the target group.

vpc-0c4132289f376383b
IPv4: 172.31.0.0/16 ▼

Protocol version

◉ HTTP1
Send requests to targets using HTTP/1.1. Supported when the request protocol is HTTP/1.1 or HTTP/2.

○ HTTP2
Send requests to targets using HTTP/2. Supported when the request protocol is HTTP/2 or gRPC, but gRPC-specific features are not available.

○ gRPC
Send requests to targets using gRPC. Supported when the request protocol is gRPC.

Health checks
The associated load balancer periodically sends requests, per the settings below, to the registered targets to test their status.

Health check protocol

HTTP ▼

Health check path
Use the default path of "/" to ping the root, or specify a custom path if preferred.

/

Up to 1024 characters allowed.

Figure 7.55 – Configuring the port, protocol, and health checks for the target group

3. **Navigate to ASG**: Once your target group has been created, go to the **Auto Scaling Groups** section of the Amazon EC2 dashboard:

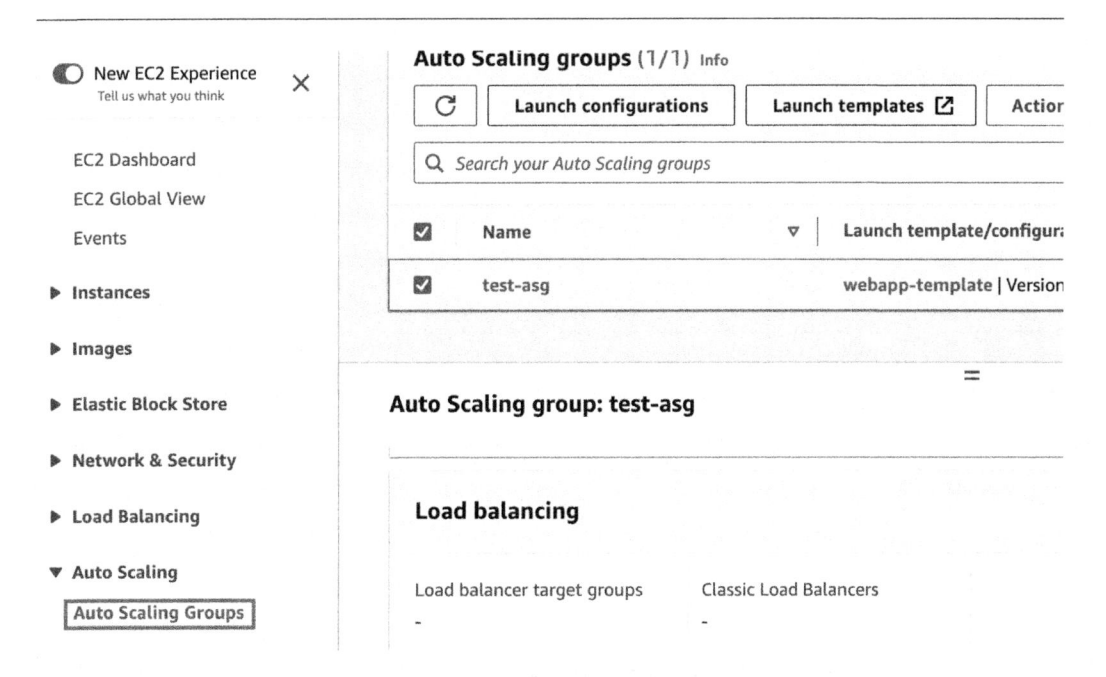

Figure 7.56 – EC2's ASG landing page

4. **Choose or create an ASG**: If you already have an ASG, select it. If not, you can follow the steps provided in the *Introduction to ASG* section to create one. In this case, I am selecting the existing one:

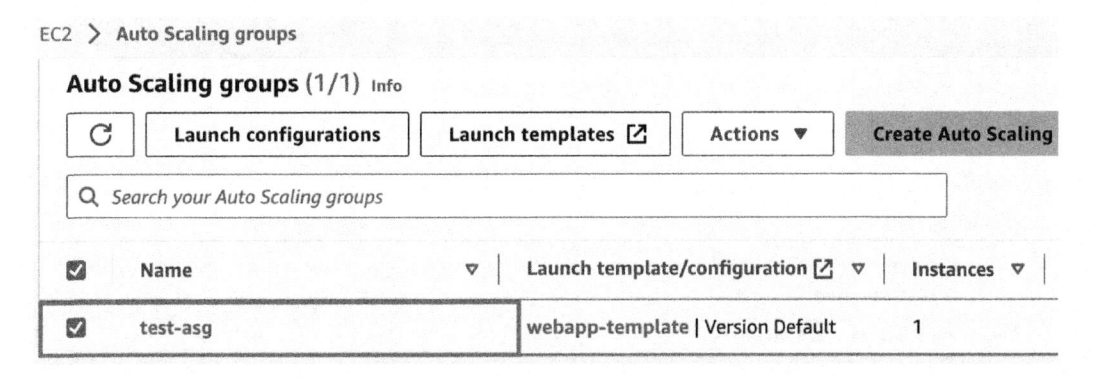

Figure 7.57 – Selecting the desired ASG

5. **Associate the target group**:

   I.   In the **Details** tab of your chosen ASG, scroll down until you see **Load Balancing**. You will find the option to **Edit**. Click on it. Here, you can associate your previously created target group:

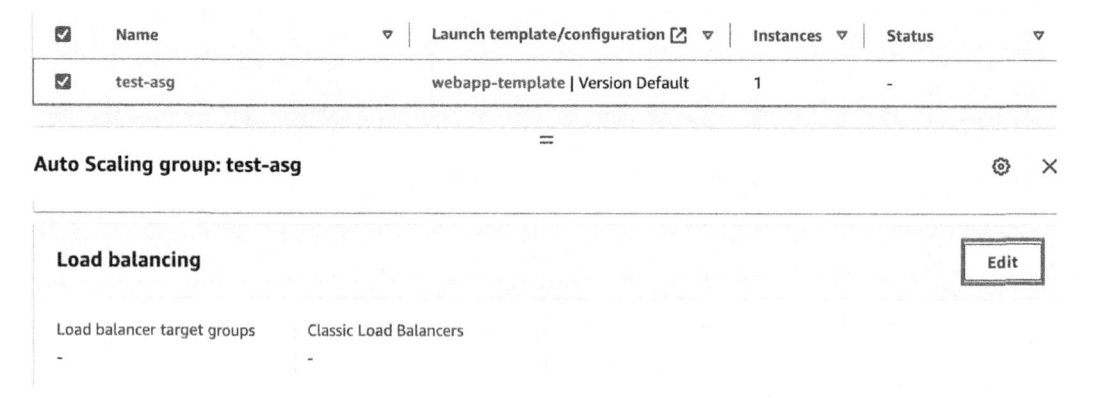

Figure 7.58 – Associating the target group with the load balancer

   II. Associate the desired load balancer with the target group, as shown here:

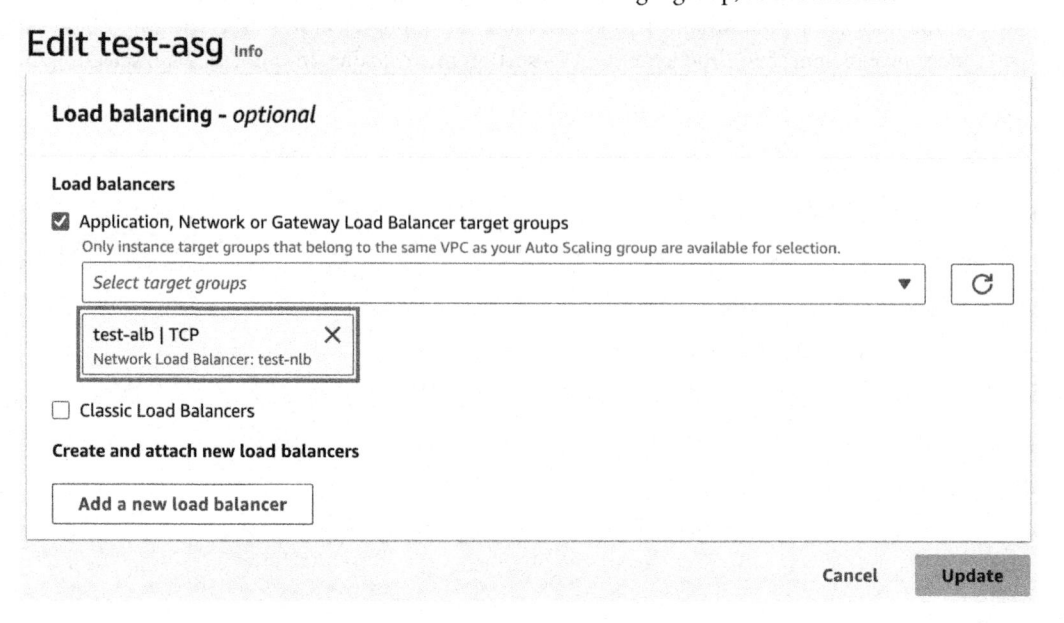

Figure 7.59 – Configuring the target group for a load balancer

6. **Save your changes**: Review your configurations and click **Update** to save your settings.

With these steps, you have ensured your load balancer is always aware of the instances it needs to route traffic to, adapting in real time to the changes ASG makes.

Next, we will look at the art of distributing traffic among instances and build expertise in the health check settings.

Distributing traffic among instances

Integrating ELB with ASG is not just about ensuring availability – it is about smartly channeling incoming requests, leading them to the most appropriate instance, balancing loads, and avoiding any single point of overload. ELB, by default, uses a round-robin algorithm (*"Round Robin is a simple cyclic scheduling technique where each task is assigned a fixed time slot in a rotating order"*) in distributing incoming traffic across all the registered instances. This might sound more straightforward, but there is more going on under the hood that can be fine-tuned for perfection.

Here are some key points regarding traffic distribution:

- **Sticky sessions**: It is beneficial for a user's requests to be directed to the instance where they began their session, especially for applications that store the session data locally. ELB allows you to enable sticky sessions, ensuring that all requests from a user during a single session are directed toward the same instance.
- **Cross-zone load balancing**: ELB can distribute incoming traffic evenly across all instances, regardless of the Availability Zone. This ensures that even if one of the Availability Zones sees more traffic, instances in other Availability Zones won't be left idle.
- **Connection draining**: If an instance becomes unhealthy or needs maintenance, connection draining ensures that an in-flight request isn't dropped. Instead, they are completed, and only then is the instance deregistered.
- **Request routing**: Complex modern applications demand routing rules for directing incoming requests. ELB supports host-based and path-based routing, ensuring that requests are forwarded to the appropriate services.
- **Weighted target groups**: For instance, if you are testing a new version of your application, you can direct a chunk of your traffic to the new version and the rest of the traffic to the stable version. This helps you with canary testing and phased rollouts.

Next, we will discuss the various health check settings to ensure your instances are always ready to serve your incoming requests when needed.

Health check settings

Health checks ensure everything stays in harmony when you're integrating ELB with ASG. It constantly evaluates whether your instances are fit to serve or need a momentary respite.

Why are health checks so vital?

Imagine orchestrating a grand symphony where every instrument plays a pivotal role. Now, envision a situation where one instrument goes out of tune. Without a mechanism to detect and rectify this anomaly, the performance could descend into chaos. That is precisely the role health check settings play in the world of ELB and ASG to ensure your application remains operational at all times. Let's dive in and understand the details of the check settings that are available so that we can make use of them:

- **Types of health checks**: There are two main health checks to consider in this setup:

  - **ELB health checks**: These determine the health of the instances registered with the load balancer
  - **EC2 status checks**: These assess the health of the EC2 instances and are carried out by the instance itself

- **Health check grace period**: After an instance comes into service, it might need some warmup time before it is ready to take on any incoming requests. This grace period prevents the instances during that time from being wrongfully marked as "unhealthy."

- **Configuring health checks**: This process includes setting the desired interval between checks, the response timeout, the number of consecutive failures to mark an instance as unhealthy, and the path for the check if it is HTTP/HTTPS based.

By diligently configuring and monitoring health check settings, you ensure that traffic is routed only to the healthiest of instances, guaranteeing the optimal performance and robustness of your application.

Now, let's understand the best practices for using ELB and ASG together.

Best practices for using ELB and ASG together

Today's digital age is defined by its relentless pace and its demand for ever-available services. Users expect the systems to always be resilient, scalable, and reliable without appreciating the sophisticated infrastructure mechanism happening behind the scenes. As we delve into understanding how to create this seamless experience for users, it becomes crucial to understand the best practices involved in integrating ELB and ASG. At the heart of this integration lies high availability, fault tolerance, and scalability:

- **High availability**: High availability refers to a system design that ensures a high degree of operational performance and reliability. Here are some methods you can use to achieve this with ELB and ASG:

  - **Multi-AZ deployments**: Ensure your ELB and ASG can span across multiple Availability Zones. It is not only helpful in distributing incoming traffic but also guarantees service availability, even if one Availability Zone faces disruptions.
  - **Health check optimization**: Configure health checks to allow only the healthier instances to receive traffic. Make it a regular exercise to evaluate and revisit your health check settings so that they align with your evolving application demand.

- **Fault tolerance**: Fault tolerance is the ability of the system to continue functioning properly in the event some of its components fail. Here are the methods of achieving this with ELB and ASG:

  - **Diversify resource allocation**: Distribute instances across multiple Availability Zones to prevent any single point of failure. If an outage or issue occurs in one Availability Zone, the traffic will be seamlessly routed to instances across other Availability Zones.

  - **Backup and recovery protocols**: Regularly back up instances and data. Implement robust recovery mechanisms in such a way that if a component fails, the system can self-heal without any intervention.

- **Scalability**: Scalability is the capacity of the system to handle increased load or demand efficiently. Here are the methods of scaling that are achieved through ELB and ASG:

  - **Predictive scaling**: Use predictive scaling to preemptively scale instances based on historic demand patterns

  - **Scheduled actions**: For predictable workloads, schedule scaling activities ahead of time

  - **Dynamic scaling**: Regularly evaluate and adjust the scaling policies to cater to real-time traffic demands, ensuring resources are used optimally

By adhering to these best practices, you can ensure a seamless experience for your users, regardless of unforeseen hitches or surges in demand.

Summary

With that, we have concluded this chapter through the interplay of ELB and ASG. We did a deep dive into understanding the nuances of this duo, which is the cornerstone of many AWS deployments worldwide. When this duo is implemented thoughtfully, they can create a resilient, efficient, and responsive digital environment.

As we close this chapter, let's pivot our attention to another cornerstone of AWS: *storage*. In the next chapter, we will demystify the intricacies of understanding and optimizing Amazon EC2 storage options.

8

Understanding and Optimizing Amazon EC2 Storage Options

In the vast landscape of cloud infrastructure, storage emerges as one of the critical components of your application. Data storage is not just about having a place to store your files, but it's also about speed, accessibility, durability, and security. As we wade into the depths of the Amazon EC2 environment, it becomes evident how diversified, dynamic, and intricate its storage offerings are. This chapter seeks to shed light on these offerings, providing you with both a macro and micro view of EC2 storage and its components.

This chapter's journey encompasses two central storage systems: Amazon **Elastic Block Store** (**EBS**), known for its block-level storage capabilities; an instance store, providing temporary storage for instances; and Amazon **Elastic File System** (**EFS**), which offers a scalable file storage system. We will also deep dive into each of these storage systems and discuss how to decide which storage type is best suited for your application. What are the nuances of their performance? How can you fine-tune and monitor them to ensure seamless operations? And so on. By the end of this chapter, you will be well equipped to answer these questions, armed with knowledge, best practices, and real-world application strategies.

The following topics will be covered in this chapter:

- Amazon EBS volumes
- Instance stores
- Amazon EFS
- Choosing the right storage option

Amazon EBS volumes

EBS is a block storage solution, essentially similar to a sophisticated cloud-based hard drive for your EC2 instance. But wait – what is block storage? **Block storage** divides data into a uniform block of storage, each with a unique identifier. Unlike file storage, where the data is stored as a file within folders, or object storage, where the data is stored as objects, allowing each block to be controlled as an individual hard drive, this type of storage is very appropriate for applications that need high performance as it enables flexible and granular control over data storage and access.

As we dive deep into Amazon EBS, you will quickly realize the pivotal role it plays in AWS. EBS offers a high-speed, reliable hard drive attached to your EC2 instances, but with the added benefits of scalability, replication, and seamless integration with supported AWS services. As we further our journey into EBS, you will notice the variety of options it offers to cater to different workloads.

In this section, we will deep dive and explore types of EBS volumes, use cases, and performance considerations for each of the volume types with practical hands-on exercises detailing how to provision and attach EBS volumes into the EC2 instance. We will then transition to understanding the backup aspect of EBS volumes with a practical hands-on exercise detailing the creation of an EBS snapshot and its lifecycle, and conclude this section with an understanding of sharing the captured snapshot across different AWS environments.

Let's now kick off this section by delving into the different types of EBS volumes that come with Amazon EC2 to handle varied demands of workloads.

Types of EBS volumes

Amazon EBS provides a range of EBS volume types catering to different storage needs and performance requirements for applications hosted in the AWS environment. These volume types include *General Purpose SSD (gp2 and gp3), Provisioned IOPS SSD (io1 and io2),* and *Throughput Optimized HDD (st1 and sc1)*, with each volume type catering to specific use cases as follows:

- **gp2 and gp3**: General Purpose SSD volumes that balance cost and performance for a broad range of workloads, from databases to boot volumes. While gp2 offers a fixed performance-to-storage ratio, gp3 offers a customizable performance independent of storage capacity.
- **io1 and io2**: Provisioned IOPS SSD volumes tailored for I/O-intensive applications such as large relational or NoSQL databases. This nature of volume offers a consistent and low-latency performance. With io2, you gain better durability and more **input/output operations per second (IOPS)** per GB.
- **st1 and sc1**: Throughput Optimized HDD volumes can be used for frequently accessed, throughput-intensive workloads such as big data, log processing, and data warehouses. This type of volume offers a lower cost per throughput performance.

Each of these types of EBS volumes has been crafted with specific workloads in mind, and choosing the right type of volume needs a clear understanding of your application's I/O patterns, performance needs, and budget constraints. As we move forward, we will uncover practical use cases, performance considerations, and operational nuances of these volumes to ensure you have the insights needed to make informed choices.

Use cases and performance considerations

With a firm understanding of EBS volume types, let's try to explore when and where to deploy each of them. The choice of EBS volume isn't just about space. It is about orchestrating a symphony of performance, durability, and cost-efficiency for your applications. As we dive into the use cases and performance considerations of EBS, you will acquire the knowledge to tailor your storage choices for optimized outcomes.

Use cases for EBS volumes

EBS volumes offer flexible, high-performance storage solutions for various use cases in the AWS cloud, with each type of EBS volume designed to meet the requirements of different workload types:

- **General Purpose SSD (gp2 and gp3)**: These volumes are ideal for workloads such as web servers, development environments, medium-sized databases, and most other use cases where you expect a balanced I/O. A classical use case is hosting a WordPress website, where the blend of read and write operations aligns well with these volumes.

- **Provisioned IOPS SSD (io1 and io2)**: These types of volumes are tailored for heavy workloads such as large relational databases, high-performance applications, and NoSQL databases such as MongoDB and Cassandra. The consistent performance delivered by these volumes ensures that the demanding I/O operations of the systems can run without any hitch.

- **Throughput Optimized HDD (st1)**: Throughput Optimized HDD volumes are suited for large datasets that require high throughput reads. Use cases such as data lakes, log processing, and data warehouses find their match here.

Performance considerations

It is essential to align your storage choices with the specific performance requirements of your application. In this section, we will look at the distinct performance characteristics of EBS volumes in terms of I/O operations, throughput, burst performance, and latency:

- **I/O operations**: Understand the IOPS requirement for your application. If that is determined to be I/O intensive, then lean toward io1 or io2.

- **Throughput**: Evaluate the MiB/s needs of your workloads. For sequential reads/writes of large blocks of data, st2 offers great value.

- **Burst performance**: gp2 and gp3 volumes come with burstable performance. So, keep a close watch on the burst balance to ensure consistent performance is delivered for your applications.
- **Latency**: If your application requires an ultra-low latency, then SSD options such as gp3 and io2 would be a more fitting option.

Understanding these nuances is critical as this is not just about the performance of your workloads but also about cost optimization. The right choice of volumes ensures you are not over-provisioning and inflating costs.

As we transition further, we will delve into the mechanics of provisioning and attaching EBS volumes, where we will discuss the operational steps involved.

Provisioning and attaching EBS volumes

With understanding and knowledge gained on EBS volume types and their suitable workloads, we are ready to dive into the operational steps. Provisioning and attaching EBS volumes is like giving your EC2 instances their personal storage wardrobes, designed precisely to fit their unique needs. Let's walk through this process step by step, starting with provisioning EBS volumes.

Provisioning EBS volumes

Provisioning EBS volumes is the initial and foundational step in their lifecycle, setting the stage before associating them with Amazon EC2 for their intended usage. Let's delve into the process and explore the key steps involved in provisioning EBS volumes:

1. **Navigate to the Amazon EC2 dashboard**: Begin by navigating to the EC2 section:

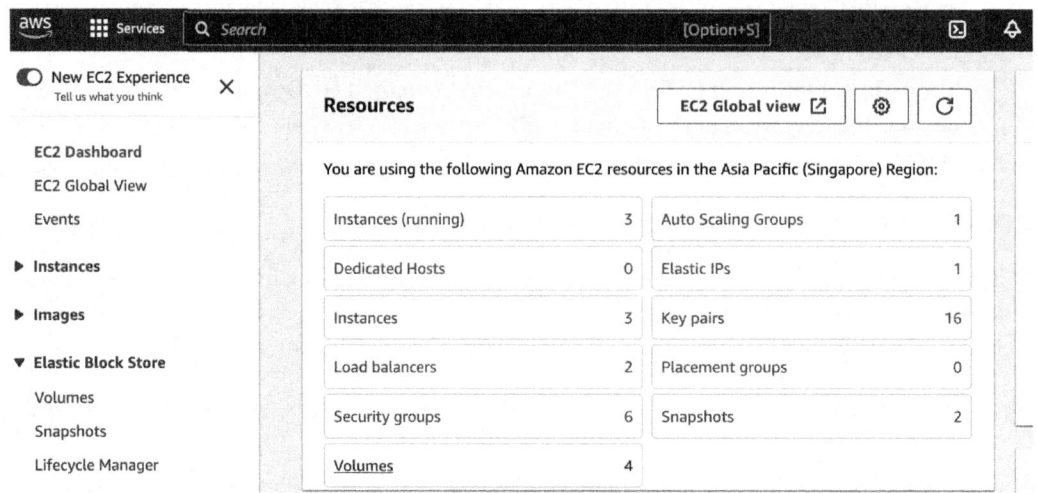

Figure 8.1 – EC2 dashboard/landing page

Amazon EBS volumes   195

2. **Access EBS volumes**: Under the **Elastic Block Store** subsection on the left sidebar, click on **Volumes**:

	Name	Volume ID	Type	Size
☐	-	vol-0916d7023962e6a6a	gp3	8 GiB
☐	-	vol-01f87e5cc08c73a96	gp3	8 GiB
☐	-	vol-00916a4a993029839	gp3	8 GiB
☐	-	vol-0de9753da67b2bcb6	gp3	100 GiB

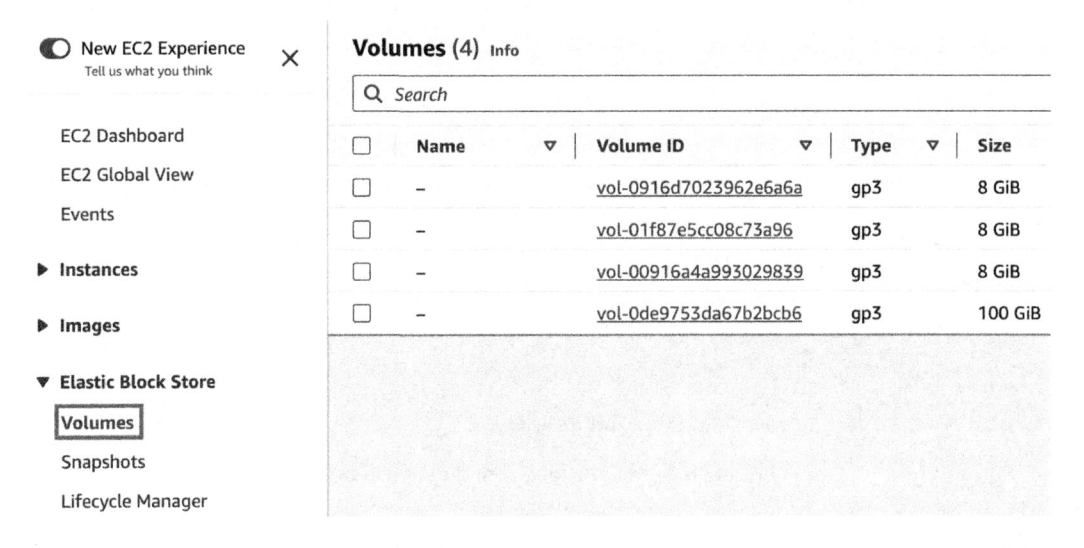

Left sidebar:
- EC2 Dashboard
- EC2 Global View
- Events
- ▶ Instances
- ▶ Images
- ▼ Elastic Block Store
  - Volumes
  - Snapshots
  - Lifecycle Manager

Figure 8.2 – Action to navigate to volumes

3. **Create a volume**: Choose **Create volume**, and this will lead you to a screen where you will be presented with various configuration options:

Volume ID	Type	Size	IOPS	Throughput	Snapshot
vol-0916d7023962e6a6a	gp3	8 GiB	3000	125	snap-0131791...
vol-01f87e5cc08c73a96	gp3	8 GiB	3000	125	snap-0131791...
vol-00916a4a993029839	gp3	8 GiB	3000	125	snap-031a7b5...
vol-0de9753da67b2bcb6	gp3	100 GiB	3000	125	-

Figure 8.3 – Action to define a new volume configuration

4. **Choose the right volume type**: Your use case and performance requirements determine this. Using the **Volume Type** dropdown, select the desired volume type (for example, gp2, gp3, io1, io2, st1) that best aligns with your use case and performance needs:

Create volume Info

Create an Amazon EBS volume to attach to any EC2 instance in the same Availability Zone.

Volume settings

Volume type Info

General Purpose SSD (gp2) ▼

Size (GiB) Info

100

Min: 1 GiB, Max: 16384 GiB. The value must be an integer.

Figure 8.4 – Volume type configuration details

5. **Specify the size**: In the **Size** field, input the desired capacity in GiB. It is crucial to forecast and accommodate potential future data growth. However, remember that EBS volumes can be dynamically resized later on:

Size (GiB) Info

100

Min: 1 GiB, Max: 16384 GiB. The value must be an integer.

IOPS Info

300 / 3000

Baseline of 3 IOPS per GiB with a minimum of 100 IOPS, burstable to 3000 IOPS.

Throughput (MiB/s) Info

Not applicable

Availability Zone Info

ap-southeast-1a ▼

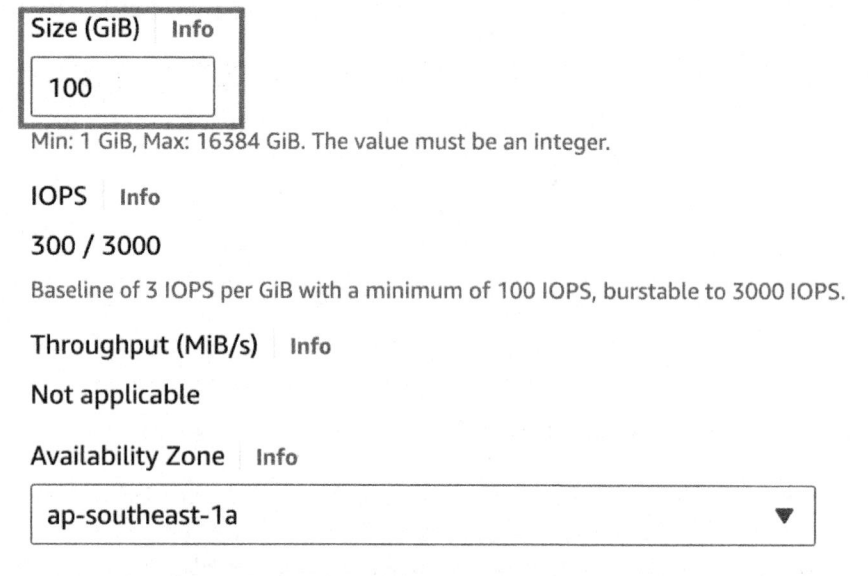

Figure 8.5 – Volume size, IOPS, and Availability Zone (AZ) configuration details

6. **Select an AZ**: In the **Availability Zone** dropdown, choose the appropriate zone:

Throughput (MiB/s) Info

Not applicable

```
Availability Zone  Info
┌─────────────────────────────────────────┐
│ ap-southeast-1a                       ▼ │
└─────────────────────────────────────────┘
```

Snapshot ID - *optional* Info

```
┌─────────────────────────────────────────┐  ┌───┐
│ Don't create volume from a snapshot   ▼ │  │ ↻ │
└─────────────────────────────────────────┘  └───┘
```

Encryption Info

Use Amazon EBS encryption as an encryption solution for your EBS resources associated with

☐ Encrypt this volume

Figure 8.6 – Volume size configuration details

7. **Configure IOPS**: If you have chosen the io1 and io2 volume type, an additional **IOPS** field will be available. Here, input the desired Provisioned IOPS SSD value to tailor the performance for your application needs:

> Volume type Info
> ```
> ┌─────────────────────────────────────────┐
> │ Provisioned IOPS SSD (io1)            ▼ │
> └─────────────────────────────────────────┘
> ```
>
> Size (GiB) Info
> ```
> ┌───────┐
> │ 100   │
> └───────┘
> ```
> Min: 4 GiB, Max: 16384 GiB. The value must be an integer.
>
> IOPS Info
> ```
> ┌───────┐
> │ 3000  │
> └───────┘
> ```
> Min: 100 IOPS, Max: 5000 IOPS (up to 50 IOPS per GiB)
>
> Throughput (MiB/s) Info
>
> Not applicable

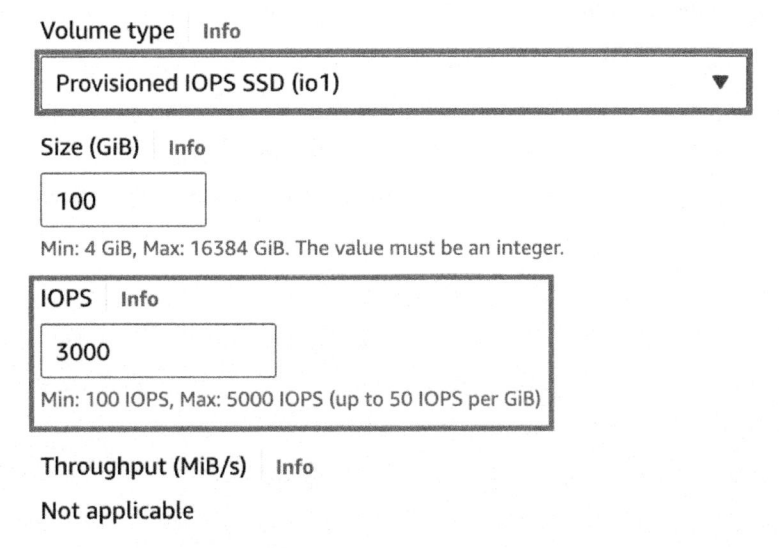

Figure 8.7 – Volume type and IOPS configuration details

8. **Create the volume**: After confirming your configurations, click on the **Create Volume** button at the bottom of the page. AWS will then begin the provisioning process; your volume will be created in a matter of moments:

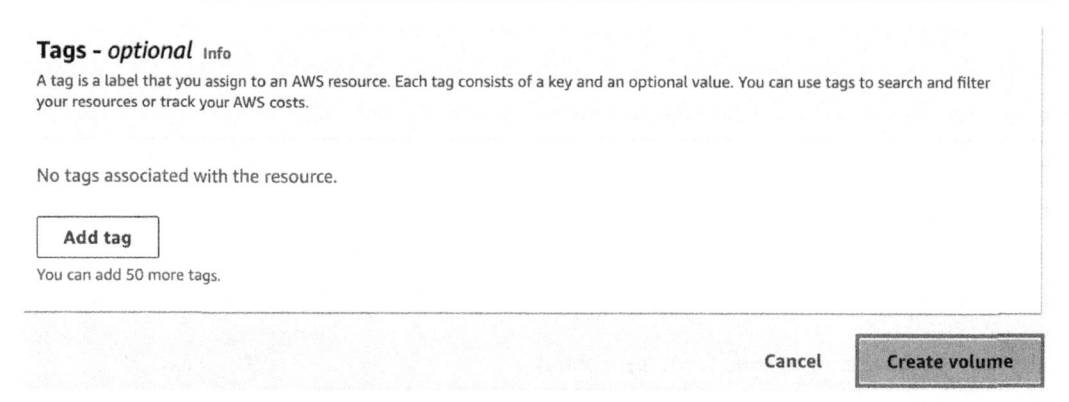

198　Understanding and Optimizing Amazon EC2 Storage Options

Figure 8.8 – Action to create an EBS volume

With the EBS volume created, we will now transition into understanding the steps involved in associating the EBS volume with an EC2 instance for its actual usage (i.e., volume).

Attaching the EBS volume to an EC2 instance

In this section, we will practically understand the necessary steps involved in associating the provisioned EBS volume with an EC2 instance:

1. **Navigate to the Amazon EC2 dashboard**: Begin by navigating to the EC2 dashboard:

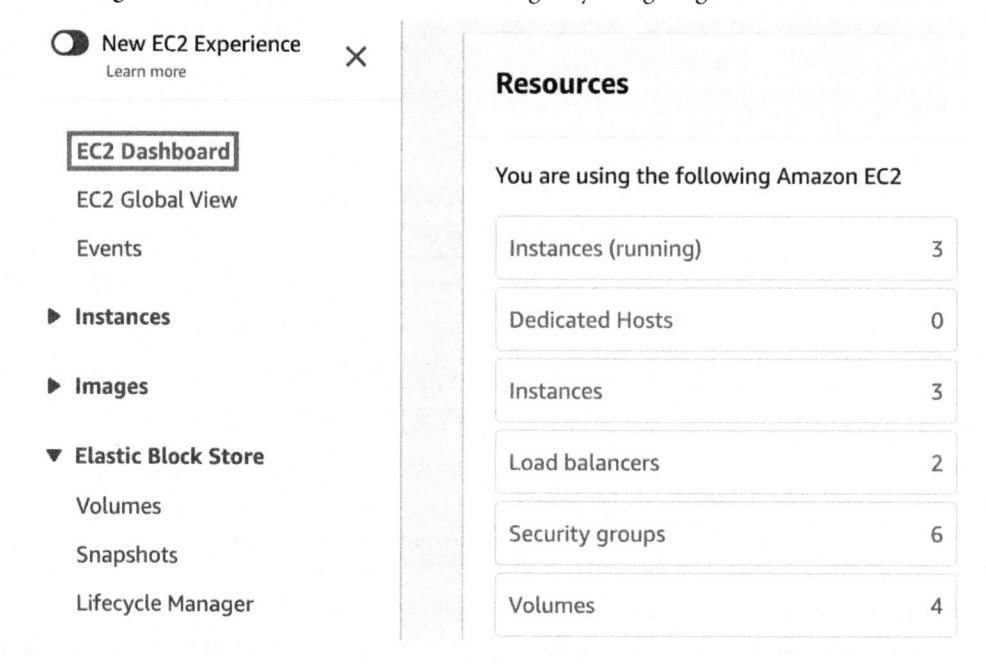

Figure 8.9 – EC2 dashboard/landing page

Amazon EBS volumes 199

2. **Access EBS volumes**: Under the **Elastic Block Store** subsection on the left sidebar, click on **Volumes**:

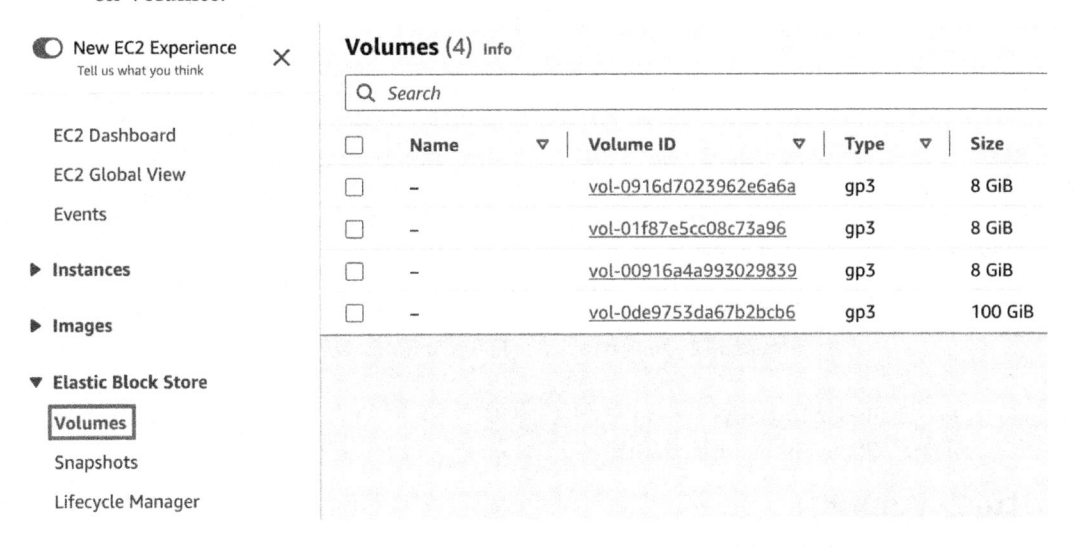

Figure 8.10 – Action to navigate to volumes

3. **Select the EBS volume**: Choose the newly provisioned volume from the list:

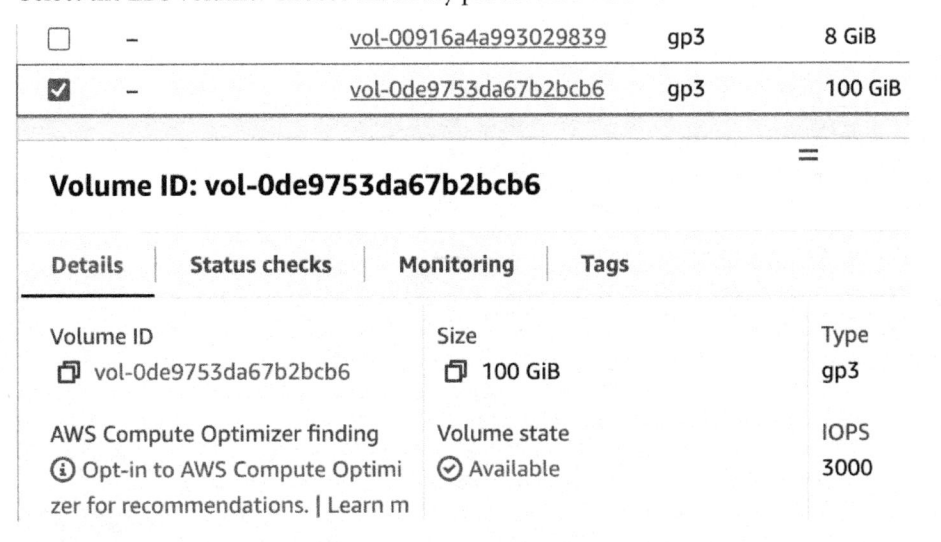

Figure 8.11 – Action to select EBS volume

4. **Actions menu**: Against the selected EBS volume, click on the **Actions** menu and choose **Attach volume**:

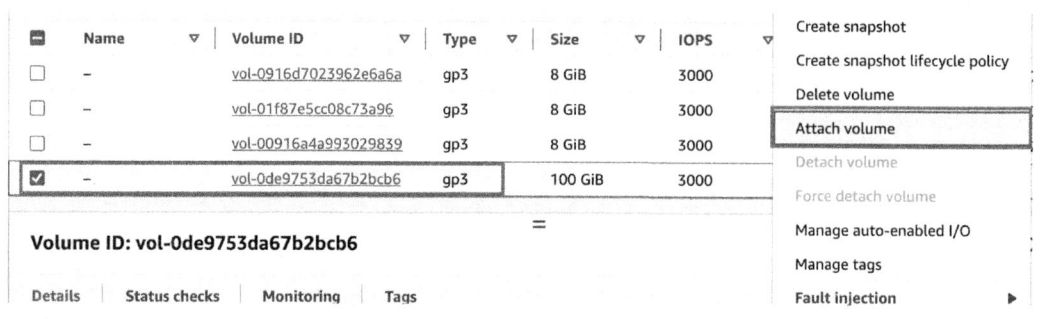

Figure 8.12 – Action to define EBS volume attachment

5. **Choose an EC2 instance**: Select the relevant EC2 instance and confirm the attachment. The volume will then be associated with your chosen EC2 instance, ready for data storage:

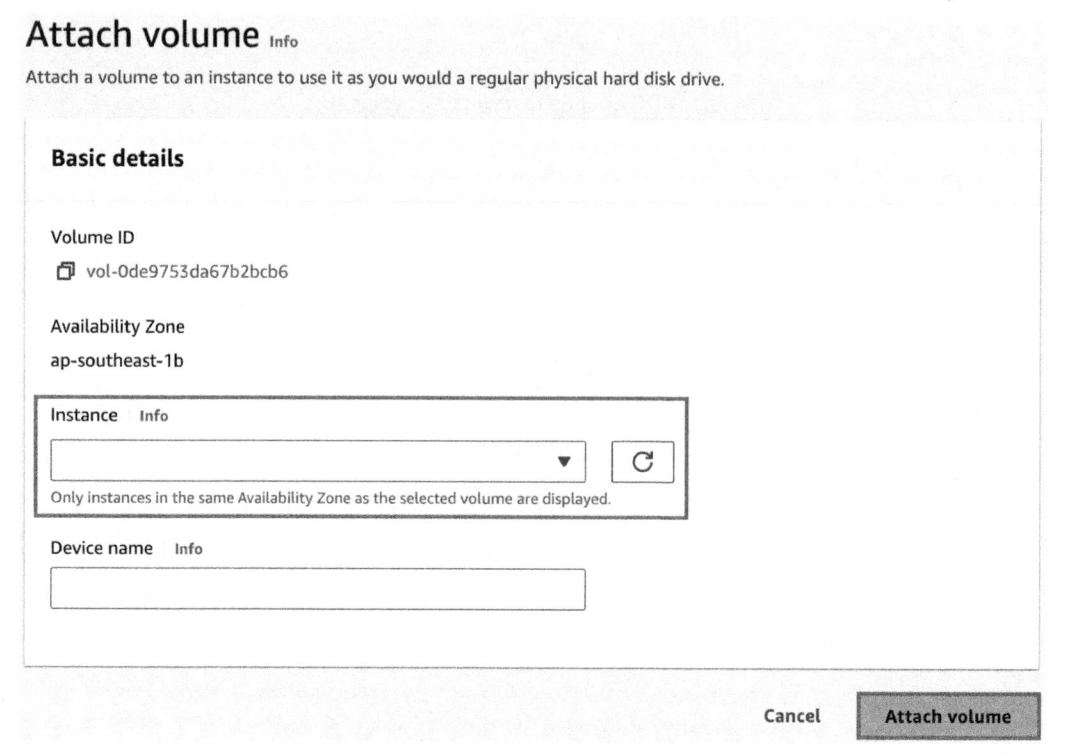

Figure 8.13 – Action to attach EBS volume

Once you attach the EBS volume to an EC2 instance, if necessary you can mount it to a specific directory.

Having understood the provisioning and attachment process, we will next explore EBS snapshots and lifecycle management. EBS snapshots are basically tools that ensure your data's continuity, safeguarding against failures and mishaps.

EBS snapshots and lifecycle management

Data is almost the lifeblood of modern business these days. **EBS snapshots** are nothing short of a marvel when it comes to data backup and recovery. But what precisely are they? In essence, EBS snapshots are a **Point-in-Time (PIT)** backup of your volumes. They capture the entire block-level data, enabling you to recover your volume to its saved state if the need arises. But there are nuances to be aware of. Let's explore!

What is an EBS snapshot?

An EBS snapshot is a PIT copy of your data. Think of it as a photograph of your volume, capturing the data as it exists in that particular moment. These captured snapshots are stored in Amazon **Simple Storage Service (S3)**, which ensures high durability and the ability to recover data if needed. Also, take note that every snapshot created after the first one will only capture the changes you made since the last snapshot, ensuring the efficient use of storage and cost savings. So, imagine you took a snapshot yesterday and another one today. Today's snapshot will only record the changes made over these 24 hours.

Why are snapshots essential?

Snapshots play a crucial role in managing and safeguarding your data within the AWS ecosystem. They are truly an indispensable resource for your **disaster recovery (DR)**, data migration, and cost management:

- **DR**: In the event that there is accidental data deletion or data corruption, snapshots can be a savior, allowing you to revert to a previous state
- **Data migration**: When you want to move data across regions or accounts, snapshots can be copied and used to create new volumes, streamlining the data migration process
- **Cost management**: With snapshots, you can move older and non-critical data to less expensive storage tiers to balance cost with performance

How to create an EBS snapshot?

In this section, we will delve into understanding the practical aspects of creating a snapshot. Let's explore the steps involved:

1. Navigate to the EC2 dashboard:

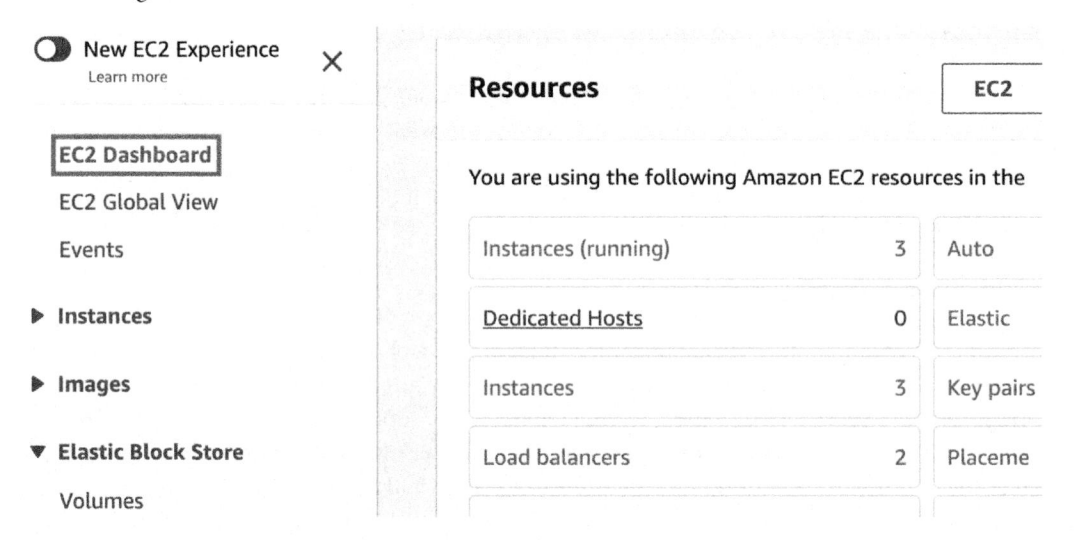

Figure 8.14 – EC2 dashboard/landing page

2. Under **Elastic Block Store**, choose **Snapshots**:

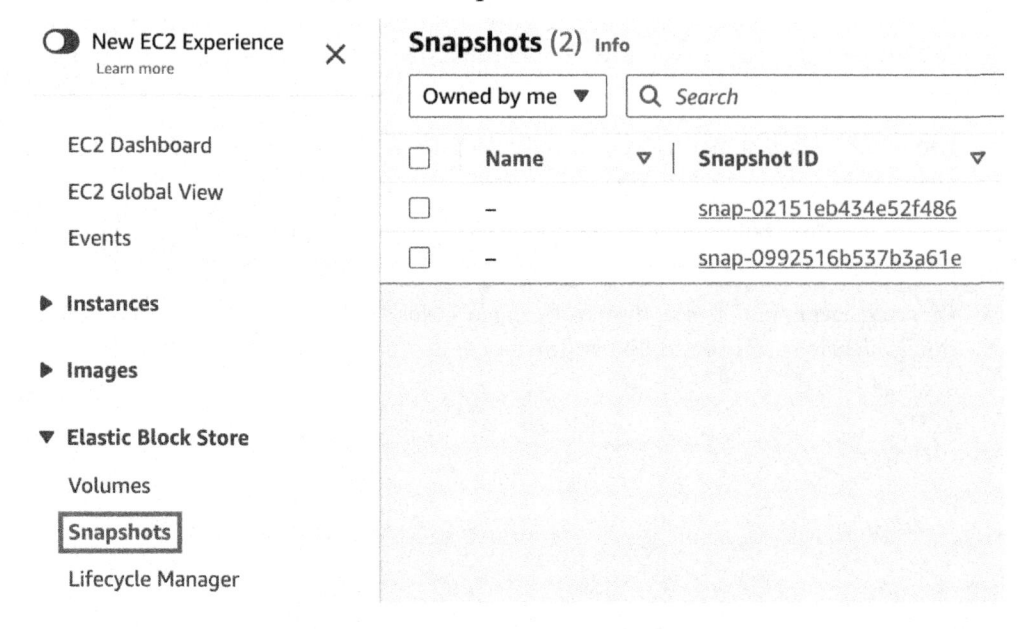

Figure 8.15 – Action to navigate to Snapshots section

3. Select **Create snapshot**, choose your volume, and add a description if needed. That's it. The creation process begins!

Volume ID
The volume from which to create the snapshot.

vol-0916d7023962e6a6a

Description
Add a description for your snapshot.

Snapshot

255 characters maximum

Encryption Info

Not encrypted

Tags Info
A tag is a label that you assign to an AWS resource. Each tag consists of a key and an optional value. You can use tags to search and filter your resources or track your AWS costs.

No tags associated with the resource.

Add tag

You can add 50 more tags.

Cancel   **Create snapshot**

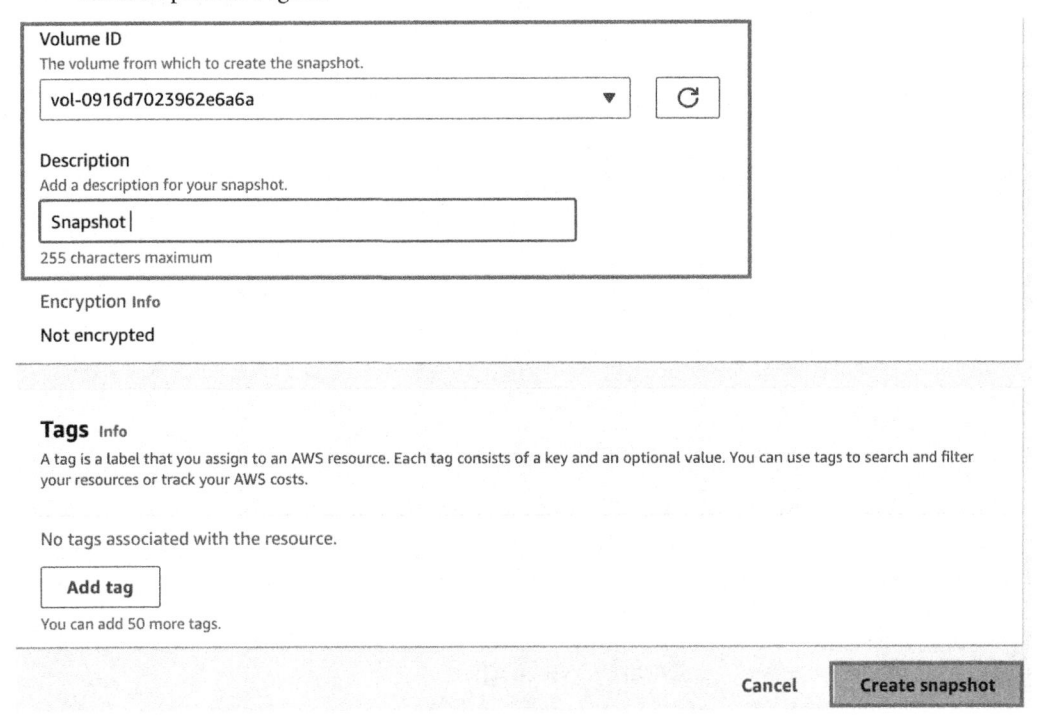

Figure 8.16 – Action to configure and create snapshots

With the creation of a snapshot, let us now transition and understand managing the lifecycle of the snapshot created.

Lifecycle management

AWS offers the ability to automate snapshots via lifecycle policies. By defining a set of rules in Amazon Data Lifecycle Manager, you can determine when to take snapshots and, more importantly, when to delete older ones. Following these actions not only saves costs but also ensures that you are not drowning in a sea of outdated snapshots. Let's now explore the steps involved in defining the lifecycle management of EBS snapshots:

1. **Access Data Lifecycle Manager (DLM) in the AWS console**: As usual, navigate to the EC2 dashboard, and under **Elastic Block Store**, select **Lifecycle Manager**:

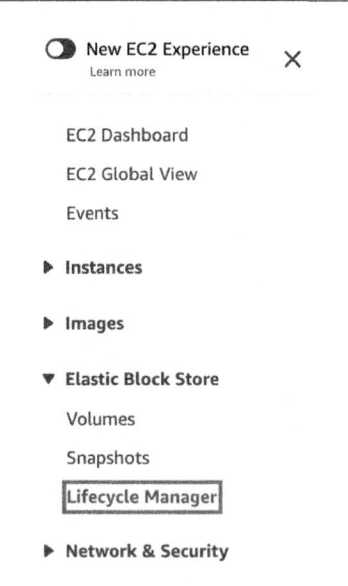

204　Understanding and Optimizing Amazon EC2 Storage Options

Figure 8.17 – Action to navigate to EBS Lifecycle Manager

2. **Create a lifecycle policy**: Click on **Create Snapshot Lifecycle Policy**. Provide a description of your policy for easy identification:

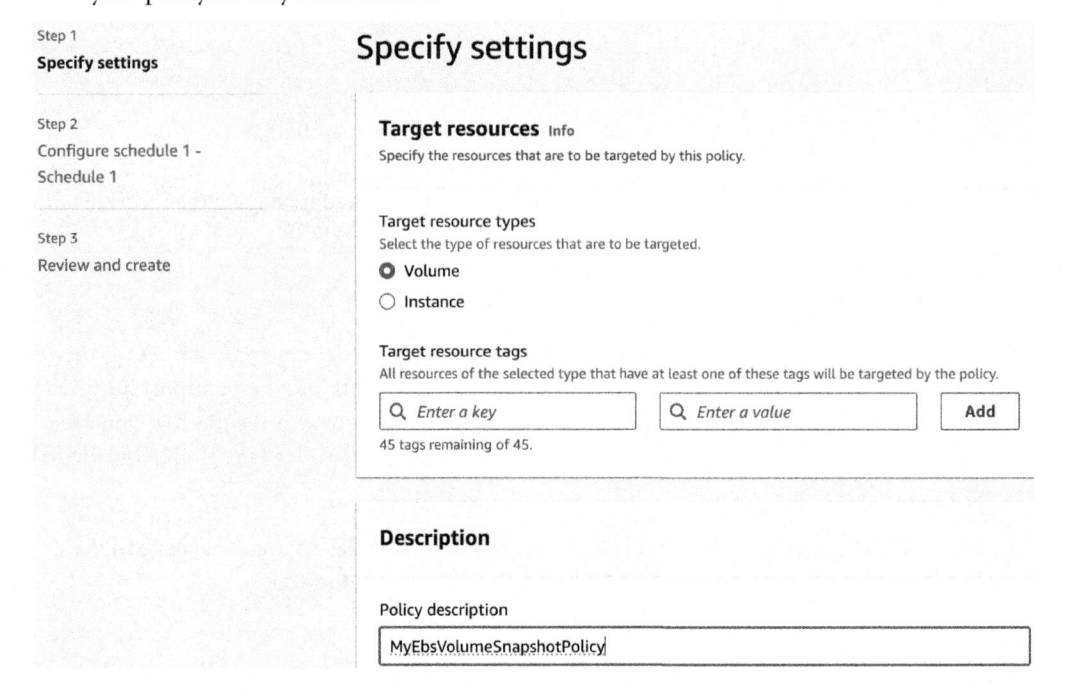

Figure 8.18 – Lifecycle policy configuration details

3. **Specify target volumes**: Specify which EBS volumes this policy should apply to. You can choose them based on resource tags or volume IDs:

Target resources Info

Specify the resources that are to be targeted by this policy.

Target resource types
Select the type of resources that are to be targeted.

● Volume

○ Instance

Target resource tags
All resources of the selected type that have at least one of these tags will be targeted by the policy.

| Q Enter a key | Q Enter a value | Add |

Name ✕
BookDraft

44 tags remaining of 45.

Figure 8.19 – Lifecycle policy configuration to define target resource type

4. **Configure snapshot tags (optional)**: You can add tags to your snapshot to categorize and manage them better. Tags are especially useful for cost allocation in a shared environment:

Tags - *optional* Info

Assign custom tags to the policy to help you identify, organize, and secure your lifecycle policies. Each tag consists of a key and an optional value.

| Key | Value - *optional* | |
| Q Name ✕ | Q DailyBauSnapshot ✕ | Remove |

Add tag

You can add 49 more tags.

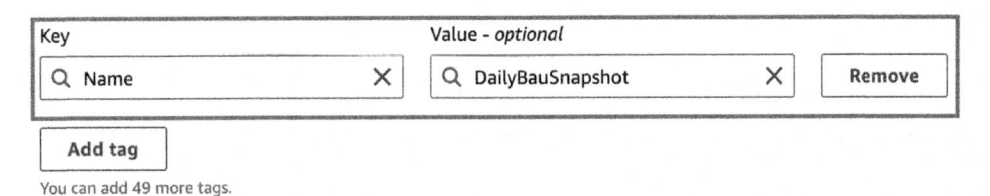

Figure 8.20 – Lifecycle policy configuration to associate tags

5. **Set up Identity and Access Management (IAM) roles**: Lifecycle Manager requires IAM roles to create and manage snapshots. You can either use an existing role with the necessary permissions or let DLM create a new one for you:

Understanding and Optimizing Amazon EC2 Storage Options

IAM role Info

This policy must be associated with an IAM role that has the appropriate permissions. If you choose to create a new role, you must grant relevant role permissions and set up trust relationships correctly. If you are unsure of what role to use, choose Default role.

○ Default role

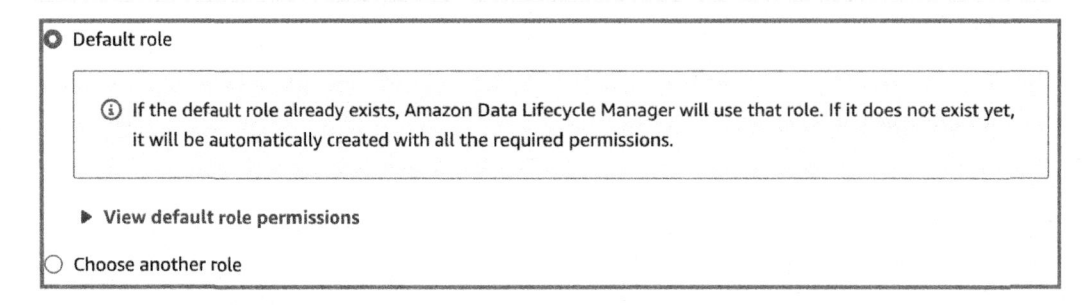

> ⓘ If the default role already exists, Amazon Data Lifecycle Manager will use that role. If it does not exist yet, it will be automatically created with all the required permissions.

▶ View default role permissions

○ Choose another role

Figure 8.21 – Lifecycle policy configuration to associate IAM role

6. **Define snapshot creation rules**: Specify the frequency (for example, hourly, daily) and the exact time you want snapshots to be taken. Also, decide on a retention strategy to define how many snapshots you wish to retain:

Schedule details Info

Schedule name: DailySnapshotSchedule

Frequency: Daily

Every: 12 hours

Starting at: 09:00 UTC

Retention type: Count

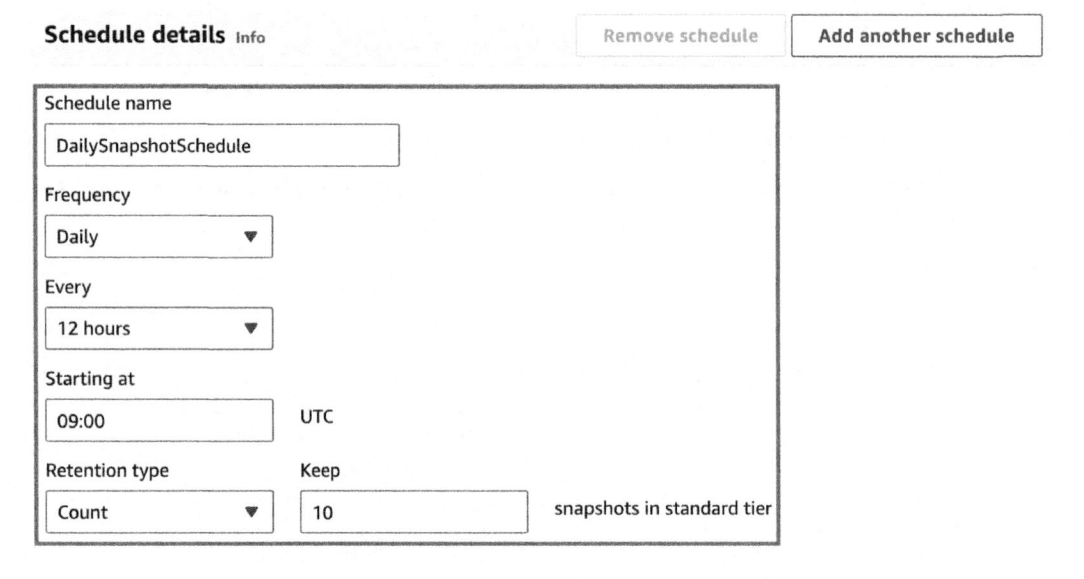

Keep: 10 snapshots in standard tier

Figure 8.22 – Lifecycle policy configuration to define snapshot schedule

7. **Review and create the policy**: Go over the policy details to ensure everything is defined as per your requirements. Click on **Create policy** to activate the lifecycle management:

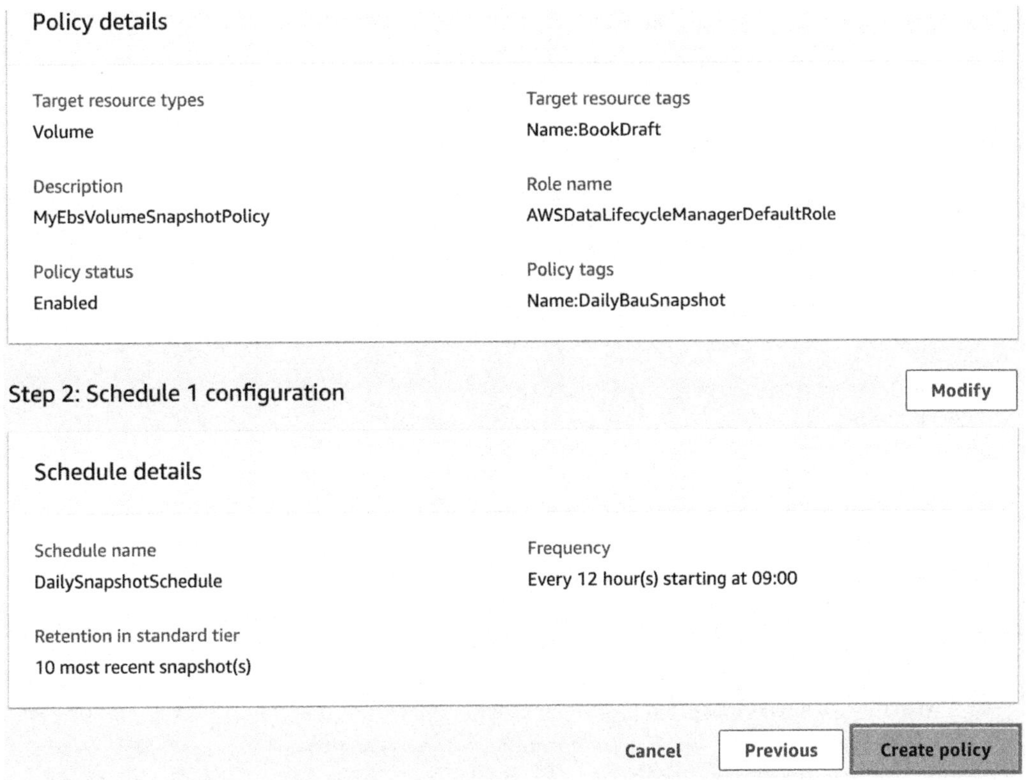

Policy details

Target resource types
Volume

Description
MyEbsVolumeSnapshotPolicy

Policy status
Enabled

Target resource tags
Name:BookDraft

Role name
AWSDataLifecycleManagerDefaultRole

Policy tags
Name:DailyBauSnapshot

Step 2: Schedule 1 configuration   Modify

Schedule details

Schedule name
DailySnapshotSchedule

Frequency
Every 12 hour(s) starting at 09:00

Retention in standard tier
10 most recent snapshot(s)

Cancel   Previous   **Create policy**

Figure 8.23 – Action to create a new lifecycle policy

By following these steps, you can effectively automate the snapshot lifecycle, ensuring optimal storage usage, consistent backups, and cost-efficiency. Let's now look into the intricacies of sharing and migration of these snapshots across accounts and regions.

Sharing and migration

Snapshots can be shared across AWS accounts or even made public, providing flexibility in data migration and collaboration. Additionally, these snapshots can be copied across AWS regions, ensuring the availability of your data when and where you need it.

Let's now explore the steps involved in making this happen:

1. **Identify the required snapshot**: Start by navigating to the Amazon EC2 dashboard, then proceed to the **Snapshots** section. Locate the snapshot you wish to share or migrate:

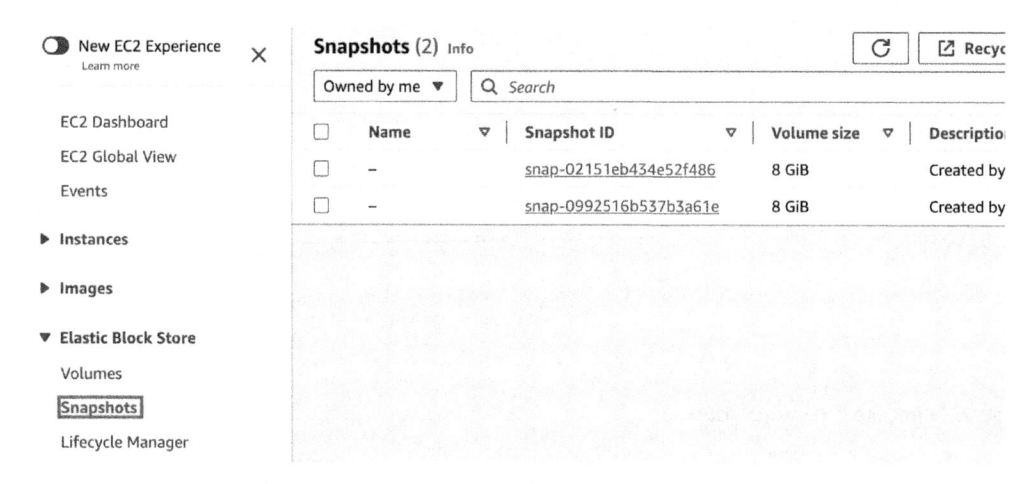

Understanding and Optimizing Amazon EC2 Storage Options

Figure 8.24 – Action to navigate to the Snapshots section

2. **Modify snapshot permissions**: For sharing the snapshot, right-click on the chosen snapshot and select **Modify permissions**. To share the snapshot with specific AWS accounts, add the respective AWS account ID. For public sharing, select the **Public** option:

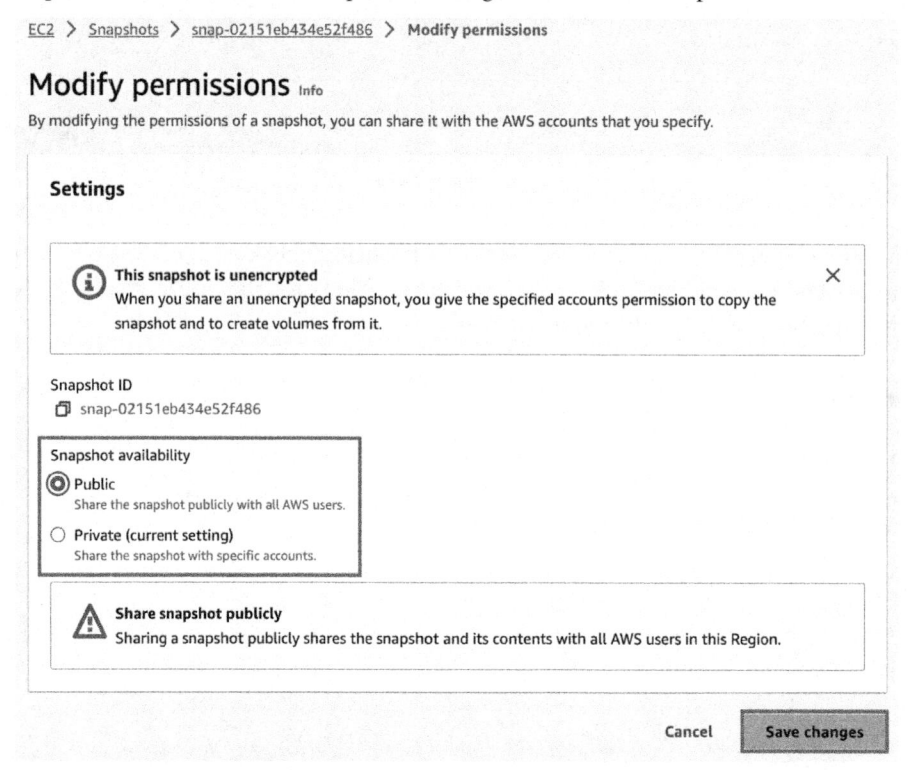

Figure 8.25 – Configuration details to share snapshots with all AWS users

3. **Enable cross-account access**: If you are sharing the snapshot with a different AWS account, then ensure the recipient AWS account has the necessary permissions to access and restore from the shared snapshot.
4. **Copy snapshot for regional migration**: Navigate back to the snapshot list and right-click on the snapshot you wish to migrate. Select **Copy Snapshot**. Choose the destination region from the drop-down menu.

   Optionally, you can encrypt the snapshot if needed by selecting an encryption method:

Figure 8.26 – Configuration details and action to copy snapshot

5. **Monitor the copy process**: Check the progress in the destination region's **Snapshots** section. It might take some time, depending on the size of the snapshot and the region's distance:

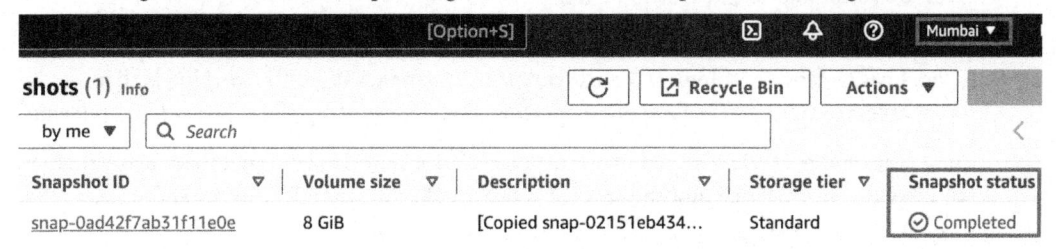

Figure 8.27 – Monitoring the progress of snapshot copy status

6. **Verify the snapshot**: Once the copying process is complete, ensure the snapshot in the new region is accessible and contains all the expected data.

7. **Implement proper management**: After the migration is complete, ensure you set up lifecycle policies or any other necessary configurations in the new region to maintain consistent management practices.

In summary, EBS offers a reliable, efficient, and versatile solution for data backup and recovery.

As we transition from EBS, our journey in the Amazon EC2 storage landscape continues. Up next, we will delve into another vital storage mechanism – the often underestimated instance store storage volume.

Instance stores

In the world of EC2, alongside popular EBS, you will encounter the **instance store** storage option. This storage option is often referred to as ephemeral storage, which provides temporary block-level storage for instances. This storage option is delivered on disks that are physically attached to the host computer. Think of it as a high-speed, local temporary storage solution directly connected to the computational machine running your instances.

Well, what is distinct about this storage option, and why should one consider using it? It's all about the specific use cases and inherent characteristics that it brings to the table. If you are chasing low latency, need a cache, or require temporary storage that should swiftly be wiped out upon cessation, then an instance store rightly offers this distinctive blend of features, and you can consider using it.

Now, let's dive deeper to understand the characteristics of instance store volumes and the scenarios where this nature of volumes can be used.

Characteristics and use cases

An instance store volume, often overshadowed by EBS, has its own unique set of characteristics that make it invaluable for specific scenarios:

- **Ephemeral nature**: Instance store volumes are inherently temporary in nature. Their lifecycle is strictly tied to the lifecycle of the hosting EC2 instance. When an instance is terminated or fails, data on the instance store is also lost. This ephemeral nature makes it ideal for temporary data such as buffers, caches, or scratch data.

- **High-speed access**: Being directly attached to the host hardware, an instance store volume offers lower latency and high I/O performance. This makes it apt for workloads that require rapid access to their data, such as **high-performance computing** (**HPC**) or video rendering.

- **No additional cost**: Data stored in an instance store volume doesn't incur any extra charges. You pay for the instance, not the storage, which makes it cost-effective for applications that need temporary storage.

The character traits of an instance store volume pave the way for its usage in the following scenarios:

- **Temporary storage workloads**: An instance store volume can be used as a storehouse for data that is frequently updated, such as session data or cache
- **High-performance applications**: An instance store volume is an ideal fit for applications that require high-speed read and write access
- **Data replicated across domains**: This can be used especially for cases where the loss of single-node data doesn't impact the system, such as certain distributed systems (for example, Apache Cassandra in a multi-node cluster)

With a clearer picture of what an instance store brings to the table, let's now delve into its performance metrics and the inherent limitations to ensure that you can make an informed choice on its applicability in various scenarios.

Performance and limitations of an instance store

The appeal of an instance store lies not only in its high I/O performance but also in its low latency. Let's dive in further to understand its performance highlights.

Performance highlights

Understanding the performance highlights of a storage option is key to optimizing application efficiency and response times. Let us understand some of the key performance highlights of an instance store volume:

- **Direct-attached storage (DAS)**: As an instance store is physically connected to the host machine, it bypasses potential bottlenecks that network-based storage might introduce. This results in incredibly fast data read and write operations.
- **Burst capabilities**: For applications that experience sporadic spikes in data access requirements, instance store volume burst performance can be a game changer.
- **Optimal for temporal workloads**: Workloads that process and discard large volumes of data, such as batch processing jobs, can benefit immensely from the quick-access nature of an instance store volume.

Of course, no system exists without caveats, and understanding the limitations of instance stores is equally critical. Let's dive in.

Limitations

Understanding the limitations of instance store volumes is equally important to make an informed decision. Let us understand some of the key limitations of instance store volumes that we should be concerned about in their usage:

- **Ephemeral nature**: As we discussed earlier, instance store volumes are ephemeral in nature, where the data storage is temporary. While this might be okay for some use cases (such as cache storage), it could end up being a disastrous option if misunderstood.
- **Limited size**: Each EC2 instance type comes with a predefined storage size for its instance store volume. Unlike EBS volumes, instance store volumes cannot be dynamically resized.
- **Data redundancy**: An instance store does not offer built-in data replication or redundancy. Any replication mechanism has to be managed at the application level.

By being aware of these potential pitfalls, businesses can make the most of what an instance store offers, aligning its capabilities with the right use cases.

Now, let's shift our attention to a practical application by exploring how one can launch instances with an instance store volume.

Launching instances with an instance store volume

In the landscape of Amazon EC2, an instance store stands out as a unique offering – a direct host-attached storage solution that often becomes the backbone for applications demanding rapid data access. Here is a step-by-step guide on how one can create and associate an instance store volume with an EC2 instance:

1. **Selecting the right EC2 instance type**: Not every EC2 instance supports instance stores. So, it is essential to choose an instance type that has instance store volumes available. AWS provides a detailed list that showcases these instances (https://docs.aws.amazon.com/AWSEC2/latest/UserGuide/instance-store-volumes.html).

2. **Specifying an instance store during launch**: While navigating the EC2 launch wizard, under the **Storage** section, you will find the **Add Instance Store** option. By selecting this, you can provision the attached storage that comes with your chosen instance type:

Instance stores 213

Instance store volumes   Hide details

Instance store volumes are not included in the template unless modified

▼ Volume 3 (Instance Type)

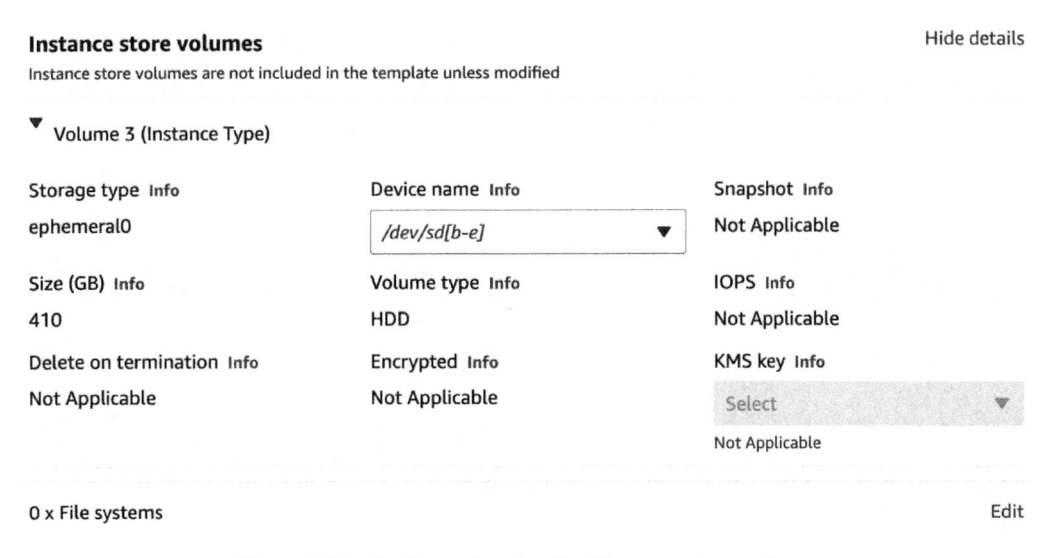

Storage type Info	Device name Info	Snapshot Info
ephemeral0	/dev/sd[b-e] ▼	Not Applicable
Size (GB) Info	Volume type Info	IOPS Info
410	HDD	Not Applicable
Delete on termination Info	Encrypted Info	KMS key Info
Not Applicable	Not Applicable	Select ▼
		Not Applicable

0 x File systems   Edit

Figure 8.28 – Configuration details of instance store volumes

3. **Configuring block device mappings**: For advanced users, by modifying block device mappings, you can dictate how instance store volumes are initialized and attached:

Instance store volumes   Hide details

Instance store volumes are not included in the template unless modified

▼ Volume 3 (Instance Type)

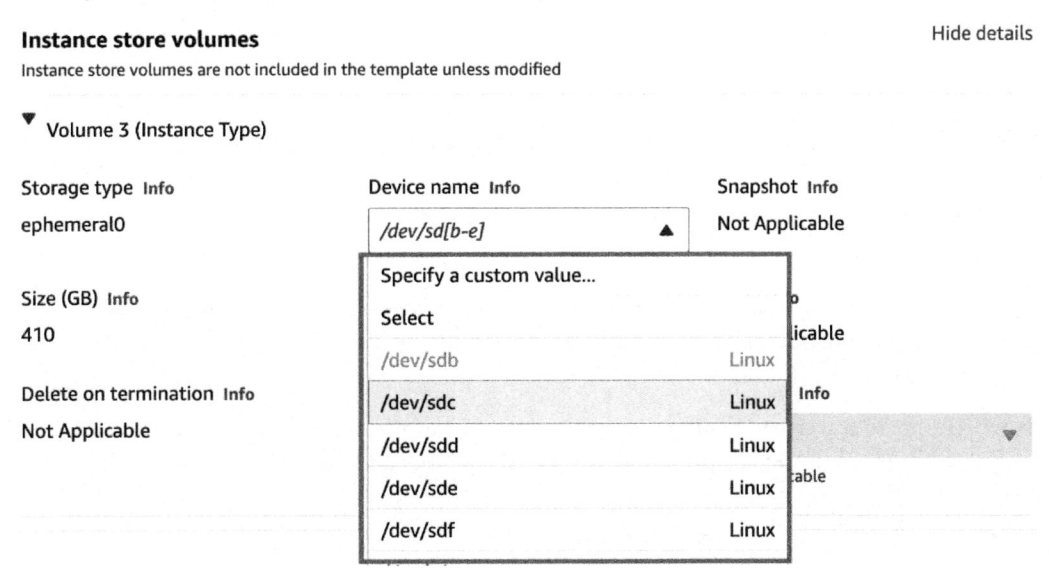

Storage type Info	Device name Info	Snapshot Info
ephemeral0	/dev/sd[b-e] ▲	Not Applicable

Specify a custom value...	
Select	
/dev/sdb	Linux
/dev/sdc	Linux
/dev/sdd	Linux
/dev/sde	Linux
/dev/sdf	Linux

Size (GB) Info
410

Delete on termination Info
Not Applicable

Figure 8.29 – Configuration details of instance store device details

4. **Filesystem selection**: Depending on your workload, choosing the right filesystem is critical. Whether it is `ext4`, XFS, or any other, ensure it aligns with your application's I/O patterns.

5. **Initialization and usage**: Once your EC2 instance is up and running, the instance store volume behaves like any other disk. You can format it, mount it, and begin utilizing its swift performance for your applications.

Having deep-dived into the provisioning aspect of instance store volumes, let's transition into understanding how to persist the data and which backup strategies you should employ. Let's dive in!

Data persistence and backup strategies

As we discussed earlier in this section, while an instance store offers stellar performance, it presents an ephemeral nature, which can be quite a double-edged sword. Data persistence and backups aren't just suggestions; they are paramount to circumvent any potential data losses. Here's what you should consider while relying on instance store volumes:

- **Synchronize with EBS**: EBS volumes are durable and persistent. So, consider relying on a mechanism to frequently sync critical data from instance stores to EBS. This way, even if the instance faces interruptions, the data will remain safe. Unlike EBS, you don't have any native snapshot functionality available for instance store volumes and you may need to rely on additional tools such as `rsync` for Linux and `robocopy` for Microsoft to copy over data to Instance store volumes.

- **Third-party solutions**: Many third-party tools seamlessly integrate with AWS to offer backup solutions tailored to your needs. Exploring this option provides an extra layer of assurance and automation. More details on third-party solutions can be found here: `https://aws.amazon.com/marketplace/search/?category=388e0eec-370f-4c12-9f92-1bb2193509d3`.

By implementing these strategies, the transient nature of an instance store becomes a strength rather than a limitation. You can confidently rely on this volume type to power high-performance applications while ensuring your data safety.

Now, it's time to traverse to another compelling storage avenue offered by AWS. Let's dive in and explore the intricate world of Amazon EFS and its capabilities and use cases.

Amazon EFS

As cloud computing continues to evolve, so do the storage solutions tailored to cater to different kinds of enterprise and developer needs. **Amazon EFS**, a unique kind of storage service, stands out as a scalable and fully managed elastic **Network File System (NFS)** filesystem. EFS offers seamless integration with applications and AWS services. Its versatility purely lies in allowing thousands of EC2 instances to connect, while also automatically scaling the storage as files are added or removed.

But what is so special about EFS? And in what scenarios one should consider using it? Hold on – to answer these questions, we will need to dive into understanding EFS and its use cases.

Understanding EFS and its use cases

EFS is inherently elastic in nature. It effortlessly expands and contracts based on the files you add or delete. This means you don't have to worry about pre-provisioning storage or incurring excess costs for unused storage space. It scales with your needs.

Moreover, it is fully managed. You can say goodbye to the complex administrative tasks of setting up and scaling file storage. AWS has got it covered for you!

Now, let's try to understand where EFS truly shines and which use cases can benefit from it:

- **Content management and web serving**: Websites and **content management systems (CMSs)** that need **high availability (HA)** and share data across instances can benefit from EFS with its robust support
- **Development environments**: Developers in need of shared storage for code repositories often prefer EFS's scalability and performance
- **Home directories**: For businesses that require centralized storage for users, EFS serves as a scalable solution

Clearly, EFS's adaptability comes as its core strength, serving everything from small-scale applications to large enterprise solutions. Beyond its adaptability, its performance metrics and durability are also commendable. Let's delve deeper into these aspects and understand the real horsepower behind EFS.

Performance and durability

Performance and durability often stand as key twin pillars of any storage solution. With EFS, both these pillars come with prime importance, allowing users to get a top-tier storage service.

Performance

The power of EFS lies in its ability to deliver consistent low-latency storage operations while being equipped to handle massive parallel workloads. EFS comes with two distinct performance modes to cater to diverse workload needs:

- **General Purpose mode**: This is the default setting in EFS. This mode is optimized for a broad spectrum of use cases such as web server environments, CMSs, and development setups.
- **Max I/O mode**: This mode is suited for workloads with a high level of aggregate throughput. This mode serves big data and analytics applications, where tens, hundreds, or even thousands of EC2 instances might be reading and writing the data concurrently.

To refine the performance further, EFS offers **Bursting throughout** and **Provisioned throughput** performance settings. While Bursting throughput scales with the size of the filesystem, Provisioned throughput lets you set your performance irrespective of your storage needs.

Durability

Data integrity and protection are at the forefront of EFS's design. Every file stored is redundantly spread across multiple AZs in a region. This not only safeguards data against failures but also ensures uninterrupted access. Natural calamities or AZ failures will no longer cause disaster to your data.

Additionally, EFS supports seamless integration with services such as AWS Backup. With AWS Backup, it is seamless for you to set up policies for scheduling routine backups, ensuring that data restoration when needed is done with just a few clicks.

Now, let's shift our focus to operational aspects. Here, we will explore how to seamlessly set up an EFS filesystem and integrate it with your EC2 instances.

Setting up EFS and mounting it on EFS instances

Let's walk through the process of setting up EFS and its integration with EC2 instances to ensure that your data can seamlessly flow between these two AWS powerhouses.

Kickstarting the EFS creation

Creating an EFS filesystem is a simple and straightforward process. Let us understand the initial steps involved in the creation of an EFS filesystem:

1. Start with the EFS dashboard in the AWS management console. Here, select **Create file system** and ensure the VPC you have chosen aligns with your EC2 instances:

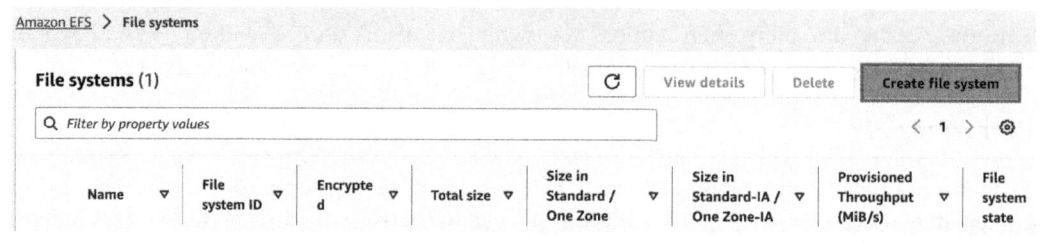

Figure 8.30 – Action to define a new EFS filesystem

2. As you proceed, verify if the **Security groups** and **Networking** configurations are associated properly as per the filesystem requirements:

Amazon EFS   217

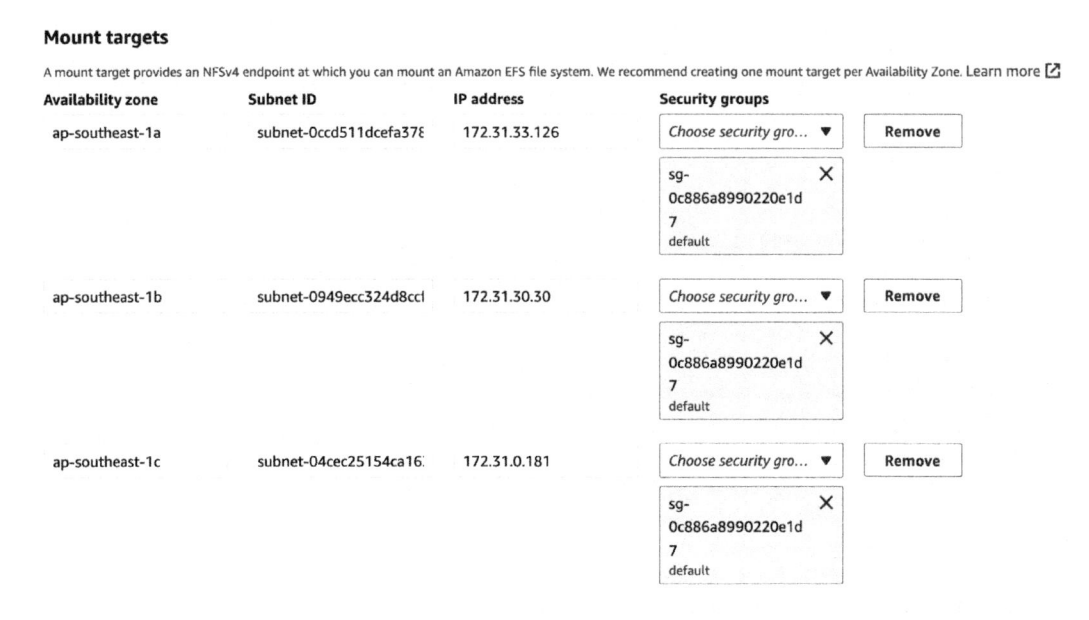

Mount targets

A mount target provides an NFSv4 endpoint at which you can mount an Amazon EFS file system. We recommend creating one mount target per Availability Zone. Learn more

Availability zone	Subnet ID	IP address	Security groups	
ap-southeast-1a	subnet-0ccd511dcefa378	172.31.33.126	Choose security gro... ▼ sg-0c886a8990220e1d7 default ✕	Remove
ap-southeast-1b	subnet-0949ecc324d8cc1	172.31.30.30	Choose security gro... ▼ sg-0c886a8990220e1d7 default ✕	Remove
ap-southeast-1c	subnet-04cec25154ca16.	172.31.0.181	Choose security gro... ▼ sg-0c886a8990220e1d7 default ✕	Remove

Figure 8.31 – Network configuration details of the EFS filesystem

Having explored the creation of an EFS filesystem, the next crucial step involves optimizing how your applications interact with the filesystem. This is where leveraging an access point becomes crucial. Let us transition and dive into exploring the process of setting up access points.

Leveraging access points

Think of access points as gateways to your filesystem. They are your sentinels managing who gets to see and interact with which directories. You can tailor multiple access points based on your application nuances. Let's look at the steps involved in leveraging access points:

1. **Initiate access point creation**: Inside the filesystem **Details** page, navigate to the **Access points** tab. Click on **Create access point**:

Metered size	Monitoring	Tags	File system policy	Access points	Network	Replication

Access points (0)   ↻   View details   Delete   **Create access point**

Q Search access points by name or ID   < 1 >

Name	Access point ID	Path	POSIX user	Creation info	State

No resources
Create access point

Figure 8.32 – Configuration of access points with EFS

2. **Define root directory**: Specify the path for the root directory. If the specified path does not exist, then EFS will create it for you. This path is where the application will be rooted when using the access point:

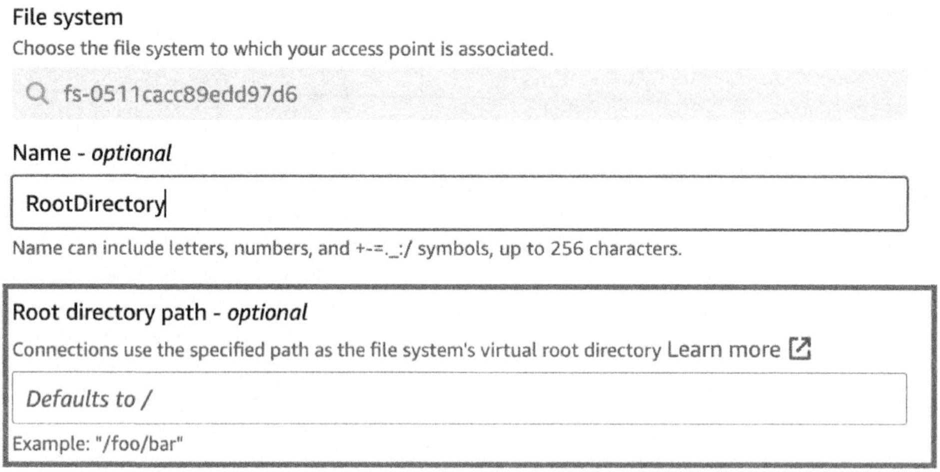

File system
Choose the file system to which your access point is associated.

    Q fs-0511cacc89edd97d6

Name - *optional*

    RootDirectory

Name can include letters, numbers, and +-=._:/ symbols, up to 256 characters.

Root directory path - *optional*
Connections use the specified path as the file system's virtual root directory Learn more

    Defaults to /

Example: "/foo/bar"

Figure 8.33 – Configuration of root directory with EFS

3. **Configure POSIX user**: Optionally, set up the user and group IDs that the application uses when accessing the filesystem. Define secondary group IDs if necessary:

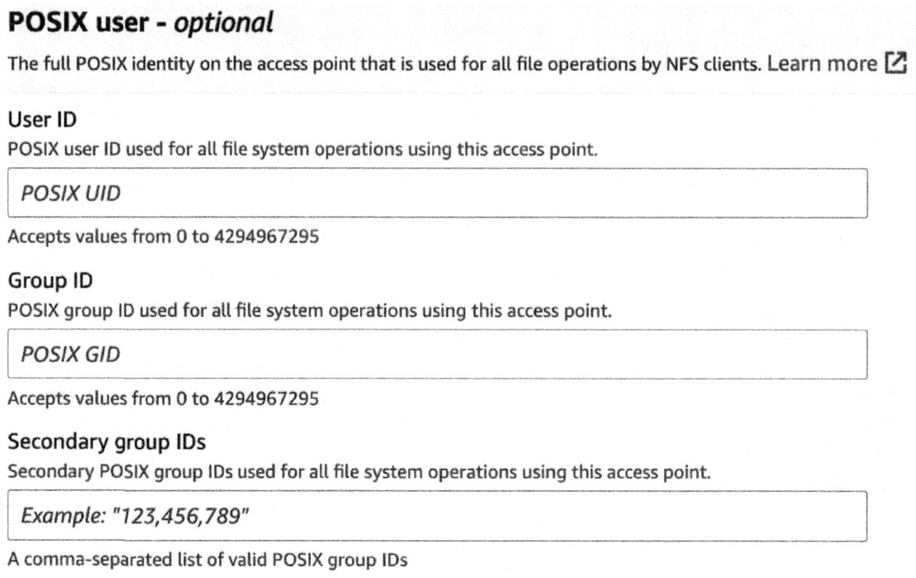

POSIX user - *optional*
The full POSIX identity on the access point that is used for all file operations by NFS clients. Learn more

User ID
POSIX user ID used for all file system operations using this access point.

    POSIX UID

Accepts values from 0 to 4294967295

Group ID
POSIX group ID used for all file system operations using this access point.

    POSIX GID

Accepts values from 0 to 4294967295

Secondary group IDs
Secondary POSIX group IDs used for all file system operations using this access point.

    Example: "123,456,789"

A comma-separated list of valid POSIX group IDs

Figure 8.34 – Configuration of user access with EFS

4. **Set permissions**: Optionally, determine the read, write, and execute permissions for the access point's root directory:

Root directory creation permissions - *optional*

EFS will automatically create the specified root directory with these permissions if the directory does not

Owner user ID
Owner user ID for the access point's root directory, if the directory does not already exist.

> POSIX user ID to apply to path

Accepts values from 0 to 4294967295

Owner group ID
Owner group ID for the access point's root directory, if the directory does not already exist.

> POSIX group ID to apply to path

Accepts values from 0 to 4294967295

Access point permissions
POSIX permissions to apply to the root directory path

> Example: "0755"

An octal number representing the file's mode bits.

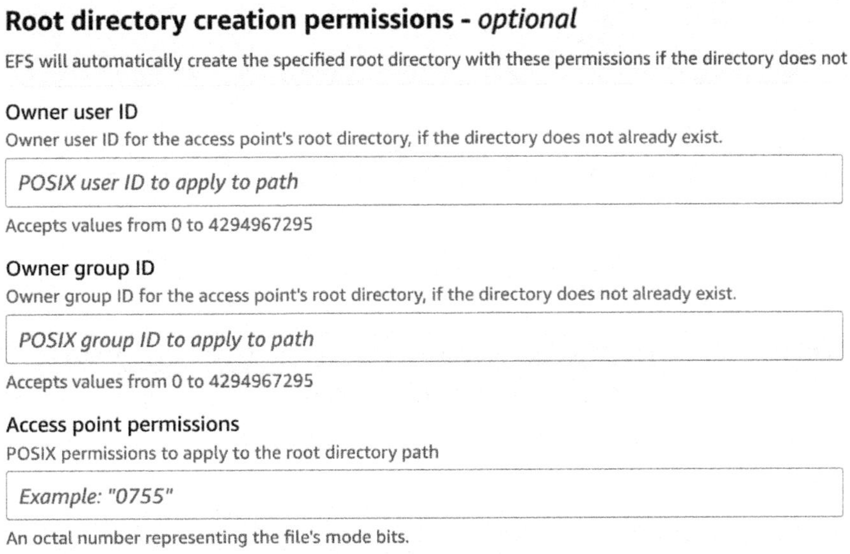

Figure 8.35 – Configuration of root directory permissions with EFS

5. **Finalize and create**: Review your configurations and click on **Create access point** to finalize the creation of access points:

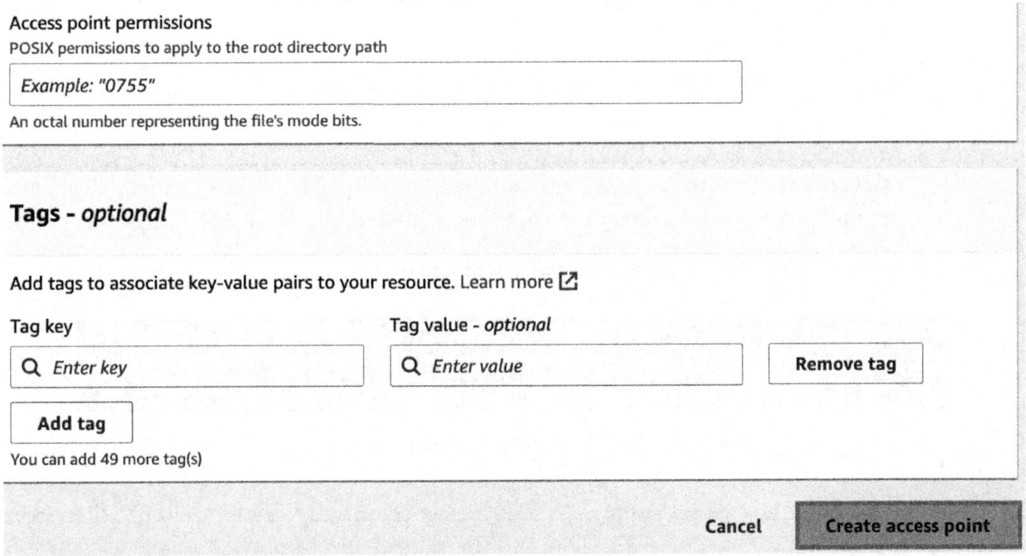

Access point permissions
POSIX permissions to apply to the root directory path

> Example: "0755"

An octal number representing the file's mode bits.

Tags - *optional*

Add tags to associate key-value pairs to your resource. Learn more

Tag key	Tag value - *optional*	
Q Enter key	Q Enter value	Remove tag

Add tag
You can add 49 more tag(s)

Cancel · **Create access point**

Figure 8.36 – Action to create an access point for EFS

6. **Integration with EC2**: When mounting the EFS on an EC2 instance, specify the access point to streamline the filesystem view for your application.

Remember – you can create multiple access points, each tailored for specific applications or sets of users, ensuring that each accesses only what is needed, making your data flow efficient and secure.

Bridging EC2 and EFS

Here are the key steps involved in establishing integration between your EC2 instances and the EFS filesystem:

1. **Verify efs-utils installation**: First off, ensure your EC2 instance houses the `amazon-efs-utils` package:

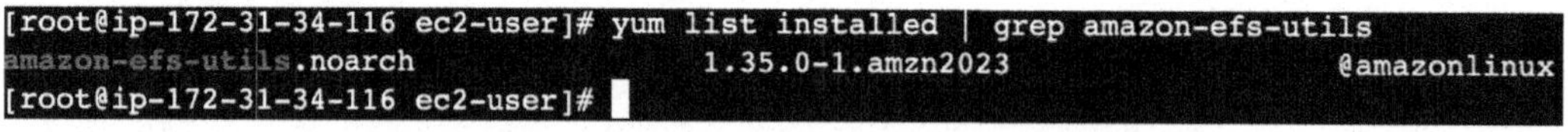

```
[root@ip-172-31-34-116 ec2-user]# yum list installed | grep amazon-efs-utils
amazon-efs-utils.noarch                    1.35.0-1.amzn2023                    @amazonlinux
[root@ip-172-31-34-116 ec2-user]#
```

Figure 8.37 – Command to verify efs-utils installation

If the package is not installed, then you can proceed with the installation with one of the commands shown next.

For Amazon Linux and Amazon Linux 2, run the following command:

```
sudo yum install -y amazon-efs-utils
```

For Ubuntu, use this command:

```
sudo apt-get install -y amazon-efs-utils
```

2. **Mount the EFS filesystem**: Use the `'sudo mount -t efs -o tls <efs-file-system-id>:/ <mount-point>'` EFS mount helper. Here, `'<efs-file-system-id>'` represents your unique EFS ID, and `'<mount-point>'` represents the desired mount location.

   I. **Create a mount point**: Before mounting, you will need a directory that will act as a mount point. Create a directory where you wish to mount your EFS filesystem:

   ```
   sudo mkdir /path/to/your/mount-point
   ```

```
[root@ip-172-31-34-116 ec2-user]#
[root@ip-172-31-34-116 ec2-user]# sudo mkdir /mount_point
[root@ip-172-31-34-116 ec2-user]#
```

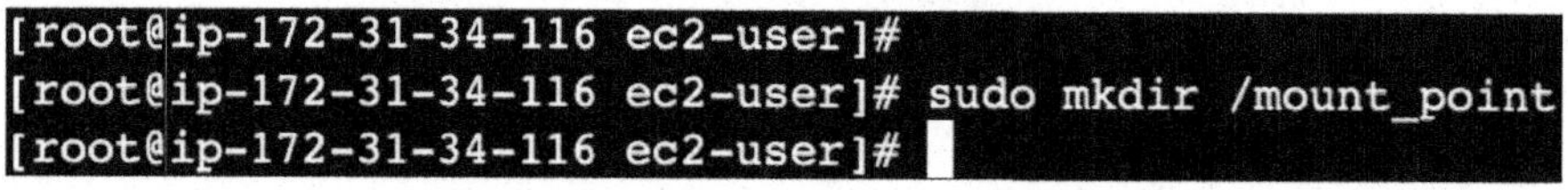

Figure 8.38 – Configuration of mount directory for EFS

3. **Mount the EFS filesystem**: Use the EFS mount helper command to mount your EFS filesystem:

   ```
   sudo mount -t efs -o tls your-efs-file-system-id:/ /path/to/your/mount-point
   ```

Replace `'your-efs-file-system-id'` with your actual EFS filesystem ID and `'/path/to/your/mount-point'` with the directory you created in *step 2*:

```
[root@ip-172-31-34-116 ec2-user]# sudo mount -t efs -o tls fs-0511cacc89edd97d6:/ /mount_point
[root@ip-172-31-34-116 ec2-user]#
```

Figure 8.39 – Command to associate EFS with mount point

Remember – always mount with the `'-o tls'` option. This ensures that data in transit between your EC2 instance and the EFS filesystem is encrypted for added security.

4. **Verify the mount**: Check and confirm the EFS filesystem is successfully mounted:

```
df -h
```

```
[root@ip-172-31-34-116 ec2-user]# df -h
Filesystem      Size  Used Avail Use% Mounted on
devtmpfs        4.0M     0  4.0M   0% /dev
tmpfs           2.0G     0  2.0G   0% /dev/shm
tmpfs           781M  8.5M  773M   2% /run
/dev/xvda1      8.0G  1.5G  6.5G  19% /
tmpfs           2.0G     0  2.0G   0% /tmp
tmpfs           391M     0  391M   0% /run/user/1000
127.0.0.1:/     8.0E     0  8.0E   0% /mount_point
[root@ip-172-31-34-116 ec2-user]#
```

Figure 8.40 – Verification of EFS mount point

5. **Automate mount on boot (optional)**: If you wish for the EFS to be mounted automatically every time your EC2 instance starts, add the mount command to the `/etc/fstab` file.

6. **Verify the connection**: Try creating a file in your EC2's mount directory. If everything is in place, you will see the same file appearing across other EFS mounts, symbolizing a successful setup.

With this operational understanding in place, let us now transition into the realm of EFS backup and understand the considerations to keep our data secure. Ready to dive in?

EFS backup and security considerations

While EFS offers ease of setup and a scalable storage solution, it is equally crucial to understand how we can ensure the data stored within is both secure and easily recoverable. Let's dive in to explore the details:

1. **Automated backups with AWS Backup**: AWS provides a fully managed service aptly named **AWS Backup**. This service seamlessly integrates with EFS, allowing for scheduled backups, retention policy management, and even cross-region capabilities.

Setting up the backup is so straightforward:

I. Navigate to the AWS Backup console (https://aws.amazon.com/backup/):

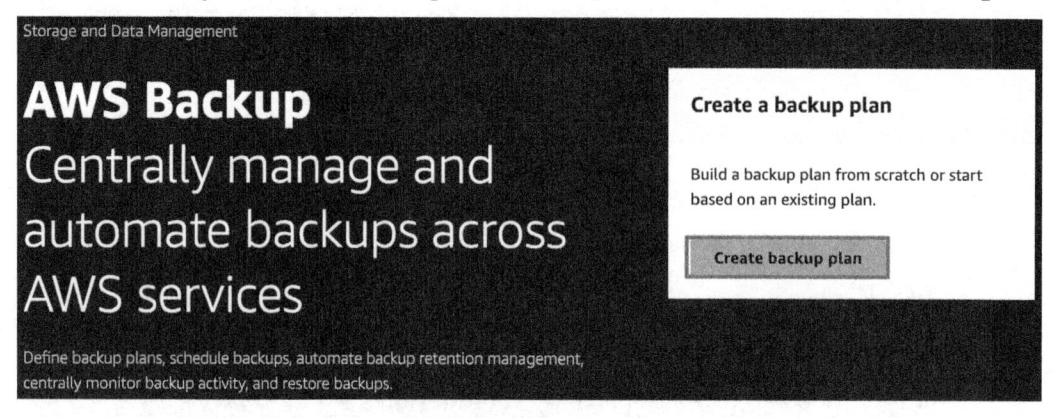

Figure 8.41 – Action to define a new backup plan

II. Create a backup plan by specifying backup frequency, backup window, and retention period:

Figure 8.42 – Configuration details of the backup schedule

III. Assign your EFS filesystems to this backup plan and click **Assign resources**:

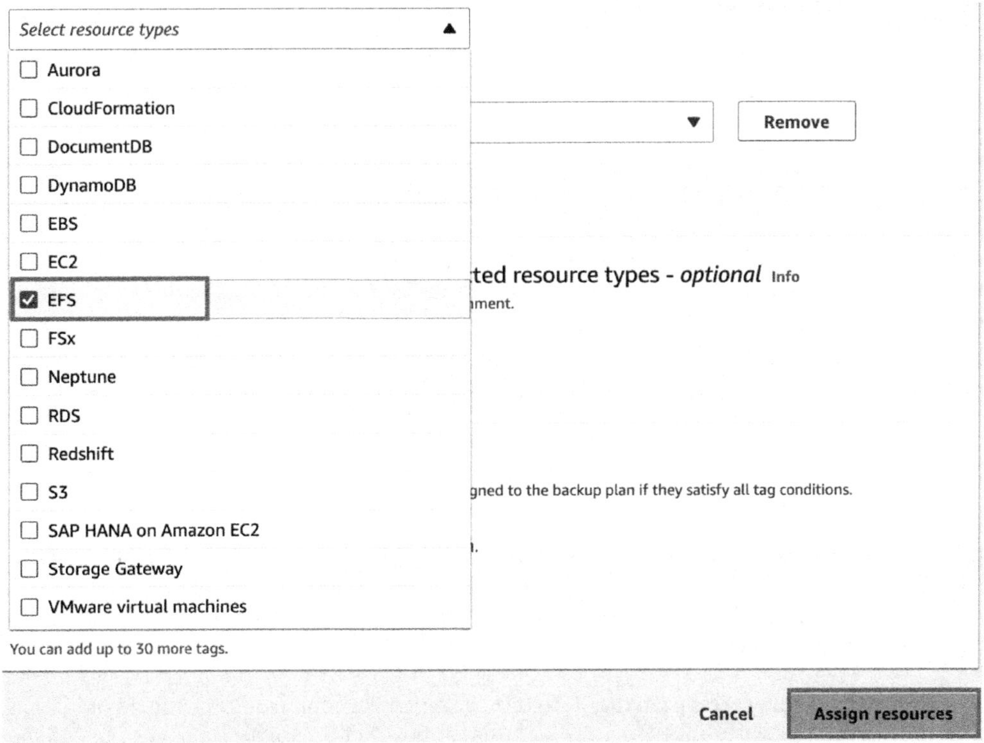

Figure 8.43 – Action to assign target resources with backup

2. **EFS lifecycle management with Infrequent Access**: EFS lifecycle management can automatically move your files to the **Infrequent Access** storage class, reducing costs while maintaining accessibility.

3. **Encryption for added security**:

    - **Data at rest**: EFS provides the option to encrypt your data at rest. This encryption uses AWS **Key Management Service (KMS)**, providing secure and seamless encryption.

    - **Data in transit**: As I mentioned earlier, always use the `-o tls` flag option when mounting your EFS volume to ensure your data between EFS and EC2 is always encrypted.

4. **Access control with AWS IAM**: EFS seamlessly integrates with AWS IAM for user access control. So, define a granular permission to control who can access and modify your filesystem. In addition to IAM, you have a security group that acts as a virtual firewall, ensuring only the desired traffic gets through.

5. **Monitoring and alerts with Amazon CloudWatch**: EFS integrates with CloudWatch, giving real-time metrics and generating alerts when there is a miss. With this, you can ensure you keep an eye on EFS's health, usage, and potential security threats.

Remember – a secure and regularly backed-up system is not just about preventing data loss; it's also about ensuring **business continuity** (**BC**).

Now that we have taken a deep dive into EFS, its setup, and guarding security posture, let's transition into making an informed storage choice where we will delve into *Choosing the right storage option* to ensure your AWS environment is not just optimized but also tailored to your unique application requirements.

Choosing the right storage option

As we navigate the intricate world of AWS storage, an important consideration emerges in understanding which storage option aligns best with your needs. In the vast AWS ecosystem, there are numerous storage solutions such as EFS, S3, EBS, and instance store options. So, making the right choice can feel overwhelming. But with a systematic approach and a clear understanding of your application demands, you can effortlessly match your requirements with the optimal storage solution.

But how do you initiate this process? It all begins with a deep dive into understanding your application nuances. So, let's start our exploration by diving into the first pivotal step: *assessing application requirements*.

Assessing application requirements

To align the storage with the application's true essence, we need to meticulously assess its requirements. Here's how you go about it:

- **Understand data access patterns**: Recognize if your application requires frequent or infrequent data access. Is the data mostly read-heavy or write-heavy? Once you determine your requirement, evaluate it against the characteristics of the storage volume types described earlier under the *EBS volumes*, *Instance stores*, and *Amazon EFS* sections and identify the right fit for your use case. For instance, if your application demands high I/O and write-intensive workloads, consider io1 or io2 EBS volume types. Otherwise, for your balanced workload needs, you can rely on gp2 or gp3.

- **Identify data lifespan**: Not all your data needs to be stored indefinitely. Understand if your application requires short-term storage (such as cache or temporary files) or long-term archival storage.

- **Determine IOPS needs**: IOPS are crucial for applications that demand high-speed data access, such as databases. Understand the requirements and pinpoint the IOPS demand of your application.

- **Scalability requirements**: Will your data storage needs grow over time? Understand if your application requires storage solutions that can scale easily without massive reconfigurations.

- **Budget constraints**: Last but not least, determine how much you are willing to spend. Balancing performance with cost is essential. So, remember the most expensive solution isn't always best for your needs.

With a clear understanding of your application storage needs, identify the right fit of your storage option with the characteristics provided against each of the storage options provided in the earlier sections. Let's now transition to diving deep into *Comparing storage options – performance, durability, and cost* to make an informed decision.

Comparing storage options – performance, durability, and cost

Here is a table highlighting the differences between different storage options:

Feature	EBS	EFS	Instance store
Performance	Best for workloads needing low latency and high throughput. Ideal for databases and high-performance applications.	Scalable performance suited for shared, concurrent file access, such as applications needing a shared filesystem.	High IOPS and low latency, apt for temporary storage and caching files.
Durability	99.99% availability. Data is replicated across storage servers in a single AZ.	99.99999999999% (11 9s) durability yearly, with automatic replication across multiple AZs.	Data persists only during the life of the associated instance; lost if the instance stops or fails.
Cost	Based on the amount of storage provisioned. Type (gp2, gp3, io1, and so on) and data transfer costs affect pricing.	Pay for the amount of data stored. No extra charges for AZ replication.	Included in the EC2 instance cost; no additional charges for storage.

Table 8.1 – Comparison of features between different storage types

The comparative insights provide a snapshot of the potential benefits and constraints of each storage type. Having compared these, it is essential to dive deeper and understand the nuances of storage configurations and best practices.

Best practices for optimizing storage configurations

Choosing a storage option is still a small part of this journey. The mastery lies in fine-tuning the configurations to ensure optimal performance, security, and cost-effectiveness. So, let's explore and unravel some of the best practices:

- **Right-size your storage**: Whether it's an EBS volume or EFS filesystem, always ensure you match your storage size with your application needs. Oversizing can result in unnecessary costs, while undersizing can hamper your storage performance.

- **Enable data lifecycle policies**: Regularly review and move your old and infrequently accessed data to a cheaper storage class or, simply better, archive them. This practice is important not only to save cost but also to declutter your primary storage.

- **Optimize I/O operations**: Especially for EBS, ensure you choose the right volume type (such as gp3, gp3, io1, or io2) that aligns with your IOPS and throughput requirements of your workload.

- **Implement proper backup and snapshots**: Regular backups and snapshots help in quick recovery, and they also provide a safety net against data loss. Also, ensure to define retention policies to avoid piling up outdated backups.

- **Encrypt data at rest and in transit**: Safeguard your sensitive data by enabling encryption. AWS offers services such as KMS for encryption and key management.

- **Stay updated with AWS announcements**: The AWS cloud landscape rapidly evolves, with new features, storage options, and cost-saving measures continuously rolled out. So, keeping a close watch on these announcements can give you a competitive edge in optimizing your storage.

By following these best practices in hand, you can maximize the potential of AWS storage solutions!

Summary

We have come to the conclusion of this enriching journey on storage where we have gone through understanding various storage options and nuances and explored how to make them work optimally for your unique workload requirements.

As we wrap up this chapter, let us now pivot our attention to harnessing the power of Amazon EC2 by diving deeper into the nuances of the next chapter, to maximize the performance of your EC2 instances while also understanding various pricing models to maximize the cost-effectiveness of Amazon EC2.

9
Optimizing Performance with Amazon EC2 Placement Groups and Pricing Model

In the intricate ecosystem of Amazon EC2, striking the right balance between performance and cost is paramount. This chapter seeks to illuminate your path in achieving that balance. We will begin by understanding the dynamics of *Amazon EC2 placement groups*, and diving deeper into their strategies and performance implications. Following that, we will transition into the world of Amazon EC2 pricing models, dissecting their variants and guiding you in choosing the apt model tailored to your needs. By the end of this chapter, you will be equipped to manage costs, ensuring an optimized EC2 experience.

The following topics will be discussed in this chapter:

- Introduction to Amazon EC2 placement groups
- Strategies for deploying placement groups
- Performance optimization with placement groups
- Understanding EC2 pricing models
- Cost optimization strategies

Introduction to Amazon EC2 placement groups

When working with Amazon EC2, ensuring optimal performance for your applications is a primary concern. This is where **EC2 placement groups** come into play. Think of placement groups as a strategy by which you can dictate how instances are positioned relative to each other within a single data center or across multiple data centers. They are tailored to suit applications that require high network throughput, low latency, or both.

AWS recognized very early that while EC2 offers immense flexibility, some workloads needed a fine-tuned environment to thrive. For tasks that demand rapid data transfer between instances or those that need to minimize the *noisy neighbor* effect, the typical EC2 environment might not suffice. Enter **placement groups**, Amazon's solution to providing a high-speed, low-latency environment by keeping the instances relatively close together.

> **Note**
>
> The noisy neighbor effect refers to a situation in a shared hosting environment where excessive consumption of resources by one user adversely impacts the performance of others in the same server or infrastructure. Overall, this leads to degraded service, slower response times, and a less reliable experience for those affected by the resource-heavy neighbor.

So, what does *close together* mean in the context of cloud computing? And more importantly, how can you leverage different flavors of placement groups to meet your specific needs? To understand this, our next discussion revolves around the diverse types of placement groups and how each type caters to distinct application requirements.

Types of placement groups

As you dive deeper into placement groups, you will quickly realize that no one size fits all your use cases. Depending on the nature and demands of your application, AWS offers three distinct types of placement groups, with each optimized for specific scenarios:

- **Cluster placement groups**: These are like high-speed lanes where all the EC2 instances reside in a single Availability Zone, ensuring the lowest latency and highest network throughput. For example, a scientific research project that requires heavy computational tasks, such as complex simulations or data processing, can benefit from the tight networking of cluster placement groups.

- **Spread placement groups**: These are your safety net. They ensure that instances are housed on distinct underlying hardware, distributing them across specified Availability Zones. This is useful for a small number of critical instances that should not share the same underlying hardware. For example, imagine having a web application with a primary and standby database. By relying on spread placement groups, you can ensure they are placed on a separate physical server for improved fault tolerance.

- **Partition placement groups**: These groups strive to strike a balance between the cluster and spread types. EC2 instances are spread across partitions, ensuring that groups of instances are isolated from each other. This provides a shield against hardware failures and is a right for distributed and replicated workloads. For example, this is suited for large distributed systems such as Hadoop, Cassandra, or Kafka, where you spread your instances across multiple partitions to reduce the impact of hardware failures or maintenance events on a single partition affecting the entire application.

Here is the illustration below describing the usecase of different types of placement group:

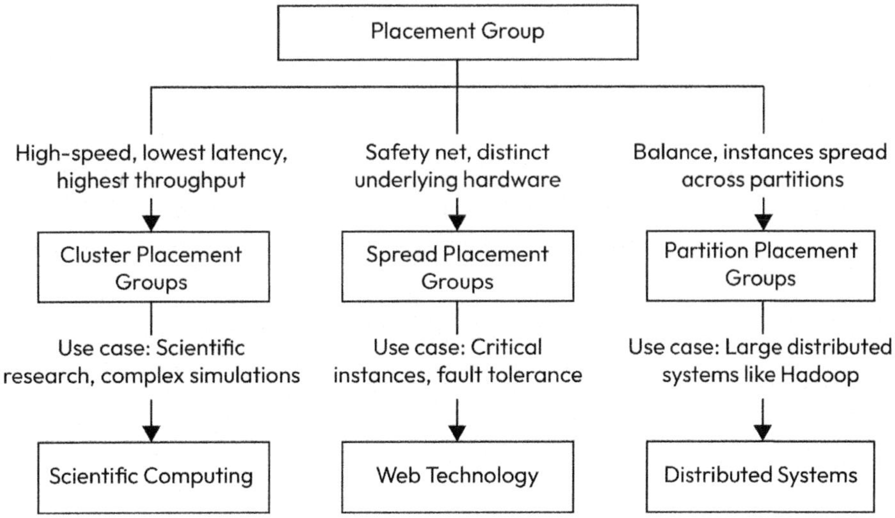

Figure 9.1 – Illustration of a placement group

But why go through the effort of understanding and selecting the right placement group type? Well, beyond the technical specifications, these groups offer some compelling advantages to your operations and the performance of your applications. Now, let's shift our focus and delve into understanding the benefits of using placement groups to see why they are such an invaluable tool in your Amazon EC2 toolkit.

Benefits of using placement groups

While architecting solutions leveraging Amazon EC2, understanding placement groups and their benefits can be a game-changer. They are tailored to enhance the performance and resilience of your applications, ensuring they run optimally. Here's why they should be a part of your design strategy:

- **Optimized performance**: With cluster placement groups, your instances get to enjoy a low-latency network, making them suitable for data-intensive tasks such as HPC and more.
- **High availability**: Spread placement groups enhance the fault-tolerant nature of your applications. By distributing instances across the underlying hardware, the risk of simultaneous failures is significantly reduced. Also, with partition placement groups, instances are isolated in partitions and even if one partition faces an outage, the others remain unaffected, ensuring uptime and high availability.
- **Predictable performance**: EC2 instances within the same partition placement group get very predictable performance, making placement groups ideal for running distributed systems such as Hadoop.

- **Efficient network**: Placement groups, especially cluster types, come with the benefit of a 10 Gbps network, ensuring high-speed communication between instances.
- **Streamlined scaling**: When growing or modifying your applications, placement groups allow for more predictable scaling behaviors, ensuring your applications can scale both effectively and efficiently.

These benefits can significantly transform your cloud operations, but it is essential to align your deployment strategy with best practices. As we transition further, let's delve deeper into the strategies for deploying placement groups to ensure our deployments are both robust and efficient.

Strategies for deploying placement groups

In the pursuit of implementing optimized cloud architecture, the action to strategically deploy EC2 placement groups is essential. It is not only about merely understanding their types and benefits but also deploying them with a strategy tailor-fitted to your application's unique demands, whether it's for latency-sensitive tasks, large-scale distributed systems, or any other specific needs. The process of selecting and managing the right placement group type significantly influences the performance of your cloud environment. So, let's dive in and explore this mastery as we choose the right type of placement group. In the next section, we will explore the factors that guide these crucial deployment decisions.

Choosing the right type of placement group

As we dive deeper into placement groups, it is paramount to understand the fact that not all placement groups are created equal. Your selection hinges largely on the workload and its specific requirements:

- **Cluster placement groups**: These are ideal for workloads that need low-latency network performance. Think of applications such as in-memory caches, high-performance computing, and big data analytics. Here, the instances are organized into a close-knit cluster format within a single Availability Zone, thus maximizing the network throughput while also minimizing latency.
- **Partition placement groups**: These are tailored for distributed, replicated workloads across several partitions where each partition within the group has its own set of racks, with each of the racks having its own network and power source. This ensures that instances in one partition don't share the same underlying hardware with instances in other partitions. Large, distributed databases such as Hadoop, Cassandra, or Kafka can notably benefit from this setup.
- **Spread placement groups**: Spread placement groups ensure that instances are placed on distinct racks with independent networks and power sources offering higher resilience. Here, the instances are spread across underlying hardware to reduce coincidental failures. This type of placement strategy is ideal for applications that require a small number of critical instances distributed across distinct hardware. Now that you have a comprehensive view of placement groups, let's optimize their usage by understanding the best practices for placement group creation and management to ensure that your placement group decisions translate to tangible and optimized outcomes.

Best practices for placement group creation and management

When it comes to placement groups, their efficiency isn't just about choosing the right type, but also about effective creation and management. Here are some best practices to guide you in this journey:

- **One size doesn't fit all**: Always assess your application's needs. High-performance apps might benefit from cluster placement groups, while those requiring high availability might lean toward spread or partition placement groups.
- **Mind the limits**: Be mindful of the limits imposed by AWS on the number of placement groups. So, planning ahead ensures that you don't hit any unexpected roadblocks.
- **Consistent instance types**: Within the cluster placement group, always opt for instances of the same type. This ensures predictable performance and improves the chances of having available capacity when adding future instances to the group.
- **Geographical awareness**: Remember, cluster placement groups are restricted to a single availability zone. Spread placement groups distribute individual instances across multiple availability zones, ensuring each instance is in a separate zone. Meanwhile, partition placement groups can span multiple zones, with the infrastructure divided in such a way that no two partitions within the zone share the same underlying hardware.
- **Monitor and re-evaluate**: Regularly monitor the performance of your instances within the placement groups. AWS CloudWatch can be pivotal here. If you notice the performance degradation, reassess, and consider reconfiguring your placement group strategy.

A correctly configured placement group can be a game changer, significantly boosting the performance and reliability of your applications. But as with any tool, its effectiveness lies in how you wield it.

Now that we have a grasp on the best practices for the meticulous management of placement groups, let's pivot our focus toward the next topic, where we'll explore how we can further optimize performance with placement groups to truly harness their power. Let's dive in!

Optimizing performance with placement groups

Within the vast toolkit of AWS, placement groups stand as pillars for applications demanding low network latency and high throughput. By tapping into the power of these groups, users can supercharge their application performance. As we dive deeper into this section, let's explore the art of reducing inter-instance latency, a cornerstone for truly harnessing the potential of placement groups.

Reducing inter-instance latency

Reducing inter-instance latency is of paramount importance in environments where every millisecond counts, especially in high-frequency trading or real-time gaming applications. Placement groups, particularly cluster placement groups, are designed with this very need in mind. Within these groups, instances are placed in close proximity, ensuring minimal network jitter and latency. This close-knit configuration ensures data is transferred between instances at lightning-fast speeds, often mirroring the performance of on-premises computing centers.

However, while reduced latency promises efficiency, what about data transfer volumes? For that, let's shift our focus to maximizing network throughput, another dimension of fine-tuning the performance of your EC2 instances within placement groups.

Maximizing network throughput

Maximizing network throughput is similar to ensuring a highway is free from traffic jams, enabling vehicles to reach their destinations swiftly and efficiently. In the context of Amazon EC2, throughput ensures data packets flow seamlessly across instances without bottlenecks. In the realm of placement groups, particularly with cluster placement types, AWS promises up to 10 Gbps of network throughput for instances, ensuring your applications aren't bottlenecked by data transfer limitations. However, achieving peak throughput requires not only the right instance type but also a well-architected application design to utilize this bandwidth effectively. Monitoring tools such as CloudWatch can assist you in keeping an eye on your network performance and ensure you are fully leveraging the potential of placement groups.

While high-speed data transfer and reduced latency are fantastic, it is also crucial to ensure that your workloads remain available in unforeseen circumstances. So, let's discuss the design aspects of placement groups that can help you improve fault tolerance. Let's dive in!

Improving fault tolerance

Improving fault tolerance within placement groups is essential for ensuring the availability and reliability of your applications, even in the event of instances or hardware failures. This especially becomes non-negotiable for applications that are very sensitive to downtime.

For instance, when using cluster placement groups, it is advisable to distribute your critical applications across different cluster placement groups. This approach enhances redundancy and availability. For higher fault tolerance within spread placement groups, the instances are positioned on distinct hardware, thereby significantly lowering the risk that multiple instances would fail concurrently. You should align the selection of your placement group with the nature of your workload, contemplating both performance requirements and the necessity for fault tolerance.

The use of Amazon EC2 Auto Scaling is also advisable as it can automatically replace any failed instance, thus contributing to the robustness and resilience of your application infrastructure.

It is also important to recognize the fact that fault tolerance is not merely the outcome of hardware and infrastructure configurations – it is also a result of well-planned architecture design and operational practices. Practices such as regularly backing up data, utilizing Amazon EC2 Auto Scaling, and leveraging ELB can further fortify your instance's fault tolerance.

The next section will delve deeper into the dynamics of pricing models, a critical component to strategizing our infrastructure both technically and economically. Let's explore how we can get the best bang for our buck in Amazon EC2.

Introduction to Amazon EC2 pricing models

In this section, we will dive deep into understanding various pricing models, including *On-Demand Instances*, *Reserved Instances*, *Savings Plans*, and *Spot Instances*. Each of these models is tailored for specific scenarios and workloads while minimizing costs and allowing you to derive the most value out of it. With a thorough understanding of each of these pricing models, you will be empowered to make informed decisions that align with your business objectives and operational needs.

Now, let's dive deep in with the first pricing model on our list: *On-Demand Instances*. This is a straightforward and easily understandable option that provides a great starting point for understanding the nuances of EC2 pricing test

On-Demand Instances

In the landscape of cloud computing, demands can be as unpredictable as the weather. For such scenarios, AWS offers **On-Demand Instances**. Think of this as a pay-as-you-go model for the cloud world. There are no long-term commitments or upfront payments involved. You are charged for compute capacity by the hour or second, depending on which instance type you run.

These types of instances are especially suited for the following scenarios:

- **Short-term workloads**: If you have tasks that are urgent and need to be processed immediately, but only for a short period
- **Variable workloads**: If you are unsure about your application usage pattern and see a fluctuation in demand, then On-Demand Instances come to the rescue by offering maximum flexibility
- **Development and testing**: Developers who need environments for short durations or sporadic testing can utilize these instances without any commitment in the long term

The major advantage of relying on On-Demand Instances is the freedom it offers from the costs and complexities of planning, purchasing, and maintaining hardware. While On-Demand Instances offer unmatched flexibility, it's also essential to note that they might not be the cost-effective option for long-running workloads or applications.

Reserved Instances

Instance predictability is crucial for many businesses. This is where **Reserved Instances** come into play. They allow you to reserve capacity for 1 or 3 years, in exchange for a significant discount compared to on-demand pricing. It is simply like reserving your seat in the cloud in advance, ensuring capacity availability and a consistent budget.

Here's why it can be a game-changer for certain types of workloads:

- **Cost-effectiveness**: For long-term projects or steady-state workloads, Reserved Instances can offer substantial cost savings, sometimes up to 75% compared to On-Demand Instances.
- **Capacity assurance**: If you are operating within a specific region or availability zone, reserving instances guarantees that you will always have the capacity you need.
- **Budget predictability**: By committing to a 1 or 3-year term, you can better forecast your cloud expenditure. This is particularly useful for budget-conscious organizations.

There are different payment options available: *all upfront*, *partial upfront*, and *no upfront*. These terms dictate whether you pay for instances in a lump sum or through monthly installments.

But what if you are looking for a balance between the spontaneity of On-Demand Instances and the commitment of Reserved Instances? Well, AWS has you covered with Savings Plans. Let's take a look.

Savings plans

Savings Plans are another approach that AWS offers you to save on your EC2 costs while maintaining the flexibility to change your instance type as required. These plans introduce a committed usage rate and are billed hourly, providing you with a discount on on-demand pricing in exchange for a commitment to a consistent amount of usage (measured in $/hour) for a 1 or 3-year period.

Here's why Savings Plans shine:

- **Flexible and cost-effective**: With a Savings Plans, there is no need to stick to a particular instance type or family, region, or size. You simply commit to an hourly dollar amount of usage and in return, you receive discounts, allowing you to adapt to changing requirements while enjoying cost savings.
- **Significant discounts**: Savings Plans offer substantial savings over on-demand pricing – up to 72% - making them an ideal option for businesses with steady-state usage or long-term projects.
- **Simplicity**: With this plan, budgeting becomes straightforward. You understand your bill with the simplicity of paying for the hourly commitment, regardless of how your use cases evolve.

Now, how does this work?

How does it work?

Let's deep dive and understand how the different Savings Plans work:

- **Compute Savings Plan**: This model provides unparalleled versatility and the highest flexibility in managing AWS compute resources. Here's how it benefits users:
  - You can commit to a specific dollar-per-hour usage across any AWS compute usage
  - You have the liberty to change instance families, sizes, tenancy, or shift between AWS regions, ensuring savings, so long as you don't exceed your committed dollar amount per hour
  - This is especially advantageous to dynamic workloads, where your compute needs might vary but you still wish to have predictable workloads
- **EC2 instance Savings Plan**: This model comes with a significant cost reduction with defined commitments. Here's how it benefits users:
  - You commit to consistent use of specific instance families in a designated region (for example, M5 in ap-southeast-1)
  - In return for this commitment, you achieve substantial discounts

This is ideal for steady-state workloads where the exact instance family and region are well-defined and unlikely to change.

While Savings Plans offer a broad spectrum of flexibility and cost savings, AWS also has an option for workloads with flexible start and end times, or that can withstand interruptions. Let's dive in and explore the next pricing model, Spot Instances, to understand how they can further optimize our AWS costs.

Spot Instances

This represents AWS's ingenious approach to optimizing unused EC2 capacity. Here, AWS allows you to tap into their surplus compute power at a cost much lower than regular on-demand pricing, making it an attractive option for flexible, temporary, or interruptible workloads.

Here's why Spot Instances stand out:

- **Budget-friendly**: By leveraging AWS's spare capacity, you can enjoy potential savings of up to 90% compared to on-demand prices
- **Ephemeral yet effective**: While the instances are reclaimed once the spare capacity diminishes, AWS offers a 3-minute warning, ensuring you can wrap up vital tasks or save your progress
- **Versatile use cases**: Whether it's batch jobs, data analysis, or even stateless web servers, Spot Instances can handle a broad array of tasks without breaking the bank

How it works

When you request Spot Instances, you bid a price. If your bid meets or exceeds the current spot price, and there's capacity available, your request is fulfilled. Remember, these instances last as long as the spot price is below your bid and capacity exists.

Next, we'll explore the next dimension of EC2 pricing – that is, choosing the right pricing model – to ensure you are not just harnessing power but doing so in the most cost-effective manner with AWS.

Choosing the right pricing model

In the world of AWS, the choice of EC2 pricing model is paramount. Each project has its unique technical and budgetary needs and understanding EC2's pricing intricacies is key to ensuring optimal performance while maintaining cost efficiency. In this section, we will deep dive into the various cost optimization strategies, the suitability of various pricing models for specific use cases, and the art of striking a balance between power and price. Let's dive in.

Cost optimization strategies

AWS pricing models offer flexibility and options designed to suit various needs and scenarios:

- **Utilize Reserved Instances and Savings Plans**: Adopting Reserved Instances for steady-state workloads and Savings Plans for fluctuating workloads can drive down costs significantly. With Reserved Instances, you commit to a specific instance type in a region, receiving a substantial discount. Meanwhile, Savings Plans offer flexibility, allowing commitment to a specific dollar-per-hour usage, allowing us to switch between instance types and still enjoy discounts.

- **Leverage Spot Instances for temporary workloads**: Spot Instances provide an economical choice for workloads that are interruptible. They allow you to use spare capacity at a potentially lower price but can be terminated by AWS with little notice if they need the capacity back.

- **Employ auto scaling for dynamic workloads**: Auto scaling adjusts your application's instance capacity for predictable performance at the lowest possible cost. It helps you maintain the right balance of instances to handle the loads of your application efficiently, reducing the cost further.

- **Monitor and analyze with AWS Cost Explorer**: The AWS Cost Explorer interface enables you to view and analyze your costs and usage. With it, you can identify areas that need attention and see trends that can shape your future strategy.

Now, let's look into specific use cases of different pricing models to understand when and how to apply these strategies effectively.

Use cases for different pricing models

Choosing the right pricing model is not only about saving money but also about ensuring optimal performance for your specific workloads. Each of the pricing models is designed with specific scenarios in mind, and understanding these can make all the difference:

- **On-Demand Instances**: These instances are best suited for short-term, irregular workloads that cannot be interrupted. This is ideal for development and testing environments or running applications that have unpredictable workloads. If your firm is new to AWS, starting with On-Demand Instances provides a pay-as-you-go rate without any upfront cost or commitment while offering maximum flexibility.

- **Reserved Instances**: This is a wise choice for predictable workloads. Reserved Instances offer up to 75% savings over the same instance charged at an on-demand rate. If you have applications that require reserved capacity, these instances provide a significant discount compared to on-demand pricing and offer a capacity reservation when used in a specific availability zone.

- **Savings Plans**: This is ideal for users with flexible workloads where savings plans offer significant savings over on-demand pricing, in exchange for a commitment to a consistent amount of compute power usage (in $/hour) for a 1 or 3-year period. It offers more flexibility as you can switch between instances, use part of your commitment toward different AWS services, and save up to 72% over on-demand pricing.

- **Spot Instances**: These are ideal for workloads with flexible start and end times. Spot Instances offer the option to capitalize on unused capacity at a potentially lower price. However, these instances can be terminated with little notice if AWS needs the capacity back.

Selecting the right pricing model is critical, but striking the ideal balance between cost and performance is equally crucial. Let's explore how to maintain this delicate balance while ensuring that your applications run smoothly and efficiently.

Balancing performance and cost

Striking the right balance between performance and cost is akin to striking gold in the cloud computing landscape. AWS offers a suite of tools and services that provide excellent performance, understanding how to harness these without unnecessary expenditure is an art in itself.

- **Prioritizing workloads**: Recognize which workloads are critical and which are less so. Core applications that form the backbone of your business operations should be allocated higher resources and hosted on instances that offer peak performance. On the other hand, sporadic, non-critical workloads can be assigned to cost-effective, interruptible workloads.

- **Employ Auto Scaling**: EC2 Auto Scaling allows you to dynamically adjust your resources based on actual demand. During high-demand periods, additional resources can be provisioned to maintain performance and during lull times, resources can be scaled down to save costs.

- **Utilizing performance metrics**: Regularly monitor key performance metrics using tools such as Amazon CloudWatch. These insights allow you to scale resources up or down based on actual usage. This allows you to ensure that you are not overpaying for unused capacity
- **Review and revise**: Regularly review your infrastructure choices. AWS continuously introduces newer instance types that might offer better performance at a similar or even reduced cost. Migrating to newer instances can help you achieve better cost-efficiency.

Let us now look into the mechanisms that will help you effectively monitor and manage your AWS expenditure.

Monitoring and managing costs

Ensuring optimal performance on AWS is only one side of the coin. The other crucial aspect revolves around managing and monitoring your expenditures. With AWS, users benefit not only from a versatile and powerful infrastructure but also from a comprehensive set of tools designed to provide visibility, insights, and control over costs. As organizations scale and diversify their AWS usage, it becomes paramount to have an eagle-eyed view of every dollar spent, ensuring alignment with budgetary constraints and organization goals. Let's embark on this journey by covering AWS Cost Explorer, an intuitive interface that provides a granular look at your AWS expenditure.

AWS Cost Explorer

As we scale and grow on the AWS platform, understanding and analyzing our cost structure becomes ever more critical. Enter **AWS Cost Explorer**, a tool that is designed to make it easier for you to visualize, understand, and manage your AWS costs and usage over time. Imagine Cost Explorer as your financial magnifying glass, enabling you to view your costs and usage patterns with an overarching lens and fine granularity.

With AWS Cost Explorer, you can do the following:

- **Identify opportunities for cost savings**: By inspecting the usage patterns, you can identify underutilized resources and make informed decisions about downsizing or terminating them
- **Forecast your future needs**: By leveraging its predictive capabilities, you can get a clearer picture of what your AWS expenditures might look like in the upcoming months
- **Analyze spending patterns**: You can break down your AWS costs by individual services, linked accounts, or even custom tags, granting comprehensive insights into where and how the resources are consumed
- **Monitor reserved instance utilization**: Ensure that you are getting the most value from your Reserved Instances by tracking their utilization and adjusting as necessary

Armed with this understanding of AWS Cost Explorer, you can streamline the budgeting, cost allocation, and financial governance of your AWS resources. However, this is just one side of it and effective budget management also lies in receiving timely alerts regarding the cost control mechanism. Let's dive in and understand how budgets and alerts act as guardians of your AWS financial health.

Budgets and alerts

As we move forward in our journey of cost management, the role of setting up the right alerts and budgets in AWS cannot be understated. They serve as an early warning system, safeguarding you from unwanted surprises in your monthly AWS bill.

AWS Budgets allows you to allocate a specific amount of resources or actions for your services. More importantly, they come with a feature of alerts. These alerts are automated notifications that are triggered when your usage crosses your budgeted amount. This can be in terms of actual cost, forecasted cost, or both.

Here are the benefits of budgets and alerts in your cost management discipline:

- **Proactive monitoring**: Instead of passively waiting to see bills at the end of the month, budgets and alerts ensure you are always in the know and can adjust resources or strategies proactively.
- **Cost management**: Defining the thresholds of your costs encourages a culture of effective resource management and ensures your cloud usage remains within your financial constraints.
- **Operational efficiency**: Alerts can also be linked to operational metrics, ensuring that you are not just cost-efficient but also operationally efficient.

Beyond this, there are comprehensive filters available for you to view cost and usage at a granular level. These filters can be defined by services, linked accounts, tags, and much more. This allows you to precisely understand your expenses, efficiently allocate resources, and strategically plan for future expenditures.

Summary

We have come to the end of this chapter, where we explored the realm of Amazon EC2 placement groups and pricing models. We have peeled the layers back on crucial aspects of AWS's pricing structure, strategies, and other vital tools that are at our disposal for effective cost management. This foundational knowledge is imperative for mastering the financial dimensions of AWS and setting the stage for cost-effective, efficient, and powerful deployment of services and resources.

With this robust understanding in place, it's time to explore the crucial arena of monitoring, logging, and maintenance when it comes to CloudWatch, CloudTrail, and Backup strategies. Prepare to deep dive into the mechanisms that ensure your AWS infrastructure is not just cost-effective but also resilient, secure, and meticulously monitored for optimal performance and reliability.

10
Monitoring, Logging, and Maintenance with Amazon CloudWatch, AWS CloudTrail, and Backup Strategies

Monitoring and management are the pivotal pillars in the cloud operations landscape. They are not merely about keeping a watchful eye but about security, optimization, and foreseeing nuances in your operating environment even before they manifest. As we navigate through the intricate channels of the Amazon EC2 environment, it is strikingly clear how robust and multifaceted its monitoring tools stand. This chapter aims to demystify these tools, offering you a panoramic yet detailed understanding of their workings and potential.

This chapter's narrative primarily revolves around two paramount entities: Amazon **CloudWatch**, popular for its real-time monitoring capabilities, and AWS **CloudTrail**, the master sentinel tracking every AWS operational activity. We will dive deep into their territories discussing what functionalities they offer, how they complement each other, and how they can be harnessed to enhance security, auditability, and performance. By the end of this chapter, you will be equipped with not just the knowledge but also the acumen to leverage these tools optimally.

The following topics will be covered in this chapter:

- Introduction to Amazon CloudWatch and AWS CloudTrail
- Amazon CloudWatch essentials
- AWS CloudTrail for auditing and security
- EC2 patch management

- Performance tuning, capacity planning, and resource management
- Backup and disaster recovery strategies.

Introduction to Amazon CloudWatch and AWS CloudTrail

In this section, we will demystify the roles of CloudWatch and CloudTrail as vigilant guardians of operational excellence and security in the cloud environment. As we unfold the narrative, you will come to clearly understand that they are not merely tools but integral companions guiding you through the realms of robust, resilient, and optimized cloud architectures. So, let us dive deep and explore the myriad of functionalities, ensuring that your cloud voyage is seamless and secure.

Overview of monitoring and logging in AWS

Monitoring in AWS provides a real-time lens into the performance of your resources, enabling swift action to maintain application health while logging the history of events, a key component for audit trails and troubleshooting.

Monitoring ensures that all your AWS resources—including EC2 instance and S3 buckets—function as expected. This proactive measure can alert you to any anomalies or potential bottlenecks, helping you to avoid downtime or degradation in service quality. It is akin to a regular health check-up, catching symptoms before they manifest as significant issues. For example, imagine caching an unexpected CPU spike in an EC2 instance before it affects your application performance.

On the other hand, **logging** is all about accountability and traceability. It allows us to ensure each action, each access, and each change in your AWS environment is documented. This comprehensive record is invaluable, especially when identifying the root cause of an issue or while ensuring that proper security protocols have been followed; for example, auditing to trace the source for an unexpected change in your IAM policy.

Both these mechanisms intervene to ensure the optimal functioning of your AWS resources, but how do they differ when we look at them through the lens of CloudWatch and CloudTrail? This basically sets the stage for the upcoming section, where we will discuss the distinct capabilities and utilities of Amazon CloudWatch and CloudTrail.

Differences between CloudWatch and CloudTrail

Navigating through the nuanced landscape of AWS's monitoring and logging tools, CloudWatch and CloudTrail each hold a distinctive use case in the realm of cloud management. CloudWatch emerges as a real-time guardian, meticulously monitoring, alerting, and visualizing operational activities to ensure the pulse of your system's health and performance remains robust. In contrast, CloudTrail acts as a meticulous historian, documenting the details of every API call meeting your requirements for audits, governance, and compliance insights.

Here's a tabular illustration that delineates their differences:

S.No	Attribute	CloudWatch	CloudTrail
1.	Primary focus	Operational monitoring	Governance, compliance, and audit
2.	Data monitored	Metrics, alarms, logs	API calls and data events
3.	Use cases	Performance tuning, resource optimization	Security analysis, change tracking, and auditing
4.	Integration	Deep integration with AWS Services	Broad coverage for AWS services (S3, CloudWatch, Lambda, Athena, and so on) for auditing
5.	Customizability	Custom metrics and dashboard	Limited to recorded events

Table 10.1 – Comparison of the key attributes of CloudWatch and CloudTrail

Having understood the differences, let's transition to a closer inspection of Amazon CloudWatch essentials, starting with its robust system of metrics, alarms, and events.

Amazon CloudWatch essentials

CloudWatch stands out not just as a mere tool but as the heartbeat of your cloud operations. You can consider it as similar to the nervous system of a living organism, capturing every fluctuation, every pulse, and every whisper of your cloud resources. By collecting these granular details, CloudWatch doesn't just tell us what's happening—it unfolds the entire story behind every metric, log, and alarm.

In this section specifically, we will embark on a journey to unveil the essentials of Amazon CloudWatch. We will begin our journey by exploring metrics, alarms, and events, which stand as the bedrock of monitoring. Moving forward, we will dive into understanding custom metrics and the monitoring of EC2 instances, CloudWatch dashboards, and visualization, as well as CloudWatch logs and log insights.

Metrics, alarms, and events

Metrics, alarms, and events are the silent narrators of your system stories. Imagine having a pulse on your application's heart, feeling every beat and rhythm in real time. That's exactly what metrics bring to the table. **Metrics** serve as a language through which your resources communicate their performance and health. They silently collect data and help you gauge the health and performance of your applications.

Alarms, on the other hand, stand as vigilant guardians and messengers, tirelessly watching over operations, ready to alert us if things are observed to be a bit off. **Events** herald the changes and operations in your environment. They encompass the array of automated responses and workflows, bolstering the resilience and reactivity of your applications.

With this foundational understanding in place, you must be curious to understand how these components interplay to create a symphony of seamless operations. This will be covered next, as we spotlight custom metrics and EC2 monitoring.

Custom metrics and monitoring EC2 instances

In Amazon CloudWatch, the standard metrics provide you with a breadth of insight, but sometimes, there's a space where you might feel that you need to venture beyond the standard. Enter **custom metrics**. They are like tailor-made suits, fitting perfectly to the unique requirements of your operational needs, allowing you to add your flavor to ensure you monitor what matters the most to you. The nature of metrics provides you with nuanced insights, amplifying the understanding of your application and system performance beyond the conventional means.

As you equip your monitoring with custom metrics, a panorama of operational clarity unveils itself. It enables you to oversee the intricacies, grasp the unseen patterns, and hone in on areas that echo potential inconsistencies or rooms for refinement. For example, imagine creating a custom metric to track the memory usage of a critical application, something not natively monitored by AWS. This metric reveals usage spikes that a standard AWS metric might miss.

As you understand the individualized insights that custom metrics bring, up next, we will step into a world where data is not just viewed but visually experienced.

CloudWatch dashboards and visualization

At its core, a dashboard is your canvas, allowing you to create a comprehensive picture of your AWS environment. Whether it is tracking your EC2 instances or monitoring S3 bucket activities, the dashboard gives you the convenience of aggregating your metrics and visualizing them in a format that resonates with your needs. It is not just about numbers or logs; it is about understanding the stories they tell when placed side by side, enabling quicker insights and faster decision-making.

The CloudWatch dashboard seamlessly integrates with various metrics and operational insights, presenting the metrics and alarms that resonate the most with your monitoring objectives. They are not merely passive displays but interactive interfaces, enabling you to sift through, scrutinize, and swiftly respond to the operational rhythms of your environment.

Let us now look into understanding the nuances of CloudWatch logs and log insights.

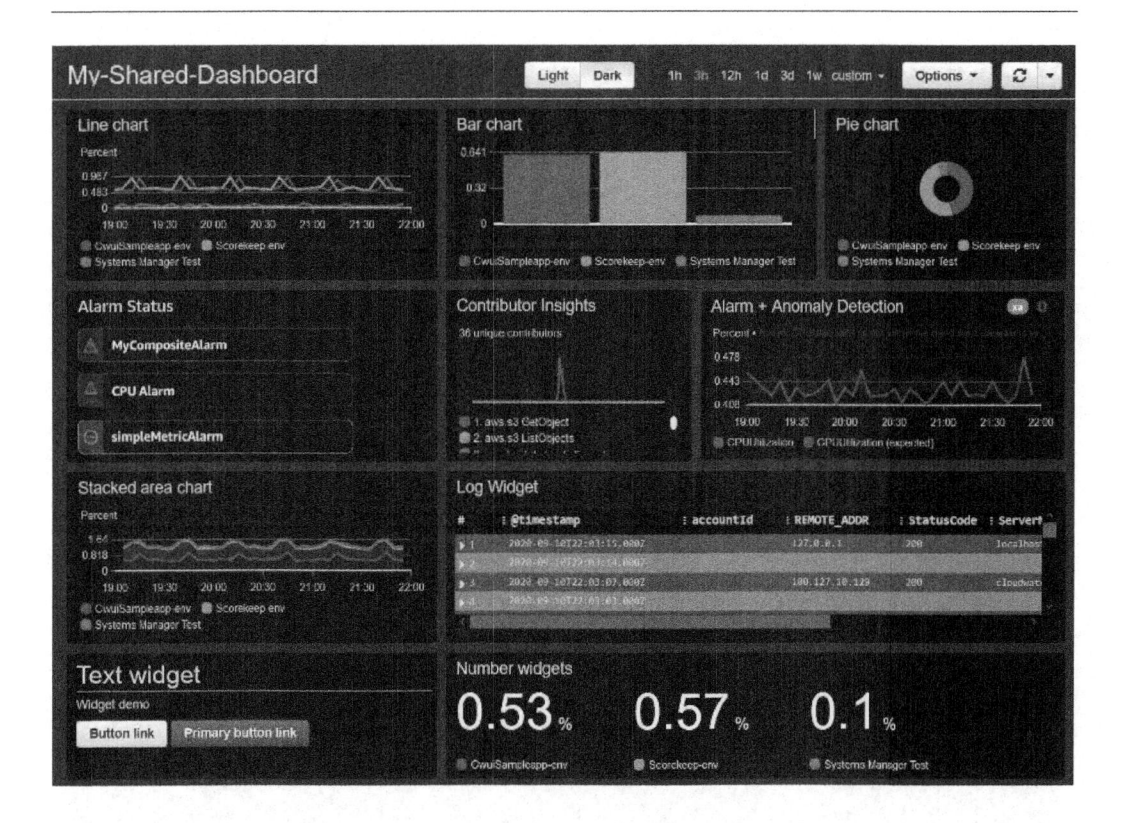

Figure 10.1 – Sample CloudWatch dashboard

CloudWatch logs and log insights

CloudWatch logs act as a diligent curator, gathering, processing, and storing data from various AWS resources. It is not just a reservoir of logs, but a dynamic landscape where logs narrate the story of application activities and health. This allows you to dive deep into the troubleshooting avenues, making sure that you are always on top of your application's performance and security.

As you traverse deeper, **log insights** emerge as the illuminating beacon in your broad and deep data pool. This acts as your ally in unearthing meaningful insights, unmasking the trends, and patterns camouflaged within the raw log data. CloudWatch log insights are also supported by potent query language, enabling you to seamlessly unravel the layers of data, revealing narratives that were once elusive, and enriching your analysis and overall decision-making process.

In conclusion, CloudWatch logs and log insights stand as monumental pillars in your expedition through Amazon CloudWatch. They equip you with tools and perspectives to translate raw, unstructured data into insightful stories and actionable intelligence.

AWS CloudTrail for auditing and security

AWS CloudTrail is a sentinel standing vigilant over the realm of auditing and security. Imagine if every footstep, every whisper, and every movement within a vast empire were chronicled meticulously. CloudTrail performs a similar role for your AWS environment, documenting each API call and giving detailed information of who did what and when. CloudTrail comes in as a gold standard for organizations to audit and ensure each and every action within AWS meets the necessary compliance requirements.

With this understanding, let us understand the intricacies of setting up and configuring CloudTrail.

Setting up and configuring CloudTrail

The following is the simplified guide to setting up and configuring CloudTrail:

1. **Log in to the AWS console**: Begin by signing into the AWS management console. Navigate to the services drop-down menu and select **CloudTrail**:

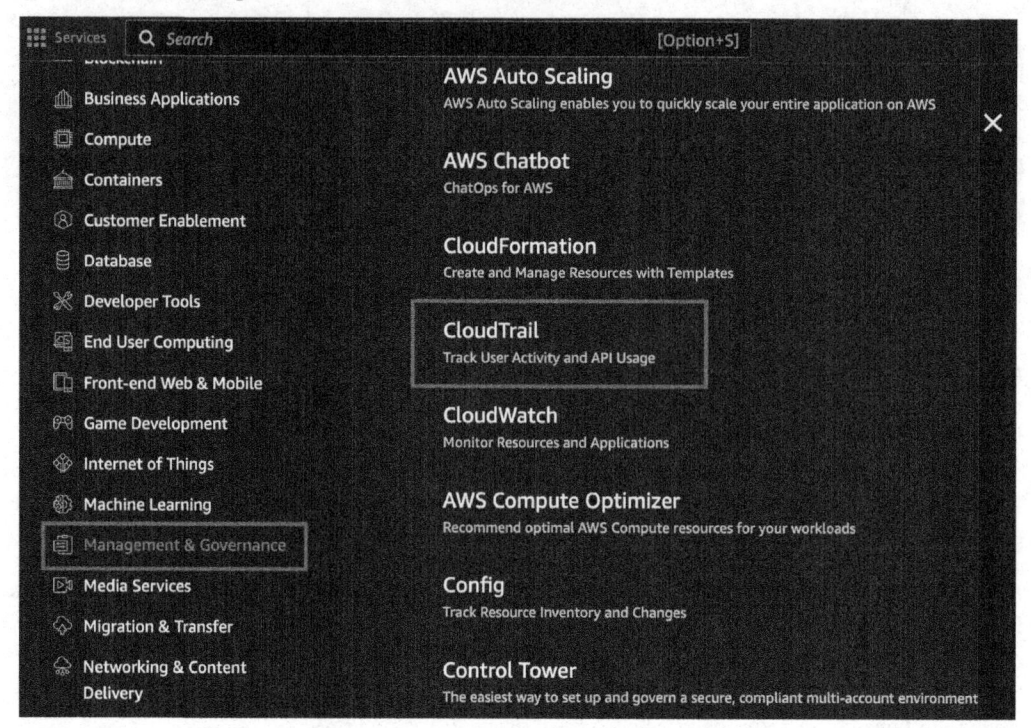

Figure 10.2 – CloudTrail service selection

2. **Create a trail**: Upon navigating to the CloudTrail dashboard, click on **Create trail**. Provide a meaningful name for your trail. This ensures that you can easily identify a specific trail among the other trails you may have created:

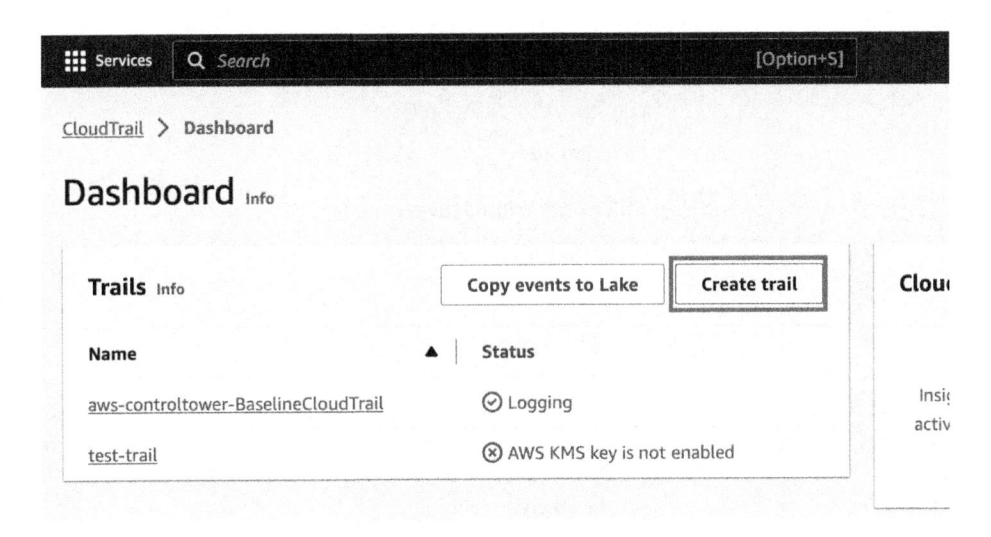

Figure 10.3 – Defining a new trail

3. **Choose or create an S3 bucket**: CloudTrail logs need storage. Here, you can either create a new S3 bucket or select an existing one. It is essential to ensure that the target S3 bucket has appropriate permissions to allow CloudTrail to write logs in it. Failing to do so will fail the delivery of logs from CloudTrail:

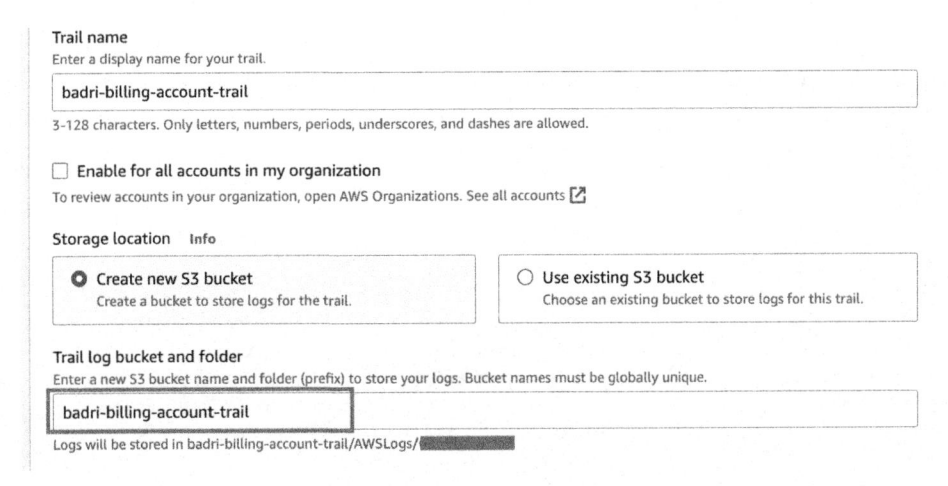

Figure 10.4 – S3 bucket details for storing trail logs

4. **Log file SSE (encryption)**: For an additional layer of security, enable **server-side encryption (SSE)** for your logs. This ensures that your logs are encrypted within the S3 bucket:

Figure 10.5 – KMS key to encrypt CloudTrail logs

5. **Enable log file integrity validation**: This feature will allow you to receive notifications when your log files are altered or deleted. It provides an added assurance to the integrity of your log files:

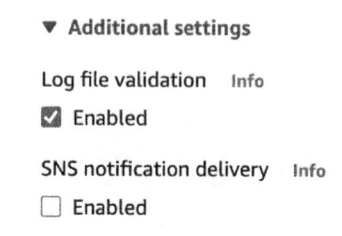

Figure 10.6 – Activating CloudTrail log validation

6. **Choose AWS Regions**: By default, CloudTrail will log events in the region where it is set up, but if you wish to capture events from all regions, ensure that you select **Apply trail to all regions**.

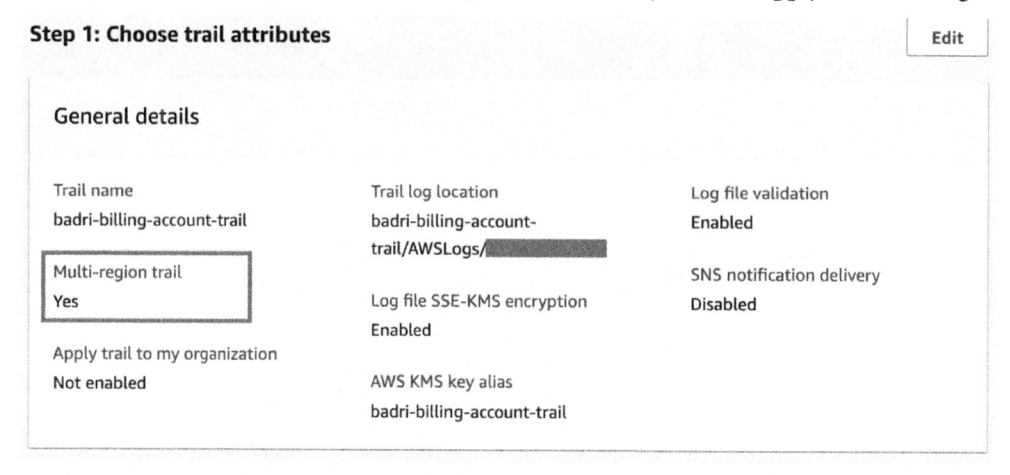

Figure 10.7 – Validation of multi-region trail activation

7. **Review and create**: Once all the settings are in place, review your configuration to ensure accuracy. Once you are satisfied, click on the **Create trail** button. Your CloudTrail will start logging events based on your setup:

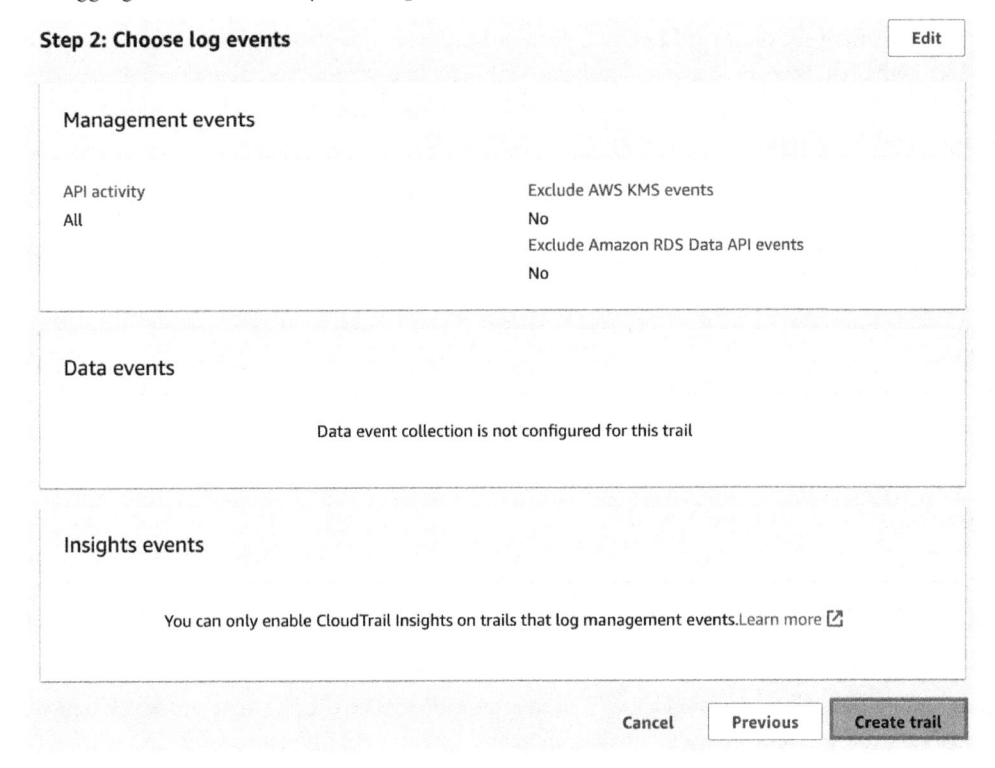

Figure 10.8 – Creating a trail

8. **Verification**: After the trail is created, it is good practice to verify its functionality. Perform some activities in your AWS environment and check the corresponding S3 bucket to see if CloudTrail logs them.

Now, with CloudTrail effectively setting up to monitor your activities, it's time to analyze logs for security and compliance.

Analyzing logs for security and compliance

Analyzing CloudTrail logs must be a routine exercise to examine and interpret the trail of API calls to unveil patterns, discern anomalies. and unearth potential vulnerabilities. Doing this not only strengthens security by facilitating early detection of suspicious activities but also fosters a robust compliance environment by ensuring that operational practices align seamlessly with regulatory requirements and organizational policies.

This analysis necessitates that we actively seek out signs of unauthorized or unusual activity. This could probably range from repeated login failures, including possible brute-force attacks, to unexpected spikes in resource utilization, pointing toward potential system vulnerabilities or misconfigurations.

Compliance analysis, on the other hand, ensures that the conduct within your cloud environment adheres to the requisite standards and policies. The activity involves validating that the resources are properly configured, access permissions are properly assigned, and the sensitive actions in your AWS environment are adequately secured, properly logged, and so on.

Let us now understand how CloudTrail integrates with other AWS services to extend its auditing capabilities.

CloudTrail integration with other AWS services

CloudTrail seamlessly integrates with essential AWS services to provide a seamless monitoring and auditing experience. It works in harmony with services such as S3, where it securely stores your log files, ensuring that they are safely kept for any future auditing or analysis. It also extends its integration with CloudWatch logs, offering a real-time glimpse into the activities across your AWS resources, ultimately enhancing your visibility and awareness.

Another noteworthy thing to mention is its integration with AWS Lambda. This integration will enable you to achieve an automatic response to a specific trail of CloudTrail events, helping to ensure immediate action is taken when something is off. CloudTrail doesn't just operate in isolation; its integration with various AWS services helps ensure that your auditing and security mechanisms operate like a well-oiled machine.

As we wrap up our discussion on CloudTrail, we transition to a new topic, maintenance best practices. This is a crucial segment where you will understand essential maintenance strategies such as patch management, performance tuning, and capacity planning.

EC2 maintenance best practices

The smooth operation and health of your AWS environment goes beyond just setting things up and lies importantly in maintaining your environment. In this section, we will dive deep into the world of AWS maintenance, emphasizing its importance and strategies to make the most of your resources.

Imagine your AWS environment as a well-tuned orchestra. Without regular practice and adjustments, even the finest instruments can sound out of tune. Similar to how the orchestra needs regular fine-tuning, your EC2 instances and other AWS resources require consistent maintenance practices to perform optimally. Ready to dive into the specifics? Let's kick off the exploration with *Patch management for EC2 instances*.

Patch management for EC2 instances

Patch management is a critical aspect of maintaining the operational health and security of your EC2 instances. AWS **Systems Manager** (**SSM**) plays a pivotal role in streamlining this process. Let's dive in further and explore how SSM can assist you in ensuring your instances are always fortified with the latest security updates and configurations.

Utilizing AWS Systems Manager

AWS SSM is a powerful tool that enables a structured and automated approach to applying patches. It facilitates centralized control, allowing you to administer patches across a fleet of EC2 instances seamlessly. It nurtures a proactive patching strategy, allowing you to schedule and deploy patches to ensure that your systems are always in adherence with compliance and security norms.

Strategizing patching activities

Strategizing patching activities requires a thoughtful approach to ensure the maintenance of optimal performance and security for your AWS resources. Let us dive in and explore the details:

1. **Assessment**: Start with an assessment for understanding what the patches available are and their relevance to your instances. Prioritize the patches based on the criticality of the vulnerabilities they address.
2. **Scheduling and timing**: Schedule the patching activity during off-peak hours to minimize the impact on your business operations. Ensure you have a structured schedule and avoid ad-hoc patches unless necessary for urgent vulnerabilities.
3. **Automation**: Leverage the SSM automation to streamline the patching process, reducing manual intervention and errors. Make use of the SSM maintenance windows to specify the pre-defined schedule for patch execution.
4. **Testing**: Before deploying patching across all of your EC2 instances, test the patches on a select group to gauge their impact and effectiveness. Make use of SSM patch baseline to curate a group of approved patches for your deployment.
5. **Review and reporting**: Regularly review the patch process and ensure it aligns with your evolving organizational needs. Make use of SSM's robust reporting feature to maintain clear visibility into the patching activities and their outcomes.

How to schedule patching for EC2 instances using AWS SSM

The following are detailed steps for scheduling simple patching for EC2 instances using AWS SSM:

1. **Navigate to the SSM console**: Navigate to the AWS SSM home page in the AWS management console:

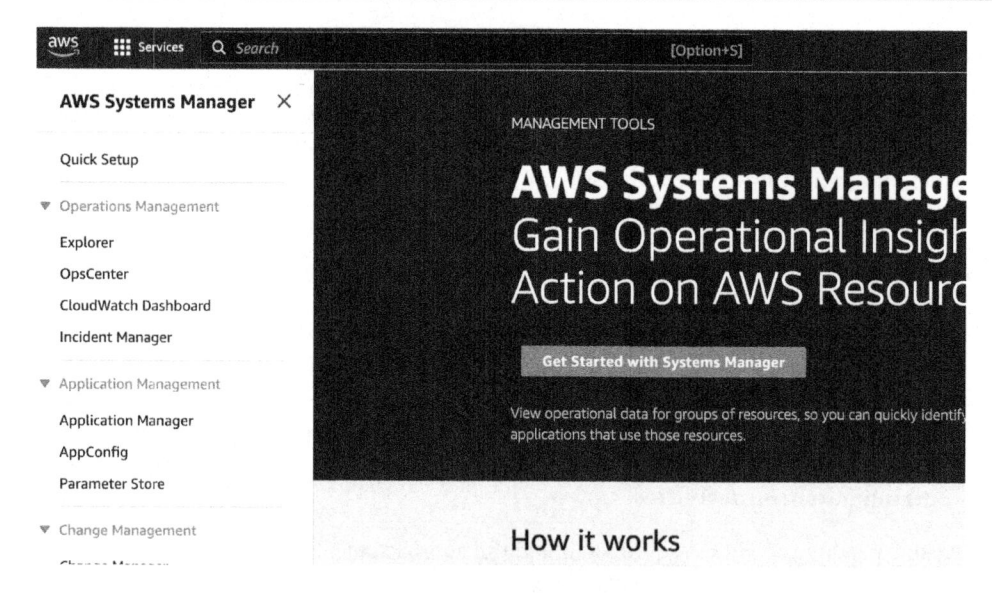

Figure 10.9 – AWS SSM landing page

2. **Access patch manager**: In the navigation pane, choose **Patch Manager** under **Node Management**:

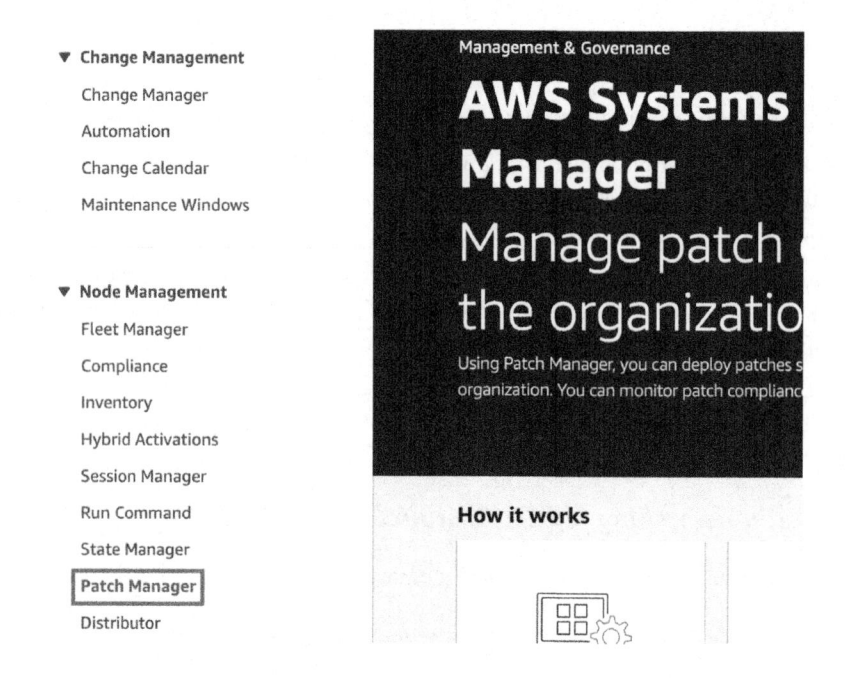

Figure 10.10 – Navigating to SSM Patch Manager

3. **Define patch baselines**: The patch baseline defines a set of rules for auto-approving patches for your system. The following steps detail the process involved in setting up the patch baseline:

   I. Go to **Patch Manager** and select **Create patch baseline**:

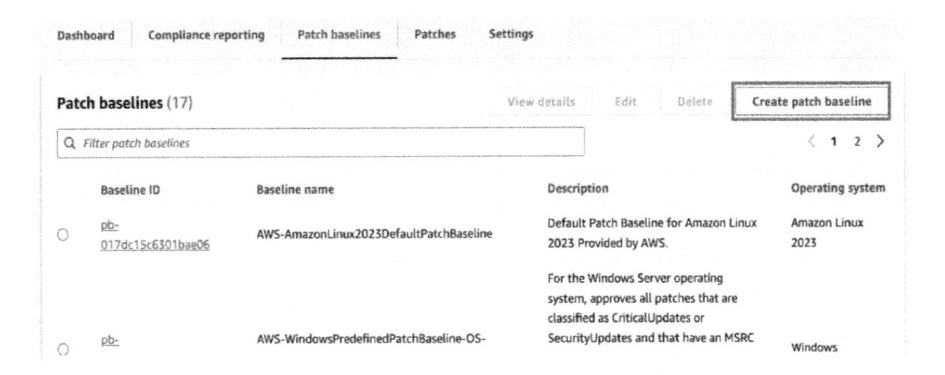

   Figure 10.11 – Defining a new patch baseline

   II. Enter necessary details such as a name, description, operating system, and approval rules:

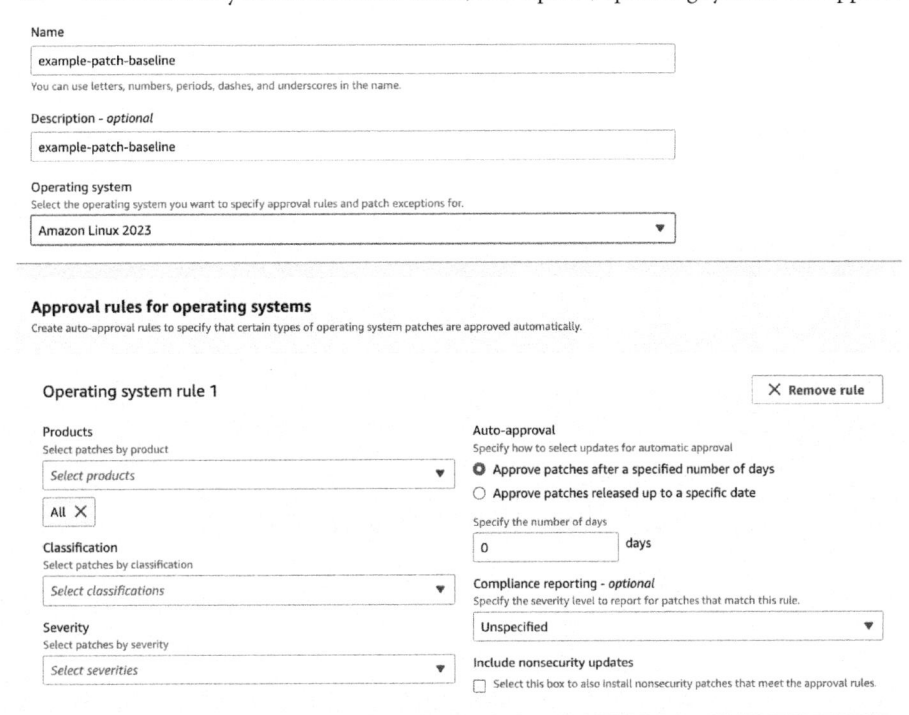

   Figure 10.12 – Patch baseline configuration details

III. Choose **Create patch baseline**:

Figure 10.13 – Creating a new patch baseline

4. **Configure the patch group**: Patch groups define a logical grouping of EC2 instances used to manage patching operations. The following steps describe the process involved in configuring the patch group:

   I. Tag your EC2 instances to define the patch group, e.g. set **Key** to **Patch Group** and **Value** to **Batch1**:

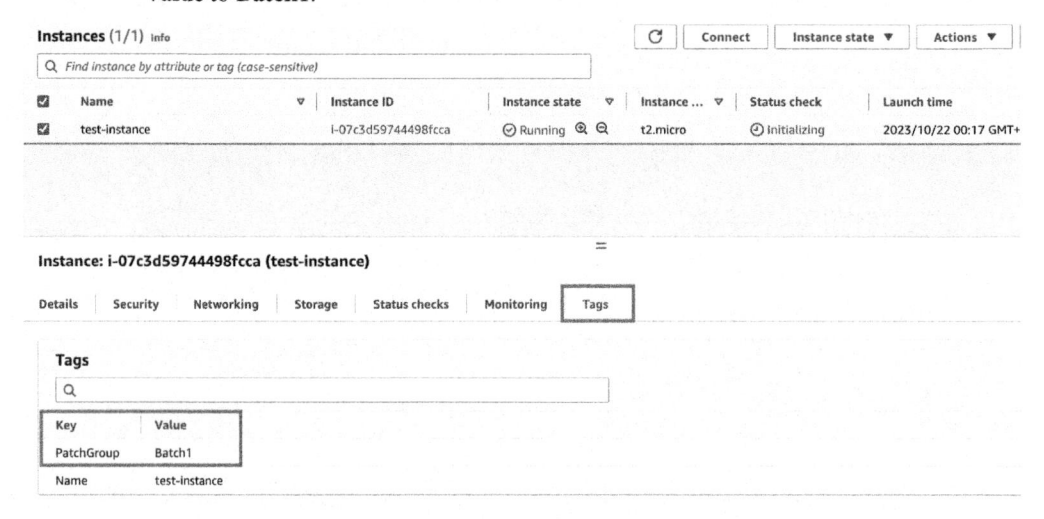

Figure 10.14 – Defining tags for an EC2 instance

EC2 maintenance best practices   255

II. Navigate to **AWS Resource Groups**, choose **Create resource group**, then define the patch group details and select **Create group**:

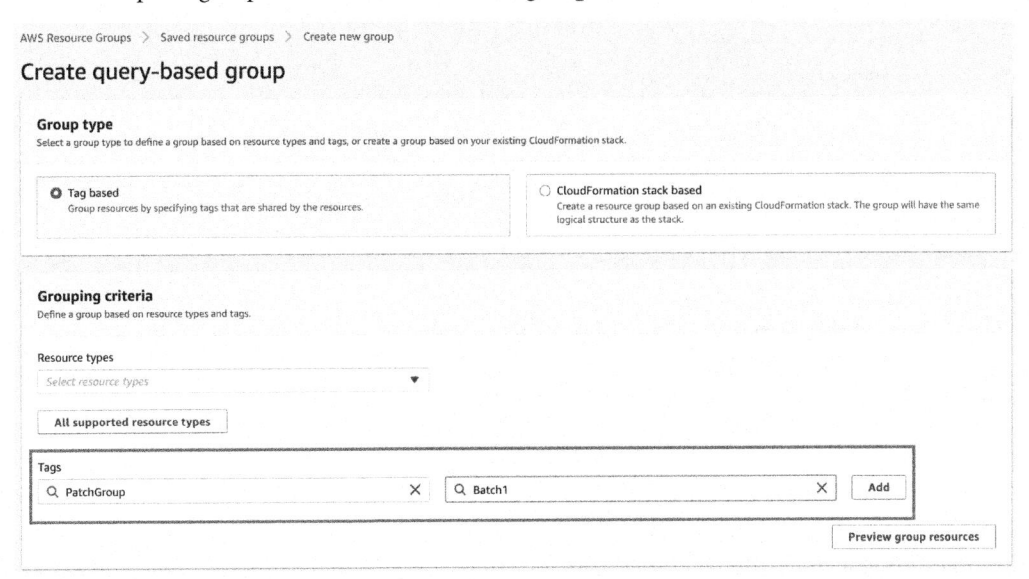

Figure 10.15 – Tag-based AWS resource group configuration

5. **Schedule maintenance windows**: Creating maintenance window allows you to define a time period to schedule patching on the underlying instances. Let's explore the steps:

   I. In the navigation pane, select **Maintenance Windows** and then **Create a maintenance window**:

Figure 10.16 – Defining a new maintenance window

II. Fill in necessary fields, such as **Name**, **Schedule**, **Duration**, and **Stop initiating tasks**:

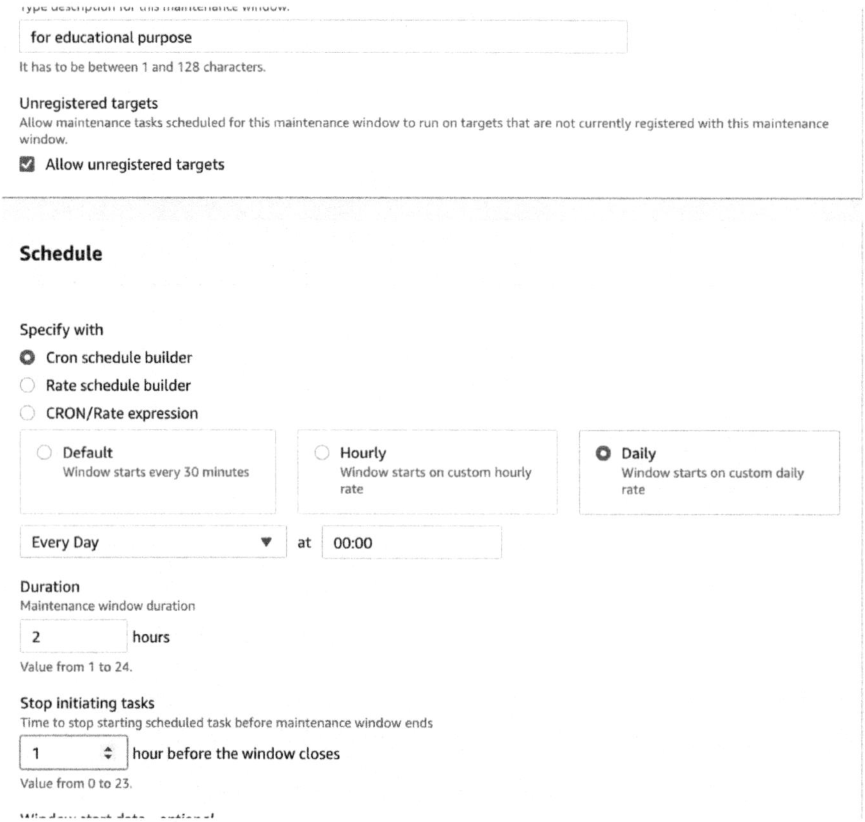

Figure 10.17 – Maintenance window configuration details

III. Choose **Create a maintenance window**:

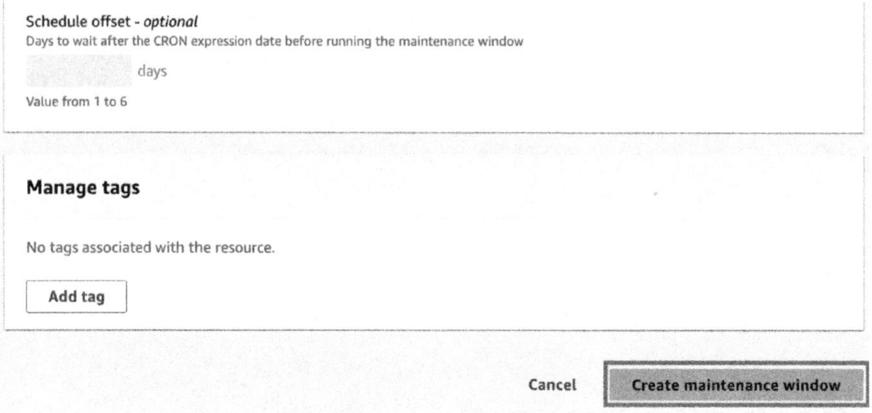

Figure 10.18 – Creating a new maintenance window

6. **Register targets**: Registering targets allows you to specify which resources should be subject to the maintenance window. Let's explore the steps involved:

   I. In your maintenance window, choose **Actions** and then **Register targets**:

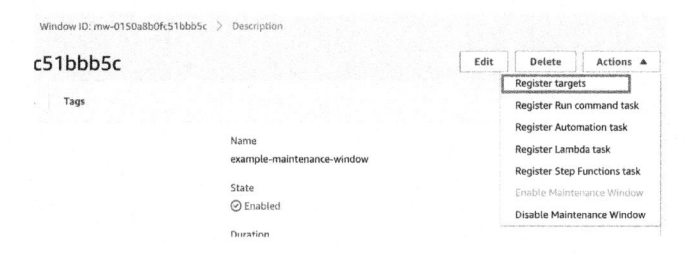

   Figure 10.19 – Defining targets with the maintenance window

   II. Enter a name and description, select **Specifying tags**, and enter the patch group. Then, choose **Register targets**:

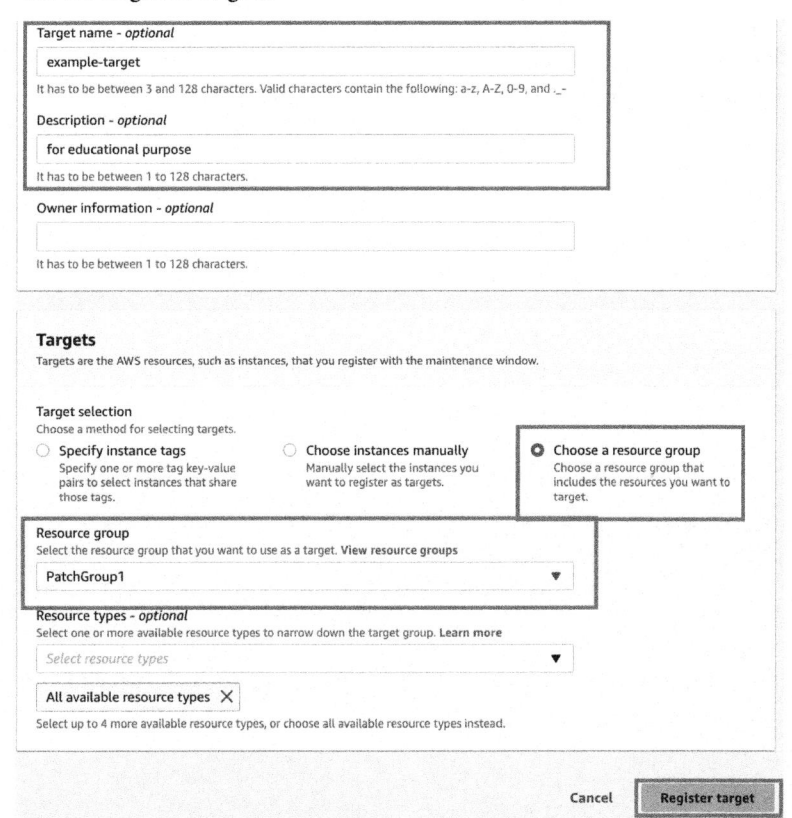

   Figure 10.20 – Target group configuration details

7. **Register a patching task**: Registering a patching task is a process where you specify the patching operation to be executed on the specified targets during a specified window. Let's dive in and explore the steps involved:

   I.   In your maintenance window, choose **Actions** and then **Register run command task**:

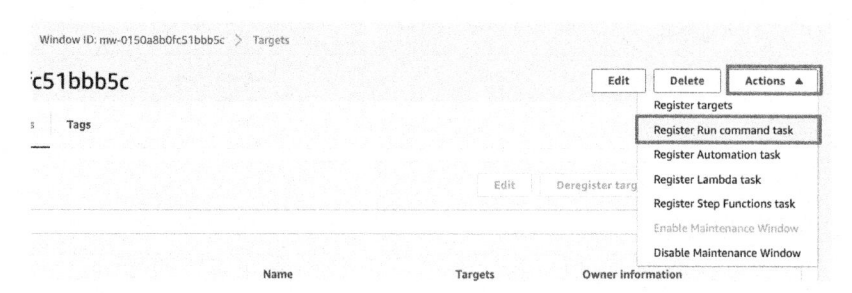

   Figure 10.21 – Defining a Run command task with the maintenance window

   II. Choose the document **AWS-RunPatchBaseline**:

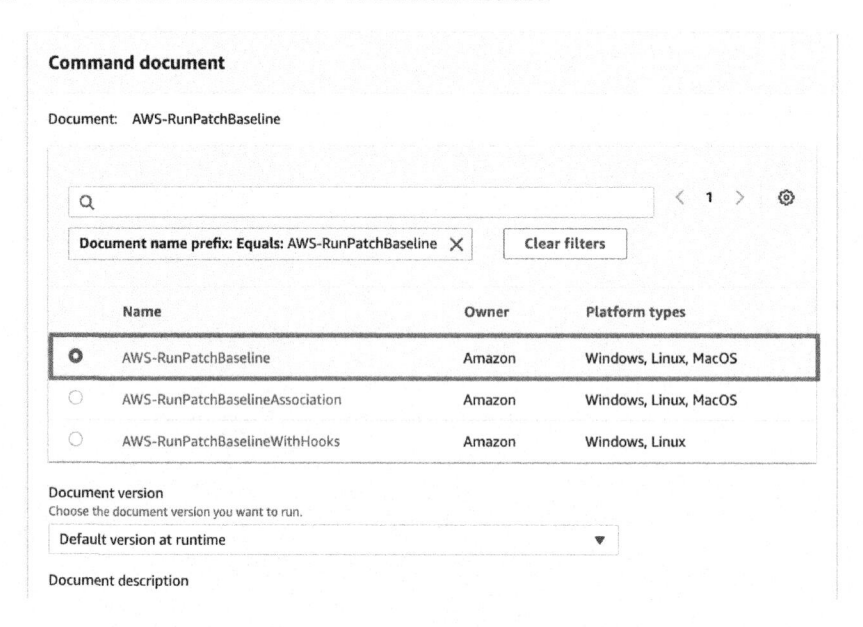

   Figure 10.22 – Run command patch baseline configuration details

III. Fill in the necessary details, such as name, role, priority, and output options:

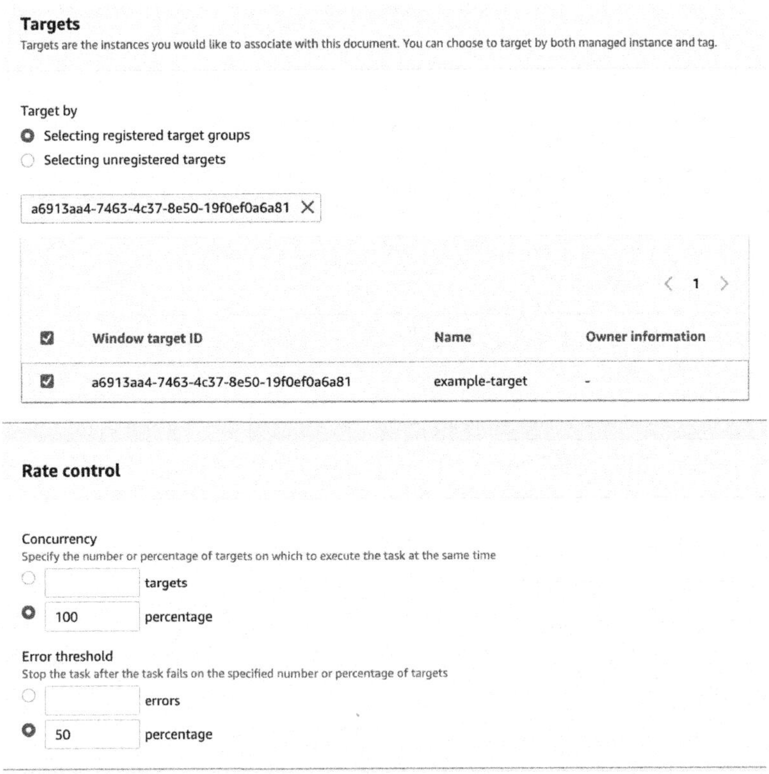

Targets

Targets are the instances you would like to associate with this document. You can choose to target by both managed instance and tag.

Target by
- ◉ Selecting registered target groups
- ○ Selecting unregistered targets

a6913aa4-7463-4c37-8e50-19f0ef0a6a81 ✕

	Window target ID	Name	Owner information
☑	a6913aa4-7463-4c37-8e50-19f0ef0a6a81	example-target	-

Rate control

Concurrency
Specify the number or percentage of targets on which to execute the task at the same time
- ○ [   ] targets
- ◉ [100] percentage

Error threshold
Stop the task after the task fails on the specified number or percentage of targets
- ○ [   ] errors
- ◉ [50] percentage

Figure 10.23 – Run command target group configuration details

IV. Choose **Register Run command task**:

CloudWatch alarm - *optional*
Add error control to this task by choosing a CloudWatch alarm.

Alarm name
The name of the CloudWatch alarm that you want to apply to this maintenance window task. **Create CloudWatch alarm**

[Choose alarm ▼] [⟳]

☐ Continue tasks if alarm status is unavailable
If Maintenance Windows is unable to retrieve information about the state of your CloudWatch alarm, the maintenance window task continues to run.

Cancel   **Register Run command task**

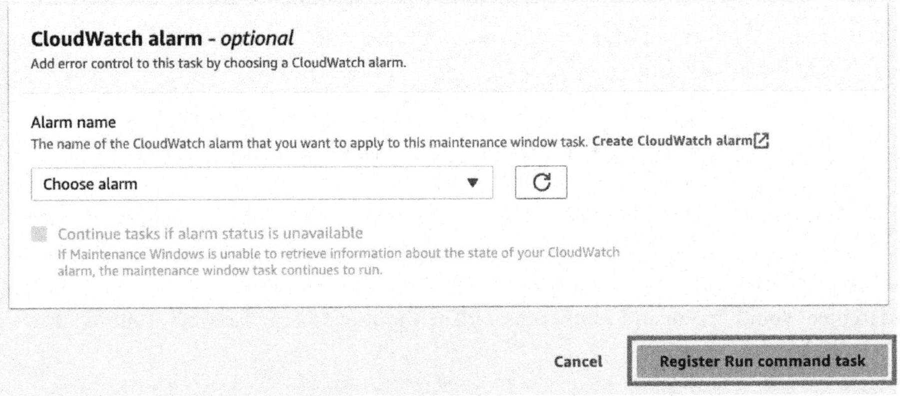

Figure 10.24 – Registering a Run command task

Overall, the integration of SSM in your patching strategy facilitates a simplified, automated, and organized patching process. Let us now unfold the strategies that hone the performance and optimization of your EC2 instances.

Performance tuning and optimization

Performance tuning is about maximizing the performance of your system, optimizing the overall system functionality, and squeezing out every bit of processing power to maximize the value of the resource you rely on. In this section, we will delve into the exploration on how to operate your EC2 instance effectively and efficiently:

- **Rightsize your instances**: Ensure you choose an appropriate instance type and size for your workload. Utilize CloudWatch metrics to monitor the performance and adjust the instance types based on the requirements.
- **Use latest generation instances**: Consider relying on the latest generation instances, as they usually offer better performance, scalability, and additional capabilities at a similar or lower price.
- **Optimize CPU and memory**: Balance the CPU and memory resources based on the needs of your applications. Ensure neither of them is a bottleneck for your application.
- **Enhance network performance**: Optimize the network by selecting an instance type that offers enhanced networking. Also, utilize VPC endpoints to connect to AWS services to enhance the bandwidth of the network path.
- **Leverage EBS optimized instances**: Utilize EBS-optimized instances to ensure consistent low latency performance for your block-level storage.
- **Auto scaling**: Implement auto scaling to ensure that your application always has the right amount of compute capacity.

After ensuring that your EC2 instances are running at peak performance, let's steer toward understanding the aspects of capacity planning and resource management to align resources efficiently with business requirements and demands.

Capacity planning and resource management

In the vast ecosystem of cloud computing, capacity planning and resource management stand as twin pillars in the robust architecture of services such as EC2 instances. They are meticulous strategies that ensure you have an optimal quantity of resources (such as storage, memory, and compute), finely aligned to meet your current and future demands without over-provisioning or under-provisioning.

Key strategies for capacity planning and resource management

Capacity planning and resource management are very important in optimizing your cloud efficiency and performance in your cloud environment. Let's explore some key strategies involved in this process.

- **Forecasting demand**: Begin by estimating the future demand for your resources based on historical usage patterns, upcoming projects, and business growth.
- **Monitor and analyze usage patterns**: Regularly monitor and analyze your usage patterns using tools such as Amazon CloudWatch. Identify the peak usage times and any recurring trends or patterns.
- **Scaling resources**: Implement auto scaling to automate the scaling of your resources based on the demand. Utilize horizontal scaling (adding more instances) and vertical scaling (upgrading an instance) as per your needs.
- **Regularly review and adjust**: Regularly review your capacity planning strategies and make necessary adjustments based on evolving business needs and technological changes.

As we wrap up this section on capacity planning and resource management, we have underscored the significance of optimizing resources to cater to both the present and future demands.

Venturing ahead, we will immerse ourselves into the realms of *Backup and recovery strategies*. From understanding the EC2 instance backups to automating backups with AWS backup, we are set to explore the comprehensive strategies that ensure our data security and resilience.

Backup and recovery strategies

In today's digital world, everyone is using computers for everything, and we all have important stuff such as photos or documents that we don't want to lose. Sometimes, things can go wrong. We might delete something by accident, or our computer might stop working. That's why it is extremely important to have backup and recovery strategies.

At its core, a backup strategy isn't just about creating copies of data but ensuring the copies can be efficiently restored when needed. The strategy becomes more complex when considering the vast array of services provided by AWS, with each of them coming with its unique backup mechanisms and best practices. However, with the challenges come the opportunities. AWS provides tools and services tailored specifically for creating and managing backups and recovering the data with very minimal downtime when a disaster strikes.

So, let's get started! We will first talk about Amazon EC2 and Amazon EBS backups.

Amazon EC2 and Amazon EBS backups

EC2 and EBS stand as the fundamental pillars in which our data resides and operates. Think of Amazon EC2 as a brain where all your applications think and make decisions, and Amazon EBS as the memory where important information resides. To ensure that your environment is resilient and data remains intact even in unforeseen scenarios, you must emphasize creating thoughtful backups. Let's explore the backup process for both these critical components:

- **EC2 AMI**: Starting with Amazon EC2, it is essential to regularly take snapshots, which are like photographs of what your data looks like at a specific moment. EC2 instance backups primarily revolve around **Amazon Machine Images** (**AMIs**) and snapshots. Creating an AMI of an EC2 instance is like taking a complete picture of the instance at a specific time, including the operating system, application server, underlying application, and related configurations. Having this AMI allows you to launch new instances, effectively cloning the original and ensuring minimal disruption.

- **EBS snapshots**: On the other side, we have EBS volumes holding crucial data. EBS snapshots play a pivotal role here. Imagine you are writing a crucial piece of information on the board. Capturing a snapshot is similar to taking a photo of a board, ensuring that the written information isn't lost even if that was erased from the board later. It is a point-in-time copy of your data that acts as a baseline for your recovery.

Armed with robust data safeguards, let us now pivot toward the section on *Disaster recovery and Automation*, where we will weave these backups into a broader strategy, ensuring our environment not only survives but thrives amidst any potential challenges.

Disaster recovery and automation

In the face of a disaster, it is important to ensure that your application's traffic is seamlessly directed to a healthy and reliable endpoint. At the forefront is **Amazon Route 53**. Useful for its health-checking features and DNS failover capabilities, Route 53 can skillfully reroute the traffic from unhealthy resources to healthy ones, fostering enhanced availability for your application.

With regard to your data durability, **Amazon S3** comes in as a perfect choice. S3 even allows for the automatic replication of data across various regions. So, even during region-specific adversaries, you can bolster your overall DR strategy by making use of S3.

With that, let's dive deep into the recovery methodologies. AWS presents a spectrum of disaster recovery strategies:

- **Pilot light**: This strategy is like a dormant gas ready to ignite. In this strategy, you keep a minimal version of your environment always running. When a disaster strikes, you can rapidly scale to handle production loads.
- **Warm standby**: Think of this as a sleeping guard dog, always present but dozing. It is a fully functional scaled-down version of your system that can wake up and react at a moment's notice, expanding to handle full operational loads as needed.
- **Backup and restore**: This is akin to the time capsule, where your data is periodically preserved and stored away. When required, you can unearth the capsule and restore its contents. Take note that this approach requires a longer recovery time.
- **Active/Active**: Imagine a team of acrobats, all performing a routine in sync. If one performer falters, the others can continue seamlessly without any interruption. In this method, you basically run identical production environments, ensuring continuous performance even if one encounters issues.

It is also worth noting that the elegance of marketplace services such as **AWS CloudEndure Disaster Recovery** helps you achieve seamless replication capabilities. CloudEndure helps you with the continuous replication of workloads and empowers your organizations by facilitating swift recovery paths and achieving minimal downtime during disruptions.

Speaking about automation, AWS Lambda emerges as a potent ally. It allows for automated responses to your system changes or hiccups, triggering essential DR workflows automatically. You can combine Lambda with AWS Step Functions to create coordinated automated tasks to achieve an efficient and resilient DR workflow. This ultimately enhances your overall system robustness.

Summary

We have now come to the end of this chapter. We started off the journey by understanding how to keep an eye on our services using Amazon CloudWatch and CloudTrail. We have learned how they can help us check the performance and security of our usage. We also discussed the practical ways to maintain our services through regular patches, tuning, and making sure we have the right amount of resources to efficiently operate our workloads. Lastly, we looked at various ways to keep our data safe through backups and recovery plans to reinstate workloads after unexpected issues.

In the next chapter, we will learn about relying on automation to manage your resources more efficiently and easily.

11
Automating Amazon EC2 – AWS CloudFormation and Infrastructure as Code

This chapter acts as a gateway to mastering the automation of Amazon EC2, a crucial aspect of effective cloud management.

We will start our trip by exploring the basics, such as what is **Infrastructure as Code** (**IaC**) and why it is so important in managing the cloud. Following this, you will introduced to AWS CloudFormation, a powerful tool that will be your companion in this automation journey.

Moving on, we will dive into the nuts and bolts of CloudFormation. Here, we will play around with templates, stacks, and resources, making sure you get comfortable with all the essential parts and pieces. This approach is similar to learning the rules of a new game, step by step. Following that, you will learn how to create and update CloudFormation stacks, where you will get your hands dirty by deploying templates and using cool tools such as the AWS Management Console, the AWS CLI, and SDKs.

We will then look into the AWS Cloud Development Kit (CDK), which is another interesting way to do IaC. This approach allows you to use different programming languages in a more dynamic way.

So, buckle up! Let's start this adventure by diving into the essentials of AWS CloudFormation and IaC and see why they are the superheroes of cloud management!

The following topics will be covered in this chapter:

- Introduction to AWS CloudFormation and IaC
- AWS CloudFormation overview
- Integrating EC2 with CloudFormation
- IaC with AWS CDK

Introduction to AWS CloudFormation and IaC

It is important to understand that in the public cloud space, infrastructure management has undergone a sea of changes, with manual configurations and deployments having become tales of yesteryears.

Imagine a world where the entire setup of servers, databases, networks, and other resources can be scripted, versioned, and treated much like software code. This not only allows for faster deployment but also ensures consistency, repeatability, and ease of scaling. Such is the magic of IaC! Within AWS, CloudFormation serves this role to help you define and deploy resources seamlessly.

By understanding the philosophy and mechanics behind these tools and practices, we basically prepare ourselves for an efficient cloud experience. Harnessing the power of IaC and CloudFormation means we are not just working on the cloud but reshaping it according to our whims and requirements.

Now, let's dive deeper and explore the very essence of IaC and understand why it is so pivotal in modern cloud management!

Why is IaC essential for cloud management?

IaC is essential because it brings unparalleled automation to the table. The practice allows complex environments to be spun up in minutes, not days. This automation also allows you to achieve repeatability and reliability – two key ingredients for today's high-velocity IT operations. No more manual setup errors or environment drifts; every setup of yours will be consistent, every configuration of yours will be repeatable, and every change will be traceable.

Moreover, IaC embodies a shift toward treating infrastructure like software. It allows infrastructure to be version controlled and reviewed as part of code review, ensuring that any changes are logged and auditable. This practice doesn't just minimize risk but also embodies compliance and governance into the very fabric of the infrastructure life cycle.

With IaC, scalability also becomes a matter of editing a few lines of code and can be aligned precisely with business needs; disaster recovery (DR) also becomes more robust and less error-prone. In essence, IaC is not just a tool but a paradigm shift that empowers teams to manage their infrastructure with the same precision and care as their application code.

Having understood the essence of IaC, let's now look into AWS CloudFormation – an AWS offering that epitomizes IaC, bringing forth a powerful and flexible way to manage AWS resources.

AWS CloudFormation overview

AWS **CloudFormation** allows developers and businesses to create a collection of related AWS and third-party resources and manage them in an orderly and predictable fashion. Imagine being able to design and deploy a virtual network, complete with a variety of interrelated resources, just by writing a script. This is the power of CloudFormation, where it turns architecture into science.

At the heart of CloudFormation is the template – a JSON- or YAML-formatted text file that describes all the resources you need (such as EC2 instances, RDS database instances, VPCs, and so on) and their configuration settings. It is exactly like a blueprint for your AWS environment. These templates can be used to duplicate environments in minutes, which simplifies the process of setting up new infrastructure or replicating existing infrastructure for testing and development purposes.

What really sets CloudFormation apart is its ability to handle dependencies and sequencing with grace. When you deploy the template, CloudFormation takes care of provisioning and configuring the resources in the right order with the right settings. It can manage updates to the stack too, and if something goes wrong, it can roll back changes to an earlier state, safeguarding your environment.

Beyond infrastructure creation, CloudFormation is instrumental in day-to-day operations, change management, and compliance. By treating your infrastructure as code, you gain consistency and control, reducing the potential for human error and enabling your infrastructure to be version controlled and reviewed just like application code.

As we wrap our minds around an understanding of the robust capabilities of CloudFormation, let's transition into understanding the specifics of these templates to master your IaC proficiency with AWS.

AWS CloudFormation basics

AWS CloudFormation is not just a tool; it is a very transformative approach to infrastructure management that encapsulates complexity and unleashes efficiency. In this section, we will unravel the fundamentals of CloudFormation and provide a solid foundation on which you can build a resilient and efficient cloud infrastructure. We will cover what CloudFormation templates are and how they function as the blueprint for your AWS infrastructure. We will explore the concepts of stacks and resources – the building blocks that bring your architecture to life. We will also dive in and explore how these elements interact and rely on one another to form complete and functioning systems within the AWS cloud. Let's dive in and explore!

CloudFormation templates, stacks, and resources

Consider the CloudFormation template as the master design of your AWS infrastructure. The template document is created in either JSON or YAML format, specifies every AWS resource required for your application, and ensures they are consistently and accurately deployed into your AWS environment.

Imagine you need to launch a web server. The CloudFormation template for this requirement might look something like the following in YAML format:

```
AWSTemplateFormatVersion: '2010-09-09'
Description: A simple AWS CloudFormation template to deploy a web
server.
Resources:
  WebServer:
    Type: 'AWS::EC2::Instance'
```

```
      Properties:
        ImageId: ami-0abcdef1234567890
        InstanceType: t2.micro
        SecurityGroups:
          - Ref: WebServerSecurityGroup
        KeyName: my-aws-key-pair
  WebServerSecurityGroup:
    Type: 'AWS::EC2::SecurityGroup'
    Properties:
      GroupDescription: Enable HTTP access via port 80
      SecurityGroupIngress:
        - IpProtocol: tcp
          FromPort: '80'
          ToPort: '80'
          CidrIp: 0.0.0.0/0
```

This template describes an EC2 instance and a security group. The instance is of type `t2.micro` and uses a specified **Amazon Machine Image** (**AMI**). The security group permits traffic on port `80`.

Coming to **CloudFormation stacks**, they form a cohesive unit of deployment. Upon submitting the template to CloudFormation, it creates a stack. The stack is a grouping of the resources specified in the template, managed as a single unit. Once the stack creation is successful, you will have a new EC2 instance running and ready to serve the web content.

As we transition to understanding CloudFormation resources, in the preceding template, `WebServer` and `WebServerSecurityGroup` are resources. `WebServer` is an EC2 instance, and `WebServerSecurityGroup` is a security group resource that defines the networking rules for your web server.

Through this example, you have seen the written document (the template) translating into actual AWS components (the stack and resources). This transition from template/code to concrete resources exemplifies the power of IaC.

Next up, we will dive into the grammar of CloudFormation – its syntax and structure. Understanding this will empower you to architect and deploy AWS resources methodically.

CloudFormation template syntax and structure

In the world of CloudFormation, templates are the master design or blueprint, telling the service precisely what to build. In this, syntax and structures are the very framework that holds our infrastructure's blueprint together. Understanding the syntax and structures is similar to learning the grammar of a new language, where each part of speech has a specific place and purpose, creating clear and executable instructions.

A CloudFormation template is structured in JSON or YAML format, providing a textual layout that describes the desired AWS infrastructure. Here's a breakdown of its anatomy:

- `AWSTemplateFormatVersion`: This declares the version of the template format. While optional, it's a good practice to include it for version control.
- `Description`: A section where you can summarize the template's purpose. It's a string, so keep it brief yet descriptive.
- `Metadata`: Any objects here provide additional information about the template, such as designer interfaces or dependencies.
- `Parameters`: These act as inputs to your template, allowing for customization each time you create or update a stack.
- `Mappings`: Similar to a `switch` statement in programming, this section matches keys to corresponding values.
- `Conditions`: Defines the circumstances in which entities are created or configured.
- `Resources`: This is the heart of the template and is a mandatory section that declares the AWS resources you are deploying.
- `Outputs`: Here, you specify the values that are returned whenever you view your stack's properties.

Here is a sample CloudFormation template that illustrates provisioning a simple EC2 instance:

```yaml
AWSTemplateFormatVersion: '2010-09-09'
Description: 'Example template to illustrate syntax and structure.'

Metadata:
  Instances:
    Description: "Information about the instances"

Parameters:
  InstanceTypeParameter:
    Type: String
    Default: t2.micro
    Description: Enter the instance type for the EC2 instance.

Resources:
  EC2Instance:
    Type: 'AWS::EC2::Instance'
    Properties:
      InstanceType: !Ref InstanceTypeParameter
      ImageId: ami-0abcdef1234567890
```

```
Outputs:
  InstanceAccess:
    Description: "The IP address of the newly created EC2 instance"
    Value: !GetAtt EC2Instance.PublicIp
```

In this example, we have a customizable parameter for the EC2 instance types, providing flexibility when creating the stack. Metadata is added for documentation purposes. The output returns the public IP address of the deployed EC2 instance, which could be handy for immediate access post-deployment.

Having explored the structural elements of CloudFormation, up next, we will tackle parameters, outputs, and mappings – these elements allow us to craft responsive and adaptable templates that cater to the varied demands of our deployment scenarios.

Template parameters, outputs, and mappings

Imagine embarking on a journey where the path you choose can vary depending on the weather or based on the sights you want to see. Similarly, when building infrastructure in AWS with AWS CloudFormation, parameters, mappings, and output provide you with the flexibility to adjust the journey without altering the map.

Parameters (the inputs for customization)

Parameters are the questions CloudFormation asks before starting the build. They are your way of saying, "Here's a choice." If you want to choose the instance type, set a parameter. If you need to specify the number of nodes, that's a parameter too.

Imagine CloudFormation parameters like the inputs you give to a vending machine. You select the snack you want, and the machine delivers. Parameters in a CloudFormation template allow you to input values such as instance sizes or AMI IDs, which the underlying template uses to provision your cloud resources.

In the following example, `InstanceTypeParameter` lets the user choose an instance type when they launch the stack, with `t2.micro` as the default option:

```
Parameters:
  InstanceTypeParameter:
    Description: Enter the instance type
    Type: String
    Default: t2.micro
    AllowedValues:
      - t2.micro
      - m3.medium
      - m3.large
```

Mappings (the predefined choices)

Mappings are static, predefined data that you can use to conditionally tailor the resources that CloudFormation creates. Mappings generally vary by region, environment type, or any variable that impacts your infrastructure setup.

In the following example, `RegionMap` helps the template decide which AMI to use depending on the AWS region where the stack is deployed:

```yaml
Mappings:
  RegionMap:
    us-east-1:
      AMI: ami-0abcdef1234567890
    eu-west-1:
      AMI: ami-0fghijklmn1234567
```

Outputs (the results of creation)

Outputs in a CloudFormation template give you information after resources are deployed. They can output anything from a database endpoint to the **Amazon Resource Name** (**ARN**) of an **Identity and Access Management** (**IAM**) role. It is basically a template telling you, "Here's the info based on what I created."

In this example, `LoadBalancerDNSName` provides the DNS name of the load balancer created by the template, which can be used by other CloudFormation stacks:

```yaml
Outputs:
  LoadBalancerDNSName:
    Description: The DNSName of the load balancer
    Value: !GetAtt LoadBalancer.DNSName
    Export:
      Name: !Sub "${AWS::StackName}-LoadBalancerDNSName"
```

Bringing it all together

Here is a simple combined example that shows parameters, mappings, and outputs in a CloudFormation template that launches an EC2 instance:

```yaml
AWSTemplateFormatVersion: '2010-09-09'
Description: A simple EC2 instance with dynamic inputs.

Parameters:
  InstanceTypeParameter:
    Description: Enter the instance type
```

```yaml
      Type: String
      Default: t2.micro
      AllowedValues:
        - t2.micro
        - m3.medium
        - m3.large

Mappings:
  RegionMap:
    us-east-1:
      AMI: ami-0abcdef1234567890
    eu-west-1:
      AMI: ami-0fghijklmn1234567

Resources:
  MyEC2Instance:
    Type: AWS::EC2::Instance
    Properties:
      InstanceType: !Ref InstanceTypeParameter
      ImageId: !FindInMap [RegionMap, !Ref "AWS::Region", AMI]
      ...
Outputs:
  InstanceID:
    Description: The Instance ID of the EC2 instance
    Value: !Ref MyEC2Instance
  InstanceDNSName:
    Description: The public DNS name of the EC2 instance
    Value: !GetAtt MyEC2Instance.PublicDnsName
```

Let's break the template down:

- The `Parameters` section lets users choose the instance type
- The `Mappings` section associates each region with the corresponding AMI
- The `Resources` section creates an EC2 instance with the selected instance type and AMI based on the region in the context
- The `Outputs` section provides the instance ID and DNS name of the created EC2 instance

Here is a simple diagram of this CloudFormation template provisioning:

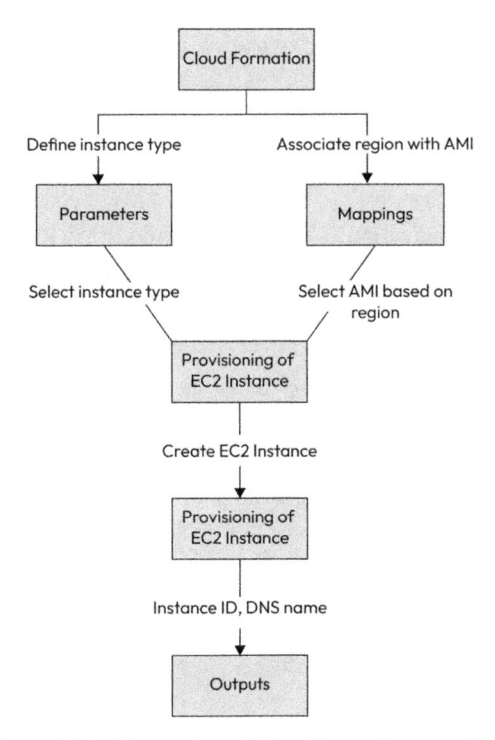

Figure 11.1 – Illustration of CloudFormation template

As we move on, we will venture into creating and updating CloudFormation stacks, where you will see how to bring a template to life and adjust it as your infrastructure evolves.

Creating and updating CloudFormation stacks

In this section, you will embark on the transformative process of turning your architectural plans into a live AWS environment. The journey begins by grasping the fundamental concept of CloudFormation stacks – the backbone of your IaC.

Understanding CloudFormation stacks

Imagine CloudFormation stacks as individual LEGO sets, where each piece represents a component of your AWS infrastructure. You have the instructions (templates) and the building blocks (resources) laid down to construct intricate structures (complete environments). AWS CloudFormation basically follows the instructions inside the template and provisions the resources with precision and ease.

Once the stack is ready, you will transition into the deployment. Here, in this section, we will delve into the practicalities of how to breathe life into these stacks. Whether you are clicking through the AWS Management Console, typing commands in the CLI, or using SDKs for a more programmatic approach, each of the pathways leads you to the same destination to fully realize your AWS infrastructure tailored to your specifications.

Deploying CloudFormation templates with the AWS Management Console, the AWS CLI, and SDKs

AWS CloudFormation has various tools at your disposal, similar to builders having different tools for different tasks. Let's take a closer look:

- **Through the AWS Management Console**: Here, you simply log in to the AWS Management Console, choose the **Create stack** option, and upload your template file:

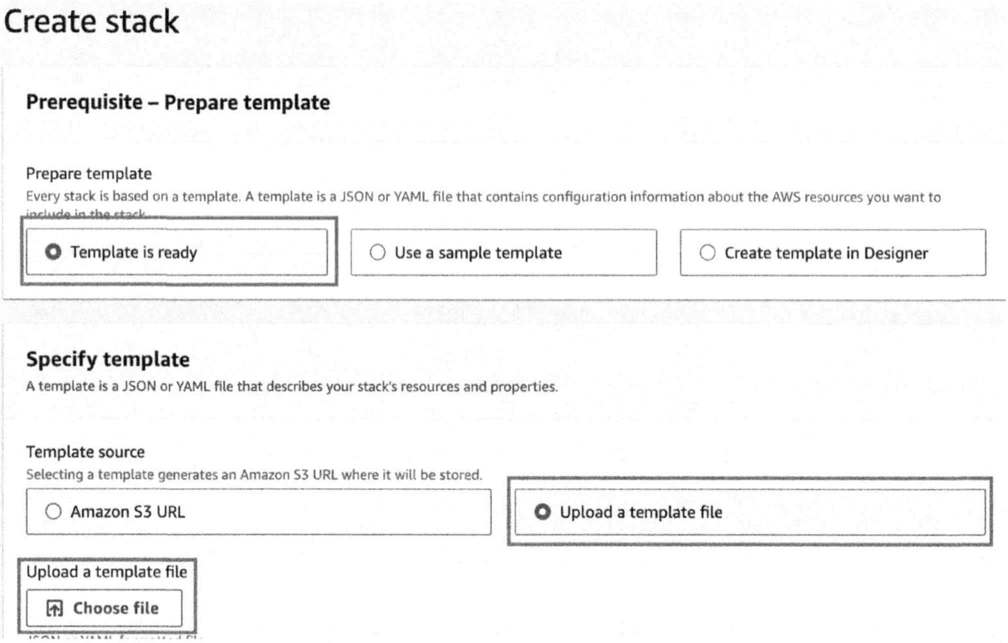

Figure 11.2 – Action to upload a CloudFormation template

Let's say you are setting up a basic web application. You select a template that defines an EC2 instance and an S3 bucket. Through the console, you input parameters such as instance type and bucket name and hit **Create**. AWS then provisions these resources for you.

- **Using the AWS CLI**: I prefer doing script over the console to improve efficiency and reduce manual work for most of my interactions with AWS, including for AWS CloudFormation. If you are like me, AWS has got you covered with the AWS CLI. For deploying the same web application, you would open your terminal and run a command such as the following:

```
aws cloudformation create-stack --stack-name mywebapp
  --template-body file://mywebapp-template.json
```

The AWS CLI processes this command and initiates the stack creation process without you needing to navigate through the AWS console.

- **With SDKs**: By relying on this approach, you enter the programmer's domain. It is like writing a custom script for a play, where each line dictates the scene on a stage. If you are using the Python SDK (`boto3`), your script would include commands like this:

    ```
    boto3.client('cloudformation').create_
    stack(StackName='mywebapp', TemplateBody=json.dumps(my_
    template)).
    ```

    This level of control allows developers to integrate CloudFormation operations into their applications seamlessly.

It is important to take note that each method has its place: the console for ease and simplicity, the CLI for efficiency and repetition, and SDKs for flexibility and integration. As we move forward, we will look into how we can update and tweak our CloudFormation stacks and ensure they stay aligned with our evolving business needs and technical requirements.

Stack updates and change sets

Understanding how to manage the evolution of your AWS infrastructure is crucial for maintaining an agile and responsive cloud environment. This is exactly where change sets and stack updates play a pivotal role.

Stack updates

Through this method, you apply changes to your infrastructure with minimal downtime. Whether you are scaling up an EC2 instance, modifying security group rules, or adding new resources, stack updates assist you in ensuring that changes are applied consistently and predictably.

For instance, if you need to increase the size of your EC2 instances from `t2.micro` to `t2.large` to handle the increased traffic, you simply edit the parameters in your template and update the stack. CloudFormation simply takes care of the rest, orchestrating the changes to make sure everything is deployed correctly.

Change sets

This method takes this one step further. Before making any actual changes, change sets allow you to preview the proposed updates and understand the impact. You create a change set, and AWS CloudFormation will show you what will be created, modified, or deleted, which helps to avoid unintended consequences.

For example, you might want to add a new Amazon RDS database instance to your stack. With a change set, you can see how this addition will affect your existing resources, costs, and deployment before you commit to implementing changes.

Both stack updates and change sets give you the control and foresight necessary to manage your cloud infrastructure effectively.

We will now shift our attention to CloudFormation best practices, ensuring that the templates we define and the stacks we deploy are not only functional but also optimized for our needs.

CloudFormation best practices

In this section, we will explore and understand the best practices that underpin a robust AWS CloudFormation strategy. We will focus on creating modular templates for reusability, nested stacks for organized resource management, and taking advantage of cross-stack references to weave different stacks together. Let us now delve into understanding the art of using modular templates, the very first step toward a sophisticated and streamlined cloud infrastructure.

Modular templates and nested stacks

In AWS CloudFormation, the principles of modularity and hierarchy are crucial. By dividing your infrastructure into modular templates, you can create reusable, maintainable, and interchangeable parts that make managing complex systems simpler. You can simply imagine this as constructing a building using prefabricated sections – they are efficient, consistent, and less error-prone.

Nested stacks in CloudFormation take this modularity a step further by allowing you to organize your modules into a clear hierarchy. Each nested stack can represent different layers of your infrastructure, such as network, security, or application layers, making it easier to update and maintain individual sections without impacting the whole.

Here is an example that illustrates this concept.

Imagine you are setting up a three-tier web application. Instead of a single, monolithic template, you split your CloudFormation templates into three parts:

- **Network stack**: This includes your VPC, subnets, and route tables
- **Security stack**: This one defines your security groups and IAM roles
- **Application stack**: Here lie your EC2 instances, load balancers, and Auto Scaling groups

Each stack is a module. The application stack would be nested within the security stack, which in turn would be nested within the network stack. This approach not only simplifies your setup and dependencies but also makes it clear where to go when a specific resource requires an update or an audit.

By embracing modular templates and nested stacks, you can ensure a well-organized and very maintainable code base. With this best practice, you can ensure your infrastructure is more transparent, manageable, and adaptable to change.

As we understand how modular templates and nested stacks contribute to establishing a sound architecture, we will now transition to understanding cross-stack references and exports. It is a glue that basically holds different CloudFormation stacks together and allows them to communicate and share resources seamlessly.

Cross-stack references and exports

CloudFormation stack references and exports emerge as a powerful duo; they basically serve as the connective tissue linking separate stacks and enable them to act cohesively together and share crucial resources. This approach not only promotes reusability but also ensures that updates in one stack can benefit dependent stacks without any manual intervention or duplication of resources.

Take, for example, a scenario where you have two stacks: one for networking components such as VPCs and subnets, and another for application resources such as EC2 instances and RDS databases. You can create an output in your networking stacks that exports your VPC ID, which can be referenced by your application stacks without hardcoding. This is not only efficient but also reduces the risk of errors during manual input. In the following examples, you will see how the VPC ID output from the networking stack is cross-referenced inside the application stack:

- **Networking stack output**

    ```
    Outputs:
      VpcId:
        Description: "The ID of the VPC"
        Value: !Ref Subnet
        Export:
          Name: { "Fn::Sub": "${AWS::StackName}-SubnetID" }
    ```

- **Application stack reference**

    ```
    Resources:
      MyEC2Instance:
        Type: "AWS::EC2::Instance"
        Properties:
          # ... other properties ...
          SubnetId:
            Fn::ImportValue: !Sub "${NetworkStackName}-SubnetID"
    ```

In the preceding example, `Export` in the networking stack outputs the VPC ID with a unique name, which is then imported by the application stack to specify the subnet ID for an EC2 instance.

By making use of such cross-stack references, you ensure that your CloudFormation stacks are both flexible and precise, like interlocking blocks that can be assembled and reassembled as per your need.

You can solidify these best practices further by making use of **AWS CloudFormation Designer**, a tool that provides a graphical interface for designing and visualizing your CloudFormation templates.

As we wrap our discussion on CloudFormation best practices, we will now pivot to another important aspect of this structure: the integration of EC2 with CloudFormation. This integration allows you to automate and manage your resources efficiently.

Integrating EC2 with CloudFormation

The ability to integrate EC2 with CloudFormation stands out as a cornerstone for seamless automation. This integration is not merely a convenience but a transformative approach that redefines how we basically interact with virtual AWS resources, manage configurations, and scale your operations. In this section, we will explore uncovering the strategic advantages of pairing EC2 with CloudFormation and how it can help us deliver a resilient, responsive, and resource-optimized environment.

Launching and managing EC2 instances and other resources with CloudFormation

Integrating EC2 with CloudFormation transforms the management of cloud resources from a manual to an automated manner. In this section, we will explore the intricacies of launching and managing EC2 instances, along with their associated security groups and other resources, within the framework of CloudFormation.

For example, consider the following YAML snippet – a boilerplate CloudFormation template, showcasing the basic structure for deploying an EC2 instance within an associated security group:

```yaml
Resources:
  MySecurityGroup:
    Type: 'AWS::EC2::SecurityGroup'
    Properties:
      GroupDescription: Allow HTTP and SSH
      SecurityGroupIngress:
        - IpProtocol: tcp
          FromPort: '22'
          ToPort: '22'
          CidrIp: 0.0.0.0/0
        - IpProtocol: tcp
          FromPort: '80'
          ToPort: '80'
          CidrIp: 0.0.0.0/0

  MyEC2Instance:
    Type: 'AWS::EC2::Instance'
    Properties:
      ImageId: ami-0abcdef1234567890
      InstanceType: t2.micro
      SecurityGroups:
        - Ref: MySecurityGroup
```

The template is a starting point, basically illustrating the deployment of a security group with SSH and HTTP access, and an EC2 instance using this security group. It is important to take note that this is just a foundational template, whereas a CloudFormation template offers a myriad of configuration options, allowing for customizations and fine-tuning to match your specific requirements.

Moving forward, we will examine how to optimize your infrastructure provisioning using CloudFormation.

Automating EC2 infrastructure provisioning with CloudFormation

Automating your EC2 infrastructure with CloudFormation allows you to manage complex environments with ease and precision. By codifying the infrastructure needed for your application in CloudFormation templates, you can automate provisioning and ensure that your infrastructure is reproducible, version controlled, and as manageable as any other code base.

Consider a scenario where you need to deploy a fleet of EC2 instances that are configured to scale based on demand, with each of them associated with a specific security group and IAM role. Here is a simplified example of how you might automate this setup with CloudFormation:

```yaml
AWSTemplateFormatVersion: '2010-09-09'
Description: Auto-scaling EC2 infrastructure with security groups &
Load balancer

Resources:
  MyAutoScalingGroup:
    Type: AWS::AutoScaling::AutoScalingGroup
    Properties:
      MinSize: '1'
      MaxSize: '5'
      DesiredCapacity: '3'
      LaunchConfigurationName: !Ref MyLaunchConfig
      TargetGroupARNs:
        - !Ref MyTargetGroup
      VPCZoneIdentifier:
        - subnet-0bb1c79de3EXAMPLE

  MyLaunchConfig:
    Type: AWS::AutoScaling::LaunchConfiguration
    Properties:
      ImageId: ami-0abcdef1234567890
      InstanceType: t2.micro
      SecurityGroups:
        - !Ref MySecurityGroup

  MySecurityGroup:
```

```yaml
      Type: AWS::EC2::SecurityGroup
      Properties:
        GroupDescription: Enable SSH access and HTTP from the load balancer only
        VpcId: vpc-1a2b3c4d
        SecurityGroupIngress:
          - IpProtocol: tcp
            FromPort: '22'
            ToPort: '22'
            CidrIp: 0.0.0.0/0
          - IpProtocol: tcp
            FromPort: '80'
            ToPort: '80'
            SourceSecurityGroupId: !Ref MyLoadBalancer

  MyLoadBalancer:
    Type: AWS::ElasticLoadBalancingV2::LoadBalancer
    Properties:
      Subnets:
        - subnet-0bb1c79de3EXAMPLE
        - subnet-0bb1c79de3EXAMPLE2

  MyTargetGroup:
    Type: AWS::ElasticLoadBalancingV2::TargetGroup
    Properties:
      VpcId: vpc-1a2b3c4d
      Port: 80
      Protocol: HTTP
```

In this template, you are not only launching EC2 instances but also defining auto-scaling parameters, security groups, and the load balancer configuration, all of which are crucial for self-healing and scalable infrastructure. This automation basically ensures that instances can be added or removed based on defined criteria, such as CPU utilization, network I/O, and so on.

Moving forward, we will delve into AWS CDK, which provides an even more developer-friendly approach to define IaC, further streamlining the process of provisioning and managing AWS resources.

IaC with AWS CDK

As your cloud environment becomes complex, the need for advanced automation becomes essential. This is exactly where AWS CDK comes into play. AWS CDK is a software development framework for defining cloud infrastructure in code and provisioning it through AWS CloudFormation. This approach basically enables developers to define their cloud resources using familiar programming languages such as TypeScript, Python, Java, or C#.

Here is a quick look at what AWS CDK offers:

- **Defining IaC**: With AWS CDK, you can define your cloud infrastructure using the constructs provided by the framework, which basically represents AWS resources as programmable entities.
- **Reusable components**: AWS CDK allows you to create and share reusable constructs that basically can encapsulate multiple AWS resources into a single unit.
- **Interoperability**: CDK seamlessly integrates with other AWS services and follows the same IaC model as CloudFormation but provides extra advantages, including the expressiveness of programming language.

Here is a simple example demonstrating AWS CDK in Python:

```python
from aws_cdk import core
from aws_cdk import aws_ec2 as ec2

class MyEc2InstanceStack(core.Stack):

    def __init__(self, scope: core.Construct, id: str, **kwargs) -> None:
        super().__init__(scope, id, **kwargs)

        # Look up the default VPC
        vpc = ec2.Vpc.from_lookup(self, "VPC", is_default=True)

        # Define the EC2 instance using an Amazon Linux 2 AMI
        ec2.Instance(self, "MyInstance",
                    instance_type=ec2.InstanceType("t3.micro"),
                machine_image=ec2.MachineImage.latest_amazon_linux(),
                    vpc=vpc)
app = core.App()
MyEc2InstanceStack(app, "MyEc2InstanceStack")
app.synth()
```

In this Python script, we define a stack that includes a `t3.micro` EC2 instance running the latest Amazon Linux 2 AMI provisioned inside the default VPC.

As you dive deeper into AWS CDK, you will discover how to compose and deploy multi-component AWS environments, establish networking resources, configure IAM roles, and so on. The journey ahead will equip you with more streamlined and automated management of AWS resources.

Summary

In this chapter, we have uncovered the transformative power of IaC with AWS CloudFormation and AWS CDK. Right from templating resources to deploying stacks, we have equipped ourselves with the tools to handle infrastructure as efficiently and effectively as code.

In the upcoming chapter, we will step into containerization and serverless computing in Amazon EC2, exploring how these technologies streamline deployment and scale applications with unprecedented efficiency.

Part 3: Advanced Amazon EC2 Concepts and Use Cases

This part focuses on advanced Amazon EC2 concepts and use cases, covering containerization, serverless computing, hybrid architectures, high-performance computing, disaster recovery strategies, and compliance, empowering you to apply your knowledge in complex, real-world scenarios.

This part has the following chapters:

- *Chapter 12, Containerization and Serverless Computing in Amazon EC2*
- *Chapter 13, Leveraging AWS Services for Hybrid and Multi-Cloud Architectures*
- *Chapter 14, Optimizing Amazon EC2 for High-Performance Computing, Big Data, and Disaster Recovery Strategies*
- *Chapter 15, Migrating, Modernizing, and Ensuring Compliance in Amazon EC2 Environments*

12
Containerization and Serverless Computing in Amazon EC2

In the ever-evolving cloud computing and technology landscape, containerization and serverless computing emerge as game-changers. Their emergence has radically altered the way we develop and deploy applications.

In this chapter, we will start by looking at containerization and serverless computing – the two buzzwords that are reshaping how we think about building and deploying applications in the cloud.

Next up, we will get hands-on with Amazon **Elastic Container Service (ECS)** and Amazon **Elastic Container Registry (ECR)**. Here, we will see how these services make deploying and managing containers in Amazon EC2 a breeze. They very much simplify what typically used to be complex tasks.

Then, we will deep dive into AWS Lambda and the world of serverless computing. Here, you will see how cutting out server management can free you up to focus more on creating great applications, all while integrating seamlessly with EC2 and other AWS services.

Finally, we will round off this chapter with a section on best practices and real-world examples. This is where the theory meets practice, showing you just how much these technologies can do.

The following topics will be covered in this chapter:

- Introduction to containerization and serverless computing
- Containerization in EC2 with ECS and ECR
- Introduction to AWS Fargate and serverless computing
- Running containers using AWS Fargate
- Best practices and use cases

Introduction to containerization and serverless computing

Containerization has been a game-changer for software delivery. It originates from the concept of isolating application environments within a single operating system. For developers, it primarily addresses the *it works on my machine* problem, ensuring consistency across various environments. Containerization gained immense popularity with the advent of Docker in 2013, offering an efficient and lightweight alternative to traditional virtualization.

Serverless computing, on the other hand, is a newer paradigm that abstracts server management and infrastructure decisions away from the developers. Launched with AWS Lambda in 2014, it introduced a way to execute code in response to events without needing to manage the underlying compute resources.

Both these technologies are not just game-changers in terms of technical capabilities – they also drastically streamline the process of software development and deployment. To their credit, they have also opened new vistas for innovation, allowing businesses to deploy faster, reduce costs, and improve their service offerings.

The next section will guide you through utilizing Amazon ECS and ECR for effective container management in the EC2 environment.

Containerization in EC2 with Amazon ECS and ECR

In this section, we will explore containerization with Amazon EC2, focusing on two cool tools: **ECS** and **ECR**. Think of this section as your guide to understanding how to manage applications that use containers in the cloud.

We will begin by exploring Amazon ECS, Amazon's proprietary container orchestration service. Imagine ECS as a smart organizer for containers, helping them work well together and scale up or down as needed. Then, we will take a look at ECR, which is similar to a GitHub repository but acts as a library for your container images. Just like how you store and manage code in a GitHub repository, in ECR, you store and manage your container images. This ensures your images are ready to go when you need them:

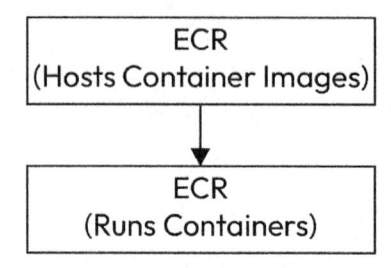

```
┌─────────────────────────┐
│          ECR            │
│ (Hosts Container Images)│
└───────────┬─────────────┘
            │
            ▼
┌─────────────────────────┐
│          ECR            │
│    (Runs Containers)    │
└─────────────────────────┘
```

Figure 12.1 – A simple illustration of ECS and ECR

And that's not all! We will also explore how to put containers into action on EC2 instances. So, get ready to dive in and see how ECS and ECR can make dealing with your containers a breeze.

Amazon ECS overview

Amazon ESC is a powerful cloud service in the AWS ecosystem that's designed specifically for managing containerized applications. ECS simplifies the overall container management process and enables you to launch, stop, and manage the life cycle of your container-based applications with simple API calls without worrying about the underlying infrastructure.

Key features of Amazon ECS

ECS offers a range of features designed for efficient container orchestration, ease of use, scalability, and robust container security measures. Let's dive in and understand the details.

- **Ease of use**: ECS is relatively easy to learn and operate compared to other container orchestration technologies. Also, it seamlessly integrates with Docker, allowing you to run Docker containers with ease.
- **Scalability**: ECS allows you to automatically scale your application up and down on demand.
- **Security**: ECS security features are designed to provide comprehensive protection and fine-grained access control to your containerized application.
- **IAM role integration**: You can assign an IAM role to your ECS tasks, providing granular control over permissions to interact with other AWS services.
- **Infrastructure security**: ECS allows for the usage of VPC endpoints. By utilizing VPC endpoints, you can be assured of private and secure communications with ECS within the AWS network.
- **Network security**: ECS allows you to associate a VPC security group to control the traffic coming in and going out of your ECS task.
- **Integration with AWS services**: ECS seamlessly integrates with various other AWS services to design and deploy a holistic container-based application in the cloud.

We will wrap up our ECS overview here and turn our attention to Amazon ECR, which we can use to securely store and manage our Docker container images.

Amazon ECR overview

Amazon ECR is a robust container image repository that acts as an integral part of the containerization landscape within AWS. It is the place where you store, manage, and deploy your Docker container images, ensuring they are both secure and easily accessible for deployment across your applications.

Key features of ECR

ECR provides a suite of features that offer secure storage, scalability, efficient image management, and high availability for container images:

- **Secure storage**: ECR provides a secure location for sharing your container images. It tightly integrates with AWS **Identity and Access Management** (**IAM**) for user access control.

- **Scalability**: Coming in as Registry-as-a-Service, it effortlessly scales to accommodate your growing container image storage needs, making it ideal for everything from small startups to large enterprise applications.

- **Pull-through cache repositories**: ECR can automatically synchronize with other container registries to cache images. So, when you pull the external images through ECR, it guarantees faster download times and reduced latency as images can be pulled from a cache closer to your deployment environment.

- **Simplified image management**: ECR simplifies the process of pushing, pulling, and managing Docker container images, streamlining your development cycles and facilitating easy deployment and rollback operations.

- **High availability and durability**: High availability and durability are at the core of ECR. The container images in ECR are stored redundantly across multiple facilities and automatically encrypted at rest, ensuring that they are always accessible and secure.

Overall, ECR simplifies the management of Docker container images, making it easier to maintain a consistent, secure, and efficient deployment process!

Now that we've explored ECR and ECS, let's look at the practical aspects of deploying containers in EC2 instances by making use of these services.

Deploying containers on EC2 instances with Amazon ECS

This method is ideal for those who are seeking to control their environment with ECS and customize the underlying infrastructure with EC2. In this process, we combine the power of Amazon ECS and the flexibility of EC2 to create a full-blown container orchestration system for our applications.

Let's try to understand the deployment process before getting hands-on and deploying the containers with ECS and EC2:

1. **Prepare your ECS environment**:

    I. Start by setting up the ECS cluster, which is a logical grouping of EC2 instances to host your containers.

    II. Ensure that the ECS agent is running on your EC2 instances. This agent communicates with the ECS service to manage containers on the instance.

2. **Create a task definition**:

    I. A task definition is a blueprint for your application. It includes container definitions, volumes, network settings, and more.

    II. Specify the Docker image to use (that is, an image hosted in ECR or any other Docker container registry), CPU and memory allocations, environment variables, and network settings.

3. **Launch an ECS service or task**:

    I. Once the task definition is ready, create an ECS service. The ECS service maintains the specified number of instances of the task definition in your cluster.

    II. Alternatively, you can run individual tasks without creating a service. This approach is typically useful for one-time or batch jobs.

4. **Load balancing and networking**:

    I. Integrate ELB to distribute traffic across your container instances.

    II. Set up appropriate networking with Amazon VPC to isolate and secure your container environment.

5. **Monitoring and logging**:

    I. Utilize CloudWatch monitoring to monitor your container instances and CloudWatch logs to aggregate your logs for easier troubleshooting and performance analysis.

The following steps are involved in deploying containers:

1. **Create an ECS cluster**:

    I. Go to the AWS ECS console and choose **Create cluster**:

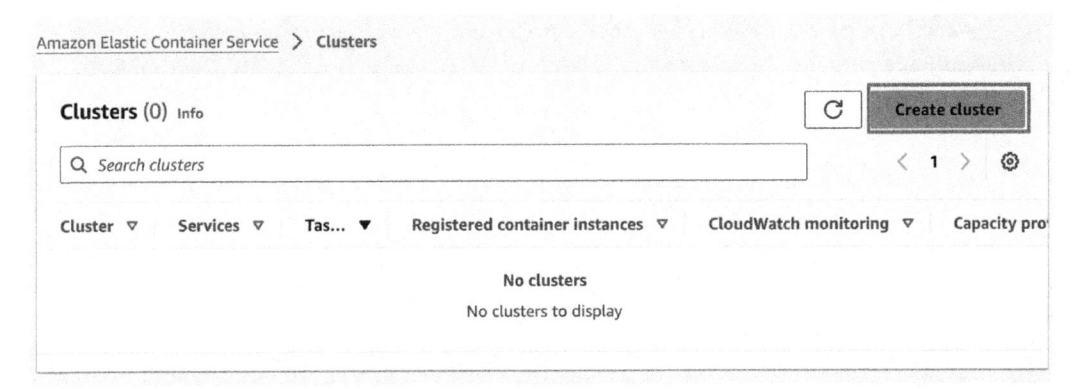

Figure 12.2 – Creating an ECS cluster

II. Name your cluster (for example, `Tutorial-Cluster`):

Cluster configuration

Cluster name

Tutorial-Cluster

There can be a maximum of 255 characters. The valid characters are letters (uppercase and lowercase), numbe

Default namespace - *optional*
Select the namespace to specify a group of services that make up your application. You can overwrite this valu

🔍 Tutorial-Cluster   ✕

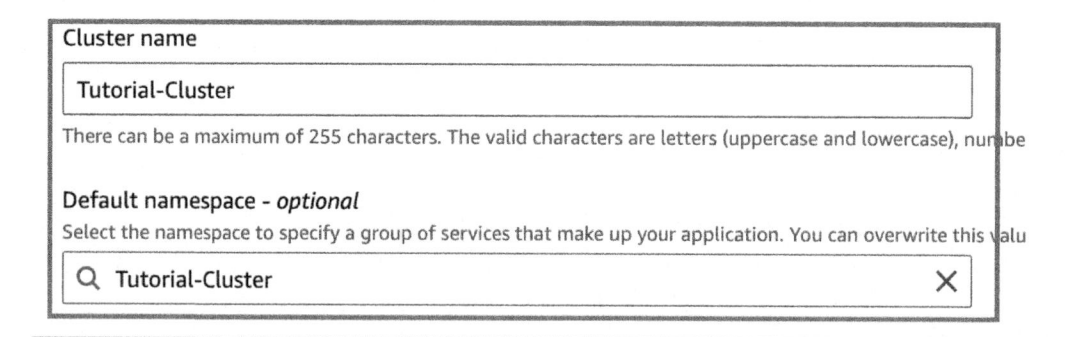

Figure 12.3 – Naming the cluster

III. Opt for **Amazon EC2 instances** instead of **AWS Fargate**:

▼ **Infrastructure** Info

Your cluster is automatically configured for AWS Fargate (serverless) with two capacity providers. Add external instances using ECS Anywhere.

☐ AWS Fargate (serverless)
Pay as you go. Use if you have tiny, batch or burst workloads or for zero maintenance overhead. The c Spot capacity providers by default.

☑ Amazon EC2 instances
Manual configurations. Use for large workloads with consistent resource demands.

Figure 12.4 – Configuring the EC2 cluster

IV. Configure the ASG settings, select an operating system and instance type, and define the capacity limits:

Use Auto Scaling groups to scale the Amazon EC2 instances in the cluster.

[Create new ASG ▼]

Provisioning model
Select a provisioning model for your instances

- ● **On-demand**
  With on-demand instances, you pay for compute capacity by the hour, with no long-term commitments or upfront payments.

- ○ **Spot**
  Amazon EC2 Spot instances let you take advantage of unused EC2 capacity in the AWS cloud. Spot instances are available at up to a 90% discount compared to on-demand prices.

Operating system/Architecture
Choose the Windows operating system or Linux architecture for your instance.

[Amazon Linux 2 ▼]

EC2 instance type
Choose based on the workloads you plan to run on this cluster.

[t3.large
x86_64
2 vCPU   8 GiB memory ▼]

Desired capacity
Specify the number of instances to launch in your cluster.

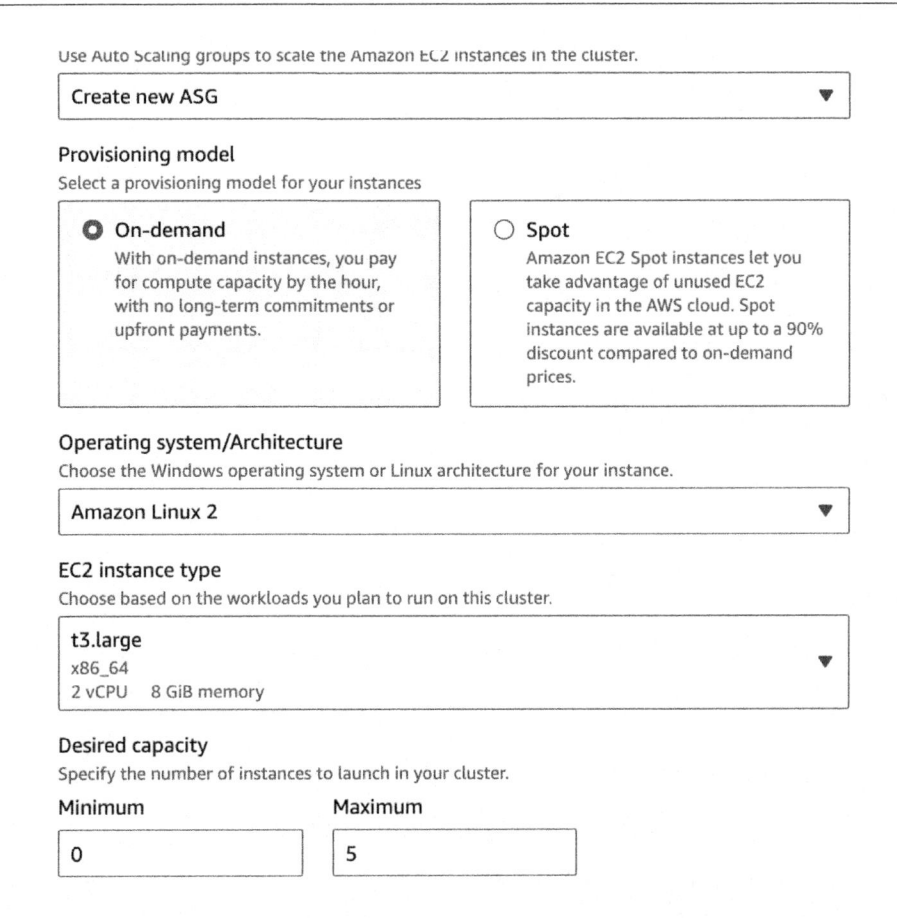

Minimum   Maximum
[0]   [5]

Figure 12.5 – ECS cluster autoscaling configuration

2. **Register a task definition**:

   I. In the ECS console, navigate to **Task definitions** and select **Create new task definition with JSON**:

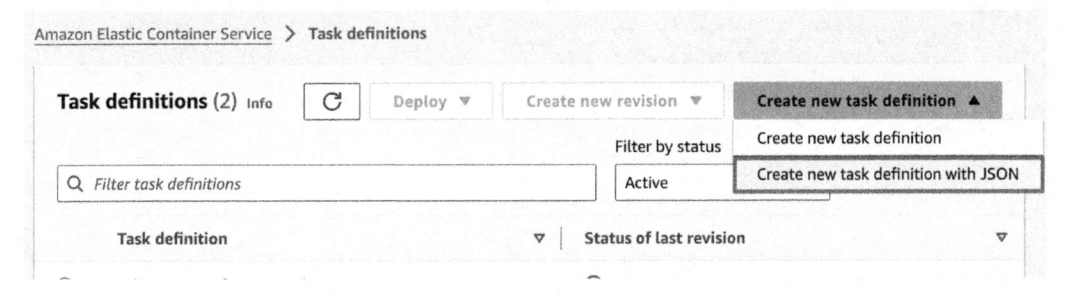

Figure 12.6 – Creating an ECS task definition with JSON

II. Choose **EC2** compatibility and input your task definition in the JSON editor. Specify your container image, memory requirements, and any other commands you wish to execute:

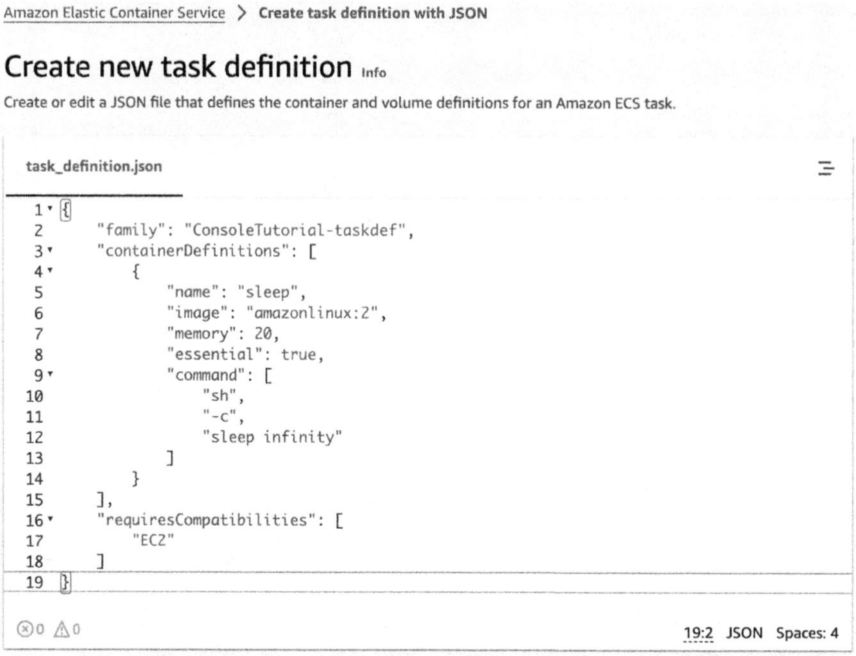

Figure 12.7 – ECS task definition JSON details

Here is the container task definition that puts your container into sleep mode, as shown in the preceding screenshot:

```
{
    "family": "ConsoleTutorial-taskdef",
    "containerDefinitions": [
        {
            "name": "sleep",
            "image": "amazonlinux:2",
            "memory": 20,
            "essential": true,
            "command": [
                "sh",
                "-c",
                "sleep infinity"
            ]
        }
    ],
    "requiresCompatibilities": [
```

```
            "EC2"
        ]
    }
```

3. **Run a task**:

    I. On the **Clusters** page, select your cluster and click **Run new task**:

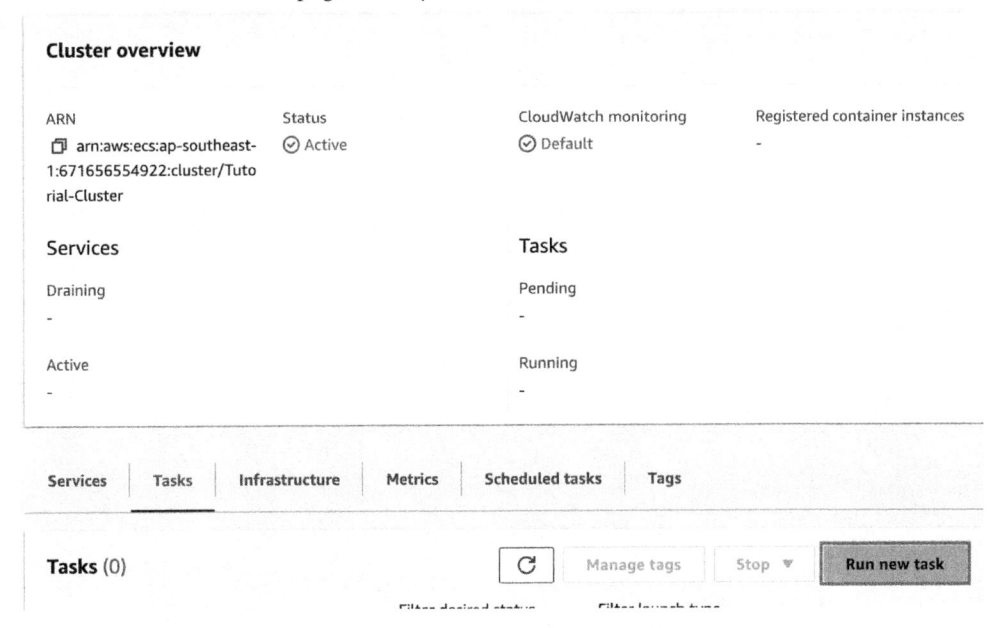

    Figure 12.8 – Running a new task

    II. Under **Compute options**, choose **Capacity provider strategy**:

    Figure 12.9 – ECS cluster advanced compute configuration

III. Set the application type to **Task**, choose your task definition, and specify the number of tasks:

Application type Info
Specify what type of application you want to run.

○ Service
Launch a group of tasks handling a long-running computing work that can be stopped and restarted. For example, a web application.

● Task
Launch a standalone task that runs and terminates. For example, a batch job.

Task definition
Select an existing task definition. To create a new task definition, go to Task definitions.

☐ Specify the revision manually
Manually input the revision instead of choosing from the 100 most recent revisions for the selected task definition family.

Family
ConsoleTutorial-taskdef

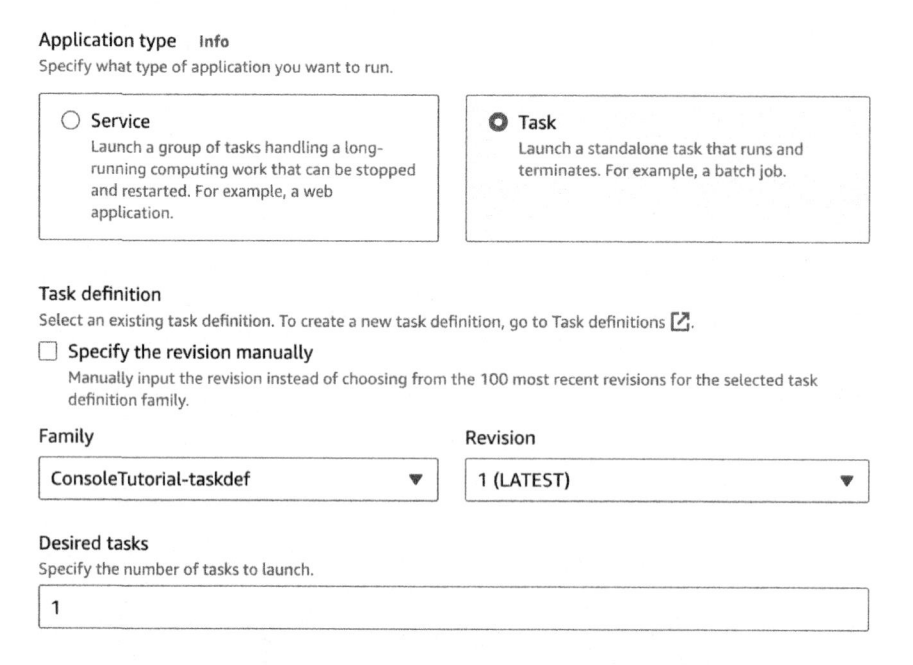

Revision
1 (LATEST)

Desired tasks
Specify the number of tasks to launch.
1

Figure 12.10 – ECS cluster task placement configuration

4. **Verify the deployment**:

   I. Monitor the deployment using CloudWatch metrics.

   II. In the ECS console, confirm that your tasks are running under the **Tasks** tab:

   26a3c2d7e4444b2792abd3d297415ce4

   Configuration | Logs | Networking | Tags

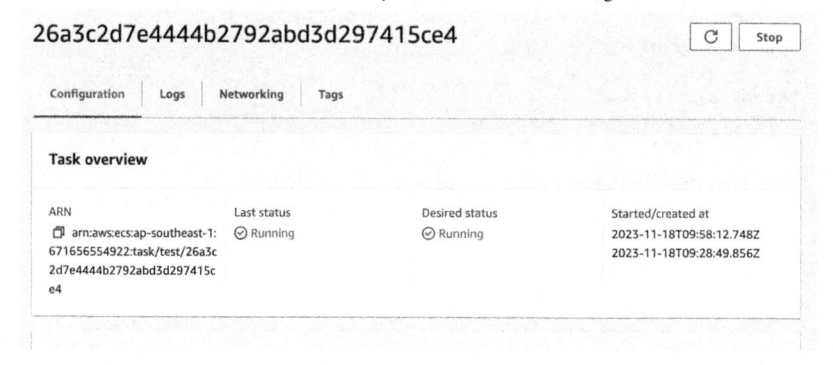

   Task overview

   ARN: arn:aws:ecs:ap-southeast-1:671656554922:task/test/26a3c2d7e4444b2792abd3d297415ce4
   Last status: ⊙ Running
   Desired status: ⊙ Running
   Started/created at: 2023-11-18T09:58:12.748Z 2023-11-18T09:28:49.856Z

   Figure 12.11 – ECS task status verification details

Next, we will explore AWS Fargate, a serverless option for running containers. This approach simplifies the deployment by managing servers and clusters on your behalf.

Running containers using AWS Fargate

In the realm of containerized application management within the AWS ecosystem, **Fargate** stands as a cornerstone, offering a streamlined, serverless approach to container deployment. The radical transformation Fargate facilitates for container users is to stop worrying about the nitty-gritty details of server and cluster management so that they can start focusing on what matters the most: their applications.

So, what exactly is Fargate?

Fargate is a cutting-edge serverless compute engine that works hand in hand with AWS ECS and EKS. Its true beauty and main quality lies in its ability to free you from the burdens of server provisioning and management. So, from the developer's perspective, they can run and launch containers with minimal fuss regarding the infrastructure underneath. Also, Fargate only charges you for the resources your applications use. Therefore, relying on Fargate for hosting your containers serves as a flexible and resource-efficient solution for running container instances.

With this understanding, let's delve into understanding the nuances of Fargate versus traditional EC2 launch types. This comparison will shed light on the distinct advantages of each of the hosting types and help you decide on the most suitable launch option for your specific containerized workloads.

Fargate versus EC2 launch types

Let's delve in and understand the key differences so that you can choose the best approach for your containerized applications:

Attribute	AWS Fargate	EC2 Launch Type
Management and scalability	Serverless; no direct server or cluster management is needed.	Requires cluster instances to be managed.
Pricing model	Pay-per-container use; aligns costs with resource usage.	You're billed for the EC2 instances, regardless of container utilization.
Control and flexibility	Less control over the hosting environment.	You have greater control and can optimize the underlying instance type for specific workloads.
Security	Enhanced isolation of containers, reducing the risk surface.	More responsibility for securing the instances.
Use case	Ideal for applications where direct control over infrastructure is less critical. It's best for batch processing or microservices.	Suited for applications requiring specific hardware configurations, high-performance computing, or when you demand granular control over the infrastructure.
Ease of use	Simplified setup.	More complex setup.

Table 12.1 – Characteristics of Fargate and EC2 launch types

With this clearer picture of when to use what, next, we will explore deploying containerized applications using AWS Fargate.

Deploying containerized applications with Fargate

AWS Fargate simplifies the deployment process of containerized applications by removing the need to manage underlying servers. Let's walk through the steps involved in deploying the sample applications:

1. **Define your task definition with a sample container**:

    I. Navigate to the AWS ECS console.

    II. Click on **Task definitions**, then **Create new task definition**:

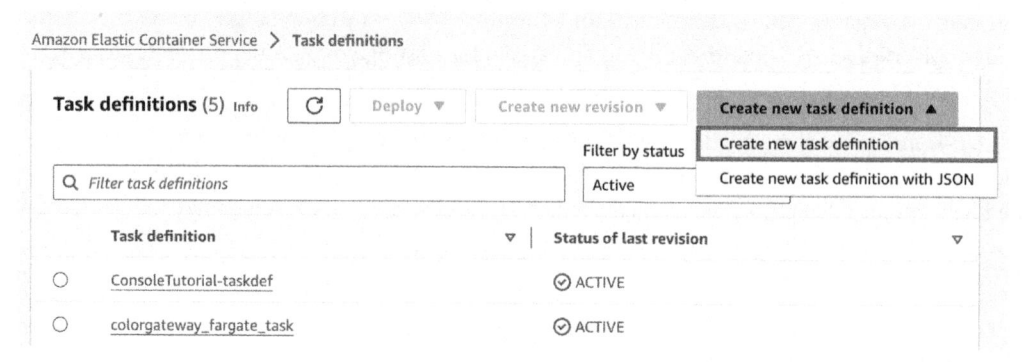

    Figure 12.12 – Creating a task definition

    III. Choose **Fargate** as the launch type:

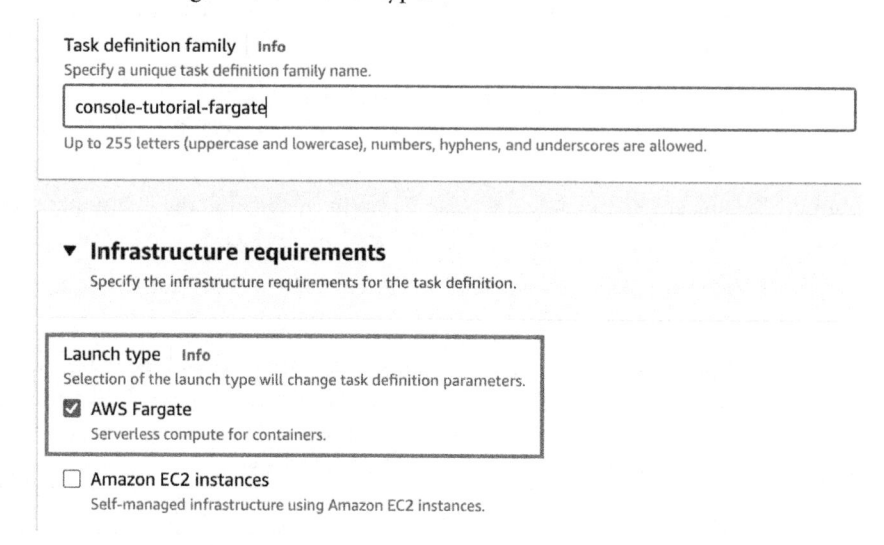

    Figure 12.13 – Choosing AWS Fargate

IV. Define your container specifications. For example, use the sample Nginx container:

- **Image**: Nginx (This uses the latest Nginx image from Docker Hub)
- **CPU**: Allocate appropriate units (for example, 0.5)
- **Memory**: Assign the necessary memory (for example, 1 GB)

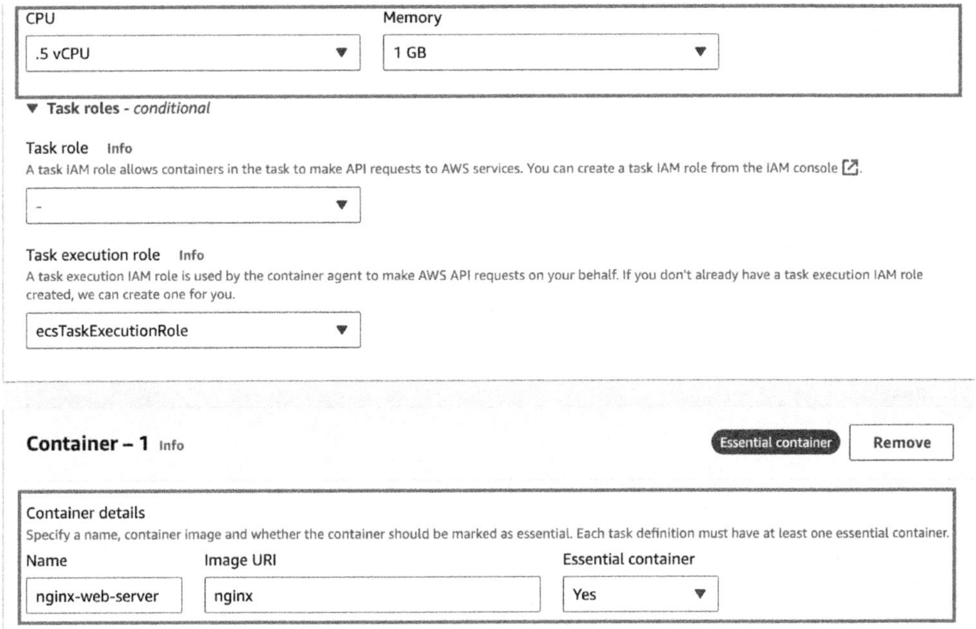

CPU	Memory
.5 vCPU ▼	1 GB ▼

▼ **Task roles** - *conditional*

Task role Info
A task IAM role allows containers in the task to make API requests to AWS services. You can create a task IAM role from the IAM console.

- ▼

Task execution role Info
A task execution IAM role is used by the container agent to make AWS API requests on your behalf. If you don't already have a task execution IAM role created, we can create one for you.

ecsTaskExecutionRole ▼

Container – 1 Info   [Essential container] [Remove]

Container details
Specify a name, container image and whether the container should be marked as essential. Each task definition must have at least one essential container.

Name	Image URI	Essential container
nginx-web-server	nginx	Yes ▼

Figure 12.14 – ECS task container resource configuration

2. **Run a task**:

   I. In the ECS cluster dashboard, navigate to the **Tasks** tab.

   II. Click on **Run new task** to start deploying a standalone task:

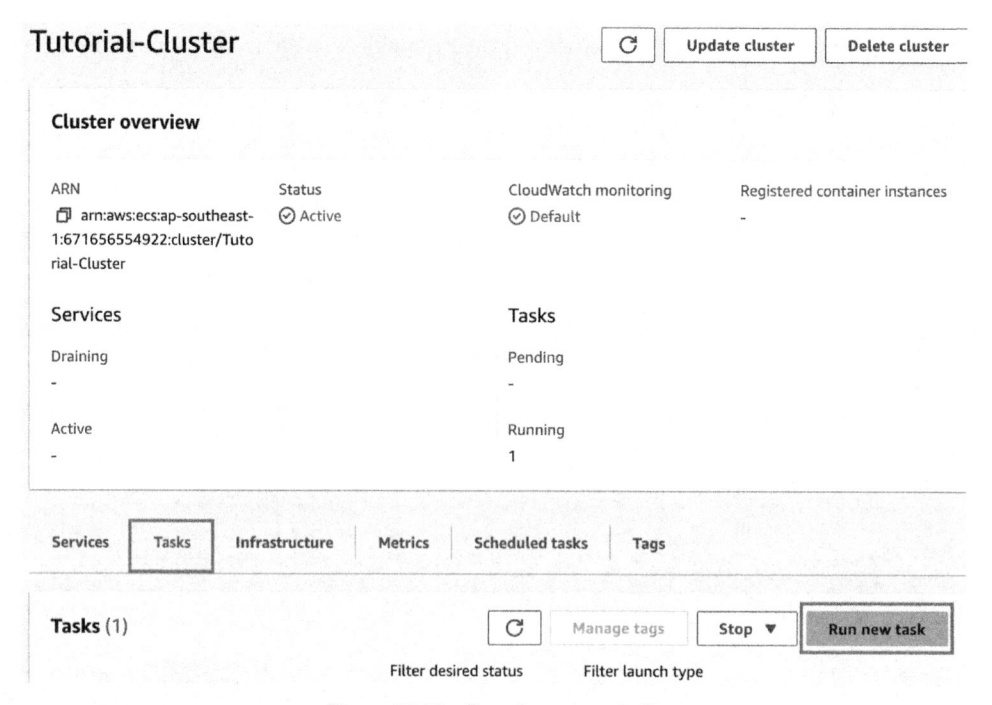

Containerization and Serverless Computing in Amazon EC2

Figure 12.15 – Running a new task

3. **Task configuration**:

   I. For **Launch Type**, choose **FARGATE**:

Figure 12.16 – ECS task launch type configuration

II. Select the existing task definition from the top-down menu.

III. Define the number of tasks you wish to run:

Deployment configuration

Application type   Info
Specify what type of application you want to run.

○ **Service**
Launch a group of tasks handling a long-running computing work that can be stopped and restarted. For example, a web application.

● **Task**
Launch a standalone task that runs and terminates. For example, a batch job.

Task definition
Select an existing task definition. To create a new task definition, go to Task definitions.

☐ **Specify the revision manually**
Manually input the revision instead of choosing from the 100 most recent revisions for the selected task definition family.

Family	Revision
console-tutorial-fargate ▼	2 (LATEST) ▼

Desired tasks
Specify the number of tasks to launch.

1

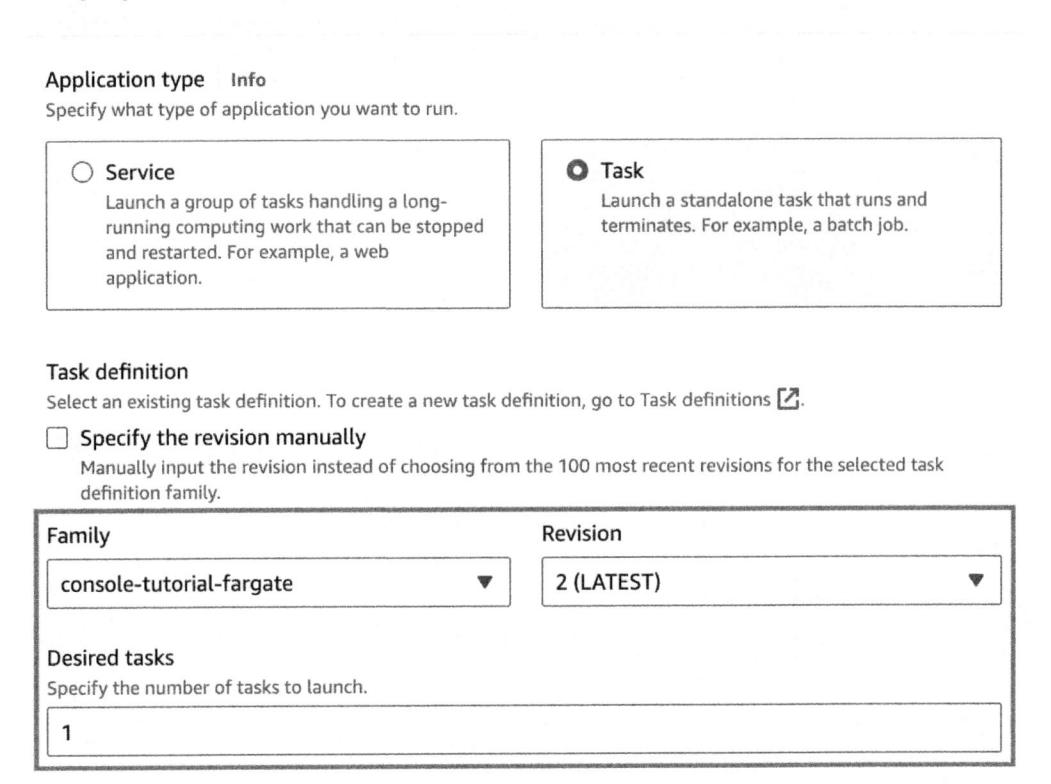

Figure 12.17 – ECS task placement definition

4. **Network configuration**:

   I. Under **VPC**, choose the appropriate VPC.

   II. Select the subnets where the task should run.

   III. Assign a security group that governs the task's network access rules:

Figure 12.18 – ECS task network configuration

5. **Running the task:**

   I. Review your settings and click **Create**:

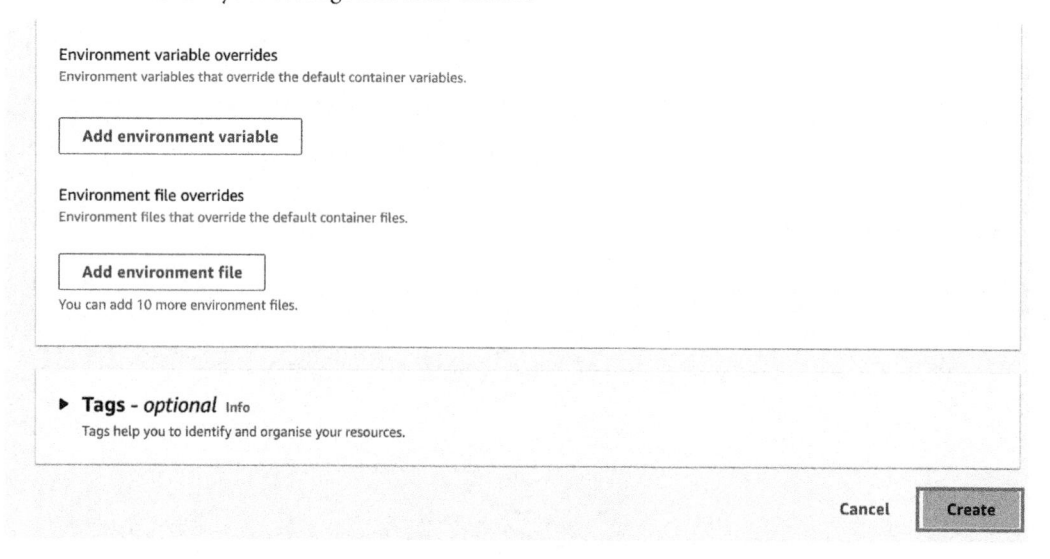

Figure 12.19 – Creating an ECS task

II. The ECS service will initiate the task based on your specifications.

III. Monitor the status of the task under the **Tasks** tab in your ECS dashboard:

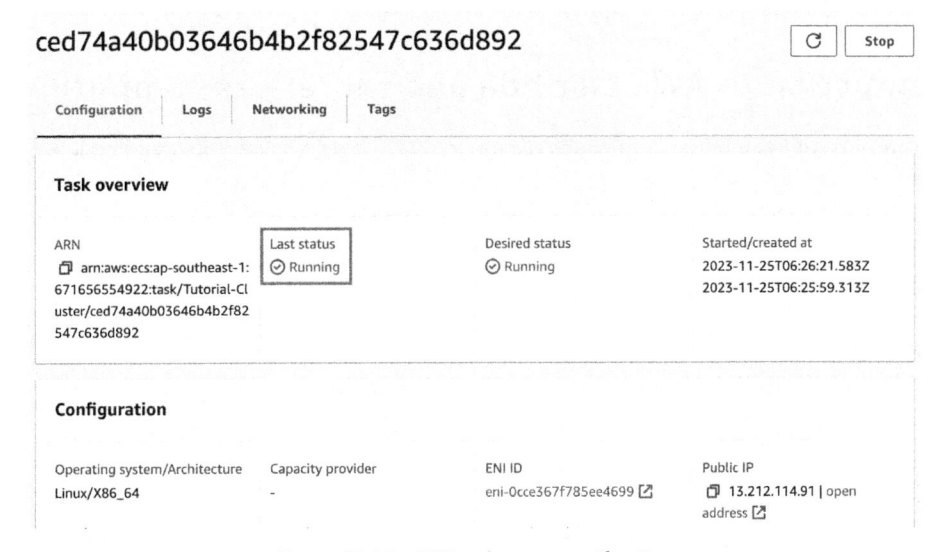

Figure 12.20 – ECS task status verification

6. **Verification**:

   I. Once the task's status is **RUNNING**, verify its functionality.

   II. Check your logs and metrics or directly interact with the application to ensure it is operating as expected:

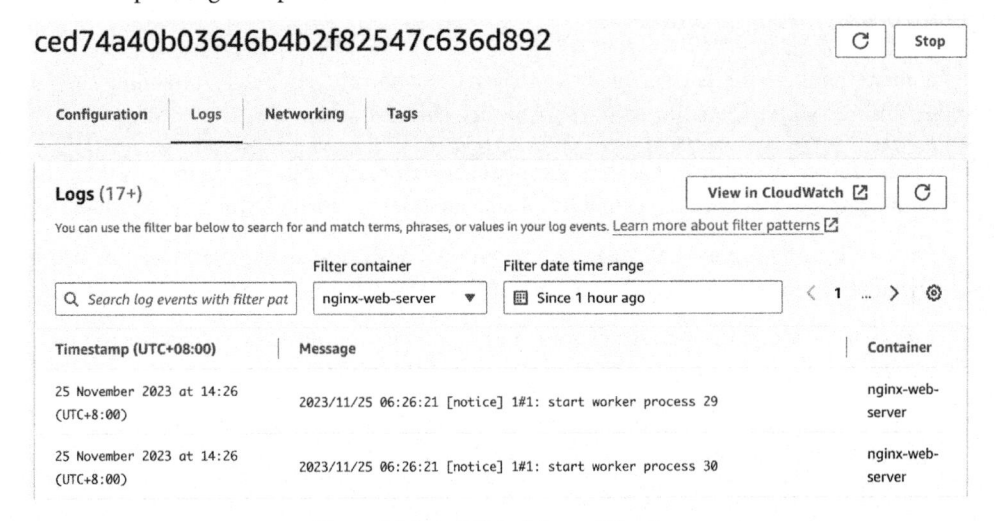

Figure 12.21 – ECS task log verification

Having set up our Fargate service, we will now delve into the realm of AWS Lambda and serverless computing and explore how to achieve even more efficient event-driven computing without managing servers. We will also explore how it integrates with EC2 and other AWS services.

Introduction to AWS Lambda and serverless computing

In this section, you will understand some of the key EC2 use cases that you could benefit from in terms of integrating with Lambda functions. But before diving into the details of Lambda functions and their use cases, let's take a moment to understand the foundation of Lambda, which is serverless computing. Serverless computing created a revolution and represented a broader paradigm shift in building and running applications without the need for server management. This paradigm shift created a huge advantage for developers to just focus on their code without worrying about the underlying infrastructure. In AWS, AWS Lambda acts as a core component of serverless computing, allowing you to run code in response to events without the traditional server management.

With this introduction, we will provide a comprehensive overview of AWS Lambda and understand its innovative features and the transformative impact it has on its application development and infrastructure management in AWS.

AWS Lambda overview

AWS Lambda stands as a pivotal component in the AWS ecosystem, and it simply redefines how we approach cloud computing with its serverless architecture. It allows you to run code in response to events, eliminating the need for server provisioning or management. AWS Lambda scales automatically and offers flexible payment by charging only for the compute time consumed by the function.

Key features of AWS Lambda

AWS Lambda stands out for its efficient, event-driven execution and scalability, providing support for multiple runtimes with the integrated security model. Here are some of its key features:

- **Event-driven execution**: Lambda simply excels in responding to various events, such as modifications in S3 buckets, DynamoDB table updates, or custom events from other services.

- **Diverse event sources**: Lambda supports numerous event-driven services, including S3, DynamoDB, Kinesis, SNS, and SQS. This enables a wide range of application scenarios.

- **Automatic scaling**: Lambda scales your application by running code in response to each event trigger, ensuring that each event is handled promptly and efficiently.

- **Resource allocation flexibility**: Lambda allows you to specify the desired amount of memory and allocates CPU power, network bandwidth, and disk I/O proportionally.

- **Multiple runtime support**: Lambda supports running various programming languages, including Node.js, Python, Ruby, Java, Go, and .NET, offering flexibility in application development.
- **Integrated security model**: You can associate the IAM role for each Lambda function, allowing you to securely access other AWS resources and maintain robust security protocols.

Lambda use cases

Here are the key use cases where AWS Lambda can be a right fit:

- Backend services for web and mobile applications
- Data processing, such as transforming files upon S3 upload
- Acting as a backend service for IoT applications to process telemetry data
- Real-time file processing, analytics, and stream processing

Simply put, AWS Lambda broadens the overall horizon of what's possible in cloud computing. As we advance, we will learn how to deploy and configure Lambda functions, focusing on their integration with EC2 and other AWS services to uncover the full spectrum of its capabilities. Let's dive in!

Deploying and integrating AWS Lambda functions

In this section, we will delve into the practical aspects of deploying, configuring, and integrating Lambda functions, ensuring seamless operation with your existing AWS infrastructure.

Deployment and configuration

The following steps are involved in deploying a Lambda function:

1. **Create a Lambda function**: Start by creating a Lambda function from the AWS management console, AWS CLI, or AWS SDK. You can write code directly in the console or upload your code as a ZIP file.
2. **Configuring triggers**: Set up triggers based on different AWS services such as S3 events and DynamoDB updates to invoke your Lambda function.
3. **Environment variables**: Use environment variables to manage your configuration settings.
4. **Memory and Timeout settings**: Adjust the memory and timeout settings based on the function's requirements to ensure efficient use of resources.
5. **Testing and debugging**: Utilize the AWS console for testing and debugging. You can integrate AWS X-Ray for in-depth tracing and analysis.

Integration with EC2 – managing your instances

Here are some key use cases of EC2 that can be a breeze to handle with AWS Lambda:

- **Automate EC2 instance management**: You can use a Lambda function to automatically start or stop EC2 instances based on a schedule using CloudWatch events. For example, you can stop all instances tagged with *Development* outside business hours.
- **Responding to EC2 state changes**: You can set up Lambda functions to respond to EC2 state changes, such as stopping or starting. Also, you can perform tasks such as creating backups or logging specific events when such changes occur.
- **Securing with IAM**: Ensure the Lambda function's IAM role has permission to manage your EC2 instances. Avoid overly permissive privileges to align with the security best practices.

By focusing on these steps and practices, you will be able to manage your EC2 instances more effectively using AWS Lambda functions. Next, we'll explore the practices and use cases for containerization and serverless computing and see how they can be applied in your AWS environment.

Best practices and use cases for containerization and serverless computing

As you may have guessed from our discussion, containerization and serverless computing are simply revolutionizing how we approach application deployment and management in the cloud. By embracing these technologies, you can significantly enhance your efficiency, scalability, and reliability. Let's dive in and explore some key practices and real-world applications.

Best practices

Here are some key best practices that you can follow while operationalizing containerization and serverless computing:

- **Optimize for scalability**: Take advantage of the elastic nature of serverless functions and container orchestration to handle fluctuating workloads effectively.
- **Emphasize security**: Secure your containers and serverless functions by following the principles of least privilege while defining security groups and IAM roles. Also, regularly update your dependencies.
- **Monitor and log**: Implement robust logging and monitoring design strategies to track performance and troubleshoot issues promptly.

Use cases

Here are the key use cases for containerization and serverless computing:

- **Microservices architecture**: Break down your complex applications into smaller, more manageable services using containerization or serverless computing to improve maintainability and scalability
- **Event-driven processing**: Utilize AWS Lambda for tasks such as image processing or data analysis (for example, perform event-driven data analysis while making use of events such as file uploads)
- **Continuous integration/continuous deployment**: Automate your deployment pipelines with containers to ensure consistent and reliable application build/deployment
- **IoT applications**: Leverage serverless computing to process the data coming in from IoT devices efficiently without worrying about infrastructure management

In conclusion, the integration of containerization and serverless computing with Amazon EC2 offers a robust platform for modern, scalable, and efficient application development.

Summary

In this chapter, we understood the essentials of containerization with ECS and ECR, explored the serverless capabilities of AWS Fargate and Lambda, and uncovered the best practices and practical use cases for these technologies.

In the next chapter, we will delve into advanced techniques for maximizing EC2's potential in specialized computing scenarios.

13
Leveraging AWS Services for Hybrid and Multi-Cloud Architectures

We start off this chapter by unraveling the definitions, significance, and distinctive features of modern cloud strategies. This will be the foundational step, setting the stage for a deeper dive into the world where multiple cloud realms can coexist and collaborate.

As we navigate further, we will look deeper into the specific AWS services that are pivotal for hybrid cloud integration. We will explore the benefits of AWS Direct Connect, AWS Storage Gateway, AWS Outposts, and AWS VPC. Each of these services offers unique capabilities to bridge on-premises infrastructure with AWS, enabling a seamless integrated cloud experience.

As we further our exploration, we will look at AWS services, such as Amazon Route 53, AWS Transit Gateway, and AWS Resource Access Manager, that facilitate multi-cloud integration. In this section, we will explore how these services play a pivotal role in bringing cohesiveness across multi-cloud environments.

We will also dive in and explore data management and migration across clouds, focusing on DataSync, AWS Transfer Family, and AWS Database Migration Service. These tools come as an essential utility in ensuring your data is agile, secure, and easily transferable across various cloud landscapes.

We will then explore AWS Organizations, AWS Security Hub, and AWS Config to help maintain oversight and fortify your cloud infrastructures against potential threats.

Finally, we will draw learning from real-world scenarios in our case studies and best practices section, learning from those who have successfully navigated the hybrid and multi-cloud architectures.

We will cover the following topics in this chapter:

- Introduction to hybrid and multi-cloud architectures.
- AWS services for hybrid cloud integration
- AWS services for multi-cloud integration
- Data management and migration across clouds
- Monitoring and security in hybrid and multi-cloud environments
- Case studies and best practices

With this overview, let us now embark on this enlightening expedition by navigating to our first stop, an introduction to hybrid and multi-cloud architectures.

Introduction to hybrid and multi-cloud architecture

In today's rapidly evolving digital landscape, understanding the nuances of hybrid and multi-cloud architectures is more than just a theoretical exercise. It's a necessity for any cloud computing specialist. So, what exactly are these architectures and why do they hold such significance in the realm of cloud computing?

Hybrid cloud architectures are basically a powerful blend of on-premises infrastructure, private cloud services, and public cloud; for example, Amazon EC2 with orchestration between various platforms. This fusion in cloud architecture provides businesses with the flexibility and scalability of the cloud while allowing them to maintain sensitive data on their private servers. It is like having the best of both worlds, tailored to fit unique operational needs.

A common use case might be a financial institution that processes transactions within its secure, private cloud but uses public cloud resources for customer relationship management or data analytics.

On the other hand, multi-cloud architecture refers to the use of multiple cloud computing service providers in a single heterogeneous architecture. This design strategy enables organizations to optimize their cloud-hosted solutions by picking and choosing from different cloud service providers to avoid vendor lock-in, enhance resilience, and optimize costs.

A common use case is for businesses to employ AWS for its robust computing infrastructure, Google Cloud for superior data analytics and AI capabilities, and Microsoft Azure for its integration with existing Microsoft products.

Why does this even matter? In a world where digital demands are constantly shifting, these architectures provide the agility and adaptability for businesses to stay competitive. This offers a customizable approach to cloud computing where you can cherry-pick the strengths of different cloud services to create a solution that is perfectly aligned with your business needs and goals.

With this foundational knowledge in place, we can now explore how AWS caters to hybrid cloud integration, offering services that bridge the gap between on-premises and cloud environments. Let's dive in and explore the AWS services for hybrid cloud integration.

AWS services for hybrid cloud integration

In this section, we will delve into and understand how AWS bridges on-premises infrastructure with cloud capabilities. We will explore the following:

- AWS Direct Connect for dedicated network connectivity
- AWS Storage Gateway for seamless on-premises infrastructure to cloud storage integration
- AWS Outposts for bringing in AWS services to on-premises environment
- AWS VPN for secure network connectivity

Each of these services plays a pivotal role in creating a cohesive and efficient hybrid cloud environment, aligning with diverse organizational needs. Let's start by diving into AWS Direct Connect and its impact on your hybrid cloud strategy.

AWS Direct Connect

AWS Direct Connect is not just a service but a bridge that connects an on-premises network to **Amazon Web Services (AWS)** over a private, high-speed link. By embarking into AWS Direct Connect, we enter into a realm where seamless integration and high-speed connectivity completely redefine our hybrid cloud experience.

Let us understand some of the significant technical facts of AWS Direct Connect before we understand its role in hybrid cloud architectures, particularly within Amazon EC2:

- **Dedicated network link**: AWS Direct Connect provides a dedicated network connection between your on-premises data center and AWS. This dedicated network link can be a 1-Gbps or 10-Gbps connection, bypassing the public internet for enhanced reliability and speed.
- **Reduced latency**: The dedicated link with Direct Connect ensures minimal network latency between your on-premises and AWS environment, which is crucial for latency-sensitive applications running on Amazon EC2 or for other services inside VPC.
- **Consistent network performance**: Unlike internet connection, Direct Connect offers more consistent network behavior, which is essential for applications that demand stable and reliable connectivity.
- **Private and secure**: By avoiding the public internet with Direct Connect, the network communication significantly reduces the exposure to potential threats, enhancing the security of data in transit.

- **Flexible connectivity**: Direct Connect supports adding multiple **virtual local area networks** (**VLANs**), allowing you to use the same connection to access public and private AWS resources.
- **Integration with other AWS services**: Direct Connect seamlessly integrates with AWS services, including Amazon VPC, allowing for smooth communication with EC2 instances.

Use case for AWS Direct Connect with EC2 in hybrid cloud architecture

Imagine a scenario where a company has a large-scale application hosted on Amazon EC2. The application deals with sensitive data and requires regular data transfer between a company's on-premises data center and AWS. By subscribing to AWS Direct Connect, the company establishes a private, high-speed, and dedicated network link to AWS and achieves the data transfer to and from EC2 instances in a fast, secure, and reliable manner.

The direct connection reduces latency significantly, making it ideal for high-performance computing tasks or applications requiring real-time data processing. It also offers consistent network experience, ensuring that data-dependent applications on EC2 perform optimally.

In summary, AWS Direct Connect provides the speed, security, and reliability needed to run complex workloads seamlessly across on-premises and cloud environments benefiting the hybrid cloud setup.

Let us now explore AWS Storage Gateway, a service that integrates on-premises IT environments with cloud storage for backup, archiving, and disaster recovery.

AWS Storage Gateway

AWS Storage Gateway is an innovative solution that comes with a range of data management capabilities that effortlessly bridges on-premises environments with cloud storage. This especially plays a crucial role in hybrid cloud architectures, particularly when it comes to data backup, archiving, and disaster recovery.

Let us now understand some of the significant technical facts of AWS Storage Gateway before we understand its role in the hybrid cloud architectures:

- **Seamless integration**: Storage Gateway seamlessly integrates with existing on-premises environments through standard storage protocols such as NFS, SMB, and iSCSI
- **Diverse gateway types**: Storage Gateway offers various types of gateways, such as file, volume, and tape gateways, with each serving different storage scenarios
- **Secure data transfer**: Data transferred through AWS Storage Gateway is encrypted offering secure data in transit.
- **Efficient data management**: Storage Gateway enables efficient data management strategies such as data caching, backup snapshots, and tiered storage mechanisms.

Use cases of AWS Storage Gateway

The following are some use cases of AWS Storage Gateway:

- **Data backup and archiving**: Organizations can make use of the file gateway to store and retrieve files in Amazon S3, providing a secure and durable solution for data backup and retrieval. This is particularly useful for organizations requiring regular data backups and long-term data retention.
- **Tape-based backup requirement**: The tape gateway feature of Storage Gateway provides a cloud-based, virtual tape infrastructure, replacing physical tape-based backups with more reliable and accessible solutions.
- **Disaster recovery**: Volume gateway offers stored and cached volumes that can be used for disaster recovery purposes. In the event of an on-premises data center failure, these volumes ensure quick data recovery and minimize overall downtime.

By now, you can understand that AWS Storage Gateway streamlines the incorporation of cloud storage into hybrid cloud architectures, offering a range of functionalities tailored to different data management needs.

We will now turn our attention to AWS Outposts, a service that brings AWS infrastructure and services directly to your on-premises facility for a truly consistent hybrid experience.

AWS Outposts

AWS Outposts is a pivotal and innovative solution that brings AWS cloud infrastructure and services directly to virtually any data center, co-location space, or on-premises facility. It is a fully managed AWS service ideal for workloads that need to remain on premises due to low latency or local data processing needs.

Let us dive in and understand some of the important benefits that it brings into your hybrid cloud environment:

- **Local data residency requirements**: For the workloads where your regulation mandates data residency, Outposts provide the necessary local processing and storage capabilities, all while keeping the data integrated with the broader AWS ecosystem.
- **Consistency across environments**: Outposts ensures a consistent operational experience, whether in the AWS cloud or on premises. This consistency is critical for businesses looking to smoothly integrate their on-premises infrastructure with the cloud.
- **Expansive services support**: With Outposts, you can use a range of AWS services locally, including EC2 instances, EBS volumes, and container-based services such as ECS and EKS, ensuring you have the necessary tools to meet your specific workload requirements.

Use cases of AWS Outposts

With this understanding in context, let us explore the use cases of AWS Outposts:

- **Low-latency applications**: Industries such as healthcare, financial services, and manufacturing, where milliseconds can make a significant difference, benefit from the low-latency performance of Outposts.

- **Hybrid applications**: Outposts facilitates a smooth transition to the cloud for organizations with legacy systems, enabling them to run hybrid applications seamlessly across on-premises and cloud environments.

Next, we will pivot into AWS VPN and explore how it complements hybrid cloud strategies by securely connecting on-premises networks to the AWS cloud environment.

AWS VPN

We will now turn our focus to **AWS VPN**, an integral service for establishing secure and private connections between AWS cloud and on-premises networks. Let us further explore the use cases and technical facets of AWS VPN and understand how it fortifies your hybrid cloud strategy. There are two types of VPN services:

- **Site-to-site VPN**: This connects your on-premises network to your AWS VPC over a secure, encrypted tunnel. It's ideal for regular, ongoing application connectivity.

- **Client VPN**: This is a client-based service enabling secure access to AWS resources and on-premises networks, suitable for remote or mobile users.

AWS VPN's technical advantages include the following:

- **Secure transmission**: AWS VPN ensures data security through encrypted tunnels, safeguarding against unauthorized access.

- **Management and integration**: AWS VPN offers seamless integration with services such as Amazon VPC and complements AWS Direct Connect for a more robust network architecture.

Additionally, AWS VPN can be seamlessly integrated alongside Direct Connect, enhancing and complementing your overall connectivity solutions. The benefits include the following:

- **Backup connectivity**: You can fortify your business continuity plan by making use of AWS VPN to serve as your failover solution for Direct Connect and ensure connectivity even if the primary Direct Connect link goes down.

- **Enhanced security**: By combining VPN with Direct Connect, you can add a layer of encryption to the data that is being transmitted over the network, thus making it ideal for transmitting secure data over network pipes without any concern.
- **Hybrid deployment**: While Direct Connect provides a dedicated connection, VPN adds a layer of flexibility and security, especially useful for remote access scenarios or when Direct Connect isn't feasible due to location constraints.

Use cases of AWS VPN

Let us now explore the use cases of AWS VPN in the hybrid cloud strategy:

- **Disaster recovery and business continuity**: AWS VPN can act as a backup to your Direct Connect connection to provide uninterrupted service to your hybrid cloud-hosted applications
- **Cost-effective connectivity**: In scenarios where Direct Connect may not be cost-effective or necessary, AWS VPN comes as a secure and scalable alternative

In summary, AWS VPN, when used alongside AWS Direct Connect, provides a comprehensive, secure, and highly available network setup. This combination is pivotal in achieving a resilient and efficient hybrid cloud architecture, offering the best of both worlds—the high speed of Direct Connect and the encrypted, flexible connectivity of VPN.

Let us now turn our attention to exploring AWS services for multi-cloud integration, diving into how AWS facilitates integration and operability across diverse cloud environments.

AWS services for multi-cloud integration

In this section, we will delve into understanding AWS's pivotal role in multi-cloud integration, focusing on services such as Amazon Route 53, AWS Transit Gateway, and AWS Resource Access Manager. These tools collectively enable seamless connectivity and resource-sharing across diverse cloud environments, underlining AWS's capability to optimize and manage multi-cloud strategies effectively.

We will explore Amazon Route 53 and understand how it directs traffic and ensures high availability across varied cloud platforms.

Amazon Route 53

Amazon Route 53 is a highly available and scalable **Domain Name System (DNS)** that is designed to give developers and businesses a reliable way to route end users to internet applications. This service effectively connects user requests to the infrastructure running in AWS, such as EC2 instances, and can also be used to route users to infrastructure outside AWS.

Here are some key features of Amazon Route53:

- **DNS management**: Amazon Route 53 efficiently handles DNS records, supporting a variety of DNS record types, which allows for effective domain management in a multi-cloud setup.
- **Health checks and traffic flow**: Route53 automatically routes users to the best endpoint for performance or health. This feature is invaluable in multi-cloud architectures for ensuring high availability and fault tolerance.
- **Geolocation routing**: Route 53 can route traffic based on the geographic location of users, which is beneficial for delivering localized content and complying with regional data policies.

Let us now explore the advantages of using Amazon Route 53:

- **Scalability and reliability**: Route 53 as a managed service automatically scales to handle large query volumes without any manual intervention, ensuring consistent and reliable performance.
- **High availability**: Route 53 is designed to be highly available. It automatically routes the users to the optimal location ensuring minimal downtime and better performance.
- **Global network**: With the global network of DNS servers, Route 53 offers low latency making it more responsive to the users regardless of their location.

With this understanding of the features and benefits of using Amazon Route 53, let us now explore where it can be effectively utilized:

- **Multi-cloud load balancing**: Route 53 can distribute loads between AWS and other cloud environments, optimizing the overall resource utilization.
- **Disaster recovery**: Route 53 can route traffic away from failed or unhealthy endpoints, aiding in effective disaster recovery strategies. As we explore Route 53 capabilities, we gain insights into how DNS and traffic routing strategies are pivotal in multi-cloud scenarios. Now, let's shift our focus to AWS Transit Gateway, which plays a key role in simplifying network architecture across multi-cloud environments.

AWS Transit Gateway

AWS Transit Gateway acts as a network hub, streamlining the way you connect multiple VPCs and on-premises networking through a single networking point. Transit Gateway simplifies your overall network architecture, especially in multi-cloud environments by offering a single gateway to manage and route your overall network traffic. Here are some key features of Transit Gateway:

- **Centralized management**: Transit Gateway enables centralized control over network routing and makes it easier to manage your network security posture and administer to your cross-network traffic

- **Simplified network topology**: By reducing the complexities of network topology, Transit Gateway facilitates smoother and more manageable connections across multiple VPCs and on-premises networks.
- **Scalability**: Transit Gateway as a managed service allows you to handle a growing number of connections without compromising the performance
- **Inter-region peering**: Transit gateway supports peering across different AWS regions, enhancing global connectivity and data sharing

Let us now explore the advantages of Transit Gateway in multi-cloud environments:

- **Unified network hub**: Transit Gateway serves as a unified hub in connecting different cloud environments and reduces the need for multiple point-to-point links.
- **Enhanced security and compliance**: Transit Gateway allows you to consistently apply network security and compliance policies across your network infrastructure in one single place.
- **Cost-effectiveness**: By simplifying your multi-cloud network architecture, Transit Gateway helps reduce operational costs associated with managing multiple discrete networks.

So, in a scenario where an organization uses multi-cloud for its operating environment (AWS for compute and another cloud provider for its niche use case), Transit Gateway ensures seamless, secure connectivity between these services, enhancing the overall network efficiency.

With Transit Gateway's capacity to unify and simplify complex network architectures, it clearly stands out as an essential tool for multi-cloud integration. We will now turn our attention to AWS Resource Access Manager, which complements these network integration capabilities by enabling the efficient sharing of resources across AWS accounts and other cloud environments.

AWS Resource Access Manager

AWS **Resource Access Manager** (**RAM**) is a service designed to simplify resource sharing across different AWS accounts within the same or different AWS organization. This feature is particularly useful for organizations with many AWS accounts where resources need to be efficiently managed and shared across different cloud environments. Here are some of the key features of AWS RAM:

- **Resource sharing**: RAM allows you to share resources such as subnets, route tables, etc. across different AWS accounts.
- **Centralized management**: RAM offers a centralized way to share and manage resources, making it easier to oversee and control access permissions.
- **Cost-effective**: By sharing resources across different AWS accounts, RAM helps you avoid duplicating resource provisioning across different AWS accounts.
- **Security and compliance**: With RAM, you can apply your organization's security and compliance policies centrally and share them with the rest of the AWS accounts. This simplifies and eases the distributed management of security and compliance policies.

Let us look at what specific advantages RAM brings to your multi-cloud environments:

- **Cross-account accessibility**: By seamlessly sharing AWS resources across different AWS accounts, it simplifies your overall operations for a multi-cloud environment
- **Flexibility and efficiency**: RAM allows your organization to optimize your resource usage by sharing necessary resources across cloud environments, thus increasing your operational efficiency
- **Enhances collaboration**: By sharing resources, RAM facilitates enhanced collaboration between different teams and departments, even when they operate in different cloud environments.

With its features and advantages in context, let us explore the use cases of RAM in multi-cloud environments.

Use cases of AWS Resource Access Manager

In a multi-cloud environment, AWS RAM is instrumental for the centralized management of AWS resources across multiple AWS accounts within the AWS ecosystem. This approach is particularly useful for organizations operating in a hybrid cloud environment such as Azure or Google Cloud, with distinct accounts for different functions or departments.

By using AWS RAM, a central account can share and manage essential AWS resources (subnets, Amazon Machine Images) with other AWS accounts. This centralized approach streamlines management, security, and compliance policies and reduces overall operational overhead. Although AWS RAM does not facilitate sharing AWS resources across different cloud service providers, it streamlines and enhances the efficiency of the AWS portion of your multi-cloud strategy. This is especially effective when combined with AWS services such as Transit Gateway with Direct Connect, where it can facilitate seamless connectivity between AWS and other cloud environments. AWS RAM thus plays a vital role in achieving cost-effective and secure resource management within AWS in a broader multi-cloud architecture.

As we move forward, we will delve into the intricacies of data management and migration across clouds, exploring tools and strategies for effective data handling in a hybrid cloud setup.

Data management and migration across clouds

Effective data management and migration are crucial in the expansive cloud landscape. This section focuses on AWS services that facilitate these processes. We will be exploring the following services:

- AWS DataSync for efficient data transfers
- AWS Transfer Family for secure file movements
- AWS Database Migration Service for seamless database migrations

These services are crucial for organizations leveraging multi- and hybrid clouds for their diverse migration needs. We will now delve into AWS DataSync and understand how it facilitates high-speed data transfers between on-premises infrastructure and cloud storage.

AWS DataSync

AWS DataSync is a highly capable data transfer service designed for efficient, high-speed transfers of large volumes of data to and from AWS services. The usage of this service is particularly advantageous for data migration, backup, and disaster recovery operations. DataSync automates and accelerates the movement of data between on-premises storage to AWS services such as **Simple Storage Service (S3)**, **Elastic File System (EFS)**, and **FSx** for Windows file servers.

Here are the key features of AWS DataSync:

- **Speed**: DataSync can transfer data up to 10 times faster than open source tools. This is achieved through an optimized network protocol and parallel data transfer.
- **Ease of deployment**: The setup involves deploying a DataSync agent in your existing on-premises environment. The agent then facilitates secure communication and direct transfer to your desired AWS storage service.
- **Data protection**: Ensuring the security of your data, DataSync offers encryption to both your data in transit and at rest with the system or service that is storing your data. This means the data is safeguarded from unauthorized access both in transit and while stored in AWS.
- **Cost-effectiveness**: With DataSync, you pay only for the data that is transferred. This pricing model makes it a cost-effective solution for your ongoing data synchronization needs.

Use cases of AWS DataSync

With this understanding of the features, let us now explore the use cases of DataSync and understand how to make the best use of it:

- **Data migration**: For migrating the data from on-premises infrastructure to AWS, DataSync simplifies and accelerates the overall process, making it ideal for large-scale migrations.
- **Regular backups**: DataSync ensures data durability and accessibility and improves business continuity by automating regular backups from on-premises to AWS environments.
- **Hybrid cloud storage synchronization**: For organizations operating in hybrid cloud environments, DataSync keeps the data synchronized between on-premises and cloud storage and ensures consistency and up-to-date data across environments.
- **Disaster recovery**: DataSync can be used to replicate data from on-premises infrastructure to AWS for disaster recovery purposes. In the event of on-premise failure, data can be simply recovered from AWS.

As we move forward, we will now explore AWS Transfer Family focusing on its capabilities to provide a secure file transfer solution to AWS.

AWS Transfer Family

AWS Transfer Family provides a robust transfer for secure and efficient file transfer into AWS cloud services, with a focus on supporting traditional file transfer protocols. This comes as an essential tool for organizations looking to leverage cloud storage without disrupting their existing file transfer workflows.

Here are some key features of AWS Transfer Family:

- **Protocol support**: It uniquely supports SFTP, FTP, and FTP protocols, making it ideal for organizations accustomed to these traditional file transfer methods
- **Cloud storage integration**: It directly integrates with Amazon S3 and EFS for direct storage and retrieval of files
- **Security and compliance**: AWS Transfer Family ensures secure file transfer with robust encryption and integrates with AWS IAM for stringent access control

Use cases of AWS Transfer Family

With these features in context, let us explore the use cases of AWS Transfer Family and how it can help with your hybrid cloud implementation:

- **Legacy system integration**: Transfer Family helps businesses with legacy systems that depend on FTP-based transfers to move files to the cloud without overhauling their existing setup
- **Cross-cloud file movement**: Transfer Family facilitates secure and protocol-compliant file transfers in multi-cloud environments

How is AWS Transfer Family different from AWS DataSync?

Let us also understand how Transfer Family differentiates itself from the DataSync-based file transfer mechanism we discussed earlier. While DataSync specializes in high-speed data synchronization between on-premises storage systems and cloud services, Transfer Family excels in protocol-based file transfers. DataSync is more suited for large-scale data migrations, periodic data sync and backup for disaster recovery, and other scenarios where high-speed data transfer is crucial. Conversely, Transfer Family is tailored for day-to-day operational file transfer, especially where traditional file transfer protocols are relied on for their file transfers.

In summary, Transfer Family complements DataSync in your hybrid cloud implementation by addressing the specific needs of businesses that rely on traditional file transfer protocols for their cloud migration and data transfer strategies.

As we move forward, we will dive in and explore AWS Database Migration Service, which offers a distinct approach to migrating databases to the AWS cloud.

AWS Database Migration Service

As we dive deeper into the realm of data management and migration across clouds, we now turn our attention to the **AWS Database Migration Service (AWS DMS)**. This service offers a seamless transition and a highly efficient pathway for migrating databases to AWS without disrupting the application performance.

Let us look at some of the key features of AWS DMS:

- **Versatile support for source and target database**: DMS supports a wide range of database sources and targets under SQL, NoSQL, and warehouse databases
- **Continuous data replication**: DMS offers continuous data replication with high availability, allowing for data migration and sync
- **Secure data transfer**: DMS employs robust security measures to protect your data during data transfer

Use cases of AWS Database Migration Service

With the features in hand, let us explore use cases where we can employ Database Migration Service:

- **Migrating to AWS databases**: DMS is ideal for organizations looking to migrate their on-premises or cloud-hosted databases to AWS-managed database services such as AWS RDS or Amazon Redshift
- **Homogenous and heterogenous migrations**: DMS supports both homogenous migrations (such as MySQL to Amazon Aurora) and heterogenous migrations (such as Oracle to Amazon Aurora or Microsoft SQL Server to RDS MySQL).
- **Disaster recovery**: DMS facilitates the creation of live data replication, which can serve as a backup for disaster recovery purposes

In summary, DMS offers a streamlined and secure way of migrating your databases into the AWS ecosystem, and it is particularly useful for organizations undergoing digital transformation looking to make use of AWS's advanced database capabilities.

As we wrap up this section, we will go ahead and explore monitoring and security in a hybrid cloud environment to understand the necessary tools and practices to ensure robust security and efficient monitoring across diverse cloud setups.

Monitoring and security in hybrid and multi-cloud environments

Monitoring and security are more crucial than ever in today's complex and hybrid multi-cloud environments. Here are some monitoring and security tools commonly used in such environments.

Starting with **Cloud Security Posture Management (CSPM)**, this tool is essentially designed to help organizations ensure that their cloud infrastructure adheres to security best practices, compliance requirements, and organization policies. They provide visibility into cloud environments, assess security configurations, and detect misconfigurations and vulnerabilities. Here are the key CSPM tools offered by the major cloud service providers:

- **AWS Config**: This helps assess, audit, and evaluate the AWS resources for their compliance with organizational policies and security standards. More on this will be discussed in the context of multi-AWS account management in the next section.
- **Azure Policy**: This allows you to enforce governance and compliance policies for Azure resources, ensuring they adhere to organizational standards.
- **Google Cloud Security Command Center (SCC)**: This offers continuous security and compliance monitoring, along with the policy enforcement capabilities of Google Cloud resources.

Cloud monitoring and management platforms are essential to any cloud infrastructure, providing insights into the performance, availability, and health of resources and applications deployed in the cloud. Here are the three key cloud monitoring and management platforms offered by major cloud service providers:

- **AWS CloudWatch**: This provides monitoring for AWS resources and applications, with features for metrics collection, log monitoring, and automated actions based on predefined alarms
- **Azure Monitor**: This offers monitoring capabilities for Azure services and applications, including metrics, logs, and alerts
- **Google Cloud Monitoring**: This is a Google Cloud Monitoring Solution for collecting, viewing, and analyzing metrics and logs for GCP resources

Also, in a hybrid and multi-cloud AWS environment, it is very natural for enterprises to make use of multiple AWS accounts, as leveraging multiple AWS accounts can provide benefits such as isolation and security, cost management, compliance, and so on. In the next section, we will pay special emphasis to it and look at several essential AWS services designed to enhance these aspects of multi-AWS account management. We will explore the following:

- AWS Organizations for streamlined access across distributed AWS accounts
- AWS Security Hub for a comprehensive security overview
- AWS Config for its detailed resource configuration auditing

Let us start with AWS Organizations and understand its role in enhancing governance and operational efficiency across your cloud landscape.

AWS Organizations

AWS Organizations is a pivotal service for managing and governing multiple AWS accounts. It enables you to consolidate billing, control accesses, comply with policies, and streamline security in a hierarchical, centrally managed environment. This service is especially beneficial for large-scale businesses or enterprises expanding into hybrid or multi-cloud architectures.

The following are some of the key features of AWS Organizations:

- **Centralized management**: AWS Organizations allows for the centralized management of multiple AWS accounts. This feature makes it easier to oversee and control your entire AWS environment.
- **Policy-based control**: AWS Organizations allows you to apply various policies (service control policies, tag-based policies, backup policies, etc.) across all your AWS accounts for security and compliance protocols.
- **Cost optimization**: Consolidated billing allows you to gain insights and optimize costs across your multi-AWS account environment.
- **Automated AWS account creation**: AWS Organizations allows you to automate and streamline the process of creating and managing AWS accounts.

Use cases of AWS Organizations

Let us now understand the use cases of AWS Organization in the distributed cloud environment:

- **Streamlining operations for large enterprises**: Large enterprises often manage numerous AWS accounts across departments or projects. AWS Organization simplifies this complexity by providing a unified view and centralized management of those AWS accounts. This eases administrative tasks such as account setup, access control, and resource allocation streamlined across the multi-AWS accounts, and it reduces operational overhead and improves your operational efficiency.
- **Enhanced security across multiple accounts**: For organizations concerned with managing robust security posture across all accounts, AWS Organizations offers a solution. AWS Organizations allows for the uniform implementation of policies, password policies, multi-factor authentication, and service control policies. This consistency is crucial for meeting your regulatory requirements and maintaining high-security standards.
- **Cost-effectiveness through centralized billing and cost management**: AWS organization offers a consolidation of billing across multi-AWS accounts and provides a comprehensive view of the organization's expenses, simplifying the billing process and aiding in budget management.

Each of the cases described illustrates the benefits of AWS Organizations in enhancing the operational efficiency and financial management of businesses operating in multi-AWS account environments.

We will now delve into AWS Security Hub, a crucial service for maintaining an overarching view of your security landscape in AWS, ensuring compliance with regulations and adherence to security best practices.

AWS Security Hub

AWS Security Hub is a powerful tool that helps you maintain a robust security posture in your hybrid and multi-cloud environments. AWS Security Hub allows you to aggregate, organize, and prioritize security alerts or findings coming in from different services. The service also supports third-party integration, providing you with a comprehensive view of your security state within AWS.

Let us look at some of the features of AWS Security Hub in detail:

- **Centralized security management**: Security Hub consolidates events from various sources such as Amazon GuardDuty, Amazon Inspector, and other third-party providers
- **Automated/scheduled compliance check**: Security Hub continuously monitors your environment using automated compliance checks based on AWS best practices and industry standards such as **AWS Centre for Internet Security** (**CIS**) foundation benchmarks
- **Actionable insights**: Security Hub not only identifies threats but also offers insights and recommendations to improve your security and compliance
- **Customizable dashboards**: Security Hub provides a customizable dashboard that offers a consolidated view of security and compliance status, enabling you to spot trends and pinpoint areas requiring action

By integrating AWS Security Hub, Organizations can streamline security monitoring and improve overall security posture. Security Hub is essentially a vital tool for Organizations that allows security insights to be lost in the noise of ever-increasing data.

Having explored the monitoring capabilities of Security Hub, let us now explore AWS Config. This service plays a pivotal role in tracking and managing the configurations of your AWS resources, enhancing your governance and compliance efforts.

AWS Config

In the intricate world of cloud computing, managing the configuration of your resources is paramount in maintaining security, compliance, and operational efficiency. **AWS Config** rule plays an essential role in achieving these objectives. It is a service that allows you to continuously assess, evaluate and audit your configurations of AWS resources. AWS Config constantly observes and logs your AWS resource configurations, enabling automated checks between recorded and preferred configurations.

Let's take a closer look at some of the features of AWS Config:

- **Continuous monitoring and configuration history**: AWS Config records and evaluates changes in your AWS environment, giving you the detailed history of configuration changes for each of your AWS resources
- **Compliance auditing**: AWS Config aids in compliance checks by assessing whether your resource configurations align with internal guidelines and external regulations
- **Customizable rules and remediation actions**: AWS Config allows you to create custom rules that define the desired configuration state of your AWS resources. If there are any deviations detected, it triggers the automated remediation actions
- **Integration with other AWS services**: AWS Config seamlessly integrates various other AWS services, enhancing compliance and security management across your AWS infrastructure

AWS config is particularly beneficial for industries where compliance and governance are critical. AWS Config provides the tool needed to maintain an audit-ready posture and respond to the changes quickly in your environment.

With our exploration of monitoring and security in hybrid and multi-cloud environments with services such as AWS Organizations, Security Hub, and Config, we have covered the vital aspects of cloud management. Up next, we will explore case studies and best practices, where we will delve into the real-world applications and best practices illustrating successful hybrid and multi-cloud implementations.

Case studies and best practices

In this section, we will delve into the real-world examples that reflect the successful implementations of hybrid and multi-cloud strategies, showcasing the flexibility and power of AWS services in helping you achieve a successful hybrid and multi-cloud implementation:

- **Financial services**: A leading global financial institution leveraged AWS to create a hybrid cloud environment. They used AWS to create a dedicated, secure connection between their on-premises data center and AWS environment. By integrating AWS Storage Gateway, they seamlessly connected their on-premises storage with cloud storage, ensuring the data was securely transferred and encrypted. This hybrid setup basically allows them to meet strict regulatory compliance while enjoying scalability and innovation in the cloud.
- **E-commerce giant**: An international e-commerce company implemented their multi-cloud strategy using AWS. It utilized Amazon Route53 for user traffic management(i.e., DNS Routing), efficiently routing traffic between AWS and other cloud environments. AWS Lambda facilitated serverless computing, enabling them to run applications with high availability without worrying about their server administration. This approach basically allowed the company to optimize its global presence, balancing cloud across various platforms while maximizing efficiency and reach.

- **Healthcare provider**: A healthcare provider needed to ensure security and compliance with their patient data across different clouds. It relied on AWS services such as Transit Gateway for establishing unified network infrastructure, connecting AWS VPCs with other cloud environments. Its use of AWS **Identity and Access Management** (**IAM**) ensured its access was strictly controlled and compliant with healthcare regulations. This setup helped the company to securely and flexibly manage patient data securely and efficiently.

The examples we have seen underscore how diverse industries leverage AWS's hybrid and multi-cloud capabilities to address specific business needs and challenges.

Summary

In this chapter, we have navigated the basics of hybrid and multi-cloud architectures, explored AWS services' support for hybrid and multi-cloud integration, and learned about data management solutions for migration across clouds, monitoring, and security solutions for hybrid and multi-cloud environments. We also uncovered their use cases and best practices. In the next chapter, we will look into advanced techniques for maximizing EC2 potential in specialized computing scenarios.

14

Optimizing Amazon EC2 for High-Performance Computing, Big Data, and Disaster Recovery Strategies

This chapter strives to equip readers with practical guidance and a comprehensive understanding of leveraging Amazon EC2 for **high-performance computing** (**HPC**) and big data applications, alongside essential **disaster recovery** (**DR**) strategies. The journey begins with laying the groundwork through the introduction of HPC and big data on Amazon EC2, highlighting specialized EC2 instances and **graphics processing unit** (**GPU**) accelerators designed for this demanding workload. The narrative then shifts to big data solutions, emphasizing Amazon **Elastic MapReduce** (**EMR**) and Amazon Redshift as pivotal tools for processing vast warehousing datasets.

Further through, the chapter will look into the intricacies of HPC and Big Data Clusters, focusing on network configurations and storage optimizations to improve performance. We will then transition into DR strategies, understanding the importance of DR and underscoring the significance of DR planning, getting acquainted with DR concepts and AWS services such as Amazon **Relational Database Service** (**RDS**), **Simple Storage Service Cross-Region Replication** (**S3 CRR**), and Global Accelerator to facilitate a robust DR setup.

Finally, in the concluding sections, we will discuss drafting a DR implementation plan, emphasizing the critical balance between **Recovery Time Objective (RTO)** and **Recovery Point Objective (RPO)** and their vital role in regular **DR plan (DRP)** testing and maintenance to ensure operational resilience.

Throughout the chapter, you are set to uncover the breadth and depth of Amazon EC2's capabilities in HPC, big data processing, and DR. So, let's begin this insightful journey with our first step into the realm of HPC and big data in Amazon EC2.

We will cover the following topics in this chapter:

- Introduction to HPC and big data on Amazon EC2
- HPC-optimized EC2 instances
- Big data solutions on Amazon EC2
- Designing and configuring HPC and Big Data Clusters
- Introduction to DR strategies
- AWS services for DR
- Designing and implementing DR strategies on AWS
- Monitoring and testing DR strategies

Introduction to HPC and big data on Amazon EC2

HPC and **big data** are transforming the landscape of computational science and big data in Amazon EC2. In this section, we will uncover the potential of these powerful computation paradigms within the EC2 environment.

HPC is revolutionizing the way complex computational problems are being solved. HPC on Amazon EC2 enables researchers, scientists, and engineers to solve intricate computational problems more swiftly and efficiently. This massive computational power accelerates advancements in various fields, from medical research to climate modeling, by processing and analyzing massive datasets at a speed once thought unattainable, thereby completely transforming the potential for discovery and insight.

Similarly, big data emerges as another cornerstone in modern computing on Amazon EC2. Especially in the era of data explosion, the ability to store, process, and analyze vast datasets is vital. Big data solutions in EC2 offer scalable and versatile platforms for handling these enormous datasets, providing insights that were previously unattainable.

The following diagram compares an HPC cluster to a traditional server:

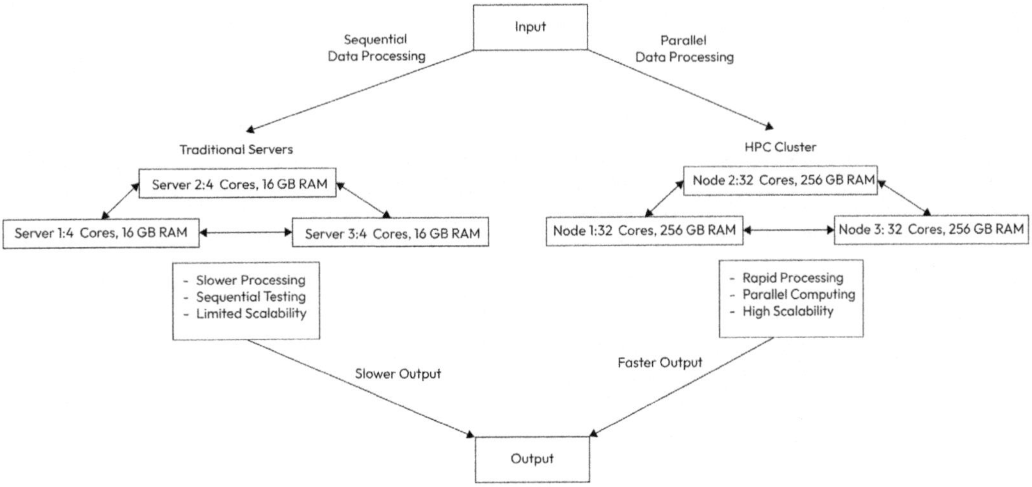

Figure 14.1 – Diagram of an HPC cluster against a traditional server

This section should help give you a solid grasp of the importance and capabilities of HPC and big data on Amazon EC2. So, let's embark on this journey, starting with an in-depth look into the importance of HPC and big data in the cloud computing realm.

Understanding the importance of HPC and big data

HPC on Amazon EC2 brings supercomputing capabilities to your fingertips, empowering you to tackle highly complex computation problems that once could be handled only at specialized research labs. With HPC, scientists and engineers can run simulations, perform advanced research in genomics, and much more at unprecedented speeds. The agility and scalability of Amazon EC2 make it ideal for handling varying characteristics of HPC tasks.

Big data, in tandem with HPC, plays a crucial role in harnessing the power of massive datasets. Whether for **machine learning** (**ML**) models or **business intelligence** (**BI**), big data solutions on Amazon EC2 provide the necessary tools to store, process, and analyze vast quantities of datasets efficiently. This process enables organizations to gain deeper insights and make data-driven decisions quickly, fostering innovation and competitive edge in their respective industries.

Together, HPC and big data represent a transformative force in cloud computing in Amazon EC2. With this understanding of their importance, let's dive deeper into key concepts and terminologies associated with HPC and big data on Amazon EC2, laying a foundation for more advanced discussions and applications.

Key concepts and terminologies

Understanding key concepts and terminologies is crucial in fully understanding HPC and big data in the context of Amazon EC2. Let's break down some of these fundamental terms:

- **Cluster computing**: This refers to the practice of using multiple computers (nodes) working together as a single system to solve computational problems. In HPC on EC2, clusters are often used to achieve high performance and scalability.
- **Parallel processing**: This refers to a computation technique where multiple processors execute or process an application or computation simultaneously. This is a core component of HPC, allowing faster processing and complex calculations.
- **GPU acceleration**: GPUs are used in EC2 instances to speed up processing in compute-intensive tasks such as ML, scientific simulations, and graphics rendering.
- **Data warehousing**: This refers to the electronic storage of large amounts of information by a business in a manner that is secure, reliable, and easy to retrieve and manage.
- **MapReduce**: This refers to a programming model and processing technique for big datasets with parallel, distributed algorithms on a cluster.
- **Batch processing**: This refers to processing high volumes of data, where a group of transactions is collected over a period of time. This is very common in HPC and big data scenarios.

Understanding these concepts is crucial as they form the backbone of how HPC and big data operate in Amazon EC2.

Up next, we will delve into the world of HPC-optimized EC2 instances, where we will explore specific instance types tailored for high-performance workloads.

HPC-optimized EC2 instances

HPC-optimized EC2 instances are designed to handle the most intensive computational tasks imaginable. They are not just a raw power but are about providing the right kind of power. Whether it is a CPU-intensive task or workloads that require low latency and high networking performance, these instances are designed to deliver optimal results.

In this section, we will dive into the specifics of these power-packed instances and explore various instance types available for HPC workloads.

Instance types for HPC workloads

Selecting the right instance type is crucial for ensuring optimal performance for your specific workloads. Each of these instance types is engineered to meet specific requirements, from general-purpose to compute-intensive tasks. Let us now look at some key HPC-optimized instance types available under Amazon EC2:

- **Compute-optimized instances (Instance types: C5, C5n)**: These instances are ideal for compute-intensive applications. They offer a high ratio of compute resources into memory. This makes them perfect for high-performance web servers, scientific modeling, batch processing, and distributed analytics.

- **Memory-optimized instances (Instance types: R5, R5n)**: These instances are tailored to specifically process large datasets in memory. They are well suited for high-performance databases, distributed web scale in-memory cache servers, and real-time analytic applications.

- **Accelerated computing instances (Instance types: P3, P4)**: These instances rely on hardware accelerators (or) coprocessors to perform functions such as floating-point number calculations or graphics processing more efficiently than the software running on the CPU.

- **Purpose-built instances (Instance types: HPC6, HPC7)**: These instances are purpose-built for running HPC workloads at scale with the best price. These types of instances are well suited for running applications that benefit from high-performance processors, such as large, complex simulations and **deep learning** (DL) workloads.

The following diagram illustrates the various instance types:

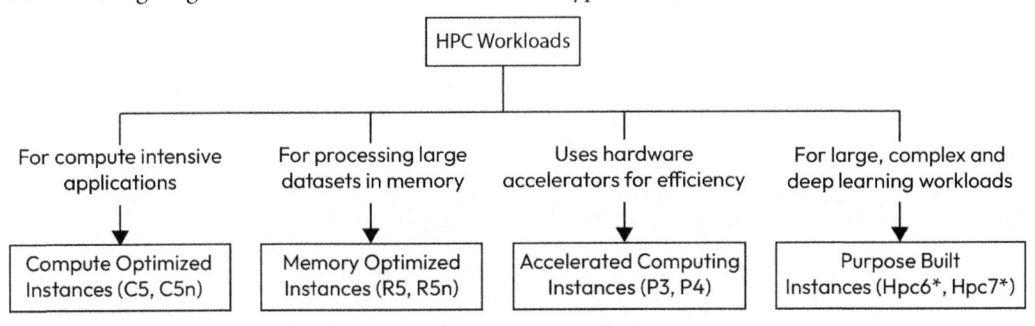

Figure 14.2 – Diagram of HPC instance types

Each of the aforementioned instance types brings its unique strength to the table, allowing you to tailor the HPC environment to your needs. Whether it is processing power, memory capacity, or specialized computing requirements such as GPU acceleration, Amazon EC2 comes with an instance type for your HPC requirement.

As we continue this journey, we will transition to understanding GPU instances and accelerators and explore how GPUs are well suited for running HPC applications.

GPU instances and accelerators

GPU instances provide a perfect blend where computing power meets high-speed processing capabilities. With GPU instances, you can handle tasks that are computationally intensive with high parallel processing power. Let's dive into key aspects of these GPU instances.

Amazon EC2 offers several GPU instance types, such as P3 and G4 instances. P3 instances are designed for general-purpose GPU computing using NVIDIA Tesla V100 GPUs. These instances are optimal for ML models and HPC applications. G4 instances, on the other hand, are optimized for graphic-intensive applications and are well suited for graphics rendering, video encoding, and **virtual reality** (**VR**) applications.

Apart from the dedicated GPU instances, Amazon EC2 also offers **Elastic GPU instances**, which allow you to attach low-cost graphics acceleration to existing EC2 instances. These are well suited for applications that demand an intermittent boost to their graphics power.

In addition to the GPUs, AWS also offers hardware accelerators such as AWS Inferentia, which is tailored for specific use cases such as ML inference and low-cost high-performance options.

In general, GPU instances are particularly useful in training complex ML models, running engineering simulations, and scientific modeling. Their high-power parallel processing capability makes them adept at running tasks that involve large volumes of data.

Here's a diagram of the GPU instance types just discussed:

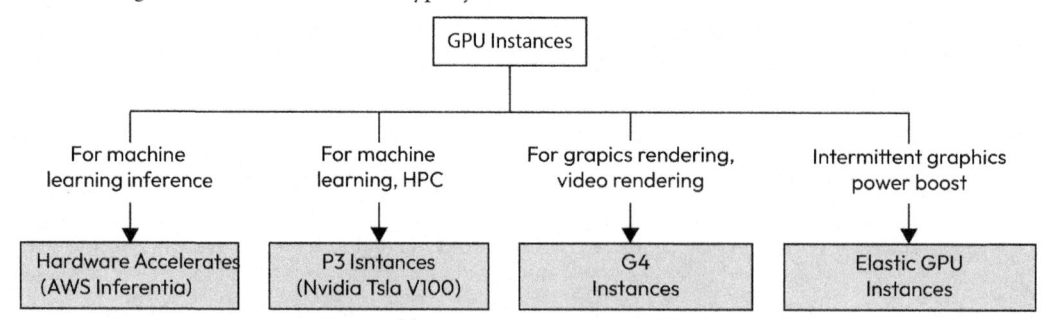

Figure 14.3 – GPU instance-type diagram

It is clear that GPU instances and accelerators are indispensable in delivering high performance in compute-intensive tasks. Their ability to process workloads in parallel at high speed makes them essential in any HPC strategy.

Next, we will delve into big data solutions on Amazon EC2.

Big data solutions on Amazon EC2

Amazon EC2 provides a versatile environment to run big data applications. With Amazon EC2, one can harness the power of extensive computing resources to process, analyze, and extract value from large datasets. Also, EC2 allows you to tailor the infrastructure for your specific big data workloads by customizing instance types, such as memory-optimized or compute-optimized options. Whether you are processing logs, analyzing clickstreams, or handling large-scale databases, EC2 offers the flexibility to handle these tasks efficiently.

EC2 offers integration with other AWS services such as Amazon S3, DynamoDB, and Data Pipeline, providing you with a comprehensive solution for big data processing and storage. This integration facilitates seamless data transfer, processing, and analysis, all within the AWS ecosystem.

Let us move on and explore Amazon EMR, a service that plays an important role in processing big data on AWS, and see how it integrates with the power of EC2 to manage and analyze large datasets.

Amazon EMR for big data processing

Amazon EMR is a cloud-native big data platform that allows you to process large amounts of datasets quickly and cost-effectively across resizable clusters of EC2 instances. EMR is adept at handling a variety of big data use cases such as analytics and ML.

Here are the key aspects of Amazon EMR:

- **Managed Hadoop framework**: EMR simplifies running big data frameworks on AWS such as Apache Hadoop and Apache Spark. EMR handles the heavy lifting of cluster setup, provisioning, and tuning, allowing you to solely focus on the analysis of data.
- **Scalability and efficiency**: With EMR, you can quickly scale your cluster up or down depending on your processing needs. This flexibility allows you to optimize costs by only paying for what is needed while delivering the required compute power.
- **Integration with other AWS services**: Amazon EMR seamlessly integrates with other AWS services such as Amazon RDS, DynamoDB, and S3, allowing you to create a comprehensive data processing pipeline.
- **Customization and flexibility**: EMR allows you to customize clusters and choose the EC2 instance type best suited for your big data workload. This customization extends to the software options, as EMR supports a vast array of big data tools and frameworks.
- **Use cases**: EMR is widely used for log analysis and ML, where processing of large datasets is essential.

Here is a simple diagram of the key aspects of EMR:

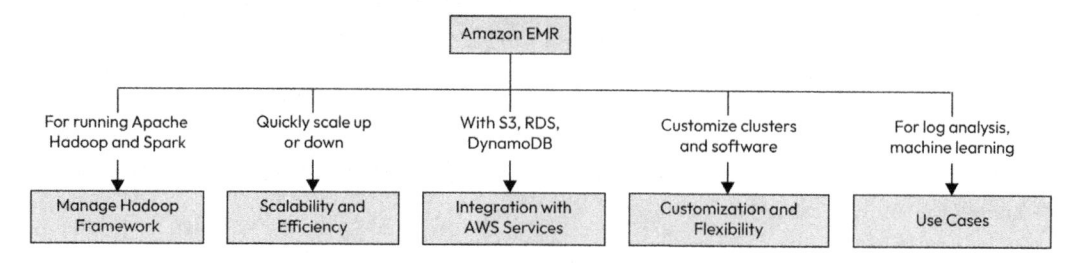

Figure 14.4 – Diagram of Amazon EMR key aspects

Having explored Amazon EMR capabilities in processing big data on EC2, we will now transition into Amazon Redshift, another powerful service in the AWS big data ecosystem that facilitates fast and scalable data warehouse solutions.

Redshift for data warehousing

Amazon Redshift is a fully managed petabyte-scale large data warehouse in the cloud that excels in large data handling by employing a columnar database storage design. The columnar storage is pivotal in data analytics as it significantly enhances the query performance by reading only necessary columns for processing, rather than entire rows. Redshift allows you to run complex data analytics queries on large datasets and integrates seamlessly with other BI tools.

Here are key features of Redshift to take note of:

- **Performance**: Redshift delivers 10 times faster processing time than other data warehouse solutions by using ML, highly distributed parallel query processing, and columnar storage on high-performance disks.

- **Scalability**: You can start with a few hundred gigabytes and scale the storage up to a petabyte or more. The `resize` API lets you add Redshift nodes as your needs change.

- **Data encryption**: Redshift encrypts and keeps your data secure in transit and rest using hardware-accelerated AES-256 and SSL encryption.

- **SQL-based**: Redshift allows you to query data using standard SQL. This capability allows Redshift to easily integrate with other BI tools.

- **Data ecosystem integration**: Redshift allows you to seamlessly integrate with other AWS services such as Amazon S3, Lambda, and Data Pipeline, allowing you to build comprehensive cloud data solutions.

- **Cost-effectiveness**: As with most other services in AWS, Redshift allows you to pay as you go; you can choose on-demand pricing with no upfront costs or long-term commitments.

Here's a diagram on the key features of Amazon Redshift:

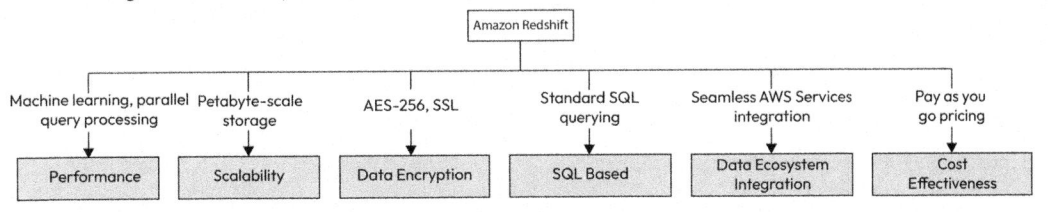

Figure 14.5 – Amazon Redshift key features

Having delved into the capabilities of Amazon Redshift for data warehousing, let us now move forward and explore the intricacies of designing and configuring big data and HPC clusters.

Designing and configuring HPC and Big Data Clusters

The design and configuration of HPC and big data clusters are pivotal in achieving the desired performance and efficiency. In this section, we will explore the foundational principles and strategies involved in creating a robust computing environment.

Here are key aspects to consider while designing HPC and Big Data Clusters:

- **Tailoring to your specific needs**: The architecture of your HPC and Big Data Clusters should align with your computational and big data requirements. This involves selecting the right EC2 instance type, storage options, and network settings.

- **Balancing performance and cost**: Optimal design choice strikes a balance between performance and cost considerations. Effective use of Reserved, Spot, and On-Demand Instances lets you influence both performance and cost.

- **Scalability and flexibility**: Clusters should be designed for scalability. They should allow for easy expansion as the cluster needs grow. Flexibility in configuration can also accommodate varying workload demands.

- **Integration with other AWS services**: Leveraging other services such as Amazon S3 for storage, AWS Lambda for automation, and AWS CloudFormation for **infrastructure as code** (**IaC**) can enhance cluster functionality.

- **Security and compliance**: Secure design principles and adhering to compliance standards are critical, especially when dealing with sensitive data. This includes implementing network security measures and data encryption.

Having set the foundation with design principles, let us now transition into exploring the specifics of network configurations for low-latency communications.

Network configurations for low-latency communication

In the specialized world of HPC and big data, the configuration of network settings is a crucial factor. In this section, we will look at the networking setup crucial for optimizing HPC and Big Data Clusters in Amazon EC2.

Here are key focus areas for consideration:

- **Low-latency networking**: Delve into the techniques to minimize your network latency. This includes understanding network topologies within Amazon EC2 and choosing the right networking options for your instances. Examples include the following:

    - Utilizing Amazon EC2 **Elastic Network Adapter** (**ENA**) to achieve 100 Gbps of network bandwidth.

> *Note:*
> *ENA is covered in great detail in Chapter 2, Understanding Core Components of Amazon EC2.*

    - Implementing placement groups to ensure that the instances are located physically close to each other, thereby reducing the network latency of HPC applications.

> *Note:*
> *Placement groups are covered in great detail in Chapter 9, Optimizing Performance with Amazon EC2 Placement Groups and Pricing Model.*

- **Enhanced data transfer speeds**: Understand how to maximize the network speed across your cluster. This involves using Amazon's high-speed networking options and understanding how to effectively distribute traffic to avoid bottlenecks. Examples include leveraging S3 Transfer Acceleration for faster download/upload speeds of larger datasets.

- **Scalable network architectures**: Get insights into building scalable network architecture that can grow with your HPC and big data needs. This includes utilizing VPC features and implementing best practices for network scalability and security – for example, setting up an Amazon VPC with multiple subnets and route tables to manage network traffic more efficiently in a scalable, multi-node HPC cluster.

These practical scenarios highlight the importance of meticulous network planning and configuration in ensuring your HPC and Big Data Clusters operate at peak efficiency.

Now, let us shift our focus to storage options and performance tuning, where we will explore how to select and optimize storage solutions for HPC and Big Data Clusters.

Storage options and performance tuning

Understanding and optimizing your storage options is crucial in the dynamic environment of HPC and big data on Amazon EC2. In this section, we will explore the most effective storage strategies to enhance your HPC and big data cluster performance.

Here are the key aspects to consider for your storage optimization:

- **Choosing the right storage type**: Understand the key difference between **Elastic Block Store (EBS)** SSDs and HDDs. SSDs offer high **input/output operations per second** (**IOPS**), ideal for database applications, while HDDs are good for sequential workloads such as database applications. Similarly, utilize **Elastic File System** (**EFS**) for file storage when you require shared access across multiple EC2 instances – a perfect choice for collaborative HPC projects.

- **Performance tuning**: Rely on EBS-optimized EC2 instances to maximize throughput between EC2 instances and EBS volumes. This will ensure that your HPC applications have the high-speed access they need. Also, fine-tuning IOPS settings based on your workload requirement can significantly improve your workload performance.

- **Data caching strategies**: Implementing in-memory caching mechanisms such as Redis or Memcached within your EC2 setup can significantly expedite your access to vital datasets, thereby boosting the overall efficiency of your big data operations.

By following these strategies, you can tailor your storage architecture to fit your unique demands of HPC and big data applications.

As we move forward, we will transition to the next section to understand the importance of DR in the cloud, looking at key concepts and terminologies.

Introduction to DR strategies

DR in the cloud encompasses a comprehensive approach to save data and applications from a myriad of potential disruptions. These disruptions could range from system failure to natural disaster, and each of the scenarios demands a proactive and resilient DR strategy.

In the following sections, we will explore the AWS services that can assist us in implementing these strategies. We will explore Amazon RDS Multi-AZ deployments for **high availability** (**HA**), S3 CRR for data durability, and Global Accelerator to maintain application performance across global AWS regions.

Importance of DR

The impact of DR extends beyond specific applications, impacting the broader landscape of cloud operations. Here are key points highlighting the importance of DR:

- **Business continuity (BC) assurance**: DR is vital for ensuring continuous business operations, even in the face of unexpected system failures or natural disasters. DR plays a crucial role in maintaining customer trust, and adherence to **service-level agreements (SLAs)** is important in maintaining a company's reputation and credibility.

- **Data protection and compliance**: An effective DR strategy protects critical data from loss or corruption, a key concern for businesses of all sizes. DR is key in meeting data protection regulations and industry standards, essential for organizations handling sensitive or personal data.

- **Minimizing financial risks**: Proper DR planning can significantly reduce the financial impact of downtime and data breaches. So, businesses must weigh the costs of implementing DR solutions against potential financial and reputational losses from inadequate disaster preparedness.

In essence, a robust DR strategy is critical for responsible cloud management, offering stability and security for digital assets and operations across various cloud scenarios.

We will next focus on some of the key DR concepts and terminologies, which will explore the foundational terms and concepts necessary for understanding and developing DR strategies in the cloud environment.

Key DR concepts and terminologies

Here are key terms that form the language and foundation upon which the effective DR strategy is built:

- **RTO**: RTO refers to the maximum acceptable time to recover the service after a disaster. It is a critical metric for evaluating the effectiveness of a DRP.

- **RPO**: RPO refers to the maximum tolerable time to which data is lost in the event of a disaster. Defining RPO allows you to define the frequency of backups, guiding how often data should be replicated to minimize potential loss.

- **Failover and failback**: Failover is the process of switching to a standby system upon the failure of the primary system. Failback is the process of returning to the original system once it is back up and functional.

- **BC plan (BCP)**: A BCP goes hand in hand with DR. It is the overarching strategy that ensures the continuity of business operations during and after a disaster.

- **Hot, warm, and cold sites**: These terms refer to the backup site used in DR planning. A hot site is a fully functional replica of the primary infrastructure, a warm site is partially equipped, and a cold site is an available space without current infrastructure.

With this solid grasp of these fundamental DR concepts, we are well equipped to explore the AWS services for DR. Let's dive in.

AWS services for DR

AWS offers a variety of services that are pivotal in ensuring your data and application are protected from any unforeseen disasters. These solutions range from data storage solutions and database replication to network optimizations, with each of the services designed to provide resilience and quick recovery in the event of system failures, data loss, or catastrophic events.

Key AWS services for data recovery include RDS for database resilience, S3 for secure and redundant data storage, and Global Accelerator to maintain performance across global networks. Let us now dive deeper into the specifics, starting with Amazon RDS Multi-AZ deployments.

Amazon RDS Multi-AZ deployments

Amazon RDS Multi-AZ deployments are a cornerstone of robust DR strategies in AWS. This service is designed to enhance RDS availability and reliability, crucial for critical workloads and applications. Here are the salient features of it:

- **Automatic failover**: RDS Multi-AZ deployments provide HA by automatically replicating the data from the primary instance to the standby instance in different **availability zones (AZs)**. So, in the event of failure, RDS automatically fails over the traffic from the primary database instance to the standby database instance, ensuring data integrity and minimizing any potential disruptions.

- **Data durability**: With synchronous replication, your data is continuously copied to a standby database instance in a different AZ. This ensures data durability and protects against any AZ-level disruptions.

- **Maintenance and backups**: RDS Multi-AZ instances handle necessary maintenance tasks such as backup and patching seamlessly. During these operations, RDS routes your workload traffic to the standby instance to avoid any downtime.

So, by leveraging Multi-AZ deployments, organizations can significantly reduce the risk of downtime, ensuring continuous operations and resilience in their database management.

Having explored the HA features of Amazon RDS, we will now turn our attention to *Amazon S3 CRR* and explore how CRR plays a pivotal role in enhancing data protection and ensuring BC across geographically dispersed locations.

Amazon S3 CRR

Amazon S3 CRR is a key feature within AWS's suite of DR services, offering enhanced data protection and BC across various geographic locations.

Here are key aspects of S3 CRR to take note of:

- **Automated data replication**: S3 CRR automatically replicates the data across different AWS regions. This process ensures the data is safeguarded by ensuring the data copy is available in another location if a region experiences data loss or an outage.
- **Compliance and data sovereignty**: For businesses with specific regulatory or legal requirements, CRR facilitates adherence to data residency laws by allowing data storage across multiple locations.
- **Optimized latency and performance**: By storing the data in closer proximity to different locations, CRR ensures the data is delivered with reduced latency and improves the application performance.
- **Simplified management**: Configuring CRR is a straightforward process, allowing you to focus on broader DR strategies without worrying about the complexities of data replication.

Overall, Amazon S3 CRR is a potent solution for organizations looking to bolster their DRP, ensuring the data is secure and accessible no matter what the circumstance is.

We will now transition into *AWS Global Accelerator* and understand how it enhances the application performance and availability, which further helps to fortify your DR strategy.

AWS Global Accelerator

AWS Global Accelerator plays a vital role in facilitating seamless traffic management across regions, automatic failover, and so on, making it an integral part of any DR strategy in AWS.

Here are some key aspects of Global Accelerator to consider:

- **Enhanced network performance**: AWS Global Accelerator improves the accessibility of your application by directing user traffic through AWS global network infrastructure. This results in a significant reduction in internet latency and packet loss, ensuring faster and more reliable access to your applications.
- **Simple IP address management (IPAM)**: Global Accelerator provides you with a static IP that acts as a fixed starting point for your application hosted on any AWS region. This simplifies the DNS management and ensures consistent user experience even during endpoint failures or regional disruptions.
- **Seamless integration with AWS services**: It effortlessly integrates with other AWS services such as **Elastic Load Balancing (ELB)**, **Elastic Compute Cloud (EC2)**, and S3. This synergy allows for a more resilient and robust application infrastructure, capable of withstanding various disaster scenarios.
- **Health checks and traffic control**: Global Accelerator continuously monitors the health of your application endpoints and automatically reroutes your traffic to healthy endpoints, minimizing downtime and enhancing overall application resilience.

With an understanding of how Global Accelerator contributes to resilient DR strategies, let's move to the next section, where we look into the crucial steps of DR planning, risk assessment, and recovery objectives.

Designing and implementing DR strategies on AWS

DR planning is an essential aspect of maintaining BC. In the AWS ecosystem, designing and implementing a DR strategy involves a comprehensive approach that includes risk assessment, risk allocation, and establishment of clear recovery objectives. The process begins with understanding the potential risks that impact your operations and then developing a plan to mitigate those risks.

AWS provides a wide range of tools that make DR planning more manageable and effective. Whether it is relying on cloud scalability to handle sudden load increases during recovery operations or relying on global infrastructure for geographical redundancy, the platform provides ample opportunities to create a robust DR strategy.

In this section, we will explore how to plan for DR, conduct a risk assessment, and set clear recovery objectives.

DR planning and risk assessment

The DR planning and risk assessment phase involves meticulously evaluating potential risks that could disrupt business operations and devising a plan to counteract those risks.

Here are some key aspects to take note of while doing DR planning and risk assessments:

- **Identify critical assets**: Begin by identifying the most critical parts of your infrastructure. Determine which data, applications, and services are critical for your business operations.
- **Assess risks**: Evaluate risk factors that could impact your critical infrastructure. This includes natural disasters, cyber-attacks, human errors, and system failures. So, understanding the impact and risk of these likelihood scenarios is crucial.
- **Impact analysis**: Conduct a **business impact analysis** (**BIA**) to understand the potential consequences of disruptions. This helps you prioritize your recovery efforts based on what is most critical to your organization.
- **Strategies for mitigation**: Develop strategies to mitigate identified risks. This includes creating data backups, implementing redundant systems, and moving to cloud-based solutions that offer greater resilience.
- **Regularly review and update**: Reviewing your risks is not a one-time activity. Regularly review and update your DRP to account for new risks and changes in your business or IT environment.

Having laid the groundwork with DR planning and risk assessment, let us now transition to understanding RPO and RTO. These metrics are vital in letting you define the acceptable downtime and data loss in case of a disaster.

RTO and RPO

Understanding RPO and RTO and setting these objectives is crucial for designing an effective DR strategy tailored to your organization's needs.

To set these objectives, we first need to understand what they are:

- **RTO**: This metric signifies the maximum acceptable time your systems and applications can be offline after a disaster. The RTO is essentially a time target for restoring your IT and business operations to a minimum acceptable level. A shorter RTO typically requires more robust and immediate failover mechanisms.
- **RPO**: RPO signifies the maximum amount of data loss measured in time. This metric indicates the age of files that must be recovered from backups for normal operations to resume. For example, a 1-hour RPO defines how your business can tolerate losing 1 hour's worth of data in the event of a disaster.

Balancing RTO and RPO is essential for businesses to ensure efficient DR, minimize data loss, and maintain operational continuity without incurring unnecessary costs. Finding the right balance involves a trade-off. More stringent RTOs and RPOs can lead to increased costs and complexity in your DR solution. So, it is essential to align these objectives with your business priorities and the criticality of different data and applications. AWS offers various services such as Amazon RDS, which provides multi-AZ deployments for HA, and Amazon S3, known for its cross-region capabilities, to help achieve desired RTO and RPO for business. Leveraging these services can effectively ensure minimal downtime and data loss in the event of any disaster.

With a clear understanding of RTO and RPO, let us now transition and explore the next crucial phase, monitoring and testing DR strategies.

Monitoring and testing DR strategies

DR is not a set-and-forget process. It demands ongoing attention and management. The process of testing, monitoring, and maintaining the DR strategy is crucial for ensuring resilience and operational continuity. Let us explore each aspect and understand how they can assist you in ensuring that they are always ready to be deployed effectively:

- **Testing and validation**: Regularly testing your DRP is crucial and it is more than just ticking the boxes. It helps you ensure that the DR strategies work as intended. This activity involves simulating various DR testing scenarios and observing how your DRP holds up. The testing should comprehensively cover all the aspects of your DRP and should account for any new changes in your environment or infrastructure.

- **Monitoring DRPs**: Continuous monitoring of DRPs is essential for early detection of potential issues that could impede your recovery during an actual disaster. This includes monitoring the replication of data, the health of your backup systems, and the performance of your failover mechanisms. Effective monitoring tools and practices give you peace of mind that your DR strategies are always operational and reliable.

- **Maintenance of DRPs**: Your DRP must evolve with your organization. As your technology grows and changes, so should your DR strategies. This means regularly reviewing and updating your DRPs to ensure they align with new technologies, business objectives, and compliance requirements. Maintaining DRPs also means training your team on any changes to DR procedures to ensure everyone is prepared in the event of a disaster.

By ensuring regular testing, monitoring, and ongoing maintenance, you can ensure that your DR strategy will function as needed when activated.

Summary

In this chapter, we have explored the intricate world of HPC, big data, and DR strategies on Amazon EC2. From understanding the critical aspects of HPC and big data configurations to diving deep into the nuances of designing robust DRPs, we have covered the spectrum of knowledge essential for EC2 and other computing needs.

As we close this chapter, be prepared to embark on the last pages of this book with the final chapter, *Migrating, Modernizing, and Ensuring compliance in EC2 Environments*. Let's dive in!

15

Migrating, Modernizing, and Ensuring Compliance in Amazon EC2 Environments

In this final chapter, we will focus on the tangible steps to transform, modernize, and navigate the compliance landscape of cloud computing environments.

We will embark on a deep dive into migrating legacy applications into Amazon EC2, laying the groundwork for a seamless transition from old to new. This section aims to demystify the migration process, providing a blueprint for reimagining legacy systems within the cloud.

As we advance further, we will explore how the applications can be refactored and re-architected for peak performance and scalability. The journey wouldn't be complete without addressing compliance and governance in EC2 environments. As the final piece in the puzzle, this section underscores the importance of security controls and a compliance framework, ensuring that your infrastructure is both robust and regulatory-compliant.

We will finally conclude this chapter with case studies and best practices, drawing insights from real-world scenarios to guide you through migration, modernization, and compliance.

The following topics will be covered in this chapter:

- Migrating legacy applications to Amazon EC2
- Modernizing applications in Amazon EC2
- Compliance and governance in Amazon EC2 environments
- Case study and best practices

Migrating legacy applications to Amazon EC2

The journey in migrating legacy applications to Amazon EC2 represents a pivotal shift toward modernization and scalability within the cloud ecosystem. This process typically begins with assessing application architecture, identifying which components can be lifted and shifted directly to EC2 and which might require re-architecture for cloud optimization. The next step involves selecting the most suitable migration strategies and tools, planning meticulously to ensure minimal disruption, and executing the migration process with precision. Let us begin our exploration into assessing the current application architecture.

Assessing the current application architecture

The first step in assessing the current application architecture involves a detailed examination of existing systems. In this phase, you will pinpoint which components can be lifted and shifted and which need re-architecting – perhaps breaking the monolith into microservices – or which could be replaced by AWS-managed services, such as **Relational Database Service** (**RDS**) for database management.

Let us consider a more detailed example involving the assessment and subsequent re-architecture of a legacy e-commerce application platform architecture for migration into Amazon EC2.

Consider a legacy e-commerce platform that runs on a monolithic architecture with its entire application stack – ranging from user interface, business logic, and database – everything hosted on a single, on-premise server.

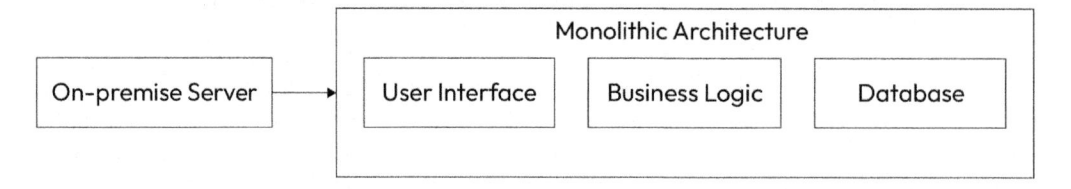

Figure 15.1 – Diagram of monolithic architecture

This setup, while initially sufficient, struggles under peak traffic loads, such as during holiday sales, leading to slow response time and potential downtimes. Moreover, making updates or scaling specific components of an application is cumbersome and risky as it requires making updates to the entire system of the application.

Let us assess the application to dive deep into the challenges and re-imagine an architecture with the AWS cloud to fix issues coming out of the assessment.

Assessment phase

In the assessment phase, after a thorough examination of a monolithic application, it reveals the following issues:

- The application's tight coupling makes it difficult to maintain and scale
- The application is reliant on a **single point of failure** (**SPOF**)
- It definitely lacks modern cloud-native features such as auto-scaling or managed services such as RDS for a database

Re-architecture strategy

Based on this assessment, a decision is made to re-architect the application into a microservices architecture. This involves breaking down the monolithic application into smaller, independently deployable services. For instance, user authentication, product catalog, and order processing components are separated into distinct services. This segmentation allows for targeted scaling and updates without impacting the entire system, significantly reducing downtime and improving deployment frequency. Let us narrow this down and explore the replacement implementation for each of the components with an AWS service:

- **User authentication service**: Recommended for migration into Amazon Cognito, enhancing security and scalability without extensive in-house development This migration offloads the heavy lifting of traditional user management to more of a managed service, thereby streamlining the overall user management and authentication process.
- **Product catalog**: Recommended for migration into EC2 instances, utilizing Auto-Scaling groups to dynamically adjust capacity based on demand, ensuring **high availability** (**HA**) during traffic surges and thereby offering a responsive and resilient product catalog service.
- **Order processing**: Recommended for re-architecture to utilize AWS Lambda for order validation and processing, allowing for cost-effective scaling per request, and integration with Amazon **Simple Queue Service** (**SQS**) for decoupling services. Overall, this facilitates a more scalable and resilient order-processing workflow.

With this architecture in place, the e-commerce platform can experience dramatic improvements in performance and reliability. It can effortlessly now scale during high-traffic time events to ensure consistent uptime and rapidly deploy new features or updates to individual services, significantly enhancing customer experience. Additionally, by leveraging AWS-managed services, the platform benefits from reduced operational overhead, enhanced security, and improved scalability.

This transformation not only addresses the initial challenges but also positions the e-commerce platform for future growth and innovation in the cloud environment.

Let us explore the strategies and tools that facilitate the migration process for a smooth transition to EC2.

Identifying migration strategies and tools

In the evolving landscape of cloud computing, identifying the right migration strategy and tools is pivotal for transitioning legacy applications into Amazon EC2. This is akin to choosing the right tools for construction projects, with each tool serving a specific purpose, ensuring the project's success.

Migration strategies

There are several strategies for migrating applications into the cloud, with each having its benefits and considerations:

- **Rehost (lift and shift)**: This involves moving the applications to EC2 with minimal changes. It's quick and cost-effective, ideal for companies looking to migrate quickly.
- **Replatform**: This involves making a slight modification to the application to leverage cloud capabilities without a full-scale re-design, such as adjusting the way the application interacts with the database to take advantage of AWS RDS.
- **Refactor/re-architect**: This is the most comprehensive approach, where applications are fully redesigned to be cloud native. It is chosen for applications needing scalability, agility and to fully utilize cloud services.
- **Relocate**: This is fairly a newly introduced strategy to assist you in migrating your workloads without impacting your ongoing operations, rewriting the application source code, or acquiring new hardware. In this strategy, you will be migrating the collection of servers from an on-premise platform such as Kubernetes to the cloud version of the same platform, such as Amazon **Elastic Kubernetes Service (EKS)**.
- **Repurchase**: This strategy involves swapping internally administered systems for third-party managed services from the **cloud service provider (CSP)**. This strategy allows the organization to retire the legacy systems and move to a consumption-based SaaS subscription model that ties the IT costs to the generated revenue. As you move toward the SAAS-based subscription model, this approach greatly reduces the operational effort of managing the infrastructure for in-house teams.
- **Retire**: In this approach, you will be identifying part of the IT portfolio that is no longer needed and can be turned off during migration.
- **Retain**: Keep certain components of the IT systems on-premises or delay their migration.

Migration tools

AWS provides a suite of tools to assist in the migration process, with each designed to simplify different aspects of the migration journey:

- **AWS Migration Hub**: Provides a central location to track the process of migration across multiple AWS and partner solutions

- **AWS Application Discovery Service**: Gathers information about on-premise data centers to plan migration projects
- **AWS Database Migration Service (DMS)**: This facilitates migrating relational databases, data warehouses, NoSQL databases, and other types of data stores
- **AWS Server Migration Service (SMS)**: This automates, schedules, and tracks incremental migration of live server volumes, making it easier to coordinate large-scale server migrations

By leveraging these strategies and goals, organizations can plan and execute a migration process that minimizes downtime and aligns with their operational goal and budgetary constraints. The chosen strategy should reflect the organization's long-term cloud objectives, balancing the need for quick wins against the desire for cloud-native advantages.

Next, we will look into the planning and execution phase of the migration process, outlining steps to ensure a smooth transition of legacy applications to Amazon EC2.

Planning and executing the migration process

The final and crucial phase in migrating legacy applications in Amazon EC2 is the planning and execution of the migration process.

Here is a high-level diagram of this process:

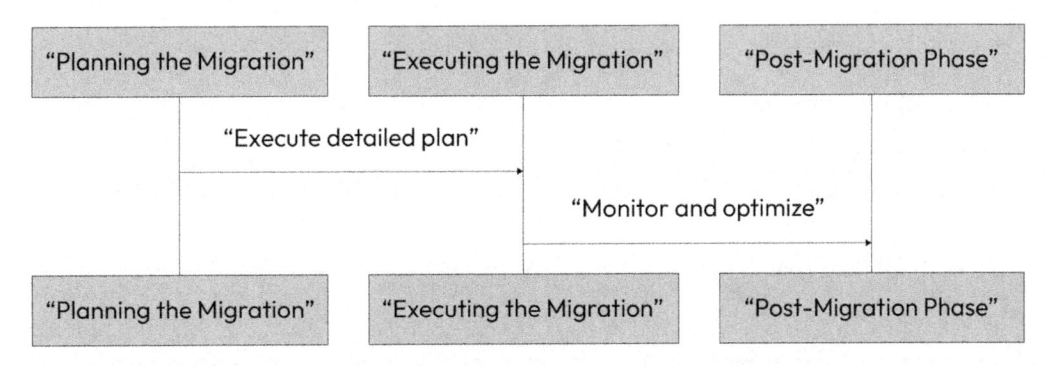

Figure 15.2 – Simple diagram of the migration process

Let us look at each aspect one by one.

Planning the migration

Here are the steps to follow while planning your migration:

1. **Comprehensive planning**: Start with a detailed plan that outlines every step of the migration, including timelines, responsibilities, and contingency plans.

2. **Application dependency mapping**: Understand and document the dependencies between your applications and services to ensure a seamless migration.
3. **Cost assessment**: Estimate the cost of running your applications on Amazon EC2 and consider using AWS Cost Explorer for budget forecasting.
4. **Security and compliance**: Ensure your migration plan adheres to your regulatory requirements and AWS best practices for security.

Executing the migration

Here are the steps to follow while executing the migration:

1. **Initial tests**: Begin with the pilot migration or move less critical applications to gauge the effectiveness of your migration processes.
2. **Leverage automation**: Utilize AWS services such as AWS CloudFormation and AWS Elastic Beanstalk to automate the provisioning of deployment of your AWS resources.
3. **Data migration**: For data-heavy applications, consider using AWS DataSync or AWS DMS to securely and efficiently transfer the data.
4. **Monitoring and optimization**: Throughout the migration process, continuously monitor application performance using AWS CloudWatch and optimize resources to ensure cost-effectiveness and performance.

Post-migration phase

Once the migration is complete, ensure you validate the completeness of the migration and optimize your AWS resources where needed by following these steps:

1. **Validation**: After migration, validate application performance against predefined benchmarks to ensure they meet the desired outcomes.
2. **Optimization**: Continuously monitor, review, and optimize your AWS resources for performance and cost.

Planning and executing the migration process with meticulous attention to detail ensures that legacy applications seamlessly transition into Amazon EC2.

As we transition from migrating and modernizing legacy applications, we will now look into the next section, where we will explore how an organization can refactor, re-architect, and revitalize their applications to fully harness the power of the cloud!

Modernizing applications in Amazon EC2

Modernization is not just about lifting and shifting existing applications into the cloud; it is about how these applications can be developed, deployed, and maintained to exploit the cloud's agility, scalability, and innovation. This process often involves refactoring, re-architecting, and embracing new operational models such as DevOps and microservices.

By modernizing applications in Amazon EC2, businesses can ensure they are not just cloud-ready but future-ready to handle the ever-evolving technological landscape. In this section, we will look at understanding the essentials of modernizing applications on EC2, highlighting key strategies, tools, and AWS services that facilitate this transformative journey.

As we begin, we will proceed by exploring the crucial steps of refactoring and re-architecting applications.

Refactoring and re-architecting applications

Refactoring and re-architecting applications within Amazon EC2 can be likened to renovating a home to enhance its efficiency, functionality, and suitability for the demands of modern living. The aim of this transformative process is to improve performance, minimize costs, and achieve greater scalability. Let us understand the process in detail:

- **Refactoring**: It is the process of modifying the application's internal structure and code without changing its external behavior. The whole process is about optimizing the code base and enhancing the application efficiency and cloud compatibility.
- **Re-architecting**: This involves more profound changes, and it might mean adopting new architectural patterns such as transitioning from monolith to microservices. This change breaks down a large monolithic application into smaller and more manageable independently deployable units, thereby improving scalability, facilitating faster development cycles, and simplifying maintenance.

It is significant for businesses to consider refactoring and re-architecting applications hosted on Amazon EC2 to fully leverage the potential of auto-scaling, managed services, and serverless computing. Practicing and implementing such exercises ensures that the applications are not just hosted but fully realize the benefit of cloud platforms.

Let us consider a practical example, such as a traditional e-commerce platform following a monolithic architecture hosted on an on-premise environment. In such cases, it is natural for applications to experience growth-related performance bottlenecks and deployment challenges due to the platform's monolithic architecture.

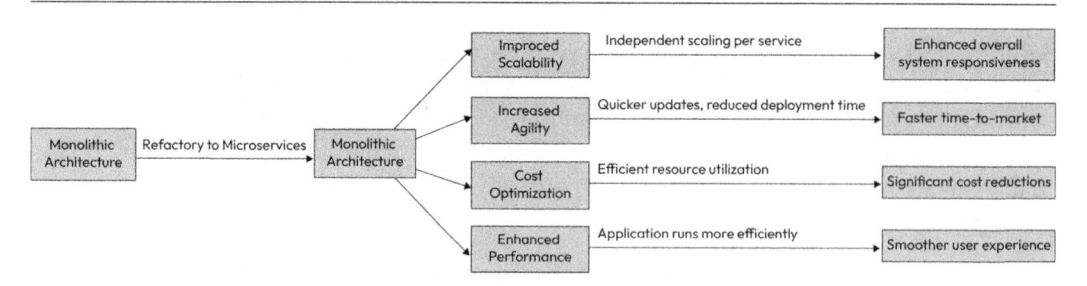

Figure 15.3 – Modernization of monolithic architecture

By refactoring the critical component into a set of microservices, such as creating an independent service authentication, inventory management, and order processing, the platform can achieve the following benefits (as illustrated in *Figure 15.3*):

- **Improved scalability**: Each microservice can scale independently in response to specific demand, enhancing the overall system effectiveness

- **Increased agility**: Independent microservices allow for quicker updates, reducing the time from development to deployment

- **Cost optimization**: Efficient resource utilization in the cloud can bring significant cost reduction in running the application in the cloud

- **Enhanced performance**: With microservices, applications run more efficiently, enhancing the overall user experience

As we delve deeper into the modernization process, we will transition and explore the role of leveraging AWS-managed services and microservices in EC2.

Leveraging managed services and microservices

Leveraging managed services transforms the way applications are built, deployed, and scaled, mirroring the shift toward more streamlined, efficient, and resilient architecture. This approach not only modernizes applications but also aligns them with the best practices of cloud-native deployment.

Let us further understand the details of managed services and microservices:

- **Managed services**: The Amazon EC2 ecosystem is rich with the availability of managed services such as AWS RDS for database management, Amazon S3 for storage, and Amazon SQS for messaging. These services abstract the complexity of managing the underlying infrastructure, allowing the developers to focus on building application logic rather than worrying about hardware, backups, or scalability.

- **Microservices**: The adoption of microservices architecture involves decomposing the application into smaller, loosely coupled services. Here, each service is responsible for a specific function and communicates with other services through well-defined APIs. This model fosters agility, making it easier to update and scale parts of the application independently.

Together, the combination of microservices and managed services offers several compelling benefits such as scalability, development velocity, and resilience.

Let us consider a practical example and understand how it realizes the benefit of leveraging microservices and managed services. For example, consider a **content delivery platform** (**CDP**) migrating to the microservices architecture with EC2. By leveraging Amazon S3 for media storage, RDS/DynamoDB for metadata storage, **Elastic Container Service** (**ECS**) or EKS for container orchestration services, with this design, the platform gains the following benefits:

- **Improved load handling**: Dynamic scaling in response to user demand ensures smooth streaming experiences during peak times.
- **Rapid feature deployment**: Independent microservices allow for quicker updates to certain aspects of the platform, such as – for example – product search or recommendation service.
- **Operational efficiency**: Managed services offload infrastructure management, reduce operational overhead, and improve platform efficiency.

Here is a diagram of the benefits we just discussed:

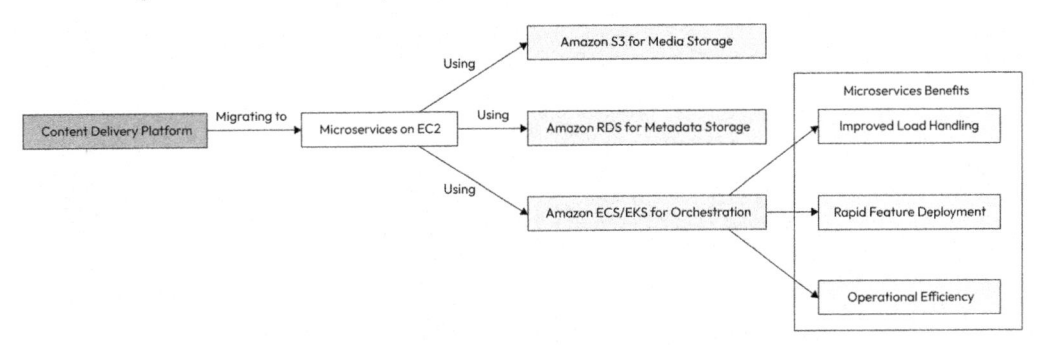

Figure 15.4 – Modernization of monolithic architecture with AWS services

Next up, we will explore the modernization journey by implementing DevOps practices for continuous improvement.

Implementing DevOps practices for continuous improvement

Implementing DevOps practices for continuous improvement within the Amazon EC2 environment marks a pivotal shift toward a culture of rapid innovation, enhanced efficiency, and increased reliability. This transition not only streamlines development activities but also fosters a collaborative environment where building, testing, and releasing software can happen rapidly, frequently, and in a more reliable manner.

The benefits of adopting DevOps practices can bring significant advantages to your team, such as the following:

- **Speed and agility**: Automating the software delivery process reduces the time from development to deployment, enabling faster feature releases and quicker response to market changes
- **Enhanced collaboration**: Bridging the gap between the development and operations teams encourages a culture of shared responsibility, improved communication, and collaboration
- **Increased reliability**: Automated testing and deployment, along with proactive monitoring, ensure that your applications are more stable and reliable, leading to a better end-user experience

Let us consider a practical example of an e-commerce platform looking to optimize its operations with DevOps practices. By implementing a **continuous integration/continuous deployment (CI/CD)** pipeline, the platform can easily deploy updates to the EC2 instances and ensure that new features and fixes are rolled out swiftly. Here is a simple diagram of what a typical CI/CD pipeline flow would look like for such an application deployment:

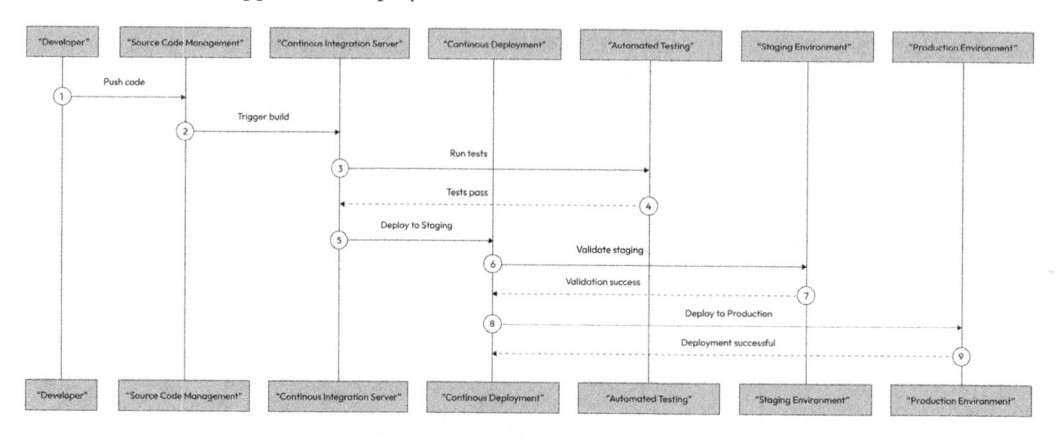

Figure 15.5 – Application CI/CD pipeline diagram

The details of the CI/CD pipeline illustrated in *Figure 15.5* are described as follows:

- **Push code**: The developer pushes code to the **source code management (SCM)** system
- **Trigger build**: The SCM system notifies the CI server, triggering a build
- **Run tests**: The CI server runs automated tests to verify the build
- **Tests pass**: If the tests pass, the process moves forward
- **Deploy to staging**: The CI server then deploys the build to a staging environment via CD tools
- **Validate staging**: The staging environment is validated to ensure the build works as expected

- **Deploy to production**: Once validation is successful, the build is deployed to the production environment
- **Deployment successful**: The production environment signals back the successful deployment

Having explored the transformative power of DevOps practices that bring in the traditional deployment, we will move forward and understand how to establish *compliance and governance in EC2 environments*.

Compliance and governance in Amazon EC2 environments

Navigating the intricacies of compliance and governance within the Amazon EC2 environment is pivotal to ensuring the security and integrity of your EC2 infrastructure. In this section, we will explore and understand the complex landscape of compliance requirements to implement robust security controls and policies. We will also look at the critical aspects of aligning EC2 deployments with regulatory standards and best practices.

Understanding compliance requirements and frameworks

AWS prides itself on its adherence to a wide array of various compliance standards. The AWS platform commitment to compliance is documented in detail under **Service Organization Control (SOC)** reports; the rigorous standards AWS meets include the **Health Insurance Portability and Accountability Act (HIPAA)**, the **General Data Protection Regulation (GDPR)**, ISO/IEC *27001* and more. These frameworks are not merely about legal compliance but also serve as a beacon of trust and security assurance for customers, showcasing AWS's dedication to safeguarding data and maintaining operational integrity.

By utilizing AWS's comprehensive suite of security and compliance resources, the EC2 environment can effortlessly meet stringent compliance benchmarks. For example, AWS **Key Management Service (KMS)** and Amazon S3 **server-side encryption (SSE)** provide strong data protection mechanisms. Access control to your AWS environment can be managed through AWS **Identity and Access Management (IAM)**, ensuring only authorized users can access specific EC2 resources. Additionally, Amazon **Virtual Private Cloud (VPC)** allows for the creation of isolated network environments, enhancing security and compliance by restricting to and from EC2 instances. The following figure gives you an illustration of security and compliance of the EC2 environment:

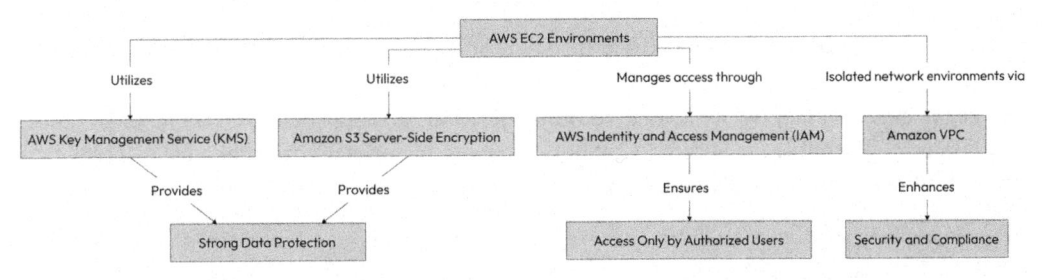

Figure 15.6 – Illustrating security and compliance of the EC2 environment

Next, we will explore the integration of the EC2 environment with AWS security services to bolster compliance efforts in your environment.

Implementing security controls and policies

AWS provides a suite of tools designed to enhance security, with each tailored to address specific vulnerabilities and threats. In this section, we will explore these tools to establish a robust security framework, ensuring that your EC2 deployments adhere to the highest standards of data protection and privacy.

At the heart of AWS security is IAM, which allows for precise control over who can access your resources and how they can interact with them. To complement IAM, a security group acts as a virtual firewall to EC2 instances, controlling inbound and outbound traffic at the instance level. For broader network security, a **network access control list** (**NACL**) offers an additional layer of defense by providing stateless filtering of traffic entering and leaving your VPC.

Moreover, you have AWS Shield for **distributed denial-of-service** (**DDOS**) protection, protecting your application from common exploits. For continuous security assessment, Amazon Inspector automatically scans your AWS resources for vulnerabilities. AWS Config monitors your overall environment and makes sure it is compliant with your defined security guidelines:

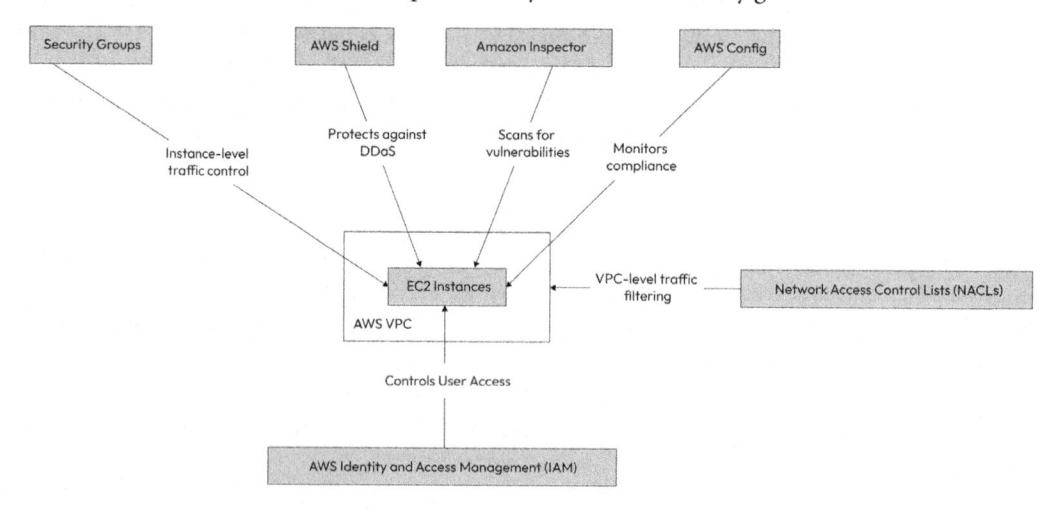

Figure 15.7 – Illustrating AWS services to ensure security and compliance of the EC2 environment

By integrating these security measures, your organization can create a fortified ecosystem around EC2 instances. This proactive approach not only ensures adherence to compliance standards but also instills confidence among stakeholders by maintaining a secure and reliable cloud infrastructure.

In the upcoming section, we will underscore the importance of persistent scrutiny and adaptation in the dynamic landscape of cloud computing, ensuring that your EC2 environment remains secure, compliant, and resilient against evolving security threats.

Auditing and monitoring for continuous compliance

Maintaining continuous compliance and rigorous monitoring is paramount in the ever-evolving cloud computing landscape. In this section, we will dive deep and understand some important suites of AWS tools at our perusal to achieve this objective.

AWS CloudTrail, for example, meticulously logs all EC2 as well as other actions across the AWS ecosystem, thus providing an indispensable audit trail for scrutinizing user activities and pinpointing any potential security vulnerabilities. Complementing CloudTrail, Amazon CloudWatch offers real-time monitoring and alerting capabilities, enabling developers and administrators to quickly detect any deviation from established operational baselines. Furthermore, AWS Config plays a crucial role in continuously recording and monitoring your AWS resource configurations and evaluating overall compliance against the configurations specified in your internal guidelines.

Together, these tools provide a robust framework for proactive compliance management, allowing organizations to quickly identify, rectify, and address any non-compliant items or configurations. The proactive stance not only ensures adherence to compliance standards but also strengthens the overall security posture of your environment:

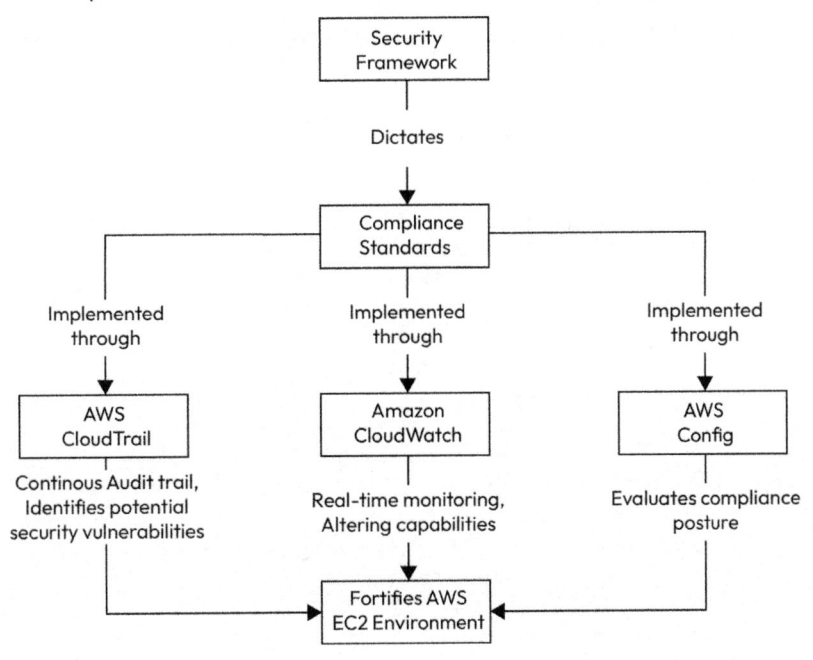

Figure 15.8 – Illustrating monitoring security and compliance in the EC2 environment

We will now move on to the next section, where we will illuminate the practical application of these principles, drawing from real-world experience to navigate through the complexities of cloud compliance.

Case study and best practices

We will now pivot to the real-world application of the theories, tools, and techniques we have explored. By examining this case study, we aim to offer a lens through which you can envision a potential roadmap for your projects, learning not only from triumphs but also from pitfalls that others have navigated.

Case study – Migrating, modernizing, and ensuring compliance

In this detailed exploration, we will spotlight the journey of a financial institution that embarked on a comprehensive migration and modernization project with Amazon EC2. This case study not only illustrates the step-by-step process involved but also highlights the significant benefits achieved through this transition.

Initial assessment and planning

The journey began through the assessment of the organization's existing on-premise infrastructure. By leveraging AWS Migration Hub, the organization gained insights into its application portfolio and identified dependencies that could impact its migration. This initial phase was critical in outlining the organization's strategic migration plan that prioritized applications based on their complexity and strategic impact.

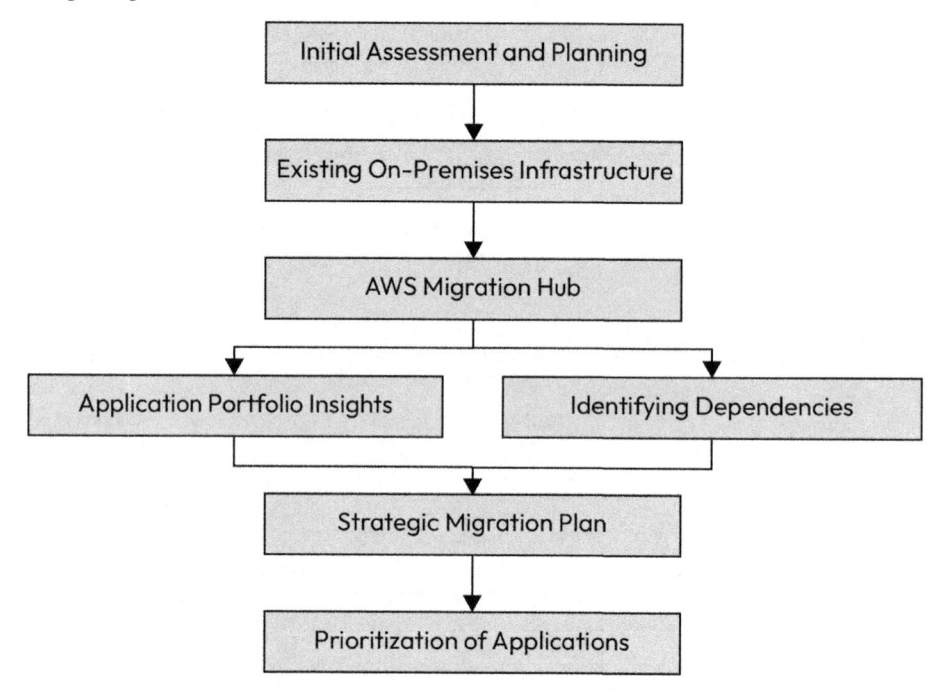

Figure 15.9 – Illustrating migration initial assessment process

Migration execution

The institution utilized AWS DMS to migrate its on-premise database to Amazon RDS, ensuring minimal downtime while maintaining data integrity. AWS SMS facilitated the seamless transfer of on-premise **virtual machines** (**VMs**) to Amazon EC2 instances. Basically, this approach allowed for phased migration, reducing risk and allowing the team to address any issues promptly:

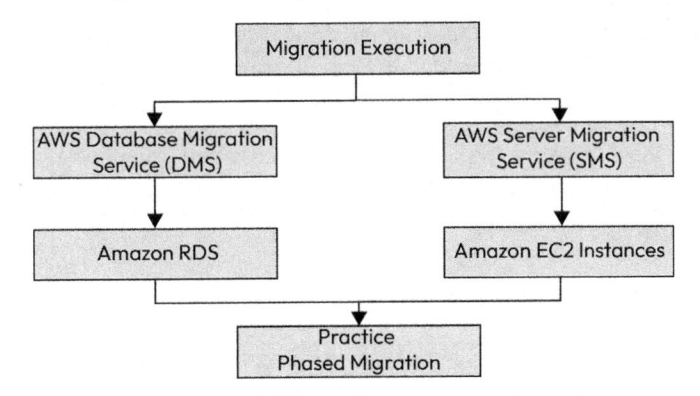

Figure 15.10 – Illustrating migration execution process

Modernization and optimization

Post migration, the institution shifted to modernizing its application landscape. The institution adopted the microservices architecture, breaking down monolithic applications into smaller, independently deployable services. This architectural shift was facilitated by Amazon ECS for container management, allowing for agile development practices and improved scalability.

Leveraging managed services

To further enhance its infrastructure, the organization embraced managed services. Amazon S3 was utilized for scalable content storage, Amazon CloudFront provided a fast **content delivery network** (**CDN**), and AWS Lambda enabled serverless computing, automating tasks and reducing operational overhead.

Compliance and security

Given the stringent compliance and security requirements, the organization implemented AWS IAM for fine-grained user access control, AWS KMS for both data encryption at transit and rest, AWS Config for continuous compliance enforcement, and so on.

Overall, the migration led the organization to reap significant benefits, including enhanced scalability, agility, and reduced operational costs. The adoption of microservices architecture improved deployment frequencies and operational efficiency. Moreover, the institution improved its security posture and ensured compliance with financial regulations, instilling greater confidence among stakeholders.

This case study, I believe, explains the systematic approach to cloud migration and modernization, demonstrating the transformative impact of AWS services in optimizing operational efficiency, security, and compliance in the financial sector.

Best practices for a smooth transition and compliance

Navigating the complexities of cloud migration and ensuring compliance requires a strategic approach. Here are some best practices that guide you through a smooth transition while maintaining stringent compliance standards:

- **Comprehensive planning**: Begin with a thorough assessment of your existing infrastructure and applications. Understand your compliance obligations and how they translate into a cloud environment. Establish clear objectives for migration and modernization activities.

- **Leverage AWS tools and services**: Utilize AWS's suite of migration tools for a more streamlined process. AWS purpose-built services such as DMS, SMS, and Migration Hub can simplify the overall transition. For compliance, services such as AWS Config and AWS Security Hub provide invaluable insights into the security posture of your application infrastructure.

- **Adopt a phased approach**: Migrate and modernize in phases to minimize risk. Start with less significant applications to gain confidence and create a replicable process for more significant migrations.

- **Continuous monitoring and testing**: Post migration, continuously monitor your environment's security and compliance. Regularly test your **disaster recovery** (**DR**) strategies and ensure they meet your RTO and RPO.

- **Invest in training and change management**: Ensure your team is well versed with AWS services and cloud best practices. Effective change management can help in addressing any cultural shifts required for adopting new technologies.

- **Engage with AWS support and partners**: The AWS ecosystem includes a vast network of partners and a robust support system. Leverage this to navigate any cloud challenges you face during your cloud journey.

With this, we have come to the end of the chapter.

Summary

In this final chapter, we dove into the practical strategies for migrating and modernizing legacy applications within EC2. From assessing the application architecture and implementing modernization techniques to embracing compliance frameworks and learning from real-world case studies, you are equipped with the knowledge to transform your EC2 environments effectively.

As we conclude this book, we have traversed through various cloud landscapes – from understanding the fundamentals of EC2 to building resilient applications on EC2 to advanced Amazon EC2 concepts and use cases. For each of those areas, you have gone through various chapters to not just inform but empower you with practical insights and actionable strategies. The journey through this book is not the end but a new beginning: a beginning where you are equipped to harness the full potential of Amazon EC2 to innovate, optimize, and secure your cloud environments with confidence.

Remember – the cloud is ever-evolving, and so should your strategies. Stay curious, keep exploring new AWS services, and never hesitate to experiment.

Index

A

access control list (ACL) 87
alarms 244
Amazon CloudWatch 241, 242
  essentials 243
  logging with 137
Amazon EBS volumes 192
  attaching, to EC2 instance 198-201
  performance considerations 193, 194
  provisioning 194-198
  types 192
  use cases 193
Amazon EC2 instances 16
  definition 16
  launch state 19
  lifecycle 19
  primary instance families 17, 18
  start state 20
  stop state 20
  terminate state 20
  types 17
Amazon EC2 networking 85
  connectivity 85
  performance 85
  scalability and redundancy 85
  security 85

Amazon EC2 pricing models 233
  On-Demand Instances 233
  Reserved Instances 234
  savings plans 234, 235
  spot instances 235
Amazon ECR
  key features 288
  overview 287
Amazon ECS
  key features 287
  overview 287
  used, for deploying containers on
    EC instances 288-294
Amazon EFS 214, 215
  access points, leveraging 217-219
  backup and security considerations 221, 223
  bridging, with EC2 220, 221
  creating 216, 217
  durability 216
  mounting, on EFS instance 216
  performance 215
  setting up 216
  use cases 215
Amazon EFS, performance modes
  General Purpose mode 215
  max I/O mode 215

Index

Amazon Elastic Compute Cloud (EC2) 4
  benefits 4-7
  best practices 358
  big data solutions 331
  compliance and security 358
  compliance, ensuring 356
  compliance, migrating 356
  compliance, modernizing 356
  initial assessment and planning 356
  integrating, with CloudFormation 278
  managed services, using 357
  migration execution 357
  modernization and optimization 357
  standout features, compared to cloud platforms 12
  versus traditional hosting 8, 9
Amazon Elastic Compute Cloud (EC2), use cases 10
  big data processing and analytics 10
  disaster recovery and backup 11
  high-performance computing (HPC) 11
  media and content delivery 11
  web application hosting 10
Amazon EMR
  for big data processing 331, 332
Amazon GuardDuty
  for threat detection 137
Amazon Machine Image (AMI) 268
  core components 27
  EBS-backed AMIs 50
  EC2 instances, launching from 61
  instance store-backed AMIs 51
  issues, troubleshooting 68, 69
  selecting 61
  types 50
Amazon RDS Multi-AZ deployments 337

Amazon Redshift
  features 332
  for data warehousing 332
Amazon Route 53 262, 313
  features 314
Amazon S3 262
Amazon S3 CRR 337
  aspects 338
Amazon Web Services (AWS) 3, 309
  logging 242
  monitoring 242
AMI issues, troubleshooting
  inaccessible AMIs 69
  launch failures 69
  permission errors 68
  storage space issues 68
AMI virtualization
  boot modes 49
  exploring 47
  types 48
  user-provided kernel 49, 50
application-level security considerations 137
application load balancer (ALB) 144, 145
  advanced routing 145
  application layer 145
  health checks 153-155
  listeners, configuring 149-151
  listeners, creating 149
  target groups 151-153
  transport layer 145
  use case 146
application resiliency 75
application security 135, 136
auditing and analysis techniques 138
automation 262, 263

Index

Auto Scaling groups (ASG) 167
  configuring 168
  ELB, integrating with 182
  health check settings 187, 188
  launch templates 168
  life cycle hooks 179
  real-world scenarios 168
  scaling policies 171
  target groups, associating with 183-186
  traffic, distributing among instances 187
  use cases and benefits 167, 168
  working 167

AWS Budgets 239
  IaC, using with 281

AWS Certificate Manager (ACM) 133, 137

AWS CloudEndure Disaster Recovery 263

AWS CloudFormation 266
  basics 267
  best practices 276
  EC2 infrastructure provisioning, automating with 279, 280
  EC2 instances, launching and managing with 278, 279
  mappings 271
  mappings, outputs 271, 272
  overview 266, 267
  resources 267, 268
  stacks 267, 268
  template parameters 270
  template provisioning 272
  templates 267, 268
  template syntax and structure 268-270

AWS CloudTrail 241, 242
  configuring 246-249
  integrating, with AWS services 250
  logging with 137
  setting up 246-249
  used, for auditing 246
  used, for security 246
  versus Amazon CloudWatch 242

AWS Config 322
  features 323
  monitoring and security 322

AWS Cost Explorer 238, 239

AWS Database Migration Service (AWS DMS) 319
  features 319
  use cases 319

AWS DataSync 317
  features 317
  use cases 317

AWS Direct Connect 121, 309
  use case, with EC2 in hybrid cloud architecture 310

AWS Fargate 295
  used, for deploying containerized applications 296-302
  used, for running containers 295
  versus EC2 launch types 295, 296

AWS Global Accelerator
  aspects 338

AWS Global Infrastructure
  reference link 5

AWS KMS
  used, for key management 133

AWS Lambda
  and serverless computing 302
  key features 302
  overview 302
  use cases 303

AWS Lambda functions
  deployment and configuration 303
  integration, with EC2 304

Index

AWS Organizations
  features 321
  monitoring and security 321
  use cases 321
AWS Outposts 311
  use cases 312
AWS Resource Access Manager (RAM)
  advantages 316
  features 315
  use cases 316
AWS Security Hub
  features 322
  monitoring and security 322
AWS service components
  order processing 345
  product catalog 345
  user authentication service 345
AWS services
  case studies and best practices 323
  for hybrid cloud integration 309
  for multi-cloud integration 313
AWS services, for DR 337
  Amazon RDS Multi-AZ deployments 337
  Amazon S3 CRR 337, 338
  AWS Global Accelerator 338
AWS services, for hybrid cloud integration 309
  AWS Direct Connect 309
  AWS Outposts 311
  AWS Storage Gateway 310
  AWS VPN 312
AWS services, for multi-cloud integration 313
  Amazon Route 53 313, 314
  AWS Resource Access Manager 315
  AWS Transit Gateway 314, 315

AWS Storage Gateway 310
  technical facts 310
  use cases 311
AWS Systems Manager (SSM) 6
  used, for scheduling patching for EC2 instances 251-260
  utilizing 251
AWS Transfer Family 318
  features 318
  use cases 318
  versus AWS DataSync 318
AWS Transit Gateway
  advantages 315
  features 314
AWS VPC
  need for 84, 85
AWS VPN 312
  benefits 312, 313
  client VPN 312
  site-to-site VPN 312
  technical advantages 312
  use cases 313

B

backup strategy 261
batch processing 328
benchmarking 80
big data
  importance 327
  on Amazon EC2 326, 327
  solutions, on Amazon EC2 331
  terminologies 328
big data processing and analytics 10
block storage 192
boot modes 49

Index   365

business impact analysis (BIA) 339
business intelligence (BI) 327

C

capacity planning 260
  strategies 261
CIDR range 86
Classless Inter-Domain Routing (CIDR) blocks 92, 93
  route table concepts 96
  route table configuration 96
CloudFormation best practices
  cross-stack references and exports 277
  modular templates and nested stacks 276
CloudFormation stacks 273
  change sets 275
  creating 273
  updating 273
CloudFormation templates
  deploying, with AWS Management Console 274, 275
Cloud Security Posture Management (CSPM) 320
cloud service provider (CSP) 346
CloudTrail logs
  analyzing, for security and compliance 249
CloudWatch dashboards 244
CloudWatch logs 245
CloudWatch visualization 244
cluster computing 328
compliance analysis 250
containerization 286
  best practices 304
  n EC2, with Amazon ECS and ECR 286
  use cases 305

containers
  running with AWS Fargate 295
content delivery network (CDN) 357
content delivery platform (CDP) 351
content management systems (CMS) 29
continuous integration/continuous deployment (CI/CD) pipeline 352
  deployment 353
  production deployment 353
  push code 352
  run tests 352
  staging deployment 352
  staging validation 352
  tests pass 352
  trigger build 352
core components 16
costs
  monitoring and managing 238
cross-zone load balancing
  implementing 164
  importance 164
cryptographic keys
  creating and managing, with KMS 133, 134
custom AMIs
  creating 52-54
  creating, best practices 67
  creating, considerations 68
  creating, use cases 55, 56
  EC2 image pipeline, leveraging to create 55
  sharing 52, 56
  sharing, with AWS Organizations 57-60
  sharing, with individual AWS accounts 56, 57
customer master key (CMK) 133
custom metrics 244
custom route tables 97

D

data at rest encryption
  for EBS volumes and snapshots 132
data encryption 132
data in transit encryption
  with TLS/SSL 133
Data Lifecycle Manager (DLM) 38
data management and migration across clouds 316
  AWS Database Migration Service 319
  AWS DataSync 317
  AWS Transfer Family 318
data warehousing 328
denial-of-service (DoS) 23
DevOps practices for continuous improvement
  benefits 352
  implementing 351, 352
DHCP option set 90
Direct Connect 89
disaster recovery (DR) 201, 266, 358
  AWS services 337
  BC plan (BCP) 336
  concepts and terminologies 336
  failover and failback 336
  hot, warm and cold sites 336
  importance 336
  RPO 336
  RTO 336
  strategies 335
distributed denial of service (DDoS) attacks 135, 354
DR planning 339
DR strategies
  monitoring 340
  testing 340

DR strategies, on AWS
  designing 339
  planning and risk assessment phase 339
  RPO 340
  RTO 340

E

EBS-backed AMIs
  advantages 50
  use cases 51
EBS snapshots 32, 201, 262
  archiving 38
  copying 35
  creating 32, 202, 203
  deleting 34
  lifecycle, automating 38, 39
  lifecycle management 203-207
  need for 201
  sharing 37
  sharing and migration 207-210
EBS volumes and snapshots
  data at rest encryption 132
EBS volume types
  Cold HDD volumes (sc1) 30, 32
  General Purpose SSD 29
  Provisioned IOPS SSD 29
  Throughput Optimized HDD volumes (st1) 30
EC2 AMI 262
EC2 applications
  architecture, assessing 344
  assessment phase 345
  DevOps practices for continuous improvement, implementing 351, 352
  managed services and microservices, using 350, 351
  migrating 344

migration process, executing 347
migration process, planning 347
migration strategies and tools,
    identifying 346
modernizing 349
re-architecting 349
re-architecture strategy 345
refactoring 349

EC2 environments
compliance and governance 353
compliance requirements and
    frameworks 353, 354
continuous compliance, auditing 355
continuous compliance, monitoring 355
security controls and policies,
    implementing 354

EC2 instance launching
setting up 179, 180

EC2 instance purchasing options 76
costs and use cases, comparing 78-80
On-Demand Instances 76
Reserved Instances (RIs) 76
Savings Plans 78
Spot Instances 77

EC2 instances
best practices, for selection 82
details, configuring during launch 62-65
IAM roles, creating and managing 127-131
launching 65-67
monitoring 244
patch management 251
reviewing 65-67
rightsizing 81
type and size 72, 73

EC2 instance terminating life cycle hook
setting up 181, 182

EC2 maintenance best practices 250
patch management for EC2 instances 251

EC2 placement groups 227, 228
benefits 229
cluster placement groups 228
creation and management,
    best practices 231
deploying, strategies 230
partition placement groups 228, 229
right type, selecting 230
spread placement groups 228
types 228
used, for optimizing 231

EC2 security 126
Elastic Block Store (EBS) 28, 50, 191, 335
benefits 28
Elastic Compute Cloud (EC2) 191, 338
Elastic Container Registry (ECR) 285
Elastic Container Service (ECS) 18, 285, 351
Elastic Fabric Adapter (EFA)
capabilities 42
features 43, 44
fundamentals 42
supported instance types 43
Elastic File System (EFS) 335
Elastic GPU instances 330
Elastic IPs 107
allocating 108, 109
associating 107-111
use cases 107
Elastic Kubernetes Service (EKS) 346
Elastic Load Balancer (ELB) 144
ALB 149
and ASG integration, best practices 188, 189
best practices 163-166
configuring 149
integrating, with ASG 182
setting up 149
Elastic Load Balancing (ELB) 23, 338

Elastic Network Adapter (ENA) 40, 334
   features 41
   use cases 42
elastic network interfaces (ENIs) 39, 107, 111
   attaching 39
   attaching, to EC2 instance 115, 116
   characteristics 112
   configuration options 39
   creating, to EC2 instance 112, 114
   detaching 39
   managing 39
   properties 39
   security and performance implications 40
   use cases 112
   use cases, for multiple ENIs 40
ELB best practices
   cross-zone load balancing 163
   monitoring and logging 166
   SSL/TLS offloading 164
enhanced networking
   benefits 40, 41
   enabling 41
   supported instance types 41
ephemeral storage 210
events 244

G

gateway load balancer (GWLB) 147
   transparent inspection 147
   use case 148
General Data Protection Regulation (GDPR) 353
Google Cloud Security Command Center (SCC) 320
GPU acceleration 328
GUID Partition Table (GPT) 49

H

hardware virtual machines (HVMs) 48
health checks 153
Health Insurance Portability and Accountability Act (HIPAA) 353
high availability (HA) 345
high-performance computing (HPC) 17, 210
   and Big Data Clusters, design and configuration 333
   importance 327
   network configurations, for low-latency communication 334
   on Amazon EC2 326, 327
   storage options and performance tuning 335
   terminologies 328
HPC-optimized EC2 instances 328
   accelerators 330
   GPU instances 330
   types, for HPC workloads 329
hybrid and multi-cloud environments
   monitoring and security 320
hybrid cloud architectures 308

I

IAM roles
   creating, and managing for EC2 instances 127-131
Identity and Access Management (IAM) 22, 127, 288, 324, 353
   in context of EC2 127
IMDSv1
   versus IMDSv2 22
infrastructure as Code (IaC) 266, 333
   essential, for cloud management 266
   using, with AWS CDK 280, 281

infrastructure resiliency 75
input/output operations per
    second (IOPS) 192, 335
instance identity documents
    examples 24
    retrieving, steps 24, 25
    used, for avoiding instance
        impersonation attacks 23
instance impersonation attacks
    avoiding, with instance identity
        documents 23
instance metadata 22
    retrieving 22
    use cases 23
Instance Metadata Service
    version 1 (IMDSv1) 22
instance profiles and policies 131, 132
instance purchasing options
    Dedicated Instances 26
    On-Demand Instances 25
    Reserved Instances (RIs) 25
    Savings Plans 26
    Spot Instances 26
instance states and instance lifecycles
    use cases for instance management 21
instance store-backed AMIs
    characteristics and use cases 51, 52
instance stores 210
    characteristics and use cases 210
    data persistence and backup strategies 214
    limitations 212
    performance highlights 211
instance store volume
    instances, launching with 212, 213
internet gateway (IGW) 88

K

key management
    with AWS KMS 133
Key Management Service (KMS) 132, 353
    used, for creating and managing
        cryptographic keys 133, 134
key pairs
    best practices 46
    secure authentication, for instances 45

L

launch templates, ASG
    features 168
    setting up 169, 170
life cycle hooks, ASG 179
    EC2 instance, launching 179
    EC2 instance, terminating 181
load balancers types
    application load balancer (ALB) 144
    gateway load balancer (GWLB) 147
    network load balancer (NLB) 146
log insights 245

M

main route tables 97
managed services 350
MapReduce 328
Master Boot Record (MBR) 49
mebibytes per second per tebibyte
    (MiB/s per TiB 30
metrics 243
microservices 350

Microsoft Azure virtual machines (VMs) 12
migration process
  executing 348
  planning 347
migration strategies
  benefits 346
migration tools 346
monitoring and logging
  implementing 166
  importance 166
multi-cloud architecture 308

N

NAT gateways/instances 89
network access control lists (NACLs) 89, 102, 134
  configuring 103-107
  creating 103-107
  overview 102
Network File System (NFS) 214
networking 74
network load balancer (NLB)
  configuring 155
  health checks, configuring for targets 161-163
  listeners, configuring 156-158
  listeners, creating 156-158
  performance 146
  setting up 155
  target groups, setting up 158-160
  use case 147
network security 134
  best practices 134, 135
NVIDIA Collective Communication Libraries (NCCL) 43

O

On-Demand Instances 76, 233
online transaction processing (OLTP) 29
Open System Interconnection (OSI) 144
operating system 135, 136
optimization 260

P

parallel processing 328
paravirtual (PV) 48
patching
  activities, strategizing 251
  scheduling, for EC2 instances with AWS SSM 251-260
patch management 136
  and updates 136
  for EC2 instances 251
performance, optimizing with EC2 placement groups
  fault tolerance, improving 232, 233
  inter-instance latency, reducing 232
  network throughput, maximizing 232
performance testing 80
  tools and techniques 80
performance tuning 260
point-in-time (PiT) 32
post-migration phase 348
predictive scaling 173
pricing model
  cost optimization strategies 236
  performance and cost, balancing 237, 238
  selecting 236
  use cases 237
PrivateLink 135

R

RAM 73
re-architecting 349
Recovery Point Objective (RPO) 336, 340
Recovery Time Objective (RTO) 336, 340
recovery strategy 261
Relational Database Service (RDS) 17, 344
refactoring 349
Reserved Instances (RIs) 76
  convertible RIs 25, 77
  scheduled RIs 25, 77
  standard RIs 25, 77
Resource Access Manager (RAM) 57-60
resource management 260
  strategies 261
rightsizing process 81
routes 96, 97
route table associations 97, 98
route table concepts 96
route table configuration 97
route tables 88, 92

S

Savings Plans 78, 234
  features 234
  working 235
scaling policies, ASG 171
  dynamic scaling 171-173
  predictive scaling 173-176
  scheduled scaling 176-178
scheduled scaling 176
secure socket layer (SSL) 132
security
  logs, analyzing for 249

security groups 99, 134
  best practices 46
  configuring 100, 102
  creating 100, 102
  virtual firewalls, for instances 45
SecurityHub 138
serverless computing 286
server-side encryption (SSE) 247, 353
server-side request forgery (SSRF) 22
service-level agreements (SLAs) 336
Service Organization Control (SOC) 353
shared responsibility model 126, 127
Simple Queue Service (SQS) 345
Simple Storage Service (S3) 38, 201
single point of failure (SPOF) 345
single root I/O virtualization (SR-IOV) 40
snapshot encryption 132
source code management (SCM) 352
Spot Instances 77, 235
  features 235
  working 236
SSL/TLS offloading
  implementing 165
  importance 164
storage option
  application requirements, assessing 224, 225
  selecting 224
  storage configurations optimization, best practices 225, 226
subnet 92
  creating 94, 95
  managing 93-96
subnets 88
Systems Manager (SSM) 251

T

threat detection
  Amazon GuardDuty for 137
time-to-live (TTL) 24
TLS/SSL
  used, for data in transit encryption 133
traditional hosting
  dedicated servers 8
  shared hosting 8
  virtual private servers 8
transport layer security (TLS) 132

U

unified extensible firmware interface (UEFI) 49
user data 22
  use cases 23
  working with 22
user-provided kernels 50

V

virtualization type 48
virtual local area networks (VLANs) 310
virtual machines (VMs)
virtual private cloud (VPC) 39
  creating 86-88
  deleting 91
  managing 86-88
  modifying 90
  overview 84
Virtual Private Cloud (VPC), settings and configuration options 88
  DHCP option set 90
  Direct Connect 89
  internet gateway (IGW) 89
  NAT gateways/instances 89
  network access control lists (NACLs) 89
  route tables 88
  subnets 88
  VPC endpoints 90
  VPC endpoint services 90
  VPC flow logs 90
  VPC peering 89
  VPN connections 89
virtual reality (VR) 330
Voice Over IP (VoIP) 42
VPC connectivity
  options 116
VPC design principles 122, 123
VPC endpoints 90, 122
  gateway endpoints 122
  interface endpoints 122
  services 90
  use cases 122
VPC flow logs 90
VPC peering 89
  concepts 117
  options 116
  setup 117-121
VPN connections 89

W

Web Application Firewall (WAF) 137
web application hosting 10
workload requirements 73
  application and infrastructure resiliency 75
  CPU analyzing 73
  memory analyzing 73
  networking and performance requirements 74, 75
  storage analyzing 73

‹packt›

packtpub.com

Subscribe to our online digital library for full access to over 7,000 books and videos, as well as industry leading tools to help you plan your personal development and advance your career. For more information, please visit our website.

Why subscribe?

- Spend less time learning and more time coding with practical eBooks and Videos from over 4,000 industry professionals
- Improve your learning with Skill Plans built especially for you
- Get a free eBook or video every month
- Fully searchable for easy access to vital information
- Copy and paste, print, and bookmark content

Did you know that Packt offers eBook versions of every book published, with PDF and ePub files available? You can upgrade to the eBook version at packtpub.com and as a print book customer, you are entitled to a discount on the eBook copy. Get in touch with us at customercare@packtpub.com for more details.

At www.packtpub.com, you can also read a collection of free technical articles, sign up for a range of free newsletters, and receive exclusive discounts and offers on Packt books and eBooks.

Other Books You May Enjoy

If you enjoyed this book, you may be interested in these other books by Packt:

AWS Observability Handbook

Phani Kumar Lingamallu, Fabio Braga de Oliveira

ISBN: 978-1-80461-671-0

- Capture metrics from an EC2 instance and visualize them on a dashboard
- Conduct distributed tracing using AWS X-Ray
- Derive operational metrics and set up alerting using CloudWatch
- Achieve observability of containerized applications in ECS and EKS
- Explore the practical implementation of observability for AWS Lambda
- Observe your applications using Amazon managed Prometheus, Grafana, and OpenSearch services
- Gain insights into operational data using ML services on AWS
- Understand the role of observability in the cloud adoption framework

Containers for Developers Handbook

Francisco Javier Ramírez Urea

ISBN: 978-1-80512-798-7

- Find out how to build microservices-based applications using containers
- Deploy your processes within containers using Docker features
- Orchestrate multi-component applications on standalone servers
- Deploy applications cluster-wide in container orchestrators
- Solve common deployment problems such as persistency or app exposure using best practices
- Review your application's health and debug it using open-source tools
- Discover how to orchestrate CI/CD workflows using containers

Packt is searching for authors like you

If you're interested in becoming an author for Packt, please visit `authors.packtpub.com` and apply today. We have worked with thousands of developers and tech professionals, just like you, to help them share their insight with the global tech community. You can make a general application, apply for a specific hot topic that we are recruiting an author for, or submit your own idea.

Share Your Thoughts

Now you've finished *Mastering Amazon EC2*, we'd love to hear your thoughts! Scan the QR code below to go straight to the Amazon review page for this book and share your feedback or leave a review on the site that you purchased it from.

`https://packt.link/r/1-804-61668-0`

Your review is important to us and the tech community and will help us make sure we're delivering excellent quality content.

Download a free PDF copy of this book

Thanks for purchasing this book!

Do you like to read on the go but are unable to carry your print books everywhere?

Is your eBook purchase not compatible with the device of your choice?

Don't worry, now with every Packt book you get a DRM-free PDF version of that book at no cost.

Read anywhere, any place, on any device. Search, copy, and paste code from your favorite technical books directly into your application.

The perks don't stop there, you can get exclusive access to discounts, newsletters, and great free content in your inbox daily

Follow these simple steps to get the benefits:

1. Scan the QR code or visit the link below

https://packt.link/free-ebook/9781804616680

2. Submit your proof of purchase
3. That's it! We'll send your free PDF and other benefits to your email directly

Printed in Dunstable, United Kingdom